Organizational Effectiveness

Organizational Effectiveness
The Role of Psychology

Edited by

Ivan T. Robertson
Manchester School of Management, UMIST, UK

Militza Callinan
Manchester School of Management, UMIST, UK

Dave Bartram
SHL Group plc, Thames Ditton, Surrey, UK

JOHN WILEY & SONS, LTD

National   01243 779777
International (+44) 1243 779777
e-mail (for orders and customer service enquiries): cs-books@wiley.co.uk
Visit our Home Page on: http://www.wiley.co.uk or http://www.wiley.com

Other Wiley Editorial Offices

John Wiley & Sons, Inc., 605 Third Avenue,
New York, NY 10158-0012, USA

WILEY-VCH Verlag GmbH, Pappelallee 3,
D-69469 Weinheim, Germany

John Wiley & Sons Australia, Ltd., 33 Park Road, Milton,
Queensland 4064, Australia

John Wiley & Sons (Asia) Pte, Ltd., 2 Clementi Loop #02-01,
Jin Xing Distripark, Singapore 129809

John Wiley & Sons (Canada), Ltd., 22 Worcester Road,
Rexdale, Ontario M9W 1L1, Canada

British Library Cataloguing in Publication Data

A catalogue record for this book is available from the British Library

ISBN 0-471-49264-7 cased

Typeset in 10/12pt Palatino from the author's disks by TechBooks, Delhi
Printed and bound in Great Britain by Antony Rowe Ltd, Chippenham, Wiltshire
This book is printed on acid-free paper responsibly manufactured from sustainable forestry,
in which at least two trees are planted for each one used for paper production.

Contents

Part III

About the Editors

Ivan Robertson is Professor of Work & Organizational Psychology at the Manchester School of Management, UMIST. He has published over 150 scientific articles in the work and organizational psychology field and over 25 books. He is co-editor (with Professor Cary Cooper) of the *International Review of Industrial and Organizational Psychology*.

Militza Callinan is Assistant Director of the Centre for Research in Work and Organizational Psychology at Manchester School of Management, UMIST.

Dave Bartram is Director of Research at SHL Group plc. He has extensive experience in work and organizational psychology and until recently was at the Department of Psychology at Hull University, where he was Dean of Science. Professor Bartram has held senior posts in the British Psychological Society (BPS) and has produced numerous publications, including the BPS *Review of Personality Assessment Instruments*.

Contributors

Beverly Alimo-Metcalfe, The Nuffield Institute, Fairbairn House, University of Leeds, 71–75 Clarendon Road, Leeds LS2 9PL, UK

John Arnold, The Business School, Loughborough University, Loughborough LE11 3TU, UK

Helen Baron, SHL Group plc, 1 Atwell Place, The Pavillion, Thames Ditton, Surrey KT7 0NE, UK

Dave Bartram, SHL Group plc, 1 Atwell Place, The Pavillion, Thames Ditton, Surrey KT7 0NE, UK

Eugene Burke, SHL Group plc, 1 Atwell Place, The Pavillion, Thames Ditton, Surrey KT7 0NE, UK

Militza Callinan, Centre for Research in Work and Organizational Psychology, Manchester School of Management, UMIST, Manchester M60 1QD, UK

Sue Cartwright, Manchester School of Management, UMIST, Manchester M60 1QD, UK

Mary Dalgleish, Occupational Psychology Division, Employment Service, Block 3, Level 3, Porterbrook House, 7 Pear Street, Sheffield S11 8JF, UK

Clive Fletcher, Department of Psychology, Goldsmiths College, University of London, New Cross, London SE14 6NW, UK

Peter Herriot, The Empower Group, 23 Buckingham Gate, London SW1E 6LB, UK

Gerard P. Hodgkinson, Leeds University Business School, The University of Leeds, Leeds LS2 9JT, UK

Rick Jacobs, SHL North America & Pennsylvania State University, State College, 300 South Burrowes Street, PA 16801, USA

Rainer Kurz, SHL Group Technology & Policy Advisor, SHL Group plc, 1 Atwell Place, The Pavillion, Thames Ditton, Surrey KT7 0NE, UK

Kevin R. Murphy, Department of Psychology, Pennsylvania State University, University Park, PA 16802, USA

Gill Nyfield, SHL Group plc, 1 Atwell Place, The Pavillion, Thames Ditton, Surrey KT7 0NE, UK

Ivan T. Robertson, Professor of Work and Organizational Psychology, Manchester School of Management, UMIST, Manchester M60 1QD, UK

Wouter Schoonman, Managing Director, Instituut voor Best Practice-4tp, Beeklaan 395, 256 2BA Den Haag, Netherlands

Paul Sparrow, Sheffield University Management School, University of Sheffield, 9 Mappin Street, Sheffield S1 4DT, UK

Phyllis Tharenou, Department of Business Management, Monarsh University, Caulfield Campus, PO Box 197, Caulfield East, Melbourne, Victoria 3145, Australia

Michael West, Organizational Studies, Aston Business School, University of Aston, Aston Triangle, Birmingham B4 7ET, UK

Richard Williams, Principal Psychologist, Assessment & Consultancy Unit, Home Office, London SE1, UK

Preface

This book originates from a gathering of senior practitioners and researchers in the field of work and organizational psychology which was held at Manchester School of Management, UMIST, UK, in September 1999. The purpose of the seminar was to discuss an open question—what is the impact of individuals' performance on overall organizational effectiveness? Of course, given that psychology is the study of individuals, the answer to that question is also about the potential applications of psychology to the pursuit of organizational effectiveness.

What emerged from the discussions that day were the beginnings of some answers to what was recognized as being a very difficult question. The difficulty is, as the following chapters testify, that while psychological knowledge and approaches hold many responses to this question, they have not really been placed together before.

Some of the most common fields of activity in work and organizational psychology have rarely been evaluated for the impact they have at the level of the organization, with intervention and evaluation remaining firmly at the level of the person. While we cannot claim to be in a position yet where we can develop a neat and coherent model, specifying elegantly the path by which individual people make organizational outcomes, collectively, the contributors have assembled a detailed picture depicting much of how individuals create the group level phenomena that make an effective organization and the psychological interventions that can aid them. The richness and breadth of the book's content is testimony to the quality, expertise and diversity of the professionals we were able to assemble for this task.

The authors' starting point was the seminar discussions, the Introduction written by the Editors, and a deadline. It is testament to their ability and effort as scholars and writers that these chapters can be seen as a collection. Each chapter can be read independently, or in the context of our collective endeavour.

The Contents of the Book

The Editors' Introduction presents a general framework of organizational functioning incorporating the role of the individual within which a psychological approach to organizational effectiveness can be viewed. Effectiveness is characterized as a multidimensional construct and a range of criteria are organized into four broad categories. The role of various stakeholders in the organization in defining effectiveness is also discussed. The potential relevance of psychological intervention at various levels of organizational functioning, from global to individual, is highlighted. Finally, the discussion, which then continues throughout the book, is opened. This discussion concerns the path by which individuals' knowledge, skills, abilities and other characteristics lead to behaviours and, collectively, to organizational level outcomes that may be considered as more or less "effective". This is discussed using the concept of competencies.

In Chapter 1, Paul Sparrow and Michael West argue that psychological research has already demonstrated a "powerful linkage between the individual, team and organizational effectiveness". The authors review research on three facets of effectiveness—productivity, innovation and mental health—at two levels of analysis—individual and group—moving on to the level of the organization and the link between HRM and organizational performance.

The next two chapters focus on some of the key issues surrounding the effective translation of research knowledge into action in organizations. The process of application and intervention is viewed as a critical area of discussion in itself because it is only through this process that the potential benefits of psychological research can be delivered.

In Chapter 2, Gerard Hodgkinson and Peter Herriot provide a thoughtful exploration of some issues in identifying opportunities to carry out psychological work in organizations. They describe some structural features of the profession of psychology that constrain and shape the type of questions addressed. They comment on the reasons why psychology has not been at the forefront of research aimed at improving organizational effectiveness, identify what they see as its real strengths for that purpose, and suggest future directions that might be taken.

Chapter 3, by Mary Dalgleish and Rick Jacobs addresses some of the practical aspects of doing psychology in organizations. With the aid of some illustrative case studies of real interventions in which they have been involved, they first identify the kinds of organizational impact that can be demonstrated and then outline a process model for psychological intervention, showing how that impact may be enhanced and maintained.

Part II of the book contains seven chapters, each specifically addressing a significant area of psychological research and practice in organizations and explaining its products in relation to their contribution to overall effectiveness.

In Chapter 4, Kevin Murphy and Dave Bartram provide a comprehensive review of the strengths and shortcomings of the most substantial area of psychology at work—recruitment and personnel selection. The assumptions underlying research on this topic are subjected to critical appraisal, particularly focusing on how those assumptions differ from the reality of how selectors make personnel decisions. The authors examine attempts to demonstrate the utility of selection at the organizational level and identify some of the problems associated with linking selection test validity with organizational effectiveness.

Phyllis Tharenou and Eugene Burke begin Chapter 5 by voicing the doubts that many organizations have about whether training does actually pay off in significant ways. In what appears to be the first published review of research addressing this question, the evidence of the impact of training on a range of individual and organizational effectiveness outcomes is described. Some explanations are then offered for the impact that training does appear to have on overall effectiveness. The final section of the chapter outlines some approaches organizations might take in order to maximize the positive benefits that accrue from training.

In Chapter 6, Richard Williams and Clive Fletcher review the area of performance management. Three types of model that come under the description of performance management are identified and described. Some issues surrounding the definition of performance are discussed. The authors distinguish between the antecedents and determinants of performance, viewing performance as being determined by the interaction between multiple person and system factors. Finally, the impact of work psychology-based interventions that come under the banner of performance management is considered.

The topic of motivation is covered by John Arnold and Wouter Schoonman in Chapter 7. The authors first trace the history of motivational concepts and approaches and then take a critical look at their usefulness. They go on to describe how some of these ideas might be applied to some conditions of modern workplaces, and highlight some areas of potential conflict between individual and organizational goals and motivations that may impact on overall effectiveness. Some new directions in the field are also outlined—in particular, a concern about the lack of attention that has been given to the self and identity in motivation research. A case study focused on individuals' values is offered as an example of a more self-orientated approach to the topic of motivation.

In Chapter 8, Sue Cartwright and Helen Baron examine the various definitions and concepts of organizational culture and some of the ongoing debates within the field about how culture is best described. The use of cultural concepts to analyse differing perceptions between organizational members is illustrated in three cases studies, each addressing a different problem. The authors also discuss cultural assessment methods, and the potential consequences of cultural consistency between individuals and organizations. They suggest some of the future challenges that may impact on the management of organizational culture.

In Chapter 9, Beverly Alimo-Metcalfe and Gill Nyfield discuss the impact of leadership on organizational functioning and review the history and progress of leadership research. The effect of gender and cultural dominance on the research process and the interpretation of findings is discussed. The authors go on to outline the new directions leadership research and practice is now taking. Issues covered include an increased focus on leaders' self-awareness and the subsequent development of 360-degree, multi-rater feedback assessment instruments, as well as the relative contribution of stable and learnt qualities to leadership ability and the implications for organizations' selection and development practices.

The final chapter in Part II, by Rainer Kurz and Dave Bartram, extends and develops the ideas presented in the Introduction on competency and performance. It presents an attempt to outline a model of performance at work that integrates academic theory and occupational assessment practices into a unifying framework that can be used as the basis for human resources management in organizations.

In Part III, the Editors have written a concluding chapter which attempts to bring together some of the themes and conclusions that have emerged in the individual chapters.

INTRODUCTION

A Framework for Examining Organizational Effectiveness

Dave Bartram, Ivan T. Robertson and Militza Callinan

This Introduction outlines an overall structure within which to consider the impact of individual performance on organizational effectiveness. The structure provides the framework for demonstrating how psychology can provide, through appropriate modes of intervention at the individual level, the means of enhancing organizational effectiveness.

ORGANIZATIONAL EFFECTIVENESS

In order to explore ways in which the behaviours of individuals at work can impact on organizational effectiveness, we first need to define what we mean by "organizational effectiveness". Both words need consideration.

There are many ways in which we could define an organization. Typical dictionary definitions focus on a number of key features:

- Organizations are structured, orderly systems—they are "organized".
- They are constructed to serve a particular end or set of objectives.
- They provide the means of controlling performance in the pursuit of those goals.
- They are primarily social arrangements—organizations are organized goal-oriented collections of people.

Within organizations, the role of individual members is varied; but for the organization to be effective, the members need to gear their activities towards defining and attaining shared goals (i.e. the organizational goals). An organization's effectiveness can be judged by the extent to which its members are successful in this endeavour. We can distinguish between primary and secondary organizational goals.

Organizational Effectiveness: The Role of Psychology
Edited by I.T. Robertson, M. Callinan and D. Bartram. © 2002 John Wiley & Sons, Ltd.

- Primary goals reflect the organization's raison d'être, and will generally be described in commercial terms (market share, profit levels etc.).
- Secondary goals are about how to achieve the primary goal, and often focus on internal organizational criteria (levels of job satisfaction, developing the "right" culture, effective internal communication and so on).

Organizations are more than just a collection of people in pursuit of some common objectives. From the perspective of individuals, their organizations have a physical dimension (it is their place of work) and provide them with physical space and resources for their work. They also provide more or less effective communication channels (formal and informal) and may be more or less effective in providing people with the information and knowledge they need as and when they need it. As has already been noted, organizations are social arrangements. This means not only that they consist of collections of people, but also that the effectiveness of the organization will be dependent on the nature and quality of relationships between those people. Organizational structures, training, selection procedures etc. can all impact on the quality of the social environment within which people work.

While the realization of collective organizational goals is dependent on the performance of people in organizations, organizations also provide people with the opportunity to meet a range of individual needs (see, for example, Fryer & Payne, 1986).

Specifically, organizations can provide people with:

- money and physical resources
- power, authority and control
- status, prestige and self-esteem
- security, support and protection
- order and stability
- meaning, relevance and purpose.

From the perspective of employees, the extent to which an organization can provide satisfaction of the needs associated with this range of variables is a major consideration in judging the effectiveness of that organization.

While the collective approach towards the pursuit of common goals is easy to identify within small organizations, as organizations increase in size, so job positions become increasingly specialized and each individual has a proportionately smaller impact on the overall effectiveness of the organization. In addition, each individual will "see" only a small part of the organization and have increasing difficulty in owning general organizational goals and objectives.

As a consequence, individuals will tend to identify with their own particular part or section of their organization. As an organization increases in size, so issues of controlling individual performance in the pursuit of collective goals become more and more complex. It may also be the case, that the goals themselves become more diffuse and complex. Not only does this make it more difficult to describe what the organization's purpose is, but it also becomes more difficult to communicate that purpose effectively to all those who work in it.

Kaplan and Norton (1992) proposed the use of a balanced scorecard approach to dealing with the need for multiple indicators of performance effectiveness. However, their approach tends to conflate stakeholder groups with categories of effect (economic or social). Kaplan and Norton proposed the measurement of performance in terms of four perspectives: Financial, Customer, Internal Process, and Growth and Innovation. Atkinson et al. (1997) have argued that this approach ignores some key stakeholder groups (notably suppliers, employees and the broader community within which the organization operates and on which it can have indirect but significant effects).

The model proposed here extends their approach and makes a separation between who is affected and how they are affected. Key to developing a framework for the consideration of organizational effectiveness is two questions.

1. What are the characteristics of an effective (as opposed to an ineffective) organization?
2. Which groups of people are affected by the success or otherwise of an organization?

These are related, in that each stakeholder group will have a different view on what may be regarded as "effective".

- Investors and shareholders look to the organization to provide a good return on investment, long-term stability and growth.
- Customers want value for money, quality of product or service, good support and after-sales care.
- Suppliers want to work with an organization that is dependable and provides them with long-term stability as a market and reliability in payment, and is aware of the constraints on the suppliers' ability to supply.
- Employees look for job satisfaction, stability of employment, career prospects, personal development, good pay and rewards.
- Others look for the impact of the organization's activities on their environment and way of life (economic, social, political, and cultural) to be positive and beneficial.

Broadly speaking we can break down effectiveness criteria into four categories:

1. *Economic*. This is fundamental, as commercial organizations that are economically ineffective will not survive. As with all other criteria, the effectiveness or otherwise of an organization in economic terms is inextricably linked with the external economic environment. Effective organizations must be able to adapt to changes in the economic climate.
2. *Technological*. Organizational effectiveness requires use of technology for internal communication as well as for service and product development and delivery. The nature of the business will impact on the roles technology can play, but effective use of technological resources can be as critical in organizational success as effective use of people.

3. *Commercial.* The nature of the commercial environment within which an organization operates is critical to its success. In this sense, one could identify competitors as another stakeholder group. Effectiveness can be defined in terms of finding or developing a specific market niche, or confronting the competition head-on and taking market share.
4. *Social.* This is intended as a broad notion of social, to include socio-political, ethical and cultural measures of effectiveness. Organizations are not only collections of people, but also impact on people (customers, suppliers, shareholders and the public at large). The effects of economic success or failure are social effects (employment, standard of living and quality of life). Organizational goals may have ethical, social and political dimensions. As such, they may conflict with purely economic goals.

Finally, we need to consider the scope of each of four categories of criteria for each of the stakeholder groups:

- internal to the organization
- within the immediate local environment of the organization
- national
- international.

By combining these various categories together we end up with a three-dimensional matrix containing 80 cells, of which most are meaningful stakeholder-by-environment-by-scope combinations.

Organizational effectiveness is a complex multi-dimensional construct. While there are some essential criteria (e.g. maintaining financial viability) for effectiveness, organizations will differ in their overall concept of "effectiveness". They will differ in terms of the emphasis they place on factors such as: internal levels of job satisfaction; pursuit of an ethical sales policy; contribution to the social development of third-world countries, and so on. Such differences will be reflected in an organization's espoused values and missions. Each organization constructs its own definition of effectiveness and its success needs to be evaluated in terms of that construction. Although each organization constructs its own success criteria, these criteria may, in some cases, be externally influenced or imposed. For example governments may prescribe effectiveness criteria for public sector organizations.

IS EFFECTIVENESS AN ORGANIZATIONAL CONSTRUCTION?

The above discussion could be taken to imply that effectiveness is a purely relative term: that there are no absolute criteria that could be applied. While it is clear that organizations differ in the degree of emphasis they place on different criteria, much of this variation can be related back to the overall nature and purpose of the organization (public or private, large or small, production or service oriented etc.). Perhaps the organization's capability to choose and balance various effectiveness criteria is in itself a contributor to overall effectiveness. Clearly, both the clarification of criteria within an organization and decisions about differences in emphasis are actually achieved through the actions of organizational members.

When we consider the characteristics of an effective organization we tend to find common themes emerging. For example, Dunphy (1981) provided the following list of characteristics that define an effective organization:

- clearly-defined goals
- structure related to goals
- constant scanning of the environment and appropriate adaptation
- consistent clear procedures that evolve purposefully
- exercise of power in a manner that recognizes mutual influence
- flexible, participate decision-making
- information openness
- initiative in external relations
- well-defined concept of social responsibility
- meaningful, varied work with learning opportunities
- commitment to personal growth (planned skills development)
- mutual trust, respect and support
- accurate timely performance feedback
- just and equitable rewards.

These can be summarized in terms of five main areas:

1. goal specification
2. clarity of goals and clear communication of objectives throughout the organization
3. awareness of the commercial environment and ability to change and evolve within it
4. a management structure that facilitates goal-related performance
5. a well-motivated workforce, valued by the organization, with competencies that are aligned with the goals of the organization.

Organizations may become ineffective in achieving their espoused goals for one of a number of reasons associated with problems in these areas. While the role of psychology might appear to be most obviously relevant in the last of these areas, psychology has a contribution to make in all of them.

INTERVENING AT DIFFERENT LEVELS

In considering organizational effectiveness, we need to look at problems that can arise at a number of levels of social aggregation, which relate to the areas outlined above.

- *At organizational level:* are the strategies being followed the appropriate ones for achieving the corporate goals, has the wider commercial and socio-political environment been understood and taken into account?

- *At inter-group level:* do the various work groups within the organization communicate and co-operate effectively and share a common understanding of the corporate goals?
- *At intra-group level:* does the organization provide the environment and resources necessary for groups to work effectively?
- *At the individual level:* is each individual role defined in a way that does not create overlap or confusion and are individual needs and competencies considered and managed?

While these may reflect different functional levels and impact on increasingly larger numbers of people within the organization, they are all fundamentally concerned with the performance of individual people.

- It is people who perform at the individual level.
- It is people within organizations who are responsible for providing the working environments for work groups.
- It is people who manage the communications within organizations.
- It is people who manage organizations, from Board level downwards.
- It is people who set the strategy, and define the goals and objectives.

Although it can be helpful and sometimes illuminating to consider organizations as a whole, it is important to remember that the "behaviour" of organizations as entities is determined by the actions of individual members, or groups of members. Organizations, as such, do not take action. Consideration of concepts such as the strategy of an organization, or the state of readiness of an organization, should not lead to the false view that organizations may be treated as independent entities, without recognition of the key causal role of the people who make up the organization.

To change an organization, you have to operate at the level of changing the behaviour of the people who make up that organization. While the role and breadth of impact of the CEO may be different from that of the receptionist, both have an impact on the effectiveness of the organization and psychologists can play a role in enhancing that impact in both cases.

HOW IS ORGANIZATIONAL EFFECTIVENESS DELIVERED THROUGH THE PERFORMANCE OF INDIVIDUALS?

At the heart of the process of managing individual behaviour is the need to direct that behaviour toward the production of results that help build towards realizing the organization's objectives.

Competencies have become an integral part of modern people management throughout the world. To manage people effectively, managers need a way of accurately assessing each individual's strengths, development needs and potential contribution. Competencies have become popular because they meet the need for increasingly sophisticated measures, while remaining firmly linked to observable behaviour.

By defining constructs in terms of clearly specified behaviours, competencies have become a powerful tool for assessing the performance of people. In addition competencies have given managers and their people a common language for discussing development and career potential issues, and a way to express the culture and values of the organization in terms of the behaviour expected of employees.

WHAT DO WE MEAN BY "COMPETENCY"?

We define competencies as *sets of behaviours that are instrumental in the delivery of desired results or outcomes*.

It is important to note the focus here is on behaviours, not on results or personal attributes. The present competency model (Figure A) distinguishes four main sets of variables:

1. *Competencies* themselves—defined as sets of desirable behaviours, where "desirable" is defined in terms of the outcomes to which such behaviours lead. Competencies reflect the behaviours that a person does in order to achieve specific business objectives—these objectives can either be actions to achieve business results or actions to support the general operation of the organization. The goal of a competency approach is to provide specific guidance regarding which behaviours organizations are encouraging among their members.
2. *Competency potential*—the individual attributes necessary for someone to produce the desired behaviours. These attributes are not always reflected in actual behaviour, since the behaviour that an individual displays is moderated by

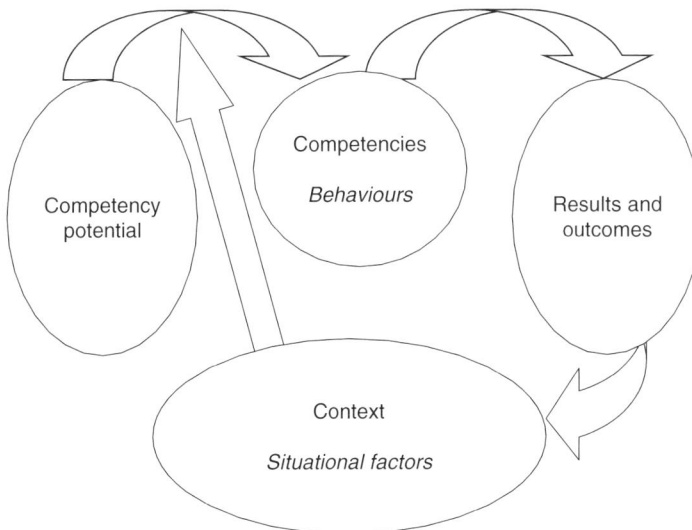

Figure A   A model of competency

the *context*. For example, an operative may have the capability to work more effectively and increase output but will not do so, because the rewards (such as recognition, praise or additional pay) are not available.

3. *Context*—the implicit and explicit situational factors, which influence individuals within a work setting to behave in certain ways and not to behave in others. In addition to instructions (e.g. the line manager's setting of an individual employee's goals), a wide range of contextual and situational factors in the work setting will also influence an individual's effort and affect the individual's ability to produce the desired sets of behaviour. Important situational factors in the workplace include: work colleagues; supervision; reward systems; physical environment. There are also situational factors outside the direct work setting which can have an impact on the competencies displayed by an individual. These include: domestic relationships and leisure pursuits.

4. *Results*—the outcomes or goals of behaviour, which have been defined either explicitly or implicitly by the individual, their line manager or the organization. The distinction between results and behaviour is important and serves as a reminder that sometimes people may be displaying many of the necessary competencies but things go wrong—perhaps due to unforeseen external events.

It is only when an individual performs within a setting that we can judge whether they are displaying the competencies required to generate the outcomes needed. As that may be too late, we need to provide organizations with effective methods of measuring competency potential.

Competency Potential

A person's potential, or capability, to behave competently in the workplace is partly a function of their personal attributes. These include underlying aspects of the individual (aptitudes, interests, values, motives and personal style) as well as their knowledge and their skills. Campbell et al. (1993) have similarly distinguished between "antecedent" person factors (personality and abilities) and "determinants" (knowledge, skills and motivation) of job-relevant behaviour.

The concept of competency potential is important in that it enables us to draw a distinction between measures that *predict* competency and measures *of* competency. This is a crucial difference that many other approaches blur. It can also appear to be blurred by the use of common language. For example, some personality questionnaires use terms such as "persuasiveness" and there are competency definitions using the same term. The new model requires us to be very clear in differentiating these: the trait describes a propensity to act in certain ways, the competency is based on evidence that a person does act in those ways.

Situational Factors

The differences between competency potential and competency arise from the impact of situations on behaviour. In any work setting, there are factors that tend to facilitate or encourage some behaviours, and factors that will inhibit or discourage other behaviours. These factors range from the communication of instructions down from line management to the physical arrangements of space within the work setting; from the relationships between work colleagues to the provision of the necessary resources and materials.

Situational factors can be divided into two types: *drivers* and *barriers*. As their names imply, drivers act to encourage or increase the likelihood of desirable behaviours being elicited. Barriers, on the other hand, act to reduce the likelihood of these behaviours occurring. In short, the same person may be able to act competently in one work setting but unable to do so in another. This is not because he or she lacks the necessary knowledge, skills and other attributes, but because the situation makes it difficult to impossible for them to be displayed. As a consequence, the desired outcomes or results are not achieved.

Characteristics of the work environment act as barriers to or drivers of behaviour both formally (e.g. through training, provision of equipment, objectives setting) and informally (e.g. through social relations, ease of communication, work place design influences on activities and so on).

The environmental factors that affect an individual's ability to demonstrate competency, given a clear set of performance objectives, range from physical and geographical factors, through provision of resources, to organizational culture and the patterns of formal and informal person relationships within the work setting.

Relationships represent the social structures that make up the surrounding of each individual. Relationships moderate the objective work demands by providing multiple perspective of authorities, peers, dependants and external relations that may be supportive of each other or conflict. Their operation is central to understanding and managing performance at work. The formal and informal structure combine to set the framework against which behaviours are shown and judged.

SUMMARY

This book is focused on building a detailed picture of how organizational effectiveness stems from the actions of individuals, and, consequently, how psychological interventions can aid its achievement. This Introduction has sketched out the structure and boundaries of a broad framework within which the link between people and their organizations can be viewed. In the following chapters, the authors have addressed the issues within the framework that relate to their own areas of knowledge and expertise.

REFERENCES

Atkinson, A.A., Waterhouse, J.H. & Wells, R.B. (1997). A stakeholder approach to strategic performance measurement. *Sloan Management Review*, spring, pp. 25–37.
Campbell, J.P., McCloy, R.A., Oppler, S.H. & Sager, C.E. (1993). A theory of performance. In N. Schmitt, W. C. Borman et al. (Eds), *Personnel Selection in Organizations*. San Francisco: Jossey-Bass.

Dunphy, D. (1981). *Organizational Change by Choice*. Sydney: McGraw-Hill [reprinted 1993].

Fryer, D. & Payne, R. (1986). Being unemployed: a review of the literature on the psychological experience of unemployment. In C.L. Cooper & I.T. Robertson (Eds), *International Review of Industrial and Organizational Psychology*, volume **1**. Chichester: John Wiley.

Kaplan, R.S. & Norton, D.P. (1996). Using the balanced scorecard as a strategic management system. *Harvard Business Review*, **73** (1), 75–85.

PART I

CHAPTER 1

Psychology and Organizational Effectiveness

Paul Sparrow
Manchester Business School, UK
and
Michael West
Aston Business School, UK

INTRODUCTION

Management should take a much broader perspective on what is meant by effectiveness. As psychologists we could concern ourselves with the many different potential contributions of the individual to the "organization" (by which we might mean its products, its processes, or its performance) or to its "effectiveness". The performance criteria applied to "effectiveness" are themselves diverse. We might mean: basic task competence or proficiency; delivery of performance against efficient or cost effective performance metrics; an impact on organizational competitiveness on different bases such as speed or time; the creation of internal or external customer perceptions of added value; longer term strategic risks or costs associated with error or inappropriate organizational decision making; or even the "collateral damage" created by current actions in terms of the future constraints on actions that they might create. If demonstrating the link between the individual and the definitions of effectiveness at the beginning of this list is difficult enough, then making organizations realize that some of the dimensions at the end of the list may be equally important areas of contribution and study will prove even more problematic. So do we have relevance, influence, both or neither? Is our knowledge base powerful enough to make relevant previously unappreciated dimensions of organizational effectiveness?

Psychologists have conducted a wealth of research relevant to issues of organizational effectiveness in recent years. To support this judgement we address what is known about issues of three facets of effectiveness (productivity, innovation and mental health) at two levels of analysis: individual and group. We then review the evidence that looks at the link between HRM and organizational

Organizational Effectiveness: The Role of Psychology
Edited by I.T. Robertson, M. Callinan and D. Bartram. © 2002 John Wiley & Sons, Ltd.

performance. Identifying the factors that determine company economic perfor-mance is a central challenge to researchers, policy makers and managers, if countries are to compete successfully in world markets. Ultimately, however, economic performance is about the contributions and constraints of human be-haviour. We therefore adopt an explicitly psychological approach.

WELL-BEING OF INDIVIDUALS, TEAMS AND ORGANIZATIONS

How well the organization makes use of employees to achieve its goals will directly affect its productivity. If the physical environment of an organization is so noxious that it causes injury or illness to employees they will be forced to withdraw their work and knowledge through illness, absenteeism or turnover. Moreover, if the way work is organized and the workload distributed is such that high levels of strain are experienced, this in turn may lead to problems of mental health with similar detrimental consequences. We examine these issues at three levels of analysis—individual, team and organizational.

Individual Well-being

We shall concentrate on three areas of research in which individual well-being has recently been linked to organizational effectiveness: the psychological contract; the creation of effective organizational cultures through organization citizenship behaviours; and perceptions of person–organization values fit. Organizations need to develop organizational cultures that create *the mental, emo-tional and attitudinal states that precede effective employee performance*. Once these states are established in a positive direction, *then* employees begin to exhibit a series of salient organizational behaviours; i.e. the behaviours that actually generate effective performance. People are attracted to specific organizational cultures, which act as stabilizers of individual behaviour. Currently, however, many organizations are using changes in work system design and business pro-cess to modify employees' work orientations and responsibilities, and there-fore the extent to which these sorts of mental, emotional and attitudinal states are seen as discretionary, or as an inherent part of the job and organizational life (Coyle-Shapiro, 1999). The most important of these states are: trust and an effec-tive psychological contract; perceived level of organizational support, fairness and justice, work motivation; job satisfaction and job involvement (de Witte & van Muijen, 1999).

The Psychological Contract

Kramer (1999) notes that trust is a complex, multidimensional psychological state that includes cognitive, affective and motivational components. People think trust and feel trust. The psychological contract has featured in recent work on effectiveness. It represents an implicit and open-ended agreement on what is given and what is received and captures expectations of reciprocal behaviour that cover a wide range of societal norms and interpersonal behaviour (Sparrow, 2000). It is based on changing perceptions of the employer–employee balance of power and is very emotive—some academics argue that you only know what the contract is when you breach it. Initially attention to the psychological contract associated with changes in the employment contract outlined the "old deal" and the "new deal". There is little consensus on the components of the "new" psychological contract (Cavanaugh & Noe, 1999) but the shift is seen generally in terms of a move from a paternalistic to a partnership relationship, and a move from relational aspects of the relationship to more transactional components. Managers' loyalty to their employer has declined (Stroh et al., 1994) and commitment to type of work and profession appears to be stronger now than commitment to organization (Ancona et al., 1996).

The psychological contract is viewed as an umbrella construct capturing a range of variables associated with trust, commitment and the exchange of expectations and obligations. Research has operationalized several psychological constructs (such as perceptions, expectations, beliefs, promises and obligations) and applied these processes to a range of outcomes (such as levels of commitment, job satisfaction, socialization, employer–employee fit and organizational climate). Research has tended to include several different psychological facets, each of which bears an unknown relationship to the other, and the contract has become an analytic nightmare (Guest, 1998). On a positive note, however, the label "psychological contract" has captured complex changes in work in times of high uncertainty. It has acted as an organization-wide frame of analysis (similar to culture or competencies) and has used a language (such as mindsets, frames of reference, schema, implicit deals, breach of trust and disengagement) that captures concerns over the new employment relationship (Sparrow & Marchington, 1998).

Employees are assumed to "input" various attributes to the "new deal", such as their work values and attitudes, motivational needs, and personal dispositions or competencies. Contract formation and breach processes (signals sent by the HRM environment about socialization, mutual exchanges, promises and obligations) lie at the heart of most research. Attention has also been turned to a series of "outputs" or outcomes, such as commitment, job satisfaction, trust and organization citizenship behaviours. Much research assumes a generic response to perceived breach of contract in terms of the impact on commitment and organizational citizenship behaviour, but research in sectors that have undergone significant amounts of rationalization, such as financial services (see, for example, Hartley, 1995; Herriot & Pemberton, 1996; Sparrow, 1996) suggests an individually-diverse response. These studies have teased out different attitudinal and contractual stances held by segments of the workforce. Individual differences are expected to return as important predictors of adaptive work behaviour in the new employment contract, with some individuals likely to pursue high intensity/variety patterns, and others seeking the opposite.

Attempts have been made to tease out the role of the social exchange elements of the contract, by concentrating on the perceived agreements between two parties (Shore & Barksdale, 1998). Therefore, although the psychological contract is highly idiosyncratic and situation-bound, it has been used to capture the impact of recent changes in the employment contract (Shore & Tetrick, 1994). Research suggests that it has additional value over other constructs such as perceived organizational support and can help us describe, understand, and predict the consequences of changes in employment (Coyle-Shapiro & Kessler, 2000). The sense of mutuality implicit in the psychological contract has proved a useful vehicle to capture the consequences of perceived imbalances of exchange in the new employment contract. Because it is evidenced in an individual's mental models of the world, it is felt to act as a deep driver of careers, rewards and commitment behaviour. Positive employer contract behaviour has been linked to outcomes such as: job satisfaction and organizational commitment (Coyle-Shapiro & Kessler, 2000; Guest et al., 1996; Robinson & Rousseau, 1994); organizational citizenship behaviour (Robinson & Morrison, 1995); and employee performance (Robinson, 1996). Social exchange theory is used to argue that different employees appear to react similarly to contract violations or fulfilment. When fulfilled, employees are assumed to reduce their indebtedness by reciprocating with more effort directed at the source of the benefits. Breach of contract is seen through three primary reactions (Hirschman, 1970; Turnley & Feldman, 1998):

- *exit behaviour*, where the individual is angered by the violation so seeks employment elsewhere
- *voice*, where the individual makes an attempt to correct the problem and salvage the employment contract, and
- *loss of loyalty*, where the individual withdraws emotionally, displays less loyalty and lower organizational citizenship behaviour.

Individual Well-being and Contextual Performance

The role of psychological contract, motivation and organizational commitment has consistently featured in the causal processes investigated or assumed by the above studies. The level of organization citizenship behaviours (OCBs)—also referred to as contextual performance—has also emerged recently as an important linking mechanism between individual well-being and organizational effectiveness.

Contextual performance plays an important part in linking individual task performance to the broader organizational and social demands (Borman & Motovidlo, 1993, 1997). Indeed, OCBs first became important as a possible explanation to the satisfaction–performance relationship. A series of important distinctions can be made. Recipients of OCBs may be interpersonal or organizational. Some OCBs may be seen as part of the job and accepted as a role requirement, others may be a personal choice and therefore seen as part of a reciprocal social exchange (Coyle-Shapiro, 1999). It is this latter element—the perception of the OCB climate within an organization—that is important in relation to effectiveness. These perceptions are rarely job specific but are rather shared across several jobs in an organization. They are a product of organizational culture and shape the individual environment (Allen & Rush, 1998). In fact, the job satisfaction–OCB link may be due to the underpinning notion of fairness or justice, given that job satisfaction is a judgement about met and unmet expectations. Therefore, justice has been seen as a direct precursor of OCBs (Konovsky & Pugh, 1994), as has the level of perceived organizational support (Wayne et al., 1997) and commitment (as a form of emotional attachment) (Meyer & Allen, 1997; Pond et al., 1997). Justice perceptions in turn appear to be preceded by—or mediated by—perceptions of trustworthiness (Mayer & Davis, 1999).

Psychologists are now trying to unravel some of the complex causation issues across these constructs. Coyle-Shapiro and Kessler (2000) have drawn attention to the role of perceived organizational support (a general perception by the employee of the extent to which the organization values their general contribution and well-being and an important element of many assessments of climate) and the subsequent fulfilment of obligations. Two questions were asked: does perceived organizational support mediate the impact that the fulfilment of obligations and promises has on important psychological outcomes? Does the psychological contract account for useful additional variance in outcome behaviours? High levels of perceived breach of contract were found and psychological contract fulfilment accounted for unique and additional variance in explaining levels of commitment and OCBs.

Person–Organization Fit

Another way of linking individual well-being to organizational effectiveness that is gaining prominence is through the study of perceptions of person–organization (P–O) fit. The literature on perceptions of P–O fit provides a bridge through which shared individual perceptions of the climate are linked to the mental, emotional and attitudinal states associated with an effective culture (Sparrow, 2001). P–O fit in terms of values—and the socialization processes that help engineer it—is also seen as a precursor to most of the previous constructs: trust, justice, perceived organizational support, contract formation, commitment and OCBs. It sets the frame for all of these mental, emotional and attitudinal states, because values are an important disposition, akin to personality traits that predispose people to trust people more or less. Attitudes define trustworthiness; perceptions of trustworthiness and disposition influence trust; and trust is exhibited through a series of behavioural intentions (Mayer et al., 1995). Values lie at the "front-end" of the beliefs (cognitions)–feelings (affect)–behavioural intention process suggested in Ajzen and Fishbein's (1980) theory of reasoned action. They are proving a useful vehicle for study. P–O fit is then seen as the congruence between patterns of organizational values and patterns of what an individual values in the organization (Chatman, 1991).

Perceptions of P–O values fit have been linked to different forms of effectiveness. For example, congruence between individual and corporate values has been found to: correlate significantly with job outcomes such as individual productivity, job satisfaction and commitment (O'Reilly et al., 1991); contribute unique variance to job satisfaction, job involvement, organizational commitment, turnover intention and optimism about the organization's future

(Harris & Mossholder, 1996); and predict turnover versus staying decisions of recruits during the early employment experience (Vandenberghe, 1999). However, the role of P–O fit can be over-stated. In some instances it is not the fit of values, but *the actual values themselves* that may be more predictive of well-being or effectiveness. Vandenberghe and Peiró (1999) found that the *actual* organizational values and individual value preferences were more predictive of outcomes such as commitment than was P–O *value fit*, which had a marginal impact. Similarly, a study on the impact of cultural value orientations and P–O fit measures of HR preference and value fit in Kenyan employees on levels of job involvement similarly found that actual values were more predictive than value fit (Nyambegera et al., 2001).

Well-being in Teams

Socio-emotional Issues over Task Characteristics

Work at the individual level has, then, laid out a series of causal mechanisms through which individual perceptions of trust, justice, organizational support, and the psychological contract obligations and promises exchange impact salient organizational behaviours (in terms of organizational effectiveness) such as commitment, involvement and contextual performance. Similar important evidence can be found at the team level. Given the centrality of team work to recent HRM strategies, organizational structures and business process redesigns, psychologists have concentrated on the task characteristics and new organizational forms and contexts that have made team-working a more important link on the road to organizational effectiveness (Sparrow, 1998). However, effectiveness at this level of analysis is also driven by the more fundamental socio-emotional requirements of team-based working. As noted in the above analysis of individual level factors, it is the sequence of causal factors at the team psychology level that leads to effectiveness.

The fundamental human drive and pervasive motivation to form and maintain lasting, positive and significant relationships helps us to understand the functioning of teams at work, and in particular the emotions and well-being manifested in work groups. Most current research and theories about the functioning of teams fail to take account of the solid evolutionary basis of our tendency to form strong attachments, and by extension to live and work in groups. Human beings work and live in groups because groups enable survival and reproduction (Ainsworth, 1989; Axelrod & Hamilton, 1981; Barash, 1977; Bowlby, 1969; Buss, 1990,1991; Hogan et al., 1985; Moreland, 1987). By living and working in groups early humans could share food, easily find mates, and care for infants. They could hunt more effectively and defend themselves against their enemies. Individuals who did not readily join groups would be disadvantaged in comparison with group members as a consequence. The need to belong, which is at the root of our tendency to live and work in groups, is manifested most profoundly in the behaviour of children and infants. Children who stuck close to adults were more likely to survive and to be able to reproduce, because they would be protected from danger, cared for and provided with food: "Over the course of evolution, the small group became the basic survival strategy developed by the human species" (Barchas, 1986, p. 212). This fundamental human motivation to belong therefore shapes much human behaviour and for our purposes helps to explain emotional reactions in teams. The absence of one or more of the characteristics of belongingness (frequent interaction, likely continuity and stability, mutual affective concern, and freedom from conflict and negative affect) will lead to conflict and disintegration within relationships and teams. For the benefits of team-working are not only improved task performance (West, 1996), but also intra-psychic and emotional benefits for team members (Carter & West, 1999; Patterson et al., 1997).

By recognizing the influence of the need to belong upon the behaviour of individuals in teams we can come to understand something of the range and underlying causes of emotions in teams. Being accepted, included and welcomed in the team will lead to feelings of happiness, elation, contentment and calm. Being rejected, excluded or ignored will lead to feelings of anxiety, depression, grief, jealousy or loneliness. Team members' emotional reactions will be stimulated by real, potential or imagined changes in their belongingness within their work team. Real, potential or imagined increases in belongingness will lead to an increase in positive individual and team level affect. Decreases in belongingness will be associated with threats to the individual and a sense of deprivation that will lead to negative affect. Below we consider the effects of the need to belong upon positive and negative emotions and attitudes.

Positive Emotions and Attitudes: Satisfaction, Trust and Well-being

When a new work team is formed, team members tend to experience positive emotions and the creation of the team is often a cause for celebration. When new members join teams there tends to be an abundance of positive affect and warm expressions of welcome which are a consequence of the increase of the sense of belonging experienced by existing members and by the new member. Indeed this positive affect itself increases attraction and social bonding within the group (Moreland, 1987).

One of the characteristics of a strong sense of belonging is the sense of mutuality in the relationships. So satisfaction in teams is also likely to be a consequence of both the costs as well as the rewards of team membership. People prefer relationships and teams within which all give and take. For example, Hays (1985) examined "relationship satisfaction" from the perspective of behaviourism, assuming that rewards would determine people's satisfaction. He found instead that satisfaction was predicted by rewards plus costs, apparently because people prefer relationships and groups in which all both give and receive support and care. Baumeister et al. (1993) report that for both those who give love without receiving it, and those who receive love without giving it, the experience is aversive. Mutuality and reciprocity appear to be necessary for positive affect, and satisfaction will be highest when the sense of mutuality in teams is strong.

Satisfaction will also be higher to the extent that the team members interact frequently, the tenure of the team is relatively enduring, there is a sense of mutual concern among team members, and there is not a high level of conflict. These propositions are, of course, easy to subject to empirical test.

We come again to the importance of trust, which will be most likely to develop in teams where there is a strong sense of reciprocal concern amongst team members. Belonging implies a sense of mutual affective concern. When this shared affective concern is developed in teams it will lead to feelings of satisfaction among team members, and particularly to trust. Holmes and Rempel (1989), reviewing the evidence on trust in relationships, concluded that trust depends on the mutual recognition of reciprocal concern and closeness. This mutual affective concern is also likely to translate into behaviour within the team and specifically to the expression of altruism. Much has been made in social psychology of the so-called "bystander effect", where bystanders in the presence of others fail to take action to help someone in distress, apparently because of a sense of diffusion of responsibility and anxiety about the personal consequences of involvement. But what is less well known is the evidence that when bystanders are members of a cohesive group, the effect is nullified (Harkins & Petty, 1982). Moreover, members of large cohesive groups are more likely to help (whereas among strangers larger numbers of bystanders leads to a lower likelihood of intervention). Social loafing (where group members exert less effort in task accomplishment in the presence of other group members) is not evident in cohesive groups where members have unique contributions, even when their contributions cannot be identified (Harkins & Petty, 1982).

Recent research evidence provides some support for the thesis we advance here. In a study of the mental health of health service workers, Carter and West (1999) compared those people who worked in teams, those who worked in pseudo-teams and those not working in teams, in the United Kingdom National Health Service. Pseudo-team members were those who reported working in a team but indicated that there were not clear team objectives, or members did not frequently work with other members of the team to achieve those objectives, or there were not separate roles, or the team was not recognized by others in the organization as a team. The sample of 2250 workers completed the General Health Questionnaire and individuals were categorized as "cases" if their scores indicated that they would benefit from professional intervention, because of high stress levels (Hardy et al., in press). The results revealed that 35% of those who did not work in teams were cases; 30% of those who were in pseudo-teams were cases; while only 21% of those who worked in real teams were cases. It appears from these data that working in teams is a significant buffer against the stresses of health service work. Further investigation revealed that the differences between these teams could be attributed to the role clarity experienced by team members, along with the high level of social support that they experienced. Moreover, working in teams appeared to ameliorate negative effects of organizational level difficulties. The findings extend to studies at the organizational level. Patterson et al. (1997) showed that in 54 UK manufacturing organizations, the extent of team-working was a predictor of the overall levels of mental health amongst employees.

Well-being of Organizations: Effective Organizational Cultures

The thesis developed at the team level should not be taken to imply that team membership is good in organizations come what may. Evidence derived from research on social participation and bad marriages suggests that being in pathological teams may be worse than being in no team at all. The same is true at the organizational level. It is the organizational culture that may lead to pathologically detrimental or highly effective outcomes. Effective performance is seen to follow from culture because the organization's culture provides (Ott, 1989):

- shared patterns of interpretations and perceptions that show employees how to act and think
- an emotional sense of involvement and commitment to organizational values and moral codes; i.e. what to value and how to feel
- defined and maintained boundaries allowing groups to identify and include members in problem solving
- learned responses to problems and commonly held understandings for organizing actions
- control systems, that in turn prescribe and prohibit certain behaviours.

Culture as the Initiator of Appropriate Mental, Emotional and Attitudinal States of Mind

The topics of organizational culture and organizational effectiveness are inextricably linked (de Witte & van Muijen, 1999). However, it is the field of organizational culture that has dominated management thinking about problems of adaptability, change and competitive success in large organizations (Kilmann, 1984; Pettigrew, 1979; Schein, 1985). Culture is presumed to create appropriate states of mind—i.e. the mental, emotional and attitudinal states that precede effective employee performance referred to earlier. The attraction of the construct is that it represents a global concept to help understand complex organizational problems.

Requests to analyse and assess organizational culture and align it with strategic options continue to be directed at academics and consulting organizations. The need to develop viable assessments of organizational culture and climate has increased for a number of reasons (Sparrow & Gaston, 1996). The 1990s witnessed a continuing revolution in the nature and shape of organizations, with the emergence of new organizational forms, concepts of business process, and basis of the employment relationship and psychological contract. As organizations have become more flexible, and traditional boundaries of hierarchy, function and geography are eroding, the boundaries that matter most are in the minds and perceptions of managers and the workforce. Culture is being seen as an increasingly important co-ordination mechanism. For example, Ruigrok and Achtenhagen (1999) have examined the shift from economic organizational forms towards network organizational forms (also referred to as cellular, individualized or horizontal structures) in four innovative German-speaking companies and found that the role of organizational culture as a co-ordination mechanism increased in importance over the period 1992–97. The same is true across European organizations (Ruigrok et al., 1999). Not surprisingly, then, the co-ordination of organizational behaviour (an important element of organizational effectiveness) is seen increasingly to rely in the management of psychosocial boundaries and perceptions, or "soft-wired" aspects of strategic change, such as the way individuals pattern authority, tasks, politics, identity, manager–subordinate relationships and subordinate–peer perceptions (Sparrow, 1994).

The Assessment of Relevant Domains

Interest in high performance organization cultures can be traced back to the 1970s when researchers and consultants at Harvard, Stanford, MIT and McKinsey began to explore the positive and negative impacts that organization culture could have. One might imagine that psychologists would by now have some clear understanding about the role of culture in creating effectiveness. Until recently, however, the usefulness of the construct of culture has not been evidenced in the ultimate financial performance of organizations. An effective performance culture *is hard to emulate* because it is embedded in a complex set of links that operate all the way from the level of organizational culture through to eventual organizational performance.

  Two issues have obscured our understanding: a lack of consensus over how best to measure culture; and debates over the relative causal path to effectiveness and organizational performance. A long list of questions still dominates attempts to assess effectiveness and culture at the organizational level today (de Witte & van Muijen, 1999). Psychologists are debating what domain of activity assessments should focus on, whose perspective (or which constituency's point of view) should be evidenced, what level of analysis should be used, what time frame is appropriate, and what types of data are appropriate. We still ask such questions in part because researchers have tried to understand culture, and so attempt to "*measure to know*" whereas consulting firms need to know whether culture can be managed, and so "*measure to change*" (Sackmann, 2001). Assessments have also tended to concentrate on yielding understanding about the organization as a human system (Schneider, 1990), rather than on the prediction of outcomes. There is a difference between domains that are predictive of performance and domains that are useful for facilitating understanding. DeWulf et al. (1999) found nine primary domains or dimensions are assessed across the most common instruments in use: hierarchical relations, peer relations, relations between sub-groups, selection, socialization, reward, relations with clients, relations with competitors, and job design. The balance of items across these domains is unequal, with hierarchical relations, rewards, job design and relations between sub-groups featured in relative order of the proportion of items dedicated to them. Moreover, the choice of these dimensions is not driven by any coherent model of domain relevance.

The Link between Cultural Values and Effectiveness

Cultural value assessments reflect and tap collective interpretations of the most important ways of perceiving, thinking and feeling (group understandings of appropriate problem solving); the norms, beliefs and justifying ideologies (the system-sanctioned behaviours); and the espoused management style and assumptions (the shared meanings) (Sparrow, 2001). The creation of a generic set of values, perceptions and behaviours does not automatically lead to superior financial performance, because the link may be destroyed at several important points. However, values do appear to represent one of the most fundamental starting points in the culture–climate–performance linkage process. They predict eventual organizational performance and are an important determinant of several of the factors that link the individual, team and organization to this eventual effectiveness.

Research has linked organizational value systems to a number of psychological outcomes associated with effectiveness. A six-year longitudinal study of organizational value systems showed that cultures emphasizing interpersonal relationships were more likely to produce lower staff turnover rates than other cultures (Sheridan, 1992), satisfaction-orientated norms are positively related to role clarity, personal satisfaction with the organization and intention to stay, whilst security-orientated norms are negatively related to these outcomes (Rousseau, 1990). Attention has shifted to the link between values and contextual performance. In a study of over 200 manufacturing employees, Goodman and Svyvantek (1999) measured the impact that both perceived and ideal culture had on contextual performance. The perceived culture (what the individual valued) accounted for a significant amount of performance, and the ideal culture accounted for a significant proportion of additional variance. Warmth, competence, reward, risk, standards, identity, customer focus and decision-making accounted for the majority of the variance in performance. In line with the person–organization (P–O) literature in general, P–O fit discrepancies accounted for 2–6% of the variance in total contextual performance, and task performance, was also linked to P–O fit.

Cultural values have been shown to be associated with superior organizational performance. Kotter and Heskett (1992) assumed that, regardless of the type of culture, it was the *strength of culture* that was the most predictive of performance. If all managers share relatively consistent values, then performance follows because of increased goal alignment, a stronger sense of motivation and intrinsic reward implicit in the "successful" cultures, and implicit controlling and sanctioning of appropriate behaviours without the need for expensive and stifling bureaucracy and co-ordination structures (Hofstede, 1980; Peters & Waterman, 1982; Schein, 1985). This argument gathered uncritical support from many senior managers during the 1980s and early 1990s. Until recently evidence for the influence of cultural values upon organizational productivity has been limited, but there is an increasing weight of evidence suggesting that high performance culture and climates can be identified.

Do employees' perceptions of the culture or climate of the organization predict company performance, and, if so, which aspects? A 15-year longitudinal research programme at the Centre for Economic Performance (CEP) at the London School of Economics (to which we return later in this chapter) has provided some support for the culture–performance link. This study examined the market environment, organizational characteristics and managerial practices that are empirically related to company financial performance of over a hundred

UK manufacturing companies (Patterson et al., 1997). Over half the companies participated in employee attitude and organizational culture surveys that explored perceptions of organizational functioning in areas such as innovation, training, concern for employee welfare, performance pressure and formalization. They also measured some of the outcomes (job satisfaction and organizational commitment) that are assumed to facilitate the link to organizational performance. An analysis of the link between employee ratings of organizational culture in 36 firms and their financial performance found that cultural factors accounted for some 10% of the variation in profitability between the two periods measured during the study. The results were even more striking in relation to change in productivity. When the results were examined in terms of predicting change in organizational performance, individual employee attitudes (commitment and job satisfaction) accounted for 11% of the variation between companies. However, some 29% of the variation between companies in change in productivity over an 18-month period could be explained by the measures of culture (Patterson et al., 1998). A significant proportion of change in productivity could be predicted by those cultural variables associated with emphasis on productivity and human relations values. It is important to note that out of 17 cultural scales, only *eight* were significantly related to performance: concern for employee welfare; autonomy; emphasis on training; supervisory support; vision; emphasis on quality; pressure to produce; and performance feedback.

INDIVIDUAL, TEAM AND ORGANIZATIONAL INNOVATION

The first section of this chapter concentrated on psychological factors that are associated with well-being at the individual, team and organizational levels. It should be noted that the causal pathways that have been revealed between key variables (such as organizational culture, value fit, trust, fairness, the social exchange of the psychological contract, commitment and contextual performance) have relevance for the final debate in this chapter, which will be about the relationship between HRM practices and organizational performance. In this section we concentrate on the role of innovation as an important element of organizational effectiveness.

Innovation is the development and implementation of new and improved products or ways of working. Innovations are intentional attempts (based on our own, or others' creativity) to bring about benefits from changes; these might include economic benefits, personal growth, increased satisfaction, improved group cohesiveness, better organizational communication, as well as the productivity and economic benefits that we usually identify. Innovations may include technological changes, such as new products, but may also include new production processes, or the introduction of new computer support services within an organization. They can also include administrative changes, such as human resource management (HRM) strategies, organizational policies or the introduction of teamwork.

Psychologists have made a contribution to understanding the innovation process at the individual, team and organization levels. This research has made it clear that innovation occurs only where there is strong practical and cultural support for efforts to introduce new and improved products and procedures. At the same time, opportunities to develop and implement skills in the workplace and to innovate are central to the satisfaction of people at work (Nicholson & West, 1988), while innovation is vital to the effectiveness of organizations in highly demanding and competitive environments (Geroski, 1994).

Individual Innovation

Much research evidence within psychology indicates that psychological safety is an important factor influencing individual innovation. Psychologists have focused their attention on two issues: the factors that facilitate innovation at the individual level, and the individual characteristics that are associated with innovation.

Factors that Facilitate the Individual's Innovative Behaviour

Innovation is inhibited when people feel insecure and unsafe at work (West & Farr, 1990; West, 1987). Just as children who have close bonds with their parents are more likely to explore in strange environments (Ainsworth & Bell, 1974); just as clients who have a sense of psychological safety with their therapists are likely to explore threatening aspects of their own experience (Rogers, 1961); so too are employees likely to risk proposing and trying out new ways of doing things when they feel relatively safe from threat as a consequence.

Psychological knowledge about individual innovation is influenced by two axioms about human behaviour. The first is that human beings are motivated to explore and manipulate their environment in ways that are essentially creative (West & Farr, 1990; West et al., 1994; Nicholson & West, 1988). Research on human development from infancy on has shown that exploratory behaviour, curiosity, competence or mastery motivation strongly influence relationships with the environment. The second axiom is that we are driven by a need to be free from threat, and to have a sense of psychological safety. Creativity occurs when individuals feel free from pressure, safe, and positive (Claxton, 1997, 1998). Experimental manipulations of stress levels have shown that higher levels of stress lead to greater reliance on habitual solutions. Psychological threats to face or identity are also associated with more rigid thinking, and time pressure increases rigidity of thinking on work-related tasks such as selection decisions (Kruglansky & Freund, 1983). Prince (1975) believed that speculation makes people in work settings feel vulnerable because we often tend to experience our workplaces as unsafe. Questioning too closely the person who comes up with an idea, joking about the proposal (even in a light way), or simply ignoring the proposal can lead to the person feeling defensive, which tends to reduce not only his speculation but that of others in the group. Where individuals are threatened they react defensively and unimaginatively, tending to stick to tried and tested routines rather than attempting new ways of dealing with their environment.

A number of other work factors influence the extent to which individuals innovate in their work, and therefore ultimately organizational effectiveness. The first two concern job design factors: intrinsically interesting work, and level of autonomy and control. Individuals are more likely to innovate when they are performing tasks which are intrinsically interesting and which represent a whole, meaningful piece of work rather than a limited atomistic piece of assembly line functioning (Amabile, 1983). People are more likely to innovate where they have sufficient autonomy and control over their work to be able to try out new and improved ways of doing things (West, 1987; Nicholson & West, 1988; Oldham & Cummings, 1996). Not only are individuals who are placed in such situations likely to be creative and innovative, but their mental health at work is likely to be positive as a result (West, 1988, 1989; Bunce & West, 1995a,b, 1996).

Individual Characteristics

Reflecting traditional concerns with selection and training, psychologists have also given attention to *who* innovates. We shall examine the link between individual characteristics and organizational performance under the issue of competency later in the chapter, but draw attention here to some important individual characteristics in the context of innovation.

The innovation process begins with the creativity of individuals. The generation of a new idea is a cognitive process, located within individuals, albeit fostered by interaction processes, for example, in teams. Thus, first and foremost, innovative individuals are both creative and innovative (i.e. they don't just have creative ideas, they also try to implement them). These are people who have a preference for thinking in novel ways; who think globally instead of locally (distinguishing the wood from the trees); who can see problems in new ways and escape the bounds of conventional thinking; the analytic abilities to recognize which ideas are worth pursuing; and the ability to persuade others of the value of their ideas (Mumford & Gustafson, 1988; Sternberg & Lubart, 1996).

To be innovative and creative we also require sufficient knowledge of the field to be able to move it forward, while not being so conceptually trapped in it that we are unable to conceive of alternative courses (Mumford & Gustafson, 1988). A legislative thinking style is required, or a preference for thinking in novel ways of one's own choosing. People who are confident of their abilities are more likely to innovate in the workplace (Nicholson & West, 1988). Perseverance against social pressures presumably reduces the dangers of premature abandonment. Minority influence theory in social psychology suggests that perseverance acts to bring about change in the views of majorities, and is a necessary behavioural style amongst innovators (for reviews see Nemeth, 1986; Nemeth & Owens, 1996). Tolerance of ambiguity, widely associated with creativity, enables individuals to avoid the problems of following only mental ruts, and increases the chances of unusual responses and the discovery of novelty (Barron & Harrington, 1981).

Innovative people tend to be *self-directed*, enjoying and requiring freedom in their work (Mumford & Gustafson, 1988). They have a high need for *freedom, control and discretion* in the workplace and appear to find bureaucratic limitations or the exercise of control by managers frustrating (West, 1987; West & Rushton, 1989). Such people need clear work objectives along with high autonomy to perform well in work.

Detailing such observations raises another contribution that psychologists have made to the understanding of effectiveness at the individual level, which is to help unravel whether organizations would be better to pursue selection or development HRM strategies in relation to important individual characteristics. Innovation has always been felt to reside at the crossroads of personality and intelligence. Is it our personality that makes us more innovative (in which case organizations might favour a selection solution), or is it more to do with the way that we think (in which case a training and development solution is appropriate)?

It was noted earlier that there was not an automatic link between working in an innovative role or job design and innovative behaviour (Guest et al., 2000). The conclusion from this work was that in terms of propensity to innovate at work, people were either innovative or not, regardless of their contractual status. So what is the role of individual differences? Patterson (1999) has developed a personality instrument, deriving items from competency analysis techniques, and has linked this to other measures of innovation and other psychological assessments. Four factors played a role: consistency of work style; adaptive problem solving style; motivation to change or typical intellectual engagement; and challenging behaviour. The link to personality measures—notably openness to experience, extraversion, conscientiousness and agreeableness—was stronger (correlations up to $r = 0.49$) than to intelligence ($r = 0.17$). Patterson concludes that there is a clear personality root to innovation. Moreover, because conscientiousness (negatively associated with innovation) is the one personality factor that organizations, wittingly or unwittingly, build into their selection systems, psychologists can show how organizations design out their source of competitive advantage.

Team or Group Innovation

We have also begun to understand the team or group level factors that are associated with innovation. This has direct relevance for organizations. Deloitte Touche, in a large-scale survey of UK organizations (1999), found that team-based working was related to growth in turnover of companies due to new products or services. Other research supports this finding (Markiewicz & West, 1997; Mohrman et al., 1995). Teams provide the sources for ideas (especially cross-functional teams) while the team-based organization also offers simultaneously centralized and distributed decision-making structures that enable successful innovation. Indeed, the extent of team-based working in organizations appears to be a good predictor of innovation (Agrell & Gustafson, 1996; Mohrman et al., 1995; West et al., 1999b). West (in press) argues that four groups of factors together determine the level of group innovation:

- external demands
- psycho-social safety
- group knowledge diversity and skills
- group processes.

Knowledge diversity, group psycho-social safety, and external demands will all influence group processes such as developing and redeveloping shared objectives, participation, management of conflict, the influence of minorities in the group, support for ideas to introduce new ways of doing things, and reflexivity.

Psycho-social Safety

External demands in the form of threat, uncertainty or high demands motivate groups (as well as individuals) to innovate at work (West, in press). Innovation implementation involves changing the status quo, which implies resistance, conflict and a requirement for sustained effort. A team which attempts to implement innovations is likely to encounter resistance and conflict among others in the organization, and therefore sustained effort is required to overcome these disincentives to innovate.

The effort required to innovate has to be motivated by external demands. For example, Borrill et al. (2000) explored innovation in 100 UK primary health care teams. Where levels of participation in the team were high, team innovation was also high, but only in environments characterized by high levels of ill-health, with strong external demands on the health care professionals. This is consistent with the general prediction that external demands will moderate the relationship between team processes and innovation outcomes.

Group psycho-social traits play a role. These refer to shared understandings, unconscious group processes, group cognitive style and group emotional tone (Cohen & Bailey, 1997). Creative ideas arise out of individual cognitive processes and, though group members may interact in ways that offer cognitive stimulation via diversity (Dunbar, 1995, 1997), creative ideas are produced as a result of individual cognitions. A wealth of evidence suggests that, in general, creative cognitions occur when individuals are free from pressure, feel safe, and experience relatively positive affect (Claxton, 1997, 1998). Group psycho-social safety enables the expression and exploration of creative ideas which threaten the status quo (West, in press).

Positive Affective Tone

Attention has recently been given to the way in which affective tone of groups impacts innovation. George (1996, p. 78) uses the term group *affective tone*, to refer to "consistent or homogenous affective reactions within a group" such as shared feelings of excitement, energy, enthusiasm, distress, mistrust or nervousness. George found that a group's affective tone determined how innovative (and effective) the group was.

Relevant to this is evidence that when individuals feel positive they tend to connect and integrate divergent stimulus materials. They are: more creative

(Isen & Daubman, 1984; Isen et al., 1985, 1987; Cummings, 1998); see inter-relatedness among diverse stimuli; and use broader, inclusive categories (Isen & Daubman, 1984; Isen et al., 1987). If all or most individuals in a work group tend to feel positive at work (the group has a "high positive affective tone"), then their cognitive flexibility will be amplified as a result of social influence and other group processes. As a result the group will develop shared (and flexible) mental models. In effect, groups with a high positive affective tone will be creative.

Group Cognitive Resources, Conflict, Team Goals and Participation

Research from both a cognitive and social psychology perspective has also enabled work psychologists to provide new insights into effectiveness at the group level. The link between cognitive diversity and effective strategic management has been examined by psychologists from a theoretical and empirical perspective (Hodgkinson, in press; Sparrow, 1994).

Innovation requires diversity of knowledge bases, professional orientations and disciplinary backgrounds (West, in press). Groups composed of people with differing professional backgrounds, knowledge, skills and abilities will be more innovative than those whose members are similar, because they bring usefully differing perspectives on issues to the group (Paulus, 2000). Divergence of views creates multiple perspectives and potentially constructive conflict. If this informational conflict is processed in the interests of effective decision-making and task performance rather than on the basis of egotistical motivation to win or prevail, or conflicts of interest, this in turn will generate improved performance and more innovative actions will be the result (DeDreu, 1997; Hoffman & Maier, 1961; Pearce & Ravlin, 1987; Porac & Howard, 1990; Tjosvold, 1985, 1991, 1998; Paulus, 2000).

Psychologists have begun to unravel the role of conflict in creating innovation. The management of competing perspectives is fundamental to the generation of creativity and innovation (Mumford & Gustafson, 1988; Nemeth & Owens, 1996; Tjosvold, 1998). Such processes are characteristic of task-related or information conflict, as opposed to conflicts of interest, emotional or interpersonal conflict (DeDreu & DeVries, 1997). They can arise from a common concern with quality of task performance in relation to shared objectives—what has been termed "task orientation" (West, 1990). Task orientation may be evidenced by appraisal of, and constructive challenges to, the group's processes and performance. In essence, team members are more committed to performing their work effectively and excellently than they are either to bland consensus or to personal victory in conflict with other team members over task performance strategies or decision options. Arguing from the perspective of social psychology, DeDreu and DeVries (1997) suggest that a homogeneous workforce in which minority dissent is suppressed will reduce creativity, innovation, individuality and independence. In a study of newly formed postal work teams in the Netherlands, DeDreu and West (2000) found that minority dissent did indeed predict team innovation (as rated by the teams' supervisors), but only in teams with high levels of participation. It seems that the social processes in the team necessary for minority dissent to influence the innovation process are characterized by high levels of team member

interaction, influence over decision-making and information sharing. This finding has significant implications too for our understanding of minority dissent
in groups operating in organizational contexts.

Finally, group processes, if sufficiently integrating, will facilitate group creativity and innovation implementation (West, in press). Research evidence from
studies of top management teams in hospitals (West & Anderson, 1996) and
of primary health care teams (Borrill et al., 2000) provides clear support for the
proposition that clarity of and commitment to team goals is associated with high
levels of team innovation. Where group members do not share a commitment to a
set of objectives (or a vision of the goals of their work) the forces of disintegration
created by disagreements (and lack of safety), diversity and the emotional demands of the innovation process are likely to inhibit innovation. Participation is
also linked to team innovation. To the extent that information and influence over
decision-making are shared within teams, and there is a high level of interaction
amongst team members, the cross-fertilization of perspectives which can spawn
creativity and innovation is more likely to occur (Cowan, 1986; Mumford &
Gustafson, 1988; Pearce & Ravlin, 1987; Porac & Howard, 1990). When people
participate in decision-making through having influence, interacting with those
involved in the change process, and sharing information, they tend to invest
in the outcomes of those decisions and to offer ideas for new and improved
ways of working (Kanter, 1983; King et al., 1992). Recent studies of health care
teams, TV programme production teams, and top management teams, support
this proposition (Borrill et al., 2000; Carter & West, 1999; Poulton & West, 1999;
West et al., 1999a).

Organizational Innovation

The final source of evidence we discuss in this section on innovation is derived
at the organizational level. As with the discussion on well-being, we begin with
research on the topic of climate and culture.

Organizational Climate

Organizations create an ethos or atmosphere within which creativity is either
nurtured and blooms in innovation, or is starved of support. Psychological research has revealed that supportive and challenging environments are likely
to sustain high levels of creativity (Mumford & Gustafson, 1988; West, 1987),
especially those which encourage risk taking and idea generation (Cummings,
1965; Delbecq & Mills, 1985; Hage & Dewar, 1973; Kanter, 1983; Kimberley &
Evanisko, 1981). Employees frequently have ideas for improving their workplaces, work functioning, processes, products or services (Nicholson & West,
1988; West, 1987). Where climates are characterized by distrust, lack of communication, personal antipathies, limited individual autonomy and unclear goals,
the implementation of these ideas is inhibited (Amabile et al., 1996). A number
of studies have shown that work demands—the level of which may be set by

external demands or the internal culture—influence innovation (Bunce & West, 1995a). For example, in a study of 10 000 health service personnel the level of work demands was not only the main predictor of stress, but also a significant predictor of individual innovation amongst NHS personnel (Hardy & West, 2000).

The challenge then for psychologists is to help organizations create climates and cultures so that innovation is enabled. While not all innovation is beneficial, the challenge is to create climates of innovation within which intelligent and wise innovation is possible. One of the most striking findings from research on managerial job change (Nicholson & West, 1989) was how the mental health of those who moved into jobs which offered them fewer opportunities than their previous jobs to be creative in their work showed a bigger decline than among those who became unemployed. The Whitehall studies too have shown how important for mental health are variety of work and opportunity to use skills (Stansfield et al., 1998). The bigger danger is that organizations remain resistant to innovation, encouraging acceptance of incompetence and ineffectiveness, and of environments that are damaging to those who work within them.

Market Environment and Environmental Uncertainty

Psychologists have entered into research at the organizational level looking at innovation from a quasi-economic perspective. We can ask: are we motivated to innovate in our organizations when we feel safe and confident about our circumstances, or are we stimulated to try new ways only when we feel threatened or in fear of losing our prosperity or plenty? Psychologists have attempted to answer this economic issue by considering company market share. The Schumpeterian hypothesis, that the social cost of monopoly power is offset by the high levels of innovative activity it enables, has many adherents. So is high company market share associated with higher levels of innovation than in companies with relatively low market share? Returning to the 10-year longitudinal study of UK manufacturing companies conducted by the Centre for Economic Performance (CEP), results revealed a clear negative association between market share and product innovation. Low market share predicted high levels of subsequent product innovation (West et al., 1999).

But maybe the explanation comes neither from considerations of plenty versus famine, nor safety versus fear, but can be found by examining the overall level of environmental uncertainty to which organizations are exposed. Perhaps innovation is simply an attempt to reduce uncertainty, a state humans generally dislike, and which organizations, in particular, strive to avoid (Burns & Stalker, 1961; Lawrence & Lorsch, 1967; Miles et al., 1978; Thompson, 1967). Firms operating in uncertain, turbulent environments must continually adapt to changing technological and market conditions and, in the more unpredictable industries, the need to innovate can be a condition of survival. Not only must they innovate in the domains of products, technology and production processes to keep abreast of technological and market change, but uncertain environments also require more flexible, decentralized and organic structures (Burns & Stalker, 1961). This is so that organizations can be readily aligned to meet changing market challenges.

Again, this is exactly what the UK Centre for Economic Performance study revealed, with companies facing high environmental uncertainty reporting higher levels of subsequent innovation in their administrative systems (work design, HRM practices and other administrative processes) (West et al., 1999).

ORGANIZATIONAL PERFORMANCE

The Early Studies

Finally, we move to perhaps what is the most important debate—the link to organizational productivity and profitability. HRM policies and practices are assumed to be linked to organizational performance through their ability to increase employee skills and abilities, promote positive attitudes and increase motivation, and provide employees with expanded responsibilities so that they can make full use of these skills and abilities (Patterson et al., 1998). Work to date has focused on assessments of perceptions of HRM effectiveness, and assessments of the presence of specific practices. The common research design has been to assess an organization's HR practices and then statistically relate these practices to a financial outcome such as profitability or shareholder wealth.

Studies of actual practice (the acknowledged presence of an HRM policy or practice) have shown significant linkage between the presence of "bundles" of high-performance practices and organizational performance (for reviews see Becker & Gerhart, 1996; Paauwe & Richardson, 1997; Rogers & Wright, 1998). The linking process has been explained in different ways, but is explained typically as follows. Business and strategic initiatives shape the HRM system, which impacts the creation of requisite employee skills, motivation and the design of jobs. In turn these generate effective employee behaviours (such as creativity, productivity and discretionary effort), which lead to better strategy implementation, which consequently determines operating performance, profits and growth and then market value (Becker & Huselid, 1998; Becker et al., 1997; Wright & Snell, 1998). Positive support has been established from a series of surveys in the US conducted in the early to mid 1990s (see Huselid, 1995b, for a review). These surveys, covering around 4000 firms, indicated a relationship (the strength of this relationship has since formed the subject of debate) between the use of high-performance work systems (HPWS) and the financial performance of the firms, such that firms that adopted a significantly greater number of HPWS practices achieved 24% higher shareholder equity and 25% higher accounting profits. In the UK studies within the manufacturing sector (Patterson et al., 1997), analyses of the 1998 Workplace Employee Relations Survey (Guest et al., 2000b), and work on the impact of new forms of work organization on the psychological contract (Guest et al., 2000a) are cited as providing support for the link. Indeed, the introduction to the recent Executive Brief from the Chartered Institute of Personnel and Development (Armstrong, 2000) positively asserts that "the outcomes of a wide range of research projects demonstrate conclusively that there is a strong, positive relationship between better people management and bottom-line performance".

Some Emerging Questions

Despite the emerging consensus that there is a link, three important questions have however emerged:

1. How many "boxes" are there in the causal process?
2. Is the relationship a linear one?
3. In which direction does the relationship go, investment in HRM to positive firm performance, or positive firm performance to investment in HRM?

The first question has been addressed in part in the previous sections where we have looked at a micro level at the "boxes" that form part of the linking process from the organizational culture, to the psychological contract, to positive outcome behaviours. The answer to how many boxes are there in the causal process is one that psychologists are perhaps peculiarly well-positioned to investigate. As we have seen, there is no agreement on how many factors consistently feature in the causal process, and there are differences across sectors. However, clearly variables such as organizational culture, value fit, trust, fairness, the social exchange of the psychological contract, commitment and contextual performance need to be featured.

On the second question of whether the relationship a linear one, the answer clearly is no. The relationship between the presence of HRM practices and organizational effectiveness is neither simple nor linear. Huselid and Becker (1996) found that there were non-linear gains (as measured by market value per employee in dollar terms) according to the level of HRM sophistication. A low level of HRM sophistication led to a significant improvement in market value (a cross-sectional design using a one-year time lag to performance measures was used). At moderate levels of HRM sophistication the financial returns fell off, but were then increased to their highest levels once very high levels of sophistication were introduced.

Assessment of *perceptions* of HRM policies and practices have been used to tease out the guiding principles that might help explain the alignment of HRM with strategy. Huselid et al. (1997) examined the relationship between organizational performance, the perceived quality of HRM in the organization, and the perceived capabilities of HRM staff, in 293 US organizations. This work demonstrated a number of important findings.

First, *perceived* effectiveness in strategic areas of HRM was significantly related to financial measures of organizational performance—between 12% and 29% of variance in financial measures of performance was predicted by measures of perceived HRM effectiveness.

Second, there are a number of areas of HRM in which the organization may be technically proficient, but which bear no relationship to organizational performance. In this study these included things such as benefits and services, compensation, recruitment and training, safety and health, employee education and training, retirement strategies, employee/industrial relations, social responsibility programs, equal opportunities for females/minorities, management of labour costs, selection testing, performance appraisal, HR information systems, and assessment of employee attitudes. Whilst these areas are "nice to have", perceived effectiveness in these areas bore no relationship to financial measures of organizational performance.

Third, there was considerable practical utility of having an effective HRM system architecture. A one standard deviation increase in overall HRM effectiveness created a 5.2% increase in sales per employee, amounting to an increase in sales of \$44 380 per employee. The nine strategic areas of HRM that were associated with superior financial performance were: teamwork; employee participation and empowerment; workforce planning—flexibility and deployment; workforce productivity and quality of output; management and executive development; succession and development planning for managers; advance issue identification/strategic studies; employee and manager communications; and work/family programmes.

The CEP Studies in the UK

The presence of high-commitment HRM in the UK is more widespread than might be assumed. Analysis of the 1990 WIRS data in the UK showed that there were four progressive styles of high-commitment management (which goes beyond the concept of HPWS by considering the forms of management aimed at eliciting commitment and relations within the organization based on trust) amongst UK firms. Whilst the use of a high-commitment bundle of policies was still relatively rare, the proportion of UK firms with medium levels of high-commitment management was significant (Wood and de Menezes, 1998). Moreover, research conducted here, though on a smaller scale, does address *some* of the recent methodological criticisms that have been levelled at the field. Wright (2000) called for research to include more variables regarding the impact of HR practices on employees (such as their skills, attitudes, behaviours, absenteeism and turnover).

In this section we re-examine what psychological research reveals about organizational performance by drawing on the CEP study described earlier, but giving more detail of the methods and findings of this 15-year study of organizations. The study (Patterson et al., 1997) first examined whether employee satisfaction predicted subsequent productivity. In studies of individual employee satisfaction and their job performance, results have repeatedly revealed that there is only a very weak relationship. Although the two tend (weakly) to go together, there are clearly many excellent performers who are not very satisfied with their work and jobs, and plenty who are content who are doing a very poor job! The CEP researchers found that some 12% of the variation in company performance was associated with employee satisfaction, measured 18 months earlier, even after controlling for prior performance. The explanation for these findings is that a community of satisfied employees is likely to have positive attitudes towards the organization and towards work colleagues. As a consequence, people may well co-operate more in the workplace, both on tasks for which they are directly responsible and on tasks that are not part of their job description. Thus requests for assistance from another department or function might be met more positively in a firm where people feel generally relatively satisfied with their lot than in one where employees feel aggrieved or exploited. In firms with more satisfied workers too, social norms may be more likely to develop which encourage good performance, thus reinforcing both satisfaction and good performance. The results of the study in relation to the role of culture and climate were discussed earlier.

Finally, the role of HRM practices was considered by the study. Do HRM practices affect company productivity and profitability? In order to answer this question the CEP study gathered detailed information about the management of people in relation to 13 areas: selection and recruitment; induction; training; appraisal; skill flexibility; job variety; job responsibility; team-working; communication; quality improvement teams; harmonization; comparative pay; and incentive compensation systems. HRM practices accounted for 18% and 19% of the variation between companies in the change in productivity and profitability, respectively, in the 18-month period subsequent to our interviews. How people were managed in these manufacturing companies predicted how the companies subsequently performed.

But which people management practices make the difference? Two clusters emerged as significant. The first was a combination of practices associated with the acquisition and development of employee skills. Where companies had in place relatively sophisticated and widely applied people management systems in relation to recruitment, selection, induction, appraisal and training, their productivity 18 months later was markedly better than those companies which had not developed these practices to the same extent. The second cluster of practices related to the design of jobs and work. Where employees were encouraged to use a wide range of skills in jobs which offered a relatively high degree of richness and responsibility, and/or where there was a relatively high use of teams to do work, companies tended to perform better.

The study also investigated the importance of other factors in predicting productivity, including the sophistication and extent of quality management systems; the sophistication of production technologies (hand tool through to robots and CNC/DNC technologies) and the extent to which each is used in the production process; managers' ratings of the effectiveness of their implementation of the various elements of their competitive strategy; and the sophistication of, commitment to and emphasis on R&D strategy. Only the latter came close to being a significant predictor, suggesting that, at least in the short (18 months) term, people management is the key lever of productivity.

This should not be taken to imply that these other factors are unimportant. The productivity pay-offs of new production technology may not be observable in such a short period and may begin to appear as the CEP team analyse productivity data for these companies over the ensuing years. Competitive strategy has been a central concern of theorists and business school gurus for many years. Their theorising is not in vain. Undoubtedly strategy affects profitability but the effects may be less apparent in the short term than the rude impact of people management on productivity. In the short term however, the influence of these factors on productivity is not apparent. Organizations are not simply buildings or products or cultures or traditions. They are all of those things of course. But most fundamentally they are groupings of human beings working together (more or less) to achieve often overlapping and sometimes shared goals. It is the management of their human needs, the release of their creativity, the co-ordination of their efforts and the creation of co-operative and effective communities that determines the productivity of organizations.

CONCLUSIONS

The HRM—organizational performance debate can be used to help draw some conclusions about work on psychology and organizational effectiveness. The field seems to be characterized by studies that have good research methodology but small-scale samples, or large-scale samples but poor method. There are also a number of debates currently raging: "while evidence mounts that HR practices are at least weakly related to firm performance, significant theoretical and empirical challenges exist with regard to furthering our understanding of this relationship" (Wright, 2000, p. 2).

It is useful to explore these challenges because of the points they make about research methodology, but also because they question some of the assumptions that we might make about the causation process. Much of the existing research that has tried to demonstrate the links between HRM and organizational performance is not yet powerful enough for us to trust the evidence, and recent criticisms on both conceptual grounds and methodological grounds should be considered by work psychologists. On conceptual grounds the attempt to link "bundles" of HRM policies with improved organizational performance, though well-intentioned, can also be a little naive—and certainly rather prescriptive. Whilst the approach by Huselid and others (Huselid, 1995a; Huselid et al., 1997) hardens the case for HRM, we have now to move beyond it (Sparrow, 1999). Many assumptions have to be built into an HRM bundles methodology. Coupled with difficult choices about the best financial performance measures to represent "effectiveness", the task of showing linkages from cross-sectional black box studies becomes impractical. Psychologists may be able to help HRM researchers unravel the "black box".

Most "raw" organizational performance measures are subject to situational manipulation—especially in the UK where return on assets has become a major focus, but may not be truly reflective on the inner strength of the organization. Moreover, simply measuring "inputs" such as HRM policies and "outputs" such as broad organizational performance, is too likely to "mask" the sophisticated set of linkages that really exist between HRM and performance (Hendry et al., 1989). These include "time shift" or "political process" issues and problems concerning differential "asset intensity" across sectors (Sparrow, 1999). Concerning time-shift issues, investments may be made in HRM policies which build up into a critical mass over time, with any positive influences not taking hold until at least two or three years into the process. Even the time-lagged studies of Schuler and colleagues could not fairly be expected to capture the fact that many HR programmes are run "politically" with clear "front-runner" policies intended to mobilize attitudes and change behaviour; i.e. there is a clear logic to the sequencing of the policies, but they do not act as a composite bundle nor across standardized periods of time. Internal performance, financial or control measures tend not to exist at the level of sophistication needed to conduct simple studies of HRM input against firm performance. This problem was noted when researchers tried to link training investments to performance in the late 1980s (Hendry et al., 1989). The internal budget processes of firms were so variable that comparing firms was like comparing apples and oranges. Secondly, the link between HRM and performance depends on the centrality of HR issues to core business processes. Organizations vary in terms of "human asset intensity" (Colf, 1997). In retail, despite the rhetoric about customer service and customer profit chain, only marginal gains are likely to be made by high staff retention rates and good customer service skills. Much more money can be made in the short term by effective use of EPOS technology, branding and store location, though the long-term costs of neglecting good people management practices are unknown.

A number of methodological challenges exist, neatly summarized by Wright (2000). The majority of evidence is based on single subjects rating the presence of a policy or practice in the organization, or the extent to which it exists, or the percentage coverage of a workforce by it. Attempts to consider the effectiveness of practices in a broader way are hard to find. Where multiple raters have been used, agreement between them is low. Moreover, studies that rely on ratees evaluating survey items suffer from subject bias. Research subjects—especially those from within the HR field—have "implicit theories" that for them explain the relationship between variables. They are likely to have incomplete knowledge of all HR practices (and certainly the quality of their actual implementation). Given what they do know about performance or core practices, they infer the existence or positive operation of other items.

Another issue raised by Wright (2000) concerns the intervening variable of strategy. Is it the bundle of HRM practices that governs financial performance, or the fit between the strategy and the HRM? When one considers the fit with strategy, then it becomes clear that assessing the presence of an HRM policy or practice is also too simplistic. There are four levels at which we could measure HRM–strategy fit: the guiding principles behind the HRM practice; the policy alternatives (different practices); the products of those practices (competencies or behaviours the practice promotes); and the practice-process (effective execution or not of the practice). No consensus exists for the level of specificity or depth of explanation that should be represented by items (for example, the use of job analysis might be progressive, or might represent a bureaucratic imposition).

Psychologists can contribute to this debate by applying both larger scale empirical studies based on the research design principles encompassed by the CEP studies, and by adopting more qualitative approaches. Qualitative research aimed at unravelling the differential causal mechanisms across sectors should reveal the perceived cause-and-effect thinking of business experts and identify the drives behind their short- and medium-term thinking about the new forms of work organization. In addition to defining the important "boxes" that should form part of empirical study, we need to identify the "influence" points at which effective people management policies have a bearing, and the criteria that are important in the decision-making that lies behind the pursuit of particular personnel interventions. The potential territory that has opened up for psychologists to explore is massive, the opportunity for them to continue to demonstrate the link between the individual and organizational effectiveness is inviting, and the research agenda that beckons is exciting.

REFERENCES

Agrell, A. & Gustafson, R. (1996). Innovation and creativity in work groups. In M.A. West (Ed.), *The Handbook of Work Group Psychology*, pp. 317–344. Chichester: John Wiley.

Ainsworth, M.D. (1989). Attachments beyond infancy. *American Psychologist*, **44**, 709–716.

Ainsworth, M.D. & Bell, S.M. (1974). Mother–infant interaction and the development of competence. In K. Connolly & J. Bruner (Eds), *The Growth of Competence*. New York: Academic Press.

Ajzen, I. & Fishbein, M. (1980). *Understanding Attitudes and Predicting Social Behaviour*. Englewood Cliffs, NJ: Prentice-Hall.

Allen, T.D. & Rush, M.C. (1998). The effects of organizational citizenship behaviour on performance judgements: a field study and laboratory experiment. *Journal of Applied Psychology*, **83**, 247–260.

Amabile, T.M. (1983). The social psychology of creativity: a componential conceptualization. *Journal of Personality and Social Psychology*, **45**, 357–376.

Amabile, T.M., Conti, R., Coon, H., Lazenby, J. & Herron, M. (1996). Assessing the work environment for creativity. *Academy of Management Journal*, **39**, 1154–1184.

Ancona, D., Kochan, T., Scully, M., Van Maanen, J.V. & Westney, D.E. (1996). *The New Organization*. Cincinnati, OH: South-Western College Publishing.

Armstrong, M. (2000). *People and Performance: Executive Brief*. London: Chartered Institute of Personnel and Development.

Axelrod, R. & Hamilton, W.D. (1981). The evolution of cooperation. *Science*, **211**, 1390–1396.

Barash, D.P. (1977). *Sociobiology and Behaviour*. New York: Elsevier.

Barchas, P. (1986). A sociophysiological orientation to small groups. In E. Lawlor (Ed.), *Advances in Group Processes*, Vol. **3**, pp. 209–246. Greenwich, CT: JAI Press.

Barron, F.B. & Harrington, D.M. (1981). Creativity, intelligence and personality. In M.R. Rosenzweig & L.W. Porter (Eds), *Annual Review of Psychology*, Vol. **32**, pp. 439–476. Palo Alto, CA: Annual Reviews.

Baumeister, R.F., Wotman, S.R. & Stillwell, A.M. (1993). Unrequited love: on heartbreak, anger, guilt, scriptlessness and humiliation. *Journal of Personality and Social Psychology*, **64**, 377–394.

Becker, B. & Gerhart, B. (1996). The impact of HRM on organizational performance: progress and prospects, *Academy of Management Journal*, **39**, 779–803.

Becker, B.E. & Huselid, M.A. (1998). High performance work systems and firm performance: a synthesis of research and managerial implications. In G.R. Ferris (Ed.), *Research in Personnel and Human Research Management*, Vol. **16**, pp. 53–101. Greenwich, CT: JAI Press.

Becker, B.E., Huselid, M.A., Pickus, P.S. & Spratt, M.F. (1997). HR as a source of shareholder value: research and recommendations. *Human Resource Management*, **36** (1), 39–47.

Borman, W.C. & Motovidlo, S.J. (1993). Expanding the criterion domain to include elements of contextual performance. In N. Schmitt, W.C. Borman et al. (Eds), *Personnel Selection in Organizations*. San Francisco, CA: Jossey-Bass.

Borman, W.C. & Motovidlo, S.J. (1997). Task performance and contextual performance: the meaning for personnel selection research. *Human Performance*, **10**, 99–109.

Borrill, C.S., Carletta, J., Carter, A.J., Dawson, J., Garrod, S., Rees, A., Richards, A., Shapiro, D. & West, M.A. (2000). *The Effectiveness of Health Care Teams in the National Health Service*. Birmingham: Aston Centre for Health Service Organization Research.

Bowlby, J. (1969). *Attachment and Loss: Vol. I. Attachment*. London: Hogarth.

Bunce, D. & West, M. (1995a). Self perceptions and perceptions of group climate as predictors of individual innovation at work. *Applied Psychology: An International Review*, **44**, 199–215.

Bunce, D. & West, M.A. (1995b). Changing work environments: innovative coping responses to occupational stress. *Work and Stress*, **8**, 319–331.

Bunce, D. & West, M.A (1996). Stress management and innovation interventions at work. *Human Relations*, **49**, 209–232.

Burns, T. & Stalker, G.M. (1961). *The Management of Innovation*. London: Tavistock.

Buss, D.M. (1990). The evolution of anxiety and social exclusion. *Journal of Social and Clinical Psychology*, **9**, 196–210.

Buss, D.M. (1991). Evolutionary personality psychology. *Annual Review of Psychology*, **42**, 459–491.

Carter, A.J. & West, M.A. (1999). Sharing the burden—teamwork in health care settings. In J. Firth-Cozens & R. Payne (Eds), *Stress in Health Professionals*, pp. 191–202. Chichester: John Wiley.

Cavanaugh, M.A. & Noe, R.A. (1999). Antecedents and consequences of relational components of the new psychological contract. *Journal of Organizational Behaviour*, **20**, 323–340.

Chatman, J.A. (1991). Matching people and organizations: selection and socialization in public accounting firms. *Administrative Science Quarterly*, **36**, 459–484.

Claxton, G. (1997). *Hare Brain, Tortoise Mind: Why Intelligence Increases When You Think Less*. London: Fourth Estate.

Claxton, G.L. (1998). Knowing without knowing why: investigating human intuition. *The Psychologist*, **11**, 217–220.

Cohen, S.G. & Bailey, D.E. (1997). What makes teams work: group effectiveness research from the shop floor to the executive suite. *Journal of Management*, **23** (3), 239–290.

Colf, R.W. (1997). Human assets and management dilemmas: coping with the hazards on the road to resource-based theory. *Academy of Management Review*, **22** (2), 374–402.

Cowan, D.A. (1986). Developing a process model of problem recognition. *Academy of Management Review*, **11**, 763–776.

Coyle-Shapiro, J.A-M. (1999). TQM and organizational change: a longitudinal study of the impact of a TQM intervention on work attitudes. In W.A. Pasmore & R.W. Woodman (Eds), *Research on Organizational Change and Development*, Vol. **12**. Greenwich, CT: JAI Press.

Coyle-Shapiro, J.A-M & Kessler, I. (2000). Consequences of the psychological contract for the employment relationship: a large-scale survey. *Journal of Management Studies* (in press).

Cummings, L. (1965). Organizational climates for creativity. *Academy of Management Journal*, **8**, 220–227.

Cummings, A. (1998). Contextual characteristics and employee creativity: affect at work. Paper presented at 13th Annual Conference, Society for Industrial Organizational Psychology. Dallas, USA, April 1998.

DeDreu, C.K.W. (1997). Productive conflict: the importance of conflict management and conflict issue. In C.K.W. De Dreu & E. Van De Vliert (Eds), *Using Conflict in Organizations*, pp. 9–22. London: Sage.

DeDreu, C.K.W. & DeVries, N.K. (1997). Minority dissent in organizations. In C.K.W. DeDreu and E. Van de Vliert (Eds), *Using Conflict in Organizations*, pp. 72–86. London: Sage.

DeDreu, C.K.W. & West, M.A. (2001). Minority dissent and team innovation: the importance of participation in decision making. *Journal of Applied Psychology*, **86** (6), 1191–1201.

Delbecq, A.L. & Mills, P.K. (1985). Managerial practices that enhance innovation. *Organizational Dynamics*, **14**, 24–34.

Deloitte Touche (1999*). Business Success and Human Resource Management Survey, Leeds*. Deloitte Touche.

De Witte, K. & van Muijen, J.J. (1999). Organizational culture: critical questions for researchers and practitioners. *European Journal of Work and Organizational Psychology*, **8**, 583–595.

DeWulf, A., Poortinga, Y., Fontaine, J., De Witte, K. & Swinnen, M. (1999). *Facetten van organisatiecultuur. Een systematische analyse van het concept, geconfronteerd met vragenlijsitems.* Unpublished licentiate dissertation, Faculty of Psychology and Pedagogical Sciences, Leuven, Catholic University of Leuven, Belgium.

Dunbar, K. (1995). How scientists really reason: scientific reasoning in real-world laboratories. In R.J. Sternberg & J.E. Davidson (Eds), *The Nature of Insight*, pp. 365–395. Cambridge, MA: MIT Press.

Dunbar, K. (1997). How scientists think: on-line creativity and conceptual change in science. In T.B. Ward, S.M. Smith & J. Vaid (Eds), *Creative Thought: An Investigation of Conceptual Structures and Processes*, pp. 461–493. Washington, DC: American Psychological Association.

George, J.M. (1996). Group affective tone. In M.A. West (Ed.), *Handbook of Work Group Psychology.* Chichester: John Wiley.

Geroski, P. (1994). *Market Structure, Corporate Performance, and Innovative Activity.* Clarendon Press: Oxford.

Goodman, S.A. & Svyantek, D.J. (1999). Person–organization fit and contextual performance: do shared values matter? *Journal of Vocational Behaviour*, **55**, 254–275.

Guest, D. (1998). Is the psychological contract worth taking seriously? *Journal of Organizational Behaviour*, **19**, Special Issue, 649–664.

Guest, D., Conway, N., Briner, R. & Dickmann, M. (1996). The state of the psychological contract in employment. In *Issues in People Management, No. 16.* London: IPD.

Guest, D., MacKenzie Davey, K. & Patch, A. (2000a). *The Impact of New Forms of Employment Contract on Motivation and Innovation. Final Research Report to the Economic and Social Research Council.* London: University of London, Birkbeck.

Guest, D., Michie, J., Sheehan, M. & Conway, N. (2000b). *Employee Relations, HRM and Business Performance: An Analysis of the 1998 Workplace Employee Relations Survey.* London: Chartered Institute of Personnel and Development.

Hage, J. & Dewar, R. (1973). Elite values versus organizational structure in predicting innovation. *Administrative Science Quarterly*, **18**, 279–290.

Hardy, G.E. & West, M.A. (2000). Interpersonal attachment and innovation at work. Unpublished manuscript, Department of Psychology, University of Sheffield.

Hardy, G.E., Shapiro, D.A., Haynes, C.E., & Rick, J.E. (in press). Validation of the general health questionnaire-12 using a sample of employees from the health care services. *Psychological Assessment*.

Harkins, S.G. & Petty, R.E. (1982). Effects of task difficulty and task uniqueness on social loafing. *Journal of Personality and Social Psychology*, **43**, 1214–1229.

Harris, S.G. & Mossholder, K.W. (1996) The affective implications of perceived congruence with culture dimensions during organizational transformation. *Journal of Management*, **22**, 527–547.

Hartley, J. (1995). Challenge and change in employment relations: issues for psychology, trade unions and managers. In L.E. Tetrick and J. Barling (Eds), *Changing Employment Relations: Behavioural and Social Perspectives.* Washington: American Psychological Association.

Hays, R.B. (1985). A longitudinal study of friendship development. *Journal of Psychology and Social Psychology*, **48**, 909–924.

Hendry, C., Pettigrew, A. & Sparrow, P.R. (1989) Linking strategic change, competitive performance and human resource management: results of a U.K. empirical study. In R. Mansfield (Ed.), *Frontiers of Management Research*, pp. 195–220. London: Routledge.

Herriot, P. & Pemberton, C. (1996). Contracting careers. *Human Relations*, **49**, 757–790.

Hirschman, A.O. (1970). *Exit, Voice and Loyalty: Responses to Decline in Firms, Organizations and States.* Cambridge, MA: Harvard University Press.

Hodgkinson, G. (2001). Cognitive processes in strategic management: some emerging trends and future directions. In C. Cooper & I. Robertson (Eds), *International Review of Industrial and Organizational Psychology*, Vol. **16**. Chichester: John Wiley.

Hodgkinson, G.P. & Sparrow, P.R. (2002). The Competent Organization: *A Psychological Analysis of the Strategic Management Process*. Buckingham: Open University Press.

Hoffman, L.R. & Maier, N.R.F. (1961). Sex differences, sex composition, and group problem-solving. *Journal of Abnormal and Social Psychology*, **63**, 453–456.

Hofstede, G. (1980). *Culture's Consequences*. Beverly Hills, CA: Sage.

Hogan, R., Jones, W.H. & Cheek, J.M. (1985). Socioanalytic theory: an alternative to armadillo psychology. In B.R. Schlenker (Ed.), *The Self and Social Life*, pp. 175–198. New York: McGraw-Hill.

Holmes, J.G. & Rempel, J.K. (1989). Trust in close relationships. In M. Clark (Ed.), *Close Relationships: Review of Personality and Social Psychology*, Vol. **10**, pp. 187–220. Newbury Park, CA: Sage.

Huselid, M.A. (1995a). The impact of human resource management practices on turnover, productivity and corporate financial performance. *Academy of Management Journal*, **38**, 635–672.

Huselid, M.A. (1995b). The impact of human resource management: an agenda for the 1990s. *International Journal of Human Resource Management*, **1** (1), 17–42.

Huselid, M.A. & Becker, B. (1996). Methodological issues in cross-sectional and panel estimates of the HR–firm performance link. *Industrial Relations*, **35**, 400–422.

Huselid, M.A., Jackson, S. & Schuler, R.S. (1997). Technical and strategic HRM effectiveness as determinants of firm performance. *Academy of Management Journal*, **49** (1), 171–188.

Isen, A.M. & Daubman, K.A. (1984). The influence of affect on categorization. *Journal of Personality and Social Psychology*, **47**, 1206–1217.

Isen, A.M., Johnson, M.M.S., Mertz, E. & Robinson, G.F. (1985). The influence of positive affect on the unusualness of word association. *Journal of Personality and Social Psychology*, **48**, 1413–1426.

Isen, A.M., Daubman K.A. & Nowicki, G.P. (1987). Positive affect facilitates creative problem solving. *Journal of Personality and Social Psychology*, **52**, 1122–1131.

Kanter, R.M. (1983). *The Change Masters: Corporate Entrepreneurs at Work*. New York: Simon & Schuster.

Kilmann, R.H. (1984). *Beyond the Quick Fix*. San Francisco: Jossey-Bass.

Kimberly, J.R. & Evanisko, M.J. (1981). Organizational innovation: the influence of individual, organizational, and contextual factors on hospital adoption of technological and administrative innovations. *Academy of Management Journal*, **24**, 689–713.

King, N., Anderson, N. & West, M.A. (1992). Organizational innovation: a case study of perceptions and processes. *Work and Stress*, **5**, 331–339.

Konovsky, M.A. & Pugh, S.D. (1994). Citizenship and social exchange. *Academy of Management Journal*, **37**, 656–669.

Kopelman, R., Brief, A. & Guzzo, R. (1990). The role of climate and culture in productivity. In B. Schneider (Ed.), *Organizational Climate and Culture*. San Francisco: Jossey-Bass.

Kotter, J. & Heskett, J.L. (1992). *Corporate Culture and Performance*. New York: Free Press.

Kramer, R. (1999). Trust and distrust: emerging questions, enduring questions. *Annual Review of Psychology*, **50**, 569.

Kruglansky, A.W. & Freund, T. (1983). The freezing and unfreezing of lay influences: effects on impressional primacy, ethnic stereotyping and numerical anchoring. *Journal of Experimental Social Psychology*, **19**, 448–468.

Lawrence, P.R. & Lorsch, J. (1967). *Organization and Environment*. Cambridge, MA: Harvard University Press.

Markiewicz, L. & West, M.A. (1997). *The Team Toolkit*. Aberdeen: Grampian Enterprise.

Mayer, R.C. & Davis, J.H. (1999). The effect of the performance appraisal system on trust in management: a field quasi-experiment. *Journal of Applied Psychology*, **84**, 123–136.

Mayer, R.C., Davis, J.H. & Schoorman, F.D. (1995). An integrative model of organizational trust. *Academy of Management Review*, **20**, 709–734.

Meyer, J.P. & Allen, N.J. (1997). *Commitment in the Workplace: Theory, Research and Application*. Thousand Oaks, CA: Sage.

Miles, R.E., Snow, C.C. & Meyer, A.D. et al. (1978). Organizational strategy, structure, and process. *Academy of Management Review*, **3**, 546.

Mohrman, S.A., Cohen, S.G. & Mohrman, A.M. (1995). *Designing Team-based Organizations: New Forms for Knowledge Work*. San Francisco: Jossey-Bass.

Moreland, R.L. (1987). The formation of small groups. In C. Hendrick (Ed.), *Group Processes: Review of Personality and Social Psychology*, Vol. **8**, pp. 80–100. Newbury Park, CA: Sage.

Mumford, M.D. & Gustafson, S.B. (1988). Creativity syndrome: integration, application and innovation. *Psychological Bulletin*, **103**, 27–43.

Nemeth, C. (1986). Differential contributions of majority and minority influence processes. *Psychological Review*, **93**, 10–20.

Nemeth, C. & Owens, P. (1996). Making work groups more effective: the value of minority dissent. In M.A. West (Ed.), *Handbook of Work Group Psychology*, pp. 125–142. Chichester: John Wiley.

Nicholson, N. & West, M. (1988). *Managerial Job Change: Men and Women in Transition*. Cambridge: Cambridge University Press.

Nicholson, N. & West, M.A. (1989). Transitions, work histories and the myth of careers. In M.B. Arthur, T. Hall & B. Lawrence (Eds), *Handbook of Career Theory*, pp. 181–201. Cambridge: Cambridge University Press.

Nyambegera, S., Daniels, K. & Sparrow, P.R. (2001). Why fit doesn't always matter: the impact of HRM and cultural fit on job involvement of Kenyan employees. *Applied Psychology: An International Review*, **50** (1), 109–140.

Oldham, G.R. & Cummings, A. (1996). Employee creativity: personal and contextual factors at work. *Academy of Management Journal*, **39**, 607–634.

O'Reilly, C., Chatman, J. & Caldwell, D.F. (1991). People and organizational culture: a profile comparison approach to assessing person-organization fit. *Academy of Management Journal*, **34**, 487–516.

Ott, S. (1989). *The Organizational Culture Perspective*. California: Brooks/Cole.

Paauwe, J. & Richardson, R. (1997). Introduction to the special issue: strategic human resource management and performance. *International Journal of Human Resource Management*, **8**, 257–262.

Patterson, F. (1999). *The Innovation Potential Indicator: Manual and User's Guide*. Oxford.

Patterson, M., West, M.A., Lawthom, R. & Nickell, S. (1997). *Impact of People Management Practices on Business Performance. Issues in People Management*, Report No. 22. London: Institute of Personnel and Development.

Paulus, P.B. (2000). Groups, teams and creativity: the creative potential of idea-generating groups. *Applied Psychology: An International Review*, **49**, 237–262.

Pearce, J.A. & Ravlin, E.C. (1987). The design and activation of self-regulating work groups. *Human Relations*, **40**, 751–782.

Peters, T. & Waterman, R. (1982). *In Search of Excellence*. New York: Harper & Row.

Pettigrew, A.M. (1979). On studying organizational cultures. *Administrative Science Quarterly*, **24**, 570–581.

Pond, S.B., Nacoste, R.W., Mohr, M.F. & Rodriguez, C.M. (1997). The measurement of organizational citizenship behaviour: are we assuming too much? *Journal of Applied Social Psychology*, **27**, 1527–1544.

Porac, J.F. & Howard, H. (1990). Taxonomic mental models in competitor definition. *Academy of Management Review*, **2**, 224–240.

Poulton, B.C. & West, M.A. (1999). The determinants of effectiveness in primary health care teams. *Journal of Interprofessional Care*, **13**, 7–18.

Prince, G. (1975). Creativity, self and power. In I.A. Taylor & J.W. Getzels (Eds), *Perspectives in Creativity*. Chicago: Aldine.

Robinson, S.L. (1996). Trust and breach of the psychological contract. *Administrative Science Quarterly*, **41**, 574–599.

Robinson, S.L. & Morrison, E.W. (1995). Psychological contracts and organization citizenship behaviour: the effect of unfulfilled obligations on civic virtue behaviour. *Journal of Organizational Behaviour*, **16**, 289–298.

Robinson, S.L. & Rousseau, D.M. (1994). Violating the psychological contract: not the exception but the norm. *Journal of Organizational Behaviour*, **15**, 245–259.

Rogers, C.R. (1961). *On Becoming a Person*. Boston: Houghton Mifflin.

Rogers, E.W. & Wright, P. (1998). Measuring organizational performance in strategic human resource management: problems, prospects and performance information markets. *Human Resource Management Review*, **8**, 311–331.

Rousseau, D.M. (1990). Assessing organizational culture: the case for multiple methods. In B. Schneider (Ed.), *Organizational Climate and Culture*. San Francisco: Jossey-Bass.

Ruigrok, W. & Achtenhagen, L. (1999). Organizational culture and the transformation towards new forms of organizing. *European Journal of Work and Organizational Psychology*, **8**, 521–536.

Ruigrok, W., Pettigrew, A., Peck, S. & Whittington, R. (1999). Corporate restructuring and new forms of organising: evidence from Europe. *Management International Review*, **39** (2), 41–64.

Sackmann, S. (2001). Cultural complexity in organizations: the value and limitations of qualitative methodology and approaches. In S. Cartwright, C. Cooper & C. Earley (Eds), *International Handbook of Culture and Climate*. New York: John Wiley.

Schein, E.H. (1985). *Organizational Culture and Leadership*. San Francisco, Jossey-Bass.

Schneider, B. (Ed.) (1990). *Organizational Climate and Culture*. Oxford: Jossey-Bass.

Sheridan, J.E. (1992). Organizational culture and employee retention. *Academy of Management Journal*, **35**, 1036–1056.

Shore, L.M. & Barksdale, K. (1998). Examining degree of balance and level of obligation in the employment relationship: a social exchange approach. *Journal of Organizational Behaviour*, **19**, Special Issue, 731–744.

Shore, L.M. & Tetrick, L.E. (1994). The psychological contract as an explanatory framework in the employment relationship, In C.L. Cooper & D.M. Rousseau (Eds), *Trends in Organizational Behaviour*, Vol. **1**. Somerset, NJ: John Wiley.

Sparks, K., Cooper, C., Fried, Y. & Shirom, A. (1997). The effects of hours of work on health: a meta-analytic review. *Journal of Occupational and Organizational Psychology*, **70**, 391–408.

Sparrow, P.R. (1994). The psychology of strategic management: emerging themes of diversity and managerial cognition. In C. Cooper and I. Robertson (Eds), *International Review of Industrial and Organizational Psychology*, Vol. **9**. Chichester: John Wiley.

Sparrow, P.R. (1996). Transitions in the psychological contract in UK banking. *Human Resource Management Journal*, **6** (4), 75–92.

Sparrow, P.R. (1998). The pursuit of multiple and parallel organizational flexibilities: reconstituting jobs. *European Journal of Work and Organizational Psychology*, **7** (1), 79–95.

Sparrow, P.R. (1999). Is HRM in crisis ? Re-engaging, deterring and regulating the modern organization. In R. Schuler & S. Jackson (Eds), *Strategic Human Resource Management: Linking People to the Firm*. New York: Blackwell.

Sparrow, P.R. (2000). The new employment contract. In R. Burke & C. Cooper (Eds), *The Organization in Crisis*. London: Basil Blackwell.

Sparrow, P.R. (2001). Developing diagnostics for high performance organization cultures. In S. Cartwright, C. Cooper & C. Earley (Eds), *International Handbook of Culture and Climate*. New York: John Wiley.

Sparrow, P.R. & Cooper, C.L. (1998). New organizational forms: the strategic relevance of future psychological contract scenarios. *Canadian Journal of Administrative Sciences*, **15**, 356–371.

Sparrow, P.R. & Gaston, K. (1996). Generic climate maps: a strategic application of climate survey data? *Journal of Organizational Behaviour*, **17**, 631–651.

Sparrow, P.R. & Marchington, M. (1998). *Human Resource Management: The New Agenda*. London: Pitman/Financial Times.

Stansfield, S.A., Head, J. & Marmot, M.G. (1998). Explaining social class differences in depression and well-being. *Social Psychiatry and Psychiatric Epidemiology*, **33**, 1–9.

Sternberg, R.J. & Lubart, T.I. (1996). Investing in creativity. *American Psychologist*, **51**, 677–688.

Stroh, L.K., Brett, J.M. & Reilly, J.H. (1994). A decade of change: managers' attachment to their organizations and their jobs. *Human Resource Management*, **33**, 531–548.

Thompson, J. (1967). *Organisations in Action*. New York: McGraw-Hill.

Tjosvold, D. (1985). Implications of controversy research for management. *Journal of Management*, **11**, 21–37

Tjosvold, D. (1991). *Team Organization: An Enduring Competitive Advantage*. Chichester: John Wiley.

Tjosvold, D. (1998). Co-operative and competitive goal approaches to conflict: accomplishments and challenges. *Applied Psychology: An International Review*, **47**, 285–342.

Turnley, W.H. & Feldman, D.C. (1998). Psychological contract violations during corporate restructuring. *Human Resource Management*, **37** (1), 71–83.

Vandenberghe, C. (1999). Organizational culture, person–culture fit, and turnover: a replication in the health care industry. *Journal of Organizational Behaviour*, **20**, 175–184.

Vandenberghe, C. & Peiró, J.M. (1999). Organizational and individual values: their main and combined effects on work attitudes and perceptions. *European Journal of Work and Organizational Psychology*, **8**, 569–581.

Wayne, S.J., Shore, L.M. & Liden, R.C. (1997). Perceived organizational support and leader–member exchange: a social exchange perspective. *Academy of Management Journal*, **40**, 82–111.

West, M.A. (1987). *The Psychology of Meditation*. Oxford: Oxford University Press.

West, M.A. (1988). Implications of chartering: innovations in the teaching of occupational psychology. *Occupational Psychologist*, **5**, 17–19.

West, M.A. (1989). Innovation among health care professionals. *Social Behaviour*, **4**, 173–184.

West, M.A. (1990). The social psychology of innovation in groups. In M.A. West & J.L. Farr (Eds), *Innovation and Creativity at Work: Psychological and Organisational Strategies*. Chichester: John Wiley.

West, M.A. (Ed.) (1996). *Handbook of Work Group Psychology*. Chichester: John Wiley.

West, M.A. (in press). Sparkling fountains or stagnant ponds: an integrative model of creativity and innovation implementation in work groups. *Applied Psyychology: An International Review*.

West, M.A. & Anderson, N. (1996). Innovation in top management teams. *Journal of Applied Psychology*, **81**, 680–693.

West, M.A. & Farr, J.L. (Eds), (1990). *Innovation and Creativity at Work: Psychological and Organisational Strategies*. Chichester: John Wiley.

West, M.A. & Rushton, R. (1989). Mismatches in work role transitions. *Journal of Occupational Psychology*, **62**, 271–286.

West, M.A., Fletcher, C. & Toplis, J. (1994). *Fostering Innovation: A Psychological Perspective*. Report of a Working Party of the Scientific Affairs Board of the British Psychological Society. Leicester: BPS.

West, M.A., Patterson, M.G., & Dawson, J.F. (1999a). A path to profit? Teamwork at the top. *Centrepiece*, **4**, 6–11.

West, M.A., Patterson, M., Pillinger, T. & Nickell, S. (1999b). *Innovation and Change in Manufacturing*. Institute of Work Psychology, University of Sheffield, Sheffield S10 2TN.

Wood, S. & de Menezes, L. (1998). High commitment management in the U.K.: evidence from the Workplace Industrial Relations Survey, and Employers' Manpower and Skills Practice Survey. *Human Relations*, **51**, 485–515.

Wright, P.M. (2000). Theoretical and empirical challenges in studying the HR practice–firm performance relationship. Paper presented at the EIASM Strategic Human Resource Management Conference, Fontainebleau, 30 March.

Wright, P.M. & Snell, S.A. (1998). Toward a unifying framework for exploring fit and flexibility in strategic human resource management. *Academy of Management Review*, **23**, 756–772.

CHAPTER 2

The Role of Psychologists in Enhancing Organizational Effectiveness

Gerard P. Hodgkinson
Leeds University Business School, The University of Leeds, UK
and
Peter Herriot
The Empower Group, UK

CONTENT AND PROCESS

The subsequent chapters of this book demonstrate the ways in which the knowledge and skills of psychologists may be applied to various organizational processes: leadership, culture and climate, recruitment and selection, performance management, training and development, and so on. Essentially, their authors demonstrate the value of the toolkit which psychologists bring with them in their attempts to address organizational issues. This toolkit consists of theories and models, concepts and research, methods and instruments which demonstrate both validity and utility (in the general senses of those terms).

Such toolkits exemplify what Argyris (1999) terms "theory in use". They represent the often unspoken values and assumptions of the profession. However, as Argyris argues, it is possible to be highly skilled in the use of our toolkit, but at the same time, incompetent. This unhappy paradox might arise if, for example, we became extremely skilled at enhancing the validity of certain organizational processes, but failed in so doing to enhance the organization's effectiveness. Argyris recommends the practice of "double loop learning" to prevent such an impasse. Double loop learning requires us to be reflexive about our practice. We need, in other words, to uncover and reflect upon our theories in use and test them out empirically.

As soon as we do so, we realize that the apparently simple terms of our professional objectives conceal a range of differing values, meanings and assumptions. For example, "enhancing organizational effectiveness" raises immediately the

Organizational Effectiveness: The Role of Psychology
Edited by I.T. Robertson, M. Callinan and D. Bartram. © 2002 John Wiley & Sons, Ltd.

questions of effectiveness by whose criteria and in whose interests? Or, to put it another way, who or what is the organization? The Editors of this volume recognize this issue clearly (see the Introduction). They argue that effectiveness can be defined only in terms of the objectives of a whole range of stakeholders, or interested parties. These include shareholders, customers, suppliers, employees, and the wider community.

It follows from the notion of stakeholders that effectiveness is essentially a construct, the meaning of which is likely to be continuously under negotiation between the various parties as they each seek to achieve their objectives (Weick, 1995). Of course, it does not follow that there is no coincidence between some of the parties' objectives. Nor, on the other hand, does it follow that the process of social negotiation of the meaning of effectiveness is a rational and/or cordial one. On the contrary, some stakeholders are likely to have a far greater influence on its construction than others are, and this is essentially because of the power which they wield. For example, it might reasonably be argued that shareholders and top management are currently the stakeholders with most power in the majority of Western corporations (Hutton, 1994). It is interesting that the Editors of this volume do not include top management in their list of stakeholders in the Introduction.

There are two important implications of our analysis so far. The first is that our construction of organizational effectiveness and of how to achieve it facilitates or blocks our own success as a profession. The second follows from the first: our key task is to engage in this construction process in such a way as to ensure our continuing viability. Since the construction of meaning is essentially a social process, the most fundamental skills, which we require, are social ones: how best to ensure that stakeholders' objectives are incorporated into a working definition of organizational effectiveness and its achievement. In sum, our task is to facilitate process as well as to provide knowledge and expertise in particular content areas (cf. Schein, 1987, 1988).

In the remainder of this chapter, we argue, first, that there are two very different approaches to producing knowledge and constructing meaning. While the first of these approaches incorporates only a few of the stakeholders whom we have identified, the second can incorporate all of them. Second, we maintain that in general the industrial, work and organizational (IWO) psychology profession has operated more within the first than the second approach. Third, we suggest that the current trend is away from the first approach and towards the second. Finally, we argue that the profession should follow this trend *up to a point*, and that this will require us to develop more fully certain competencies which, hitherto, we have not emphasized.

KNOWLEDGE PRODUCTION PROCESSES AND THE CONSTRUCTION OF MEANING: EMERGING TRENDS AND CONSEQUENCES

At the extreme risk of over-simplification, we characterize these two approaches as those of "scientific inquiry" (or "mode 1 production") and "problem solution" ("mode 2") (Gibbons et al., 1994). An immediate response to these labels would be to ask rhetorically how scientific inquiry could ever conceivably be construed as anything other than problem solution. Whilst there are some differences in the activities and the mental processes involved, however, we argue that these differences are due to social relationships. Specifically, we argue that the scientific inquiry approach to IWO psychology limits its range of stakeholders in such a way as to determine the nature of the knowledge constructs produced. Problem solution, on the other hand, operates with very different processes and outcomes, and this is because of the greater range of stakeholders involved.

Scientific Inquiry

Traditional scientific inquiry is, for many IWO psychologists, the bedrock of their profession. They note that part of the construction of the concept of profession is that it is based upon a body of scientific evidence. Medicine, for example, is based upon the biological sciences, engineering upon the physical ones. They also note that entrants to a profession are expected to have studied these scientific foundations to a certain level of competence, thereby adding to its exclusivity. They point to other so-called professions, for example, management, and claim that their perceived poor performance is a result of their failure to develop a sufficiently secure bedrock of scientific knowledge to support their practice.

What constitutes such secure science? Becher (1989) suggests that there are four dimensions along which scientific disciplines differ. These are:

• hard vs. soft, defined in terms of the degree to which a single agreed paradigm exists
• pure vs. applied, or the degree of concern for application to practical problems
• convergent vs. divergent, or the degree to which common assumptions and values are shared
• urban vs. rural, or the degree to which the discipline addresses a relatively few well-defined research problems.

The first-mentioned pole of each of these continua is more characteristic of the physical sciences. Some social scientists, however, have aspired to move towards these poles (e.g. Pfeffer, 1993). Part of their reasoning is that only when the supporting science is "secure" will professional practice become effective. Thus the scientific inquiry approach to knowledge creation takes a traditional view of the relationship between sound, generalized fundamental science and transitory, specific application. It makes a firm distinction between fundamental and applied, with the principal tasks of the former being explanation and prediction; those of the latter, design and craft.

Which stakeholders are implicated in the scientific inquiry approach? Clearly, in the case of certain physical sciences, the range of stakeholders is immense. The Human Genome Project, for example, must include among its stakeholders not only other biological scientists, but also pharmaceutical companies, the medical profession, and indeed governments representing their citizens.

| Research in the sub-discipline of applied psychology | → | Dissemination of this research | → | Application of its findings |

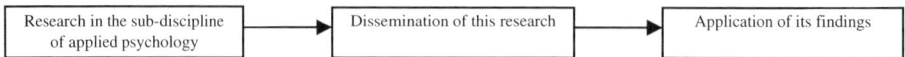

Figure 2.1   The scientific-inquiry approach to knowledge production

However, in the case of IWO psychology, the same range of stakeholders is not apparent. An investigation into the nature of publications in a range of leading IWO psychology journals by Sackett and Larson (1990) indicates that by far the majority of articles have taken the form neither of theoretical advance nor of application to real world problems. Rather, they have consisted of replications or minor extensions of previous research. The problems addressed by the authors, in other words, have been derived from the work of other researchers.

Rather than addressing issues from the world of work, IWO psychology researchers tend to treat other researchers as their prime stakeholders. They cite peer review as the necessary guarantee of scientific soundness, and in general seek to move towards hard, pure, convergent, and urban science. Their articles have become ever more methodologically sophisticated and quantitative. Moreover, current developments in the funding of science are exacerbating the narrowness of the range of their stakeholders. Psychology departments are more likely to receive funding from their universities the more they accept the norms and values of other more "respectable" sciences. Furthermore, their funding depends partly upon ratings of research performance. These ratings are based upon research published in reputable journals, and journal reputation often derives from being methodologically sophisticated. In sum, the stakeholders of most scientific research in IWO psychology (and the other areas of applied psychology) are currently other researchers, universities, and very indirectly, the citizens who provide funding through taxation (Anderson et al., 2001).

The overall model of knowledge production and application implied by the scientific inquiry approach is, then, a simple and linear one, as shown in Figure 2.1. The unresolved difficulties with this model are as follows:

• The problems addressed are derived from a very limited set of stakeholders.
• Dissemination is delayed, and is addressed primarily to this same set of stakeholders.
• The process of translation from dissemination to practice is not specified.
• Practice has little effect upon subsequent issues addressed (there is no feedback).

Solving Problems

An alternative approach (Tranfield & Starkey, 1998; Starkey & Madan, 2001) to the process of knowledge creation in the applied social sciences takes an entirely different stance on all of these issues:

| Stakeholders define the problem together | → | Team solves the problem by means of eclectic theory and interventions | → | Stakeholders communicate solution and method |

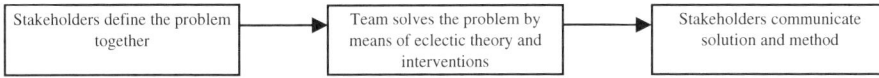

Figure 2.2   A problem-solving approach to knowledge production

- A much wider range of stakeholders is potentially involved in the process of knowledge creation: top management, employees, trades unions, government, psychologist practitioners, management consultants, pressure groups, and other professional bodies, to name but a few. As a result, the origin of the problems addressed is likely to be found in the working life and experience of these stakeholders.
- Consequently, the definitions of organizational effectiveness and of the specific problem to be addressed will necessarily result from a process of social negotiation between the stakeholding parties.
- Since real-world problems seldom come discipline-shaped, the team addressing the problem is likely to be multi-disciplinary. Moreover, it is also likely to contain representatives of most of the relevant stakeholder groups.
- The process of knowledge creation does not move from a stage of fundamental disciplinary theory testing to subsequent application. Rather, it involves a continuous flow back and forth between eclectic, multi-disciplinary theoretical advance and the practical concerns (i.e. outcomes of various interventions) of those stakeholders driving the process forward.
- Rather than seeking to make general theoretical propositions on the basis of evidence, the problem-solving approach claims only to have addressed a particular problem within a specific context.
- The problem solution is arrived at directly rather than subsequently inferred. It is immediately diffused via its users, who have already successfully employed it to solve their problem.
- However, the solution is not necessarily transferable to other situations, and the transferable learning is more likely to be of a processual nature (how the problem was addressed) rather than outcome-based (the specific solution).

In summary, the knowledge creation process implied by the problem-solving approach might be represented as shown in Figure 2.2. This system constitutes a more socially distributed form of knowledge production (Tranfield & Starkey, 1998, p. 348) in which knowledge is generated in the context of application by multi-stakeholder teams; is drawn from a range of backgrounds that transcend traditional discipline boundaries; and results in immediate or short time-to-market dissemination or exploitation (see also Starkey & Madan, 2001).

From Scientific Inquiry to Problem Solving

A wide variety of environmental changes are currently resulting in a general trend away from the scientific inquiry and towards the problem-solving approach in many of the applied social sciences.

The first of these is *the changing nature of demand*. Stakeholders are interested in addressing urgent problems which often threaten the very survival of organizations. The globalization of business and technological change are resulting in new problems which must be urgently addressed if competitiveness is to be maintained. Speed of solution and impact are often considered to be of the essence, and solutions are valued which are "good enough" rather than those which are "correct".

Second, not only are the problems often new ones; they are also highly *ambiguous and difficult to define*. It is seen to be imperative to have a variety of perspectives from which to construct a view of what the problem is. Unfortunately, more often this construction follows after action has been taken, and serves to justify and make sense of what has been done rather than to address it (Weick, 1995).

Third, there is a far greater *distribution of research skills* than hitherto. Increasingly, large corporations and consultancy firms are engaging in applied social science research, attracting by virtue of their superior resources individuals who would previously have only considered academic careers in universities. These employers control and direct research activities so as to address their own or their clients' "real" problems.

There is also a wider *dissemination of knowledge* than hitherto. Much of the knowledge that traditionally has been available only in highly technical journal articles has recently been made comprehensible to non-academics and disseminated via the Internet.

COGNITIVE INERTIA AND THE WIDENING ACADEMIC–PRACTITIONER DIVIDE: LESSONS FROM SELECTION AND ASSESSMENT

In general, IWO psychologists have been relatively slow to adapt to these fundamental changes and there are worrying signs of a deep schism beginning to open up between the science and practice of our profession (see, for example, Anderson, 1998a,b; Anderson et al., 2001; Campion et al., 1986; Dunnette, 1990; Hodgkinson et al., 2001; McIntyre, 1990; Sackett et al., 1986). The validity of this assertion is perhaps best supported by considering one particular area of substantive theory/research and application: the area of selection and assessment.

This is one of the oldest and most mature areas of IWO psychology, both from a research point of view and in relation to the world of practice. Accordingly, it represents an ideal case in point for illustrating the problematic nature of the science–practice interface within our field in general and is a good example of the failure of our profession to adapt quickly enough to its changing environment (Anderson et al., 2001; Herriot, 1992, 1993; Herriot & Anderson, 1997; Hodgkinson et al., 2001).

Essentially, the theory, research, and practice of selection, the crown jewel of IWO psychology, has been based upon theoretical constructs derived primarily from academic stakeholders. Concepts of validity and utility have developed from researchers' views of what organizational clients ought to want, rather than from the discovery of what they did want. An example is to be found in the nature of the traditionally accepted validity criterion: job performance. Research has demonstrated that organizational clients consistently fail to use the most valid tools (by this criterion), preferring instead to select by means of traditional interview procedures (Bartram et al., 1995; Hodgkinson & Payne, 1998; Robertson & Makin, 1986; Shackleton & Newell, 1991, 1994; Smith & Abrahamsen, 1992). This is partly because they are interested in selecting those who will fit the prevailing organizational culture.

Now if validity criteria were determined by means of stakeholder negotiation, between employers, employees, and psychologists, for example, a different set of validity criteria would probably emerge. Employers might stress cultural fit as well as job performance, although psychologists might question them about the degree of conformity or of innovation that they were expecting from employees. Employees might well be interested in the fairness and transparency of processes, and in the extent to which they could own and use the assessment outcomes for themselves.

Moreover, the traditional methods and concepts have become inappropriate for the rapidly changing organizational environment:

- Flexible work roles are taking the place of jobs described by a set of tasks.
- Teamworking and organizational fit are of increasing importance.
- Movement between organizational positions is more frequent.
- A much wider range of flexible employment contracts is available.
- Terms, conditions, and careers differ radically amongst employees within organizations.
- More organizations are becoming international, and processes which accord with employees' assumptions and values in the organization's country of origin may be unacceptable in other cultures.

These contextual changes have fundamental implications for selection theory and practice:

- Predictive validation cannot occur over long periods in most organizations, since job roles change and people change jobs.
- People can no longer be selected on the basis of selection criteria of knowledge and skills which may not be so important for success in the future, despite their predictive power for present job performance.
- Team fit and organization fit are likely to become as important validity criteria as individual performance.
- What is valid will need to be renegotiated and rediscovered in different cultures, rather than cumulated from meta-analytic studies based largely on North American samples.

Theory and practice are catching up too slowly with these new external realities, realities that could and should have been anticipated, if only the appropriate stakeholders had been consulted and new definitions of employee effectiveness had been agreed beforehand.

THE WAY FORWARD FOR INDUSTRIAL, WORK AND ORGANIZATIONAL PSYCHOLOGY

Learning from Professional Competitors

What is the key to avoiding this scenario in the many new areas of theory, research and practice that are emerging in response to the dramatic changes within the world of work? How, in sum, might we enhance our strategic influence in organizations over the longer term? Extrapolating from our experience in the area of personnel selection and assessment, the fundamental solution is to involve a sufficient range of stakeholders in the knowledge production process to ensure that we discover and address the "right" problems. Should we fail to do so, as has so often been the case in the past, top managers will look elsewhere for organizational solutions; i.e. independently of industrial, work and organizational psychologists.

One major source of top managers' organizational change initiatives aimed at addressing their urgent problems has always been their counterparts in other organizations. Rather than attempting to construct a solution from scratch, many top executives model their solutions on those used by "leading edge" or "best of class" organizations (Porter, 1980). Alternatively, they access their personal networks of others at the same level as themselves who have faced similar issues, and seek to learn from their experience (Spender, 1989).

However, members of other professions have succeeded in establishing themselves as valid stakeholders in the people-related elements of the management of organizations. It is instructive to note how these professionals have annexed occupational territory for themselves (Abbott, 1988). Accountants, management consultants, and human resource professionals are all cases in point.

First, none of these professions claim to be based on hard, pure, convergent or urban basic sciences. Management, for example, recognizes that its underpinning research is soft, applied, divergent, and rural (Starkey & Madan, 2001; Tranfield & Starkey, 1998). As a consequence, no one base discipline dominates the field. Rather, researchers address problems from a range of perspectives.

Second, these professions positively search out ways in which they can claim to meet the needs of key stakeholders. They may well limit their attention too much to the particular stakeholder who happens to be the paying client, often top management. Nevertheless, they present themselves as giving top priority to the client's needs. In their efforts to be involved in business strategy, for example, human resource professionals have claimed that the key tasks of their profession are to fit HR processes coherently together so that they support the achievement of strategic objectives (Anthony et al., 1999; Baron & Kreps, 1999; Schuler & Jackson, 1987).

Third, all of these professionals are normally willing and able to collaborate with other professionals and clients in the development of definitions and solutions to an individual client's problems. To the extent that they fail to treat these problems as unique and attempt instead to sell packaged single-discipline solutions, they lose credibility and reputation as professionals.

The success of accountancy as a profession is quite phenomenal. The large accountancy practices even subsume general management consultants, HR consultants, and psychologists within their organizations. This is because they have reached agreement in defining business effectiveness in financial terms, and can incorporate people factors within the ubiquitous bottom line (Armstrong, 1989). A measure of their success in persuading others of this definition is how rarely it is ever challenged.

In sum, we argue that these other professions are well and flourishing compared with industrial, work and organizational psychology because they have adopted a problem-solving rather than a scientific-inquiry approach to their production of knowledge. In doing so, they are acting more in accord with the trends in the organizational environment than we are.

Combining the Best of Both Worlds

We do not, however, recommend that IWO psychologists adopt an extreme problem-solving approach to addressing issues of organizational effectiveness. The most immediate and topical problem should not invariably occupy our attention. Rather, we maintain that there are elements of the culture of applied psychology which are hard to find elsewhere. In marketing terms, we have some unique selling points that differentiate us from other professionals and give us different perspectives on organizational problems. As key elements of the management profession also have recognised (Huff, 2000), we need to place ourselves somewhere between the two approaches (cf. Murphy & Saal, 1990).

What, then, are the features of today's problems that IWO psychologists are particularly suited to address? The first, we suggest, is the difficulty of defining and addressing the problem collaboratively. As we have argued throughout, the context of today's problems is complex and constantly changing; and the stakeholders are several and often have different interests. Whilst other social science professions and disciplines, such as economics and sociology, are skilled at analysing the broader context, psychologists are (or should be) capable of facilitating dialogue between stakeholders.

Unfortunately, dialogue is certainly not the dominant mode of recognizing and defining problems. Instead, top management typically seeks to persuade employees both of the nature of the problem and of its solution. To achieve this persuasion, they use the tools of marketing and rhetoric (Legge, 1995). Therefore, there are two social skill sets necessary: political skills to persuade top management that dialogue is a more effective way of defining and addressing problems than rhetoric; and facilitation skills for eliciting the perspectives of different stakeholders and enabling them to agree a problem definition and work together towards a solution.

The second skill set which psychologists in particular have to offer is that which is required for what Argyris (1999) terms "scholarly consultancy", major elements of which have also been termed "action research". The outputs of scholarly consultancy are propositions about the effects of actions. Such propositions are valid *and* actionable; they are both generalizable *and* applicable to the specific case. They are produced in real-world situations, and the ultimate criterion for their validity is that they work for those involved in their production and implementation. However, the practical nature of this mode of knowledge production emphatically does not imply that the usual scientific principle of falsifiability is not relevant. On the contrary, it is more important than ever that alternative outcomes to those intended in the implementation of the propositions are both possible and tested for.

Argyris' definition of "scholarly consultancy" has much in common with the second, problem solution approach to knowledge production which we described above. For example, it stresses the importance of the social construction and solution of real-world problems by stakeholders. However, it contains certain additional features which play to the strengths of the culture of applied psychology. The first of these is the insistence on falsifiability, the bedrock of scientific method (Popper, 1962). Psychologists place a strong value on the importance of evidence and of the scientific method in evaluating it. They are good at devising ways of testing propositions empirically. Many IWO psychologists have noted the impossibility of evaluating the effectiveness of a number of recent management fads, given the way in which they were described and implemented. It is impossible to falsify their propositions if their failure to have the desired outcomes, and their production of undesirable ones, can always be attributed to a failure to implement them properly.

The second feature of scholarly consultancy which differentiates it from problem solution, and which also plays to psychologists' strengths, is Argyris' insistence on generalizability as well as applicability in individual cases. However, any such generalizability depends upon scholarly consultants being completely clear and explicit about those conditions under which their results hold, and, therefore, those that others will have to replicate in order to achieve the same outcomes. Generalizability thus depends upon practicality or "actionability"; it is, after all, practitioners who seek to generalize. Selecting or setting up the situation in which intervention is likely to be successful is just as important as the intervention itself.

Now psychologists have long realized the importance of the context of behaviour. We have typically favoured contingency theories and moderating variables in our research designs. What we have not done so well is to ask why these contextual features exist in the first place—why, for example, one organization has this sort of culture another that. Nevertheless, the recognition of the importance of context combining with persons in the production of behavioural outcomes is a consequence of interactionist psychology, and is part of psychologists' intellectual heritage. The recognition that it is individuals' *perceptions* of context and of themselves, derived from interactions with others, which are more predictive has emerged from social psychology more recently (Fiske, 1995; Fiske & Taylor, 1991). Hence, the recognition of the limits of generalizability, as well as its desirability, should inform psychologists' interventions in organizations. We are, hopefully, unlikely to recommend packaged "solutions" to organizational problems. Instead, we will be intervening in tailored ways which result in "individuals or organizations that are capable of integrating diagnosis, intervention, production, and evaluation" (Argyris, 1999, p. 319). In short, we will be helping people to learn for themselves.

Moreover, as the remainder of this book demonstrates, psychologists have a set of explicit theories and models which are of potential use in collaborative work with others from different professions in addressing organizational problems. For example, if those responsible for designing and implementing business process re-engineering had been made forcefully aware of socio-technical systems theory and practice, they would not have been compelled to write a subsequent apologia admitting that they had ignored people factors. Considerable unintended and unanticipated damage to employment relationships in organizations would also have been avoided.

BLENDING SCIENTIFIC INQUIRY WITH PROBLEM SOLVING: THE CASE OF STRATEGIC MANAGEMENT

Before concluding this chapter, we consider by way of example an area of applied psychology where we can help to draw a balance between the traditional scientific inquiry and the more recent problem-solving approaches: the area of strategic management. As we will seek to demonstrate, psychological work in this area exhibits many of the features of problem solving. It embraces a variety of stakeholders in the enterprise, it engages with other disciplines in research and practice, and is beginning to result in immediate tools to assist in the development of problem solutions. However, psychologists can also contribute valuable elements derived from the "scientific inquiry" approach.

The psychology of strategic management is still in its infancy. It lies at the interface between traditional IWO psychology and several interrelated subfields of management, especially strategy and marketing. Arguably, strategic management is one of the most important but also one of the least understood areas of organizational life (Mintzberg et al., 1998). Whereas other areas of management deal with routinized, operationally specific issues of a short-term nature, strategic management addresses organization-wide issues of a fundamental nature. Such issues, by definition, tend to be relatively ambiguous, complex, and surrounded by risk and uncertainty:

> Strategy is the direction and scope of an organization over the long term, which achieves advantage for the organization through its configuration of resources within a changing environment, to meet the needs of markets and to fulfil stakeholders' expectations.
> (Johnson & Scholes, 1997, p. 10)

Over the last two decades or so, there has been a growth of interest among management consultants, organizational researchers, and strategy scholars in the application of psychological concepts, theories, and techniques to the field of strategic management (see, for example, Eden & Ackermann, 1998; Eden & Spender, 1998; Flood et al., 2000; Huff, 1990; Huff & Jenkins, 2002). Their aim has been to refine theoretical and practical understanding in areas that have traditionally been the preserve of industrial organization economists and organizational sociologists. At the heart of these developments has been a fundamental shift away from a preoccupation with traditional "content" issues in strategy; for example, questions about the merits of various strategies such as organic growth versus mergers and acquisitions, related versus unrelated diversification, and so on. Concern is now much more with "process" issues, regarding *how* particular strategies come to be formulated and implemented within organizations. For example:

- By what processes and mechanisms do industry and market boundaries and competitive practices evolve and change?
- How do the information processing limitations of decision-makers impact upon their understanding of strategic issues and problems?
- How do the mental representations of strategic issues and problems held by senior managers and other stakeholders impact upon decision processes and individual and organizational performance?
- As organizations seek to expand across national borders, how can they ensure that their employees and managers think globally, yet act in a manner that is sensitive to the local culture in which they must operate on a day-to-day basis?
- How does the CEO make a difference to the strategy and performance of the organization?

These are just some of the many complex process issues confronting business organizations that require psychological expertise, but defy simplistic analysis from the perspective of any one basic social science discipline (including psychology). If the potential contribution of IWO psychology to the field of strategic management is to be fully realized, we must as a profession be more willing to collaborate with, and learn from, other groups of social scientists and stakeholders than has been the case hitherto. Here is a rare opportunity for applied psychologists to contribute to a new perspective within an important multidisciplinary field. Such a contribution could greatly enhance our standing and credibility in the eyes of top management, while breaking the vicious cycle of non-involvement in organizational strategic decision-making that has so bedevilled our profession.

One of our greatest assets in this context is our skill in research design and statistical analysis, derived from the "scientific inquiry" approach. As noted earlier, research into the psychological aspects of strategic management is still in its infancy. Much of the work has hitherto been characterized by limited research designs in which poor or non-existent controls prohibit causal inference. Moreover, a number of methodological hurdles have yet to be overcome if we are to develop satisfactory procedures for the analysis of actors' representations of strategic issues and problems (Hodgkinson, 1997, 2001a, b). In recent years the strategy field and the organizational sciences more generally have witnessed a dramatic proliferation in the development of "cognitive mapping procedures". These have been used both as research tools in theory building and theory testing for the purposes of eliciting actors' mental representations; and as bases for intervening in processes of strategy formulation and implementation. Unfortunately, however, reliability and validity issues associated with these procedures have received scant attention, and virtually no systematic studies have been undertaken in order to formally evaluate their efficacy for use in practical settings (Hodgkinson, 2001a; Hodgkinson & Sparrow, 2002).

In fairness, this state of affairs has probably arisen from the fact that the majority of researchers currently investigating psychological aspects of strategic management are non-psychologists. Many come from research traditions where considerably less importance has been attached to measurement issues. Consequently, they have downplayed the importance of reliability and validity issues in generating evidence to be used either for theory building and testing or as a basis for management practice. In the final analysis, however, if research into the psychology of strategic management is to fulfil its ultimate potential, the procedures employed for mapping strategic thought must meet the same requirements of psychometric rigour applicable to any other method of psychological assessment.

In pursuing greater methodological rigour, however, a careful balance needs to be struck. We do have to ensure that our constructs and techniques are sufficiently reliable and valid to generate robust results. On the other hand, we must not lose sight of the fundamental reason for engaging in the process of knowledge production: to help practitioners to improve their practice and thereby enhance organizational effectiveness. Herein lies the fundamental difference between strategic management and assessment and selection. IWO psychologists can make a difference to the former by contributing their methodological skills to a multi-disciplinary endeavour. They have fallen behind in the latter by over-concentrating upon those methodological skills and ignoring the concerns of relevant stakeholders. By failing to combine rigour with relevance, they have alienated many top managers and consigned our profession to the ranks of operational technicians (Anderson, 1998b).

CONCLUDING REMARKS

In this chapter we have argued that the field of IWO psychology is approaching a critical stage in its development. The dramatic changes that are presently occurring within the world of work, centring on globalization and the impact of new technology, are resulting in radically new forms of work and organization. These in turn require those who study organizations and the people who work within them to rapidly and creatively reconsider their research agendas (Cooper & Jackson, 1987). As Cascio (1995, p. 937) has observed:

> There are great opportunities for industrial and organizational psychologists to contribute to the betterment of human welfare in the context of these changes. To lead change rather than to follow it, however, will require a break with traditional practices and a focus on rigorous research that addresses emerging trends.

Anderson (1998a,b) has cogently summarized the likely consequences for our field, should we fail to heed this well-placed advice and allow the issues which are currently predominating our scientific endeavours in several of our more traditional topic areas to continue apace (see also Anderson et al., 2001; Hodgkinson et al., 2001). In the short term, practitioners and academics alike are likely to survive by continuing to pursue their increasingly disparate agendas independently of one another. Over the longer term, however, the consequences of allowing the divide that is beginning to open up within our ranks to widen further would be equally catastrophic for academics and practitioners alike. In the final analysis, as noted by Dunnette (1990, p. 2) in his introductory remarks in the second edition of the classic *Handbook of Industrial and Organizational Psychology*:

> Advances in industrial and organizational psychology must come from both scientists and practitioners and, in particular, from those who successfully blend both science and practice.

Ultimately, we are a knowledge-based profession and, accordingly, at this critical juncture, it is vital that we take the necessary steps to ensure that the academic–practitioner divide that has become so apparent over recent years is quickly eradicated in order to secure our continuing viability. A major requirement in this regard is to ensure that our scientific endeavours are centred on issues that matter to those whose effectiveness we seek to better understand and enhance: the individuals and groups who constitute the organizations in which we enact our professional roles.

We must also be ever mindful of the fact that organizational effectiveness is a socially constructed phenomenon, defined and pursued in a variety of contexts by groups of people with different perspectives and interests. The skills which industrial, work and organizational psychologists need if we are to be used and valued more than at present are, therefore, processual as well as content-based; we need to be able to reflect on action, and help others to do so, as well as acting ourselves. We currently underestimate the importance of processual skills in our practice and in our training and development programmes, with a marked emphasis on substantive psychological knowledge, research design and statistics. Nevertheless, the process know-how and associated skills that are ultimately required if we are to survive the dramatic changes that are currently taking place within the world of work are to be found within our intellectual heritage, and, suitably combined with our traditional competencies, should afford us considerable competitive advantage in the professional marketplace.

REFERENCES

Abbott, A. (1988). *The System of Professions: An Essay on the Division of Expert Labour*. Chicago: University of Chicago Press.

Anderson, N. (1998a). The people make the paradigm. *Journal of Organizational Behavior*, **19**, 323–328.

Anderson, N. (1998b). The practitioner–researcher divide in work and organizational psychology. *Occupational Psychologist*, No. **34**, 7–16.

Anderson, N., Herriot, P. & Hodgkinson, G.P. (2001). The practitioner–researcher divide in industrial, work and organizational (IWO) psychology: where are we now and where do we go from here? *Journal of Occupational and Organizational Psychology*, **74**, 391–411.

Anthony, W.P., Perrewe, P.L. & Kacmar, K.M. (1999). *Human Resource Management: A Strategic Approach*, 3rd edn. Fort Worth: Dryden.

Argyris, C. (1999). *On Organizational Learning*, 2nd edn. Oxford: Blackwell.

Armstrong, P. (1989). Limits and possibilities for HRM in an age of management accountancy. In J. Storey (Ed.), *New Perspectives on Human Resource Management*. London: Routledge.

Baron, J.N. & Kreps, D.M. (1999). *Strategic Human Resources: Frameworks for General Managers*. New York: John Wiley.

Bartram, D., Lindley, P.A., Marshall, L. & Foster, J. (1995). The recruitment and selection of young people by small businesses. *Journal of Occupational and Organizational Psychology*, **68**, 339–358.

Becher, A. (1989). *Academic Tribes and Territories: Intellectual Enquiry and the Cultures of Disciplines*. Milton Keynes: Society for Research into Higher Education and the Open University Press.

Campion, M.A., Adams, E.F., Morrison, R.F., Spool, M.D., Tornow, W.W. & Wijting, J.P. (1986). I/O psychology research conducted in nonacademic settings and reasons for nonpublication. *The Industrial–Organizational Psychologist*, **24** (1), 44–49.

Cascio, W.F. (1995). Whither industrial and organizational psychology in a changing world of work? *American Psychologist*, **11**, 928–939.

Cooper, C.L. & Jackson, S.E. (1997). Introduction. In C.L. Cooper & S.E. Jackson (Eds), *Creating Tomorrow's Organizations: A Handbook for Future Research in Organizational Behavior*. Chichester: John Wiley.

Dunnette, M.D. (1990). Blending the science and practice of industrial and organizational psychology: where are we and where are we going? In M.D. Dunnette & L.M. Hough (Eds), *Handbook of Industrial and Organizational Psychology*. Palo Alto, CA: Consulting Psychologists Press.

Eden, C. & Ackermann, F. (1998). *Making Strategy: The Journey of Strategic Management*. London: Sage.

Eden, C. & Spender, J.-C. (Eds) (1998). *Managerial and Organizational Cognition: Theory, Methods and Research*. London: Sage.

Fiske, S.T. (1995). Social cognition. In A. Tesser (Ed.), *Advanced Social Psychology*. Boston, MA: McGraw-Hill.

Fiske, S.T. & Taylor, S.E. (1991) *Social Cognition*, 2nd edn. New York: McGraw-Hill.

Flood, P.C., Dromgoole, T., Carroll, S. & Gorman, L. (Eds) (2000). *Managing Strategy Implementation*. Oxford: Blackwell.

Gibbons, M., Limoges, C., Nowotny, H., Schwartzman, S., Scott, P. & Trow, M. (1994). *The New Production of Knowledge: The Dynamics of Science and Research in Contemporary Societies*. London: Sage.

Herriot, P. (1992). Selection: the two subcultures. *European Work and Organizational Psychologist*, **2**, 129–140.

Herriot, P. (1993). A paradigm bursting at the seams. *Journal of Organizational Behavior*, **14**, 371–375.

Herriot, P. & Anderson, N. (1997). Selecting for change: how will personnel and selection psychology survive? In N. Anderson & P. Herriot (Eds), *International Handbook of Selection and Assessment*. Chichester: John Wiley.

Hodgkinson, G.P. (1997). The cognitive analysis of competitive structures: a review and critique. *Human Relations*, **50**, 625–654.

Hodgkinson, G.P. (2001a). The psychology of strategic management: cognition and diversity revisited. In C.L. Cooper & I.T. Robertson (Eds), *International Review of Industrial and Organizational Psychology*, Vol. **16**, pp. 65–119. Chichester: John Wiley.

Hodgkinson, G.P. (2001b). Cognitive processes in strategic management: some emerging trends and future directions. In N. Anderson, D.S. Ones, H.K. Sinangil & C. Viswesvaran (Eds), *Handbook of Industrial Work and Organizational Psychology: Vol. **2**. Organizational Psychology*, pp. 416–440. London: Sage.

Hodgkinson, G.P., Herriot, P. & Anderson, N. (2001). Re-aligning the stakeholders in management research: lessons from industrial, work and organizational psychology. *British Journal of Management*, **12** (Special Issue), S41–S48.

Hodgkinson, G.P. & Payne, R.L. (1998). Graduate selection in three European Countries. *Journal of Occupational and Organizational Psychology*, **71**, 359–365.

Hodgkinson, G.P. & Sparrow, P.R. (2002). *The Competent Organization: A Psychological Analysis of the Strategic Management Process*. Buckingham: Open University Press.

Huff, A.S. (Ed.) (1990). *Mapping Strategic Thought*. Chichester: John Wiley.

Huff, A.S. (2000). Changes in organizational knowledge production. *Academy of Management Review*, **25**, 288–293.

Huff, A.S. & Jenkins, M. (Eds) (2002). *Mapping Strategic Knowledge*. London: Sage.

Hutton, W. (1994). *The State We're In*. London: Jonathan Cape.

Johnson, G. & Scholes, K. (1997). *Exploring Corporate Strategy*, 4th edn. London: Prentice Hall.

Legge, K. (1995). *Human Resource Management: Rhetorics and Realities*. London: Macmillan.

McIntyre, R.M. (1990). Our science-practice: the ghost of industrial–organizational psychology yet to come. In K.R. Murphy & F.E. Saal (Eds), *Psychology in Organizations: Integrating Science and Practice*. Hillsdale, NJ: Erlbaum.

Mintzberg, H., Ahlstrand, B. & Lampel, J. (1998). *Strategy Safari: A Guided Tour Through the Wilds of Strategic Management*. London: Prentice Hall.

Murphy, K.R. & Saal, F.E. (1990). What should we expect from scientist-practitioners? In K.R. Murphy & F.E. Saal (Eds), *Psychology in Organizations: Integrating Science and Practice*. Hillsdale, NJ: Erlbaum.

Pfeffer, J. (1993). Barriers to the advance of organizational science: paradigm development as a dependent variable. *Academy of Management Review*, **18**, 599–620.

Popper, K. (1962). *Conjectures and Refutations*. London: Routledge & Kegan Paul.

Porter, M.E. (1980). *Competitive Strategies: Techniques for Analyzing Industries and Competitors*. New York: New York Free Press.

Robertson, I. & Makin, P. (1986). Management selection in Britain: a survey and critique. *Journal of Occupational Psychology*, **59**, 45–57.

Sackett, P.R., Callahan, C., DeMeuse, K., Ford, J.K. & Kozlowski, S. (1986). Changes over time in research involvement by academic and nonacademic psychologists. *Industrial–Organizational Psychologist*, **24** (1), 40–43.

Sackett, P.R. & Larson, J.R. (1990). Research strategies and tactics in industrial and organizational psychology. In M.D. Dunnette & L.M. Hough (Eds), *Handbook of Industrial and Organizational Psychology*. Palo Alto, CA: Consulting Psychologists Press, pp. 419–489.

Schein, E.H. (1987). *Process Consultation: Vol. II. Lessons for Managers and Consultants*. Reading, MA: Addison-Wesley.

Schein, E.H. (1988). *Process Consultation: Vol. I. Its Role in Organizational Development*, 2nd edn. Reading, MA: Addison-Wesley.

Schuler, R.S. & Jackson, S.E. (1987). Linking competitive strategies with human resource management practices. *Academy of Management Executive*, **1**, 207–219.

Shackleton, V. & Newell, S. (1991). Management selection: a comparative survey of methods used by top British and French companies. *Journal of Occupational Psychology*, **64**, 23–36.

Shackleton, V. & Newell, S. (1994). European management selection methods: a comparison of five countries. *International Journal of Selection and Assessment*, **2**, 91–102.

Smith, M. & Abrahamsen, M. (1992). Patterns of selection in six countries. *The Psychologist*, **5**, 205–207.

Spender, J.-C. (1989). *Industry Recipes: The Nature and Sources of Managerial Judgement*. Oxford: Blackwell.

Starkey, K. & Madan, P. (2001). Bridging the relevance gap: aligning stakeholders in the future of management research. *British Journal of Management*, **12** (Special Issue), S3–S26.

Tranfield, D. & Starkey, K. (1998). The nature, social organization, and promotion of management research: towards policy. *British Journal of Management*, **9**, 341–353.

Weick, K.E. (1995). *Sensemaking in Organizations*. Thousand Oaks, CA: Sage.

CHAPTER 3

Maximizing and Maintaining the Impact of Psychological Interventions

Mary Dalgleish
Employment Service, UK
and
Rick Jacobs
SHL North America
and Pennsylvania State University

INTRODUCTION

It is clearly important that practitioners do what they can to maximize and maintain the impact of their work. In this way, they can also make explicit their value and develop their own practice as well as contributing to the evidence-base for the science as a whole.

This chapter sets out a continuous improvement loop showing the steps taken by a practitioner. The cycle includes: analysis of the problem (drawing on their professional expertise, taking into account the demands and constraints of the organization, and relevant external factors); design of the intervention; delivery of the intervention; evaluation of the process (or formative evaluation) which leads to an improvement cycle, feeding in to a re-analysis and possible redesign; and finally evaluation of the overall impact (summative evaluation). The impact evaluation can also feed back into a review of the original analysis and redesign.

The chapter provides a range of examples of interventions, focusing on the specific processes in the model:

- evaluating overall impact, including examples of utility analysis
- maximizing impact through evaluating process
- maximizing impact through ensuring effective delivery, and
- maximizing impact through analysis and review.

Organizational Effectiveness: The Role of Psychology
Edited by I.T. Robertson, M. Callinan and D. Bartram. © 2002 John Wiley & Sons, Ltd.

   The diversity of approaches highlights the need for practitioners to be "creative scientists" in order to meet customer needs, and to identify opportunities to contribute to the development of their discipline.

THE IMPACT OF PSYCHOLOGICAL INTERVENTIONS

The twentieth century saw the rise of applied psychology and the evolution of the scientist-practitioner. This blending of logic, methodology, tools, and creativity we know today as industrial, organizational, occupational or work psychology has intervened in countless organizations solving numerous problems faced by people at work. We need only look at the array of solutions to realize the richness of our discipline. They span the employment life-cycle from attracting individuals to the workplace to retiring those who spent careers working to further the goals of their organization. We have created recruiting programmes and strategies; realistic job previews; selection tools and associated methodologies; processes to make the on-boarding of new employees more rewarding; training and development programmes; compensation plans; motivational models and practices; performance appraisal and feedback systems; and opportunities for those in their final career phase to stay involved and provide the benefits of their experience back to the organization. All of these efforts are designed not only to help corporations enhance effectiveness but also to improve the lives of each member of the organization.

   While our discipline is characterized by variety, there are, however, underpinning processes which are common to the way we work. When a practitioner is first invited to assist an organization, there will always be an initial analysis or problem-solving stage. The practitioner brings his or her professional knowledge, experience and skills, and must find out about the organization's expectations: its values, culture and ways of working. The practitioner may need to bear in mind external constraints: for example in designing an external recruitment system, knowledge of the likely candidate pool and equal opportunities legislation will be essential. All of these factors will be critical in coming to an analysis of the issue with the client, and in agreeing on an acceptable and workable solution. The practitioner then designs an intervention to meet the requirement, ideally with extensive client involvement to ensure organizational fit and buy-in, and facilitates its delivery.

   Sometimes, unfortunately, that is as far as the practitioner is able to go. Some commissions seek the development of an intervention—say an appraisal system, or a training course designed to motivate managers—but do not involve the practitioner in embedding the system within the organization, checking its effectiveness and ensuring it has the desired impact. Since the solution that has been provided will (hopefully) be based on competent and expert diagnosis, thorough analysis of the internal and external environment and agreed with the client, it may not be unreasonable to *assume* it will be effective. After all, that is why the "expert" was approached in the first place.

   When we go to the doctor and receive tablets for an infection, we are unlikely to question the effectiveness of the treatment if the symptoms are ameliorated, at least partly. In fact, of course, we may have recovered anyway, without the treatment. Worse, if the symptoms persist, we may begin to doubt the competence of the doctor. Even if we fail to follow carefully the instructions on the dosage and timing of the prescribed drug, we may blame the treatment for being ineffective, rather than recognizing we have not implemented it properly. We would probably return and seek a re-analysis of the situation (a re-diagnosis), and another treatment. Or perhaps try an alternative practitioner. Similarly, if the organizational problem is not resolved, the competence of the psychologist may be thrown into doubt whereas what may be needed is the opportunity to review and redesign the intervention for maximum impact.

Often there is simply neither the time nor the opportunity to evaluate or improve the impact of an intervention. The necessity for speedy implementation can make it difficult to capture measures *before* the intervention takes place, or to identify a control or suitable comparison group, in order to have evidence against which to judge results. Further, the ever-increasing pace of change in organizations reduces the purity of comparison or follow-up measures. There are endless practical obstacles for a practitioner to overcome in order to systematically evaluate their efforts, not the least of which is pressure on their own time. And once an intervention is complete, and the investment has been made, the organization will be moving on and may simply not be interested in supporting an activity which may bring little direct benefit to themselves.

The scientific grounding received by psychologists as part of their training ensures that practitioners are aware that they *should* be systematically evaluating the effectiveness of their work. Most students will learn about the famous Hawthorne experiments, as a demonstration that things are not always what they seem. In these studies, the determining factor in the outcome was not the nature of the changes imposed, but the fact that the group of workers had become a focus of interest. Performance improvements may not result from our intervention itself, but perhaps from increased motivation felt by people involved in the work, or wider, unrelated changes in the organization generally. This means it is not enough simply to measure overall impact on the organization. Ideally we should be looking to understand why an intervention has worked the way it has: that is, to understand the process as well as the outcome.

There is no simple formula for assessing the impact of applied psychological programmes. Rather, it is a process of using the rigour and skills of the scientist alongside the creativity of the practitioner in a kind of "art-science" (Becker, 1997). It is not unusual to see reports documenting the degree to which new recruitment practices have increased the number of job applicants. We also see numerous validity reports documenting the relationship between selection test scores and job performance. We can find many examples of how performance appraisal and feedback programmes have affected subsequent on-the-job performance. There are many examples of the effectiveness of training programmes in changing employee behaviour, impacting employee morale, or improving employees' overall work effectiveness. Our discipline conceptualizes, develops and implements solutions for organizational and people issues, but we also need to work hard to understand the degree to which our solutions are effective. Just as evidence-based practice is increasingly seen as essential to improving quality in

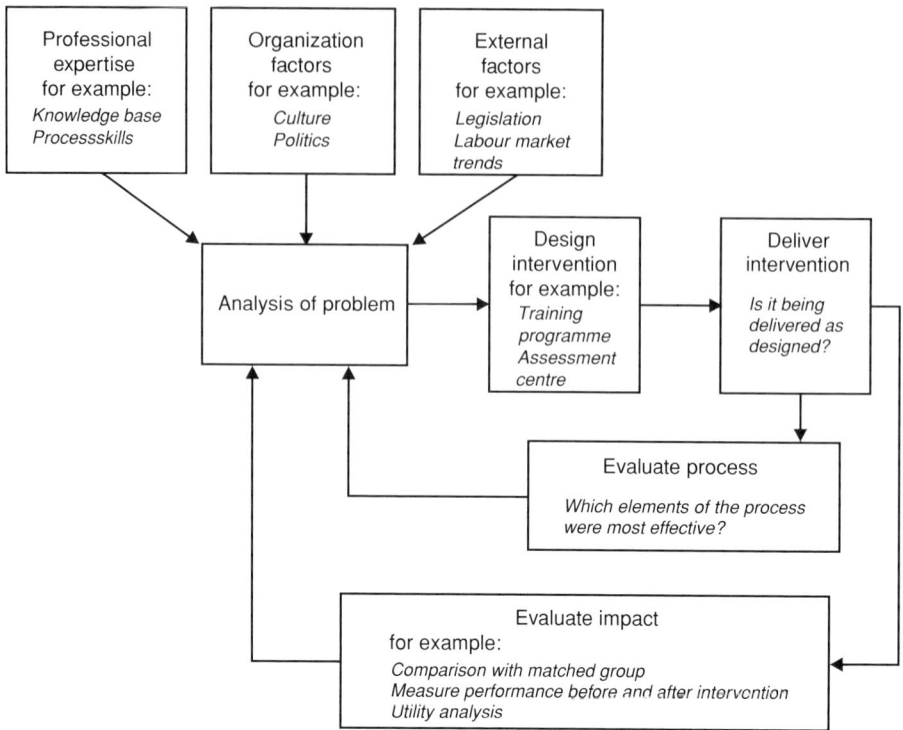

Figure 3.1 Continuous improvement loop to maximize and maintain the effectiveness of psychological interventions

health care, so there is increasing acceptance of this view within applied psychology practice (Briner, 1998).

This chapter provides examples of a variety of ways in which impact has been captured in real-world settings. It also looks at situations where the effectiveness of interventions has been developed and maintained. These examples focus on understanding the processes underpinning the intervention to determine which elements are critical in achieving results.

The elements of this discussion are captured in a simple model (Figure 3.1). This shows the feedback loops which allow incremental improvements, based on evaluation of process (formative evaluation) or impact (summative evaluation). As indicated above, some practitioners may find that their work rarely takes them beyond the "delivery" box: so they *analyse* the situation with the client, bringing their own expertise to bear alongside the organizational and external demands and constraints; they *develop* an intervention; and then *deliver* that. They may get little opportunity to carry out either an *evaluation of process*, in order to modify and improve the intervention as it is being developed, or an *evaluation of overall impact*, as their commission has ceased. This means the vital feedback loop is missing, where both types of evaluation feed into a review of the analysis, which may suggest developments to the original design. Further, the practitioners lose the benefit of feedback on the efficacy of their own professional skills.

Different examples in the chapter focus on different parts of the model. We begin with two straightforward examples focusing on *evaluating the overall impact* of interventions, in terms of improving the efficiency of training programmes, or changed manager behaviours. The analysis of impact is then extended to utility analysis, and capturing the financial impact of interventions in two selection scenarios.

These examples begin to demonstrate the value of going beyond overall impact to *evaluating processes* in developing the effectiveness of interventions. This is extended with two more examples. The first, on selecting bus drivers, highlights the need to keep an eye on how changes in the external environment lead to a need to review the analysis and design of the intervention. The second example demonstrates an iterative approach to reviewing applicant flow to an executive search organization.

Next, we describe two examples where failing to deliver an intervention as designed can be seen to have a key impact on its effectiveness. One of these demonstrates how such problems can be addressed through putting in place quality assurance procedures.

Finally, we end with two broader examples that demonstrate the operation of the model, in particular the importance of *revisiting the analysis* of the problem and the *design* of the intervention in the light of changes in external factors.

EVALUATING OVERALL IMPACT

Example 1: Increasing training programme occupancy

A public sector organization was concerned at the under-use of expensive training places to assist unemployed people into work. Although their advisers were instructed to encourage clients to attend, many of the clients referred to the programmes, and agreeing to attend, were failing to turn up. Programmes were running at only half their capacity. A psychologist was called in to help tackle the problem.

In analysing the problem, the psychologist discussed the issues with the advisers, and also observed a number of adviser and client interviews. The discussions with advisers highlighted lack of knowledge on the part of advisers. They were unclear about what exactly the training programmes, to which they were referring clients, actually involved. This meant it was difficult for them to provide full and detailed information to clients. Observations of advisers' interviews with clients showed that advisers' own lack of understanding of the programme meant they were not convincing in explaining the benefits of the training for clients. They were not able to "sell" clients the notion that there could be real benefits to be gained from attending the courses, partly because they themselves were not clear about them, but also partly because they were unaware of the best way to do this. For example, while advisers thought they were getting clients to agree to attend, they were not always aware of the signals indicating that the client was not engaged. Often the client was simply *not disagreeing* with the adviser's suggestion, rather than actively assenting. The analysis suggested that advisers needed not only more factual information about the training pro-grammes, but also enhanced skills in working with customers and in influencing outcomes.

In response to this analysis, and following discussion with senior managers about what would be practical, given constraints on advisers' time, it was agreed that an appropriate intervention would be to develop and deliver a workshop for advisers. This would not only cover the knowledge aspects, but also provide an opportunity to develop and practice influencing skills.

The workshops were designed and delivered by the psychologist (ensuring delivery captured the essential elements of the design). Feedback from partici-pants on the process was obtained immediately following the workshop. This was very positive. This is important, in that an enjoyable experience is more likely to engage people and hence to be memorable and effective. It also encouraged other advisers to attend the workshop on their colleagues' recommendations. But positive evaluation of the process of delivery of the workshops did not, in itself, demonstrate the value of the intervention.

Information on the overall impact on advisers' performance was obtained by collecting data on the number of clients referred for training, and the number actually turning up in the weeks prior to the workshops, and in the weeks following the workshops. Following the workshops, advisers were considerably more successful in their work with clients. More than 80% of clients referred now attended the programme, compared with only 50% prior to the workshops.

Subsequently a similar problem was identified in another part of the country. Following a critical analysis of that specific situation (by a different psychologist, who had seen reports of the above events), it was agreed that a similar inter-vention would be appropriate. A series of workshops was delivered, building on the original model, and a similar impact achieved. In both parts of the coun-try, the increased occupancy of the training courses meant considerable savings on the cost of training delivered to clients.

Example 2: Changing manager behaviour

In another example of non-monetary, yet organizationally meaningful impact, an organization identified a problem with the way some team leaders were managing their people. Changes in the business had resulted in less need for a "command and control" style of management, and more need to encourage people to work on their own initiative. Senior managers wanted to encourage their team leaders to be more empowering, approachable and facilitative.

In the analysis stage, psychologists worked with a range of employees to iden-tify characteristics of both the "old" and the "new" management style. While senior managers expected the latter to result in improved organizational per-formance, their aim for this intervention was simply to have their team leaders demonstrate more of the "new" behaviours. It was agreed that this informa-tion should be turned into an individual development tool, comprising a set of statements about usual behavioural styles. Both the individual manager, and their team members (anonymously), rated the manager on this set of behaviours, enabling a comparison of self-ratings against those provided by their team members. The feedback process was facilitated by a psychologist, who helped consider specific and practical action to address any areas for improvement.

The intervention itself therefore included the whole process of issuing and scoring the questionnaires to teams, the feedback process, discussion of development needs, and providing guidance on possible development action. Following delivery of the intervention, team leaders' views were sought on how the process was received. This led to some modifications: for example, team leaders preferred to receive written feedback on their scores prior to the meeting in order to have a chance to assimilate the information. This enabled them to make better use of the development discussion.

In order to capture whether the intervention had had the desired impact of making a difference to team leaders' behaviour, the process was repeated some months later. Changes were identified in the majority of these managers, as assessed by their teams. These changes included:

- improved communication
- more attention given to staff development
- wider shared decision-making
- more frequent positive feedback given for good performance
- making the time to gain a better understanding of the business
- developing a culture of openness.

While this is not a measure of impact on the organization's bottom line, it does demonstrate the required change in team leaders' behaviours in the desired direction.

A criticism of this approach might be that those team leaders most in need of the intervention may be those who are least likely to put themselves forward. The process was voluntary, and it may be that those willing to participate would be those most likely to be responsive to feedback and most willing to change their behaviour. Such self-selection would considerably reduce the overall impact on the organization.

There has been a great deal of work on ways to identify more tangible benefits from psychological interventions, including translating impact into a monetary value. We turn to this next.

EVALUATING IMPACT: UTILITY ANALYSIS

For almost as long as we have been intervening in organizations and evaluating our efforts, there have been efforts to quantify for businesses how our work impacts organizational efficiency and profitability. There is a substantial history to this particular line of work dating back to the 1930s when Taylor and Russell (1939) put forth their utility model. They identified the percentage of successful individuals resulting from a selection system under specific conditions regarding base rate, validity, selection ratio and definitions of success. Twenty-five years later Naylor and Shine (1965) built on the fundamental ideas of their predecessors to provide a more applicable model of utility. Between these two monumental works which allowed us to better understand the impact of our selection programs, Brodgen (1946, 1949) and Cronbach and Gleser (1965) added to our arsenal by translating percentage of successful individuals into a monetary estimate of productivity improvement. Since these works have been put into practice, refinements have been plentiful and have increased our understanding of the financial impact of our work. Among the notable contributions in this arena are those by Schmidt et al. (1979), Cascio and Ramos (1986), Landy et al. (1982) and Murphy (1986). We have a rich and growing methodology to support our contention that what we do for organizations impacts the bottom line. Two examples follow.

Example 3: Selecting project managers

A major computer systems organization was seeking better to understand a key position and plan for ways of improving performance for those in that position. In this set of projects the organization was looking to develop an assessment centre for project managers, the key organizational role for the company. It was hoped that the assessment centre could help develop current project managers and assist in the identification of high-quality project managers for the future.

In this organization, project managers were responsible for developing and implementing projects for clients which range in financial stature from as little as $10 thousand to over $10 million annually. When the work began, there were over 750 individuals in this job title worldwide. It was estimated that the number would grow to well over 1000 within three years. In addition to recognizing an opportunity for enhancements and utility in the selection process, the company was dedicated to the development of those already occupying the role. Our studies and analyses documented massive paybacks for any investments made to more effectively select and develop project managers. It was the presentation of this information back to corporate decision-makers that convinced the organization initially to support the development and monthly administration of the 2.5-day assessment centre. The steps in this project followed those in Figure 3.1.

The analysis stage included job analysis of the position of project manager. Over 200 project managers participated in survey work to document the duties and responsibilities of the position. Analyses were conducted overall and on subgroups better to understand the way the job changed as a function of contract size, type of work being performed and experience of the project manager. The outcome was a competency model that assisted in understanding how the job is performed and how to best measure key competencies.

The intervention involved creation of an assessment centre. A multi-day, multi-measure series of exercises, surveys and presentations was assembled with role specifications for assessors and candidates. Logistics including physical layout, equipment, candidate flow, and assessor responsibilities was created. Training of assessors was designed and implemented replete with scoring processes and feedback forms/protocols. The 2.5-day format was implemented monthly with candidate nominations and 360-degree performance appraisals required 60 days in advance of the actual assessment.

Evaluating overall impact included an estimation of the value of the position to the organization. A structured survey was created and administered to 50 vice-presidents and presidents within the organization. Following the Schmidt and Hunter methodology for estimating the standard deviation of performance in dollars, values for project managers of various sized projects were determined. Several findings were of great interest. First, the value of this job was exceedingly high—in some cases, estimates approached one million dollars. Next, the value of all types of project management jobs easily exceeded the annual salary. Finally, the distribution was not symmetric, as the difference between an average and poor performer was consistently twice that of the difference between an average and an outstanding performance. What we learned was that a poor performer can impact project performance in a negative way far more than a strong performer can help project effectiveness.

This fed back into a re-analysis, which indicated that the intervention should be extended to include an assessment of the capabilities of current project managers. A performance evaluation system was implemented, based on the competency model identified during the job analysis, to assess the performance of the current group of project managers. One interesting outcome of the evaluation of the processes at this stage was the finding of a nearly normal distribution of performance. This indicated to us that we had much to gain by targeting the current group of project managers for development. Clearly, improving the performance of some of the lower rated project managers could greatly enhance the effectiveness of the organization. This, coupled with the knowledge that the project management staff would grow by at least 33%, gave ample opportunity for overall impact of our programme.

A further re-analysis suggested the need to create the means for improving performance. In conjunction with the organization's director of employee development, a series of interventions was created ranging from on-line courses, to seminars and opportunities for mentoring. Project managers were informed of ways to become involved in the various programmes and records were kept with regard to which programmes were most requested. Estimates of the impact of these programmes were gathered from management and from programme participants.

Overall impact was assessed through utility analysis of the various strategies for performance improvement. To better understand the outcomes of this intervention, the above information was assembled and subjected to a formal utility analysis as recommended by Schmidt and Hunter. Our findings were quite surprising and very convincing to those who were in control of budgets. The estimated first year saving from the programme was calculated to be in excess of one million dollars. In the first two years of the programme over 300 project managers were assessed and given feedback. Each manager was given a detailed performance review and development plan. The programme has been modified since its inception but continues to benefit the organization.

Example 4: Selecting customer service representatives

This example comes from a major insurance company in the US that hires hundreds of customer service representatives each and every year. Their desire was to develop a full simulation along with a traditional selection test battery better to understand applicant fit to the job. The total selection system was desktop-based resulting in uniform application across all offices. The results were staggering in terms of enhancements to productivity as well as reduction in time of training. The overall savings to the organization within the first six months of implementation paid for the development and use of the selection system for five full years. Again, the elements of the project followed the model outlined earlier (Figure 3.1).

Initial analysis included a job analysis. The job of customer service representative was surveyed from both the incumbent and supervisor perspectives. A detailed competency model was generated that allowed for the specification of ability tests, work styles inventory, and structured interview. Additionally, materials were gathered to allow for the creation of a video-based, computer-generated simulation of job tasks. This also served as a realistic job preview of the tasks performed by customer service representatives.

With the benefit of the competency model, such predictors as customer service orientation, verbal comprehension, and basic computer skills were linked to the job. In each case predictor measures were identified that tapped into the important underlying skills and abilities of the job. Since the job involves interacting with both the public via telephone and the computer in real time, the simulation created featured both audio and video input with the required computer actions to respond to the input.

The design of the intervention involved creating simulations using current employees and replicating actual job tasks. Rules for the conduct of job activities were given and could be accessed during the assessment. Candidates were required to play the role of a customer service representative for several different job activities. None of the activities required prior training or knowledge of procedures. These simulated activities not only provided the organization the opportunity to assess candidates, they also allowed for the candidate to decide if the requirements of the job matched individual preferences for work.

One element in the evaluation included a concurrent validation study. Several studies were conducted to evaluate the degree to which scores on the test battery elements as well as the overall evaluation were related to on-the-job performance. Validity coefficients were strong and significant and indicated that, even within a selected population, the assessment devices were able to identify the best performers. While such evidence is often the first and only type of data collected for such a selection programme, this organization wanted more information regarding the benefits of the selection process.

Further evaluation involved a follow-up study of new hires. In an interesting and important review of selection system outcomes, it was found that those candidates achieving the top scores (upper 25% on the selection battery) were ready to perform the job three weeks earlier than their selected counterparts. This represented a 30% reduction in training time, resulting in returns on hiring in a much more expedient time frame. It is important for organizations to conduct such analyses better to understand the strengths of their interventions. If such a finding were not realized, individuals who were ready to perform the job would have remained in training and thereby reduced the benefit of the selection process.

MAXIMIZING IMPACT THROUGH EVALUATING PROCESSES

Examples 3 and 4 show that evaluation of impact can demonstrate significant outcomes, including financial benefits, to an organization and provide convincing information to encourage organizations to invest in psychological expertise. Both examples also show how process evaluation can identify factors that can significantly improve or develop an intervention. In the last example, by identifying that top scorers needed less training, an additional saving to the organization was achieved, as well as tailoring the intervention more specifically to individual needs. This section reviews two further examples of improving impact through evaluation of process.

Example 5: Selecting bus operators

A project carried out in 1993 for the American Public Transportation Association aimed at developing a bus operator selection programme that would be applicable for bus companies across the country. Working with 10 pilot organizations across the US and in Canada, a selection programme has been developed and implemented and is currently in use in 35 cities. This project involved the same steps of analysis, design, delivery, evaluation and review (re-analysis).

Again, job analysis formed part of the initial analysis. Bus operators and their supervisors (300 and 50, respectively) provided input regarding the tasks and responsibilities as well as the important abilities and characteristics for the job. As a result a tripartite theory of the job was generated specifying the key roles of attendance, safety and customer service inherent in the position. Tasks were assigned to responsibility areas and responsibility areas could be factored into the three job components. Additionally, performance scales were created to map to the responsibility areas. Finally, an experimental predictor battery was assembled to include measures that were conceptually related to the responsibilities.

The intervention was designed as a predictor battery. It was designed to include such measures as time sensitivity, safety orientation and customer focus which were identified in the literature. Additionally, measures of cognitive abilities, personality, and biographical information were created for inclusion in a concurrent validation study of bus drivers from across the US and Canada.

Process evaluation included a concurrent validation study. In excess of 800 bus drivers provided predictor information while their supervisors evaluated their job performance. Additionally, each bus organization provided data on operator attendance and accidents as well as customer service indicators. Results from the

testing of incumbent bus drivers were correlated with both supervisory evaluations and archival data. Strong relationships were uncovered between predictors
and criterion as well as some surprising "non results". Cognitive abilities did
not play a role in forecasting bus driver performance. Biographical data regarding attendance and timeliness were strongly related to on-the-job attendance.
Personality dimensions were good indicators of job performance. One interesting finding was that bus operators who were business oriented were rated as
better performers. The underlying explanation is that those operators who saw
their bus as their personal business took a greater interest in being on time,
driving safely and satisfying their client/riders. Additionally, those operators
who were internally driven were better performers while their externally motivated counterparts were seen as substandard performers. All of these findings
not only documented the efficacy of the selection programme, but also gave us
a firmer understanding of the job so as to enhance training of future operators
and maintain the effectiveness of the selection process.

Utility analysis was carried out as part of the overall analysis of impact. The
initial validation study with over 800 bus drivers showed potential reductions in
absence rates at approximately 10 days per year per bus driver hired. In addition
to reducing absence and thereby increasing driver availability, archival data indicated a reduction of 16 accidents per year per 100 drivers hired. The savings
accruing from such outcomes can be astronomical. As an example, New York
City hires between 800 and 1200 drivers per year. The average cost of a day
of absence in 1995 was estimated at $160. When you do the math, the saving
from absence reduction alone is astounding. Accident reduction not only saves
money it can save lives. The utility of the programme is clearly profound. Similar
projects have recently been completed for train and subway operators as well
as conductors with equally impressive outcomes. With such clear indications of
value, the organizations using the programme are encouraged to continue its
use. In the transit industry word spreads quickly and other organizations will
begin using the selection process so as to enhance their success.

An important follow-up to this programme demonstrates the need for re-
analysis of the intervention in the light of external changes. While the success of
the bus operator selection programme is clear to those who conceptualized it,
those who developed it and those involved in the initial implementation, recently
individual bus organizations have questioned its efficacy. While not doubting
the existing data from the initial studies, more recently bus organizations have
seen an increase in drop-out rates for training classes, increased turnover of
newly trained bus operators, and an increase in absences. These are all counter
to the data collected during the studies, and indicate a need to look again at the
analysis of the problem. What has caused such a change of fortune?

In reviewing the data for several organizations it was found that external factors were responsible, with a change in the skills of the relevant labour market.
New hires were, on average, achieving lower scores than those hired three to
four years ago. Further review uncovered a declining level of candidate availability. In 1995 it was estimated that one in eight candidates were hired for the
job. More recently that ratio has changed to one in two. For some organizations the number of vacancies routinely exceeds the number of candidates. This

change in external factors means that the selection problem has turned into a candidate flow problem, and rather than focusing on selection the organizations experiencing this problem must move to more active recruiting programmes. Without such clear and available data the ability to continue with a successful selection programme would be inhibited.

Example 6: Developing an executive search database

A slightly different example, one demonstrating the value of taking an iterative approach to managing unexpected developments, can be seen in work for a worldwide executive search firm. The firm had recently moved down the organizational ladder to create a programme for helping companies identify and hire individuals who will fill mid-level management positions. The key challenge here was to develop a database of available and pre-qualified candidates who could be presented to clients. Following analysis of the issues, we developed a website replete with assessment tools to build up the candidate pool. Our estimate was that we could have complete data on approximately 4000 qualified candidates during the first year. We were wrong. The candidate pool reached 24 000 within 90 days and the ability for the client organization to launch its business was not only advanced several months, but the estimate of revenues during the first year was doubled and the five-year revenue was projected to approximate 95 million dollars. This is all in addition to the positive benefits to client organizations to hire more quickly more qualified applicants and for the applicant pool members to move on to more fulfilling and lucrative positions. This project involved the usual steps.

The analysis stage led to the design and development of a website to attract candidates. The blending of technologists and psychologists was necessary to design a website that could attract individuals from various job families (including sales/marketing, IT, and finance) and provide a platform for basic assessment of background, skills and abilities. The site needed to be informative and interesting so as to lead not only to a casual browsing but also to a more detailed interaction of up to 40 minutes. The goal here was to gather enough information to effectively sort candidates and categorize them according to their strengths and interests.

The intervention also required the creation of a database to allow for the organization of candidates. Once again technology and psychology were put together to effectively organize the incoming data in a way that allowed for merging electronic information into meaningful, job-related, dimensions. The key criterion for system effectiveness was ease of use as many of the database users would be new to this process. What was needed was a system that incorporated the users' knowledge of human resource management but did not assume high levels of software expertise.

In addition, the intervention was extended to include training on how to use the database. Menu-driven programs were developed to introduce the users to the system and to facilitate their transition from paper and pencil resumés to the on-line information regarding candidates. Help menus and help desk services with knowledgeable individuals were available to all system users. Periodic reviews of help desk requests provided listings of most frequently asked questions that were then incorporated into additional help menu material. Users were regularly surveyed regarding system use, issues and ideas for improvement.

Process analysis involved analysis of the applicant flow through this process. Here the question of how to maintain programme effectiveness was multifaceted. Reviews were conducted to better understand time frames for completion of information by candidates, why candidates failed to complete all the requested information, and how to best capture candidate interest. Candidates' databases were also reviewed to ensure that all necessary information was being interpreted accurately and promptly transferred from the initial programme that captured the data to the system used by recruiters to identify viable candidates during the job search phase of their work. The entire project can best be described as iterative in that continuous efforts were made to review both the operation of the system and how the system was being used by the recruiters. Without the constant analysis and updating, the viability of this system would have been limited.

MAXIMIZING IMPACT THROUGH EFFECTIVE DELIVERY

The way an intervention is delivered can be critical to its success. One of the challenges facing large organizations is to deliver the same information to many thousands of employees. New training initiatives may be carefully designed to promulgate specific messages in specific ways. However, sometimes the process of roll-out, or cascade training, can mean that the training actually received by the majority of employees bears little resemblance to the carefully designed package put together at some cost by an experienced trainer or psychologist. One advantage of computer-based training is that there is built-in quality assurance: it is clear what each person is receiving. However this may not be suitable for all types of training, especially the development of skills where practice can be essential.

For evaluation purposes, as the model in Figure 3.1 makes clear, it is important to establish if an intervention is being delivered as designed. Evaluation captures the effects of the intervention *as delivered*, and this may not always be *as designed*. This section of the chapter looks at two examples where delivery is critical to maintaining the effectiveness of interventions. Although both of these involve training-type interventions, this principle applies equally to other psychological interventions. For example, assessment centres may be well researched and designed, but delivery can founder through an organization being unwilling to invest enough in the training of assessors. The design may be good, but the delivery will not be, and the overall impact will be severely reduced.

Example 7: Helping unemployed people into week

The introduction of Job Clubs in the UK Employment Service in the 1980s produced impressive initial success. They were designed—as our model indicates—following a process of analysis. The Employment Service was keen to investigate an initiative that had proved successful in other countries. Job Clubs were developed by psychologists in the US based on tried and tested job hunting techniques, with the objective of getting each member the best possible job in the shortest possible time. The leader took a directive style, serving to coach members in job hunting techniques and providing motivation by celebrating members' successes. Members had access to a range of facilities including phones, paper, stamps and vacancies.

Having established the needs of the Employment Service, and taking account of acceptability to clients, UK psychologists designed an adapted version of the US counsellors Manual and set up three sites for pilot Job Clubs. The delivery of the pilots was monitored closely. These pilot Job Clubs achieved a much higher success rate than other comparable Employment Service measures at that time: 75% of participants in the pilots obtained jobs (Price, 2000). Job Clubs expanded rapidly over the following years, but as they did, their success rate—while still impressive—was not as high as the original pilots.

A study in the early 1990s went beyond the evaluation of overall impact provided by measure of the percentage of participants gaining work, to look at processes. It examined differences between more and less effective Job Clubs. This work showed clearly that those that adhered most closely to the original, tried and tested model, achieved greater success. The lesson here is the need to identify the key elements of effectiveness and to ensure these are incorporated in future interventions, through some kind of quality assurance.

In this particular example, the process evaluation highlighted the importance of delivering the intervention as designed. Certain aspects of the process were key to its effectiveness. The results obtained from pilot initiatives are often higher than those obtained from a national programme. This may be due to the enthusiasm of those chosen—or volunteering—to be involved in a special initiative. In addition there is often greater attention to training and iterative process evaluation, or action research, to keep the pilot on track and learn lessons for wider roll-out. However, it is unlikely that a good part of the reduction in effectiveness was because the intervention as designed became less effective. Rather, the programme *as delivered* over time increasingly failed to include all the critical elements for success.

Example 8: Reducing re-offending behaviour

Another slightly different example where quality depends on delivering tried and tested approaches is the introduction of cognitive skills programmes by Prison Service psychologists. A considerable amount of research over the past decades has looked at the effectiveness of rehabilitation programmes for offenders. Through meta-analysis, characteristics of interventions that can effectively reduce re-offending have been isolated. The most successful are skills-based, cognitive approaches, usually involving the use of behavioural and social learning principles of interpersonal influence, skill enhancement and cognitive change (McGuire, 1995).

This evidence base was available to Prison Service psychologists in analysing possible solutions to the Prison Service's concern to reduce re-offending behaviour. In conjunction with the requirements of officials, the evidence base enabled them to develop programmes incorporating elements that research had demonstrated should lead to maximum impact.

Evaluation of impact is difficult in the short term (re-offending rates amongst prisoners who have been through the programme will take some time to establish). It is certainly much more difficult than in the Job Clubs scenarios to keep track of overall impact. In the absence of quick information on impact, the quality of these programmes has been maintained by the introduction of an accreditation process to ensure each course meets the criteria shown by research to reduce re-offending. In addition, to ensure effective delivery of these courses as designed, psychologists contribute to a kind of process evaluation through a quality assurance role, including selecting, training and providing ongoing supervision and monitoring of the tutors, and overseeing the progress of participants (Blud, 1999).

MAXIMIZING IMPACT THROUGH ANALYSIS AND REVIEW

The preceding sections of the chapter have provided examples that focus on different aspects of the model outlined in Figure 3.1. This section provides two final examples, which demonstrate the value of reviewing and refining interventions to maximize and maintain effectiveness. In particular, they show clearly the impact of changing environmental influences. The changing environment within which organizations operate makes it essential to review and re-analyse interventions to ensure they are still well tailored to an organization's requirements.

Example 9: Police officer selection

The first example here is taken from the selection arena. Police officer selection, where simultaneous goals of maximizing validity and reducing adverse impact against protected groups must be considered, is an area where we have spent the past 20 years refining our selection methods. The substantial challenge is not only one of enhancing validity and reducing adverse impact, but also to do so in a way that is fast and efficient. In the competitive job market of today, police departments want selection programmes that can be implemented in very short periods of time. Since public funds are being used, those programmes must be conducted at a minimum of cost. In some jurisdictions as many as 25 000 candidates are tested each time jobs become available. Analysis of all of these requirements have caused scientist-practitioners to question the fundamental assumptions inherent in the civil service testing model that has dominated this arena.

Based on attempts to maximize and maintain effectiveness we have seen a shift from designing interventions focusing on the exclusive use of written tests of cognitive abilities, to more broad-based assessment programmes including work styles, biographical data, and oral/interactive skills. While the content has shifted dramatically in efforts to reduce adverse impact and enhance validity, we have also seen a shift in the way tests are administered and funded. In several police departments, testing has shifted from an event that occurs once every year or once every other year to testing throughout the year on a monthly basis, or even more frequent. We are seeing the traditional large format test events replaced by individually administered tests at regional test centres. Finally we are seeing the funding of the testing programmes shifting from being completely the responsibility of the police department to a shared burden requiring the candidate to pay a fee to become a candidate. The future is likely to see even more changes as the testing of police officers nationwide could move to a model where a candidate can take one test battery and simultaneously apply for jobs in multiple police departments. As the needs of the client base changes so must the solutions we provide.

From the process evaluation perspective, the movement from one testing format to another has created a great deal of excitement as we have repeatedly documented substantial rises in validity while simultaneously increasing the number of minority group members selected for the job. The savings in this particular area are multi-dimensional and not restricted to financial matters. They include the very positive outcome of a more diverse and representative workforce resulting in more minority group members to improve recruiting of others and more minority group members available to act as community representatives where ethnicity is critical. Additionally, lower probability of litigation as a result of reducing adverse impact translates into huge dollar-based savings for the appointing jurisdiction. Finally, by bringing in more minority group members at the entry level, the pool of available, high-quality officers for promotion is increased. It has been a win–win–win outcome for the candidates, the police department, and the public they serve. This work has been praised by the United States Department of Justice as a model for the future selection of police officers.

In relation to our model, effective hiring is a multi-dimensional process that embodies speed, cost-consciousness, accuracy and diversity of outcome. In response to these goals, analysis has led to the design of programmes to raise validity, reduce adverse impact and do so in a way that minimizes cost and time. Such programmes require the co-operation and support of a wide variety of individuals and groups ranging from the police officer union, civil service organizations, legal groups, and the citizenry to former aggrieved parties. The process by which selection of police officers has occurred in the past is well documented and follows traditional selection methods. This process was modified to support more fully the new hiring goals. While the new process is still being worked out from city to city and from implementation to implementation, certain principles are emerging. As the implementations are occurring, we are able to see what is meeting our expectations and what needs to be changed. This evaluation is aiding in the development of new hiring programmes that more fully respond to the challenges of accuracy, diversity, speed and cost-effectiveness.

Example 10: Introducing behavioural competencies

A final example aims to demonstrate the applicability of the model to a less specific, organization-wide initiative. A large UK government organization required a new competency framework in 1996 as a result of feedback from employees that the existing performance appraisal system failed to value "how" people went about their work, but only whether their tasks were achieved. As part of the analysis stage, and as a first step towards developing a new, input-based, competency framework, repertory grid techniques and critical incident analyses were used with people at all levels throughout the organization. The work established the behaviours that distinguished particularly effective performers from those that were less effective. A framework of desirable "working styles" was developed as a basis on which to design new human resource processes.

However, changes in external factors meant it was not possible yet to leave the analysis stage. A change of government in 1997 brought about major changes in how the organization was expected to work. There was an increased emphasis on collaborative partnerships with stakeholders. There was a new focus on high standards of customer service. There was a concern to promote a more collaborative, empowered culture within the organization itself. In order to make explicit this change in direction, the entire workforce were involved in a widespread consultation to identify core organizational values.

It was clear that the framework of working styles, although robust and empirically developed, had been overtaken by events. Being "pre-values" it no longer commanded the credibility required to be acceptable. To improve its impact, therefore, and meet the new organizational requirements, further analysis work was carried out to link the behavioural indicators from the working styles framework and any new indicators emerging as a result of the changed business, to the newly agreed organizational values. The set of behavioural indicators produced was then grouped into eight "personal competencies" linked to the five values.

These competencies were then embedded in the design of a number of interventions: human resource processes. These included appraisal, internal vacancy filling and 360-degree feedback. These were initially delivered as pilot programmes to enable the processes to be evaluated. Lessons from these formative (process) evaluations were fed via further analysis, into the final design of the HR processes, before they were finally promulgated throughout the organization. For example, in piloting performance appraisal, the process evaluation showed that competencies were favourably received but there were practical issues. For example, people reported that they needed more space on the appraisal form to provide evidence. Also, links with training and development needed clarifying. These changes were incorporated into the final process. We also identified from the pilots that delivery of training on the new competencies varied greatly between trainers. A video was developed, to support the existing open learning pack that had been issued to every member of the organization to help understand the new competencies. The video described and demonstrated the new competencies, and was used in the training sessions to ensure the delivery was as intended, and that clear and consistent messages were sent.

The overall impact of the changes was captured in a number of ways. The growth of awareness of the values and reporting of values-linked behaviours was monitored through the annual staff survey, to keep track of the changing culture and identify whether there are particular places or job roles where particular attention was required. Over the past three years, there have been significant increases in key values areas—for example, the percentage of people agreeing their line manager is living the values and that the organization is committed to particular ways of working required by the values. In addition, aggregating responses to the 360-degree feedback exercises gives an overall picture of how the organization performs against values-linked behaviours, and identifies key areas where additional training and development efforts for the organization should be targeted. Finally, independent evaluation studies of the work of the organization have commented favourably on the changed culture, indicating the impact of the values and competencies.

What emerges from this and the other examples is the critical importance of reviewing interventions while they are being developed, as part of a wider analysis of changes in the internal and external environment. This particular example captures a number of key elements that contributed to maximizing the impact of the new competencies. These are noted below because they are critical in maximizing and maintaining the impact of any major organizational change:

- *Commitment from the top.* There was Board level commitment to embed the new values and competency framework which was reinforced by Board members in communications at every opportunity.
- *Responding to the changing organizational culture.* In this case this was achieved by linking the interventions closely to the organizational values as described above. The competencies were designed to provide a unified and consistent framework, and simplified message.
- *Organizational ownership.* The competencies and the values were developed following widespread consultation and work with individuals and groups throughout the organization. This process itself was well publicized, so that the language and content of the competencies became familiar to people and was "owned".
- *Simple, consistent messages.* The competencies were designed as a common currency. They were derived from the organizational values, rather than as a separate framework. In addition to using the competencies in performance appraisal, internal vacancy filling and 360-degree feedback, this was reinforced by building the competencies into external recruitment to ensure selection of those displaying the desired competencies.
- *Persistence.* Bringing about major organizational change at the same time as meeting inevitable pressures of business operations means it can be difficult to maintain everyone's enthusiasm all the time. Solid support from the top helps here, as does emphasizing the value of the culture change.

CONCLUSIONS

Finding creative ways to assess systematically the impact of applied psychological interventions in real-world settings plays to the combination of scientist-practitioner skills that are highly valued in Industrial/Organizational psychologists. There is no formulaic approach to capturing the effectiveness of interventions. In this chapter we have tried to show something of the range and diversity of psychological interventions that a practitioner might come across, and the corresponding variety in approaches to assessing, maximizing and maintaining impact.

However, while the content of our work varies widely, there are key common elements underpinning our approach. We have tailored the model of process and impact evaluation to describe the continuous improvement loop required to maximize and maintain the impact of psychological interventions.

As every practitioner knows, there are usually good reasons why a standard intervention cannot be adopted wholesale in a particular organization: our skill is in developing tailored solutions based on critical analysis, and inevitably this affects the scientific purity of comparative evaluations. Organizations are continually changing as are the environments in which they operate: it is inevitable that the effectiveness of many organizational change initiatives is difficult to capture because they have been overtaken by the next wave of change. It is often difficult for the practitioner to afford the time required to collect evidence of impact before moving on to their next assignment; and indeed their client may be less willing to participate in evaluation studies once the desired changes have been achieved. We value our creativity in working with clients to devise solutions to their requirements which most effectively meet their needs. To facilitate our discipline's continued excellence, it is clear that, as scientists, we need to exploit our creativity in doing what we can to build evaluations of our practice into our work as a matter of course. This requires consideration at the design stage of the intervention.

We owe it to our clients to be as clear as we can about our impact: they need reliable information in order to make decisions about whether, and how much, to invest in our products and services. We owe it to our profession to collect robust information on the factors leading to specific outcomes. We have a responsibility to build a sound evidence-base for our own future practice. We owe it to ourselves, as professional psychologists, to be able to continually improve the worth of our own work.

REFERENCES

Becker, H.A. (1997). *Social Impact Assessment: Method and Experience in Europe, North America and the Developing World.* London: UCL Press.

Blud, L. (1999). Cognitive skills programmes. In G. Towl & C. McDougall, *What do Forensic Psychologists do? Issues in Forensic Psychology 1.* Leicester: British Psychological Society.

Briner, R. (1998). What is an evidence-based approach to practice and why do we need one in occupational psychology? *Proceedings of the 1998 British Psychological Society Occupational Psychology Conference,* 39–44.

Brogden, H.E. (1946). On the interpretation of the correlation coefficient as a measure of predictive efficiency. *Journal of Educational Psychology,* **37**, 65–76.

Brogden, H.E. (1949). When testing pays off. *Personnel Psychology,* **2**, 171–183.

Cascio, W.F. & Ramos, R. (1986). Development and application of a new method for assessing job performance in behavioral/economic terms. *Journal of Applied Psychology,* **1**, 20–28.

Cronbach, L.J. & Gleser, G.C. (1965). *Psychological Tests and Personnel Decisions,* 2nd edn. Urbana, IL: University of Illinois Press.

Landy, F.J., Farr, J.L., & Jacobs, R.R. (1982). Utility concepts in performance measurement. *Organizational Behavior and Human Performance*, **30**, 15–40.

McGuire, J. (1995). Reviewing 'what works': past present and future. In J. McGuire (Ed.), *What Works: Reducing Reoffending*. Chichester: John Wiley.

Murphy, K.R. (1986). When your top choice turns you down: effect of rejected offers on the utility of selection tests. *Psychological Bulletin*, **99**, 133–138.

Naylor, J.C. & Shine, L.C. (1965). A table for determining the increase in mean criterion score obtained by using a selection device. *Journal of Industrial Psychology*, **3**, 33–42.

Price, D. (2000). *Office of Hope*. London: Policy Studies Institute.

Schmidt, F.L., Hunter, J.E., McKenzie, R.C. & Muldrow, T.W. (1979). Impact of valid selection procedures on work-force productivity. *Journal of Applied Psychology*, **64**, 609–626.

Taylor, H.C. & Russell, J.T. (1939). The relationship of validity coefficients to the practical effectiveness of tests in selection: discussion and tables. *Journal of Applied Psychology*, **23**, 565–578.

PART II

CHAPTER 4

Recruitment, Personnel Selection and Organizational Effectiveness

Kevin R. Murphy
Pennsylvania State University, USA
and
Dave Bartram
SHL Group plc, UK

RECRUITMENT AND PERSONNEL SELECTION

There is an extremely large body of research dealing with personnel selection; for example, Schmidt and Hunter's (1999) review summarizes the results of several thousand studies of the validity and utility of personnel selection methods. This literature focuses almost exclusively on the links between improved personnel selection and individual performance. However, there is very little research looking at the processes of attraction and initial recruitment.

Before reviewing the evidence relating selection to organizational effectiveness, it is worth considering the cycle of events involved in recruitment and selection. The process starts with the advertising of a job or position. This is generally followed by an initial sifting of applicants, often solely on the basis of information contained in an application form or résumé. Having created a short (or long) list of applicants, selection assessment tools are used to identify those with the highest job potential. The main focus of research has been on this latter stage of the hiring process, and on the validity of the assessment tools themselves rather than the validity of the process within which they are used.

It is worth considering the impact these earlier stages can have on the quality of applicants entering the final selection assessment stages of the hiring process (Bartram, 2001). Effective job advertising involves providing information about a job vacancy in such a manner that relevant applicants come to know about it and are attracted to apply. The effectiveness of later stages of assessment and testing in the selection process is directly dependent upon the size and quality of the applicant pool. That, in turn, is directly affected by the effectiveness of the job advertising process.

It should also be noted that the process of recruitment does not rely solely on the advertisement of positions. Increasingly, potential applicants are entering into a relationship with organizations they aspire to work for. They will register on that organization's web career site, provide unsolicited résumés, and so on. Organizations, in turn, are making use of this by nurturing those people who they regard as good potential employees—even when there is no current vacancy.

As will be seen later in this chapter, we now know a great deal about the effectiveness of various assessment methods for selection. We know very little, however, about the factors determining the effectiveness of the overall recruitment and selection process; about how the experience of that process affects applicants' decisions to remain in or withdraw from it; and about how organizational effectiveness may act directly to affect the attractiveness of the organization to potential new hires. It can be argued that there is a virtuous circle relating attraction, recruitment and selection to organizational effectiveness. Effective organizations are seen as desirable ones to work for. Hence, this engenders competition amongst the best candidates for positions in such organizations. In turn the organizations are then enabled to select from the best people and so ensure that effectiveness is maintained or enhanced. This model follows an assumption, commonly made in this area of research, that improvements in individual performance will translate directly into improvements in organizational effectiveness. Indeed, it is not unusual to draw inferences about the links between better personnel selection and national productivity (Hartigan & Wigdor, 1989; Hunter & Hunter, 1984).

The assumption that improving personnel selection will lead to improved organizational effectiveness seems reasonable. Hiring "better" employees not only implies that their own individual tasks will be done better and more effectively, it also implies that organizations might have more flexibility in how they use workers. For example, organizations that succeed in hiring intelligent, motivated, conscientious workers are more likely to be able to adapt to complex and turbulent work environments and to take advantage of the flexibility provided by the increasingly unstructured nature of jobs, work roles, and organizations (Committee on Techniques for the Enhancement of Human Performance, 1999; Ilgen & Pulakos, 1999). However, there is surprisingly little research directly examining the links between personnel selection and organizational effectiveness (Schneider et al., 2000). Moreover, there are reasons to question whether the links between successful personnel selection and enhanced organizational effectiveness are as strong or as simple as has traditionally been assumed.

There are two critical problems in linking research on the validity and utility of selection devices with conclusions about organizational effectiveness. First, selection decisions in the field often bear little relationship to the decision process assumed in studies of selection validity and utility. For example, estimates of the impact of selection tests on productivity and financial performance

(Hunter & Hunter, 1984; Schmidt & Hunter, 1999) are usually based on the assumption that selection decisions are made strictly and solely on the basis of test scores. In fact, selection decisions are almost always made on the basis of multiple assessments (e.g. interviews, tests, work samples; see Murphy & Shiarella, 1998, for a discussion of models for estimating multivariate validity and utility). Furthermore, selection rarely involves a one-way decision process. Rather, organizations must make decisions about who should receive job offers, and individuals must make decisions about which offers to accept or reject. As Murphy (1986) showed, applicants' decisions can sharply limit the effects of selection tests on productivity.

Second, the relationship between the attributes of the workers hired using particular tests and assessments and the effectiveness of the organizations in which they work is likely to be more complex than the simple linear forecasts that characterize most selection research. An organization that hires the "best" applicants may get workers who learn more quickly, who make fewer errors, etc., but they can also get workers who are more easily bored, who are more likely to leave the organization for better opportunities, who respond differently to styles of leadership that have been effective with less select groups of workers, who perform differently (perhaps better, perhaps worse) in teams, etc. Selection research has typically been characterized by the assumption that if you hire people who are better on some attribute (e.g. their level of general cognitive ability), their job performance will change, but everything else will stay the same. This is obviously not true, but there are few models that allow us to fully capture the effects of changing the attributes of people hired through the application of particular methods of personnel selection. More generally, organizations are complex systems, and improvements in one particular area do not necessarily translate into system-wide improvements (Schneider et al., 2000). For example, improvements in production will not necessarily lead to enhanced organizational effectiveness if the organization is unable to market its goods, to distribute what it has sold, etc.

Although the links between selection and organizational effectiveness are likely to be complex and uncertain, it is nevertheless reasonable to assume that selection will contribute, perhaps substantially, to the success of your organization. There is compelling evidence that the use of structured assessments can contribute substantially to the quality, efficiency, and fairness of personnel selection decisions. In particular, there is little doubt that the appropriate use of selection tests will aid in identifying the individuals who are most likely to perform their jobs well. The transition from individual performance to organizational effectiveness may be a complex one, but it is nevertheless reasonable to believe that organizations that can successfully identify the best candidates will in the long run be more effective than organizations that do not succeed in this regard. In the sections below, we will first review research on the validity and utility of selection tests as predictors of individual performance, then discuss the difficulties involved in linking this evidence to the broader question of how selection contributes to the effectiveness of organizations.

PERSONNEL SELECTION AND INDIVIDUAL PERFORMANCE

Introduction

The validity of the tests or assessment devices used in personnel selection is usually assessed in terms of the correlation (r_{xy}) between scores on a test and scores on some performance measure. There have been literally thousands of studies of the validity of selection tests (for reviews of validation research see Hunter & Hirsh, 1987; Hunter & Hunter, 1984; Schmidt et al., 1992), and there is also a substantial body of methodological research aimed at achieving the best possible estimate of r_{xy} (Landy et al., 1994). The validity coefficient provides one rough index of how good a job you are likely to do in selecting among applicants, and when combined with a number of other parameters of selection decisions (e.g. selection ratios, costs of testing) helps provide an estimate of the utility of these tests (Boudreau, 1991; Boudreau et al., 1994).

Throughout much of the history of personnel selection research, substantial attention has been devoted to the study of the validity of various selection *techniques*. Several influential reviews, notably by Reilly and Chao (1982) and Hunter & Hunter (1984), compared the validity of written tests, interviews, biodata instruments, and other selection instruments. Other important reviews have concentrated on evaluating the validity and utility of one specific method or family of methods (e.g. Gaugler et al., 1987, reviewed research on assessment centres).

In recent years, the focus of research and theory in the prediction of job performance has shifted somewhat from a focus on methods or techniques to a focus on underlying constructs. Broad consensus has been reached in two areas. First, cognitive ability appears to be relevant to predicting performance in virtually every job studied (Hunter & Hunter, 1984; Nathan & Alexander, 1988; McHenry et al., 1990; Ree & Earles, 1994; Schmidt et al., 1986). Second, there are broad personality traits that show generalizable validity across a wide range of jobs. For example, Barrick and Mount (1991) suggested that the dimension "conscientiousness" was a valid predictor of performance across many jobs. Other analyses (e.g. Tett et al., 1991) have suggested that other similarly broad personality attributes might also show generalizable validity, and have confirmed the finding that individual differences in conscientiousness appear to be consistently related to job performance.

Standardized tests of abilities, skills, and personality characteristics are extensively used in personnel assessment, and have been the focus of a very substantial body of research (Schmidt & Hunter, 1999; Murphy & Davidshofer, 1998). Approximately two-thirds of all large companies in the US, the UK and some of the other European countries use written tests as aids in making hiring and promotion decisions; standardized tests are especially common in evaluating applicants for clerical and administrative jobs, but they are used across a broad spectrum of occupations. Usage of tests varies considerably between countries and as a function of organizational size (DiMilia et al., 1994; Shackleton & Newell, 1994; Gowing & Slivinski, 1994; Schuler et al., 1993). Small companies rely far more on unstructured assessment process and personal recommendations (Bartram et al., 1995).

Cognitive Ability Tests

Research in personnel selection has focused most heavily on tests of cognitive ability (sometimes called intelligence tests). Hundreds of studies dealing with the relationship between scores on ability tests and performance on the job, success in training, and other organizationally-relevant criteria have led to a consistent set of conclusions. Scores on standardized tests of cognitive ability are related to measures of performance and success in virtually every job studied (see Schmidt and Hunter, 1999, for a review). Furthermore, the relationship between measures of ability and measures of performance and success is stronger in jobs that are more complex and demanding (e.g. computer programmer, systems analyst) than in jobs that are relatively simple and repetitive (e.g. assembly line worker).

If evaluated solely in terms of their validity and practicality, cognitive ability tests would almost certainly be the preferred method for evaluating job applicants. Compared with other methods of assessment, cognitive ability tests are relatively inexpensive, are easy to obtain (well-validated tests can be purchased and used "off-the-shelf"), have a clear track record of validity, and they need not be time-consuming (e.g. the *Wonderlic Personnel Test*, a widely-used and well-validated measure of general cognitive ability, can be administered in 12 minutes and scored in a matter of seconds). However, there are some features of cognitive ability tests that can limit their attractiveness to organizations.

First, average scores on cognitive ability tests are likely to vary as a function of race and ethnicity (Gottfredson, 1988; Jensen, 1980; Neisser et al., 1996). The causes and the meaning of differences in average test scores across groups have been among the most widely researched and contentious issues in the field of psychological testing, and no ready resolutions of the controversies in this area are in sight. The practical implications of these differences, however, are clear. Organizations that rely heavily on cognitive ability tests to screen applicants are likely indirectly to discriminate against members of a number of protected groups. It is often possible to mount a successful defence of such tests, especially when they are part of a thorough programme that includes a careful job analysis, judicious selection of tests, careful validation, and deliberate consideration of alternatives. In countries where adverse impact may lead to litigation, organizations often prefer to avoid discriminating in the first place, rather than being forced to defend what appear to be discriminatory procedures. As a consequence, they may opt not to use standardized ability tests.

Personality Inventories

The use of personality inventories as predictors of job performance has been a subject of controversy for nearly 30 years. An influential review by Guion and

Gottier (1965) concluded that the research available at that time did not support the validity of personality measures as selection instruments. As a result of several recent reviews of research on the validity and practicality of personality inventories (Barrick & Mount, 1991; Hough et al., 1990; Tett et al., 1991), this view has changed.

There is evidence that a variety of personality characteristics are consistently related to job performance. In particular measures of agreeableness, conscientiousness, and openness to experience appear to be related to performance in a wide range of jobs. Average validities for measures of these traits are typically not as high as validities demonstrated by cognitive ability tests, but the evidence does suggest that personality inventories can make a worthwhile contribution to predicting who will succeed or fail on the job.

An issue often raised in relation to the use of personality inventories in personnel selection is that many of these inventories are susceptible to faking (e.g. job applicants may distort their responses to appear more dependable or agreeable than they really are). Research on the effects of response distortion suggests that it does not substantially affect the validity of personality inventories as predictors of performance (Hough et al., 1990), but that it can have an influence on which candidates are accepted or rejected (Rosse et al., 1998).

The concern about faking is, however, generally considered out of context. Research is needed on the conditions under which people may choose to fake, and the extent to which personality inventories are more or less susceptible to this behavior than other self-report methods (biodata forms, application forms, references, interviews etc.). Any selection process can be considered to involve an "honesty contract" being made between applicants and recruiters. This contract is based on each party's understanding of the risks associated with not being open and honest with the other. These risks can be managed by the hiring organization through the design of the selection procedures, including the introduction of appropriate checks on the accuracy of information provided. Faking is not just something that occurs on the applicant side of the contract. Organizations also fake, for example through misrepresenting the organization itself or the positions for which they are recruiting.

Empirical Methods of Using Biodata to Predict Performance or Success

Selection decisions almost always involve the collection and perhaps the evaluation of biographical information, usually in the forms of application blanks or résumés. Résumé screening methods, even those that involve careful expert reviews of applicants' strengths, weaknesses, etc., represent a very limited use of biographical and background information to evaluate candidates. There is a stream of research going back at least fifty years that suggests strong and systematic links between the information presented on application blanks and résumés and future job performance and success (Mumford et al., 1992; Owens, 1976; Reilly & Chao, 1982). This research suggests that the methods by which this information is evaluated and scored are critical to the success of assessments based on biodata. The résumé screening methods described below often do little more than scratch the surface in terms of getting useful information from biodata. Empirically-based strategies for evaluating and scoring biodata have the potential to provide highly valid predictions of future performance and success.

There are two different empirically-based strategies for using background data in selection:

- the development of empirical keys, or data-based systems for scoring résumés and application blanks, and
- the classification of applicants into groups that are homogeneous with respect to biographical information, but differ in terms of expected job performance.

The empirical keying strategy is the older of the two; to date, many of the papers reporting substantial correlations between background data and job performance have followed this strategy. However, more recent research on the use of background data in predicting job performance has moved in the direction of theories that classify persons on the basis of their patterns of past behavior and that predict future performance on the basis of those classifications (Mael, 1991; Mumford et al., 1992, Owens & Schoenfeldt, 1979; Stokes et al., 1994).

The empirical method of scoring biographical information blanks rests on the assumption that successful workers (defined in terms of performance, tenure on the job, salary, etc.) systematically differ from unsuccessful workers in a number of ways and that at least some of the variables on which they differ can be measured by standard application blanks and résumés. If an applicant's responses to a biographical item are highly similar to those of successful workers and dissimilar to those of unsuccessful workers, the likelihood that the applicant will also succeed increases. On the other hand, a person whose responses are highly similar to those of the unsuccessful group is on the whole more likely to fail. Thus, it is possible to assign scores to each person's set of responses to a standard application blank (or to the information obtained from a résumé) that measures the degree to which responses to the entire set of items are similar to those given by successful workers, as opposed to those given by unsuccessful workers. There is considerable evidence that biodata scores of this type can be used to predict both job performance and turnover (Cascio, 1976; Reilly & Chao, 1982).

One critique of the empirical method described above is that it is based solely on consistencies in the data, and does not reflect any underlying theory of how or why biographical items predict success. In recent years, there has been considerable interest and progress in identifying the constructs that underlie responses to biodata items (Mael, 1991; Mumford et al., 1992). Stokes et al. (1994) suggest that biodata systems can provide useful measures of introversion vs. extroversion, social leadership, independence, achievement, motivation, maturity, adjustment, academic achievement, health, scientific/engineering pursuits, work values, organizational commitment, professional skills, and career development (this list is far from exhaustive; there is evidence that many additional attributes can be measured using biodata).

The emergence of construct-oriented models for evaluating biodata provides a basis for a broader and more defensible use of biodata as an assessment tool. Rather than examining individual responses to items on an application blank or a résumé in an attempt to differentiate good from poor performers, this approach encourages researchers to classify persons into groups with similar life histories and to search for differences in performance among these groups. The classification of persons rather than items allows one to take into account considerable amounts of data from different sources, rather than relying on an arbitrary classification of present or past workers into successes or failures. At a more fundamental level, these models provide a scientific rationale for the use of background information in predicting job performance. The model encourages one to view biodata as an indicator of what a person has done, which in turn provides a solid basis for predicting what the person will do.

Empirically-validated systems for evaluating and scoring biodata hold a great deal of promise as assessment tools. Biodata inventories are consistently identified as among the most valid and cost-effective methods of assessment for personnel selection (Reilly & Chao, 1982; Stokes et al., 1994). However, there are some difficulties in applying this method of assessment. First, biodata scoring schemes are usually custom-developed for each job, organization, etc. One reason for this is that the content of résumés or applications for different jobs, organizations, etc., often varies. More fundamentally, the links between biodata and success are not always the same across jobs or organizations. Aspects of a person's background and experience that predict failure in one organization may predict success in another. There is evidence that biodata scoring systems developed in one organization can hold up well in others (Carlson et al., 1999), but the limits to the generalizability of biodata scoring systems are not yet well-understood. Organizations may find it difficult to obtain valid and useful biodata scoring systems off the shelf, and may have to invest time and resources to develop scoring systems that are appropriate and valid.

A more fundamental problem with the use of biodata as an assessment tool is the risk that assessments based on biodata will lead to direct or inadvertent discrimination against members of protected groups (Sharf, 1994). Suppose, for example, that in your organization, workers who are 45 or older receive low ratings from their supervisors, while workers 25 or younger receive high ratings. An empirically keyed biodata system will give applicants who are 45 or older a lower score than applicants who are 25 or younger. It would be very difficult, on either legal or ethical grounds, to defend a selection system that screened out workers solely on the basis of their age. Even if care is taken to remove items that directly reflect age, gender, race, etc., it is still possible to discriminate on the basis of biodata. For example, studies of biodata often show that factors such as owning your home vs. renting, or owning a car vs. relying on public transport predict both performance and turnover in a number of jobs. Unfortunately, the likelihood of owning a house, a car, etc., varies substantially as a function of race, gender and age, and reliance on biodata attributes that are facially neutral can still lead one to screen out members of particular protected groups. Even when unintended, discrimination on the basis of background factors can be very difficult to defend.

Interviews

Although there is considerable diversity in the types of tests and assessments used in making personnel selection decisions, there is one nearly universal component of all systematic personnel selection strategies (i.e. the interview). Surveys suggest that for many countries well over 95% of all employers use interviews as part of the selection process. However, this figure has been reported to be as low as 50–60% in some European countries—notably Germany (Shackleton & Newell, 1994; Schuler et al., 1993). The number of interviews conducted yearly may run as high as 20 per person hired (Landy & Trumbo, 1980). Not only is the interview widespread, it also appears to have a substantial effect on selection decisions. The majority of the firms surveyed by Miner and Miner (1978) identified the interview as the single most important component of their selection programme. More recent studies (e.g. Ahlburg, 1992; DiMilia et al., 1994; Shackleton & Newell, 1994; Gowing & Slivinski, 1994; Schuler et al., 1993) attest to the continuing popularity of the interview. It is therefore no surprise that the employment interview has been the focus of a tremendous amount of research.

From the 1940s to the 1980s, research on the reliability and validity of the employment interview portrayed a consistently negative picture (Arvey & Campion, 1982). Validity coefficients for interviews (i.e. the correlations between interview ratings and measures of performance or success) rarely exceeded the teens and were often embarrassingly close to zero (Hunter & Hunter, 1984; Reilly & Chao, 1982). Indeed, one of the most interesting research questions in the early 1980s was why organizations continued to rely so heavily on such an invalid method of making selection decisions (Arvey & Campion, 1982).

More recent research suggests that interviews can indeed be a useful and valid method of selecting employees, as long as structure is imposed (Campion et al., 1988; Wiesner & Cronshaw, 1988). Most of the interview research cited in earlier reviews had focused on unstructured interviews, in which different interviewers might ask different sets of questions, or in which the same interviewer might ask different questions of different applicants. Interviews of this sort are widely regarded as poor predictors of future performance; although as McDaniel et al. (1994) note, they can show higher levels of validity than was suggested in earlier reviews. However, when care is taken to develop a consistent set of job-related questions and a consistent method for scoring or evaluating responses, interviews can show very respectable levels of validity.

Latham et al. (1980) recommended an extremely structured interview format, referred to as a "situational interview", in which examinees are asked to describe how they would behave in several hypothetical but critical situations. For example, an applicant for a baker's job might be asked what he or she would do if two oven thermometers gave readings that varied widely. Responses are independently rated by multiple interviewers, and composite ratings are used to make decisions about examinees. Although this structure may not be optimal in all settings, it represents a clear advance over the unconnected series of spontaneous questions that an untrained interviewer tends to ask (Wiesner & Cronshaw, 1988).

An alternative is to structure interviews around discussions of past behavior on the job (Janz, 1982). Rather than asking what a person might do in a hypothetical situation, interviewers might ask what he or she did do in specific situations encountered previously on the job. McDaniel et al.'s (1994) review suggests that such job-related interviews show higher levels of validity than unstructured interviews, but lower validity than the situational interview method described above.

Campion et al. (1997) note that, while adding structure to an interview generally improves its reliability and validity, there are many ways that one might add structure. They review the effects of 15 components of structure (e.g. standardizing the set of questions, tying questions to a job analysis, rating each answer on a fixed scale, using multiple interviewers). Just about all methods of adding structure seem to help, and there is no professional consensus about which methods of structuring interviews are best or worst.

Interviews are probably most useful when they cover areas that are not already covered by paper-and-pencil tests or other assessment devices. A number of researchers have suggested that interviews should focus on competencies (i.e. desired work-related behaviors), rather than attitudes or skills (Janz, 1982; Motowidlo et al., 1992; Orpen, 1985). Competency-based interviewing is becoming increasingly popular in practice, and there is evidence that a clear focus on behavioral information increases the reliability and criterion-related validity of measures obtained on the basis of interviews.

Structured interviews might prove particularly useful for assessing "soft skills". First, the interview is itself a social interaction, which allows the interviewer to obtain a sample of behaviors that may prove quite predictive of future behavior in work settings. Applicants who are unwilling or unable to communicate clearly with the interviewer or who cannot interact productively with interviewers may show similar behaviors on the job. Second, situational or behavioral interviews can be tailored to focus on the sorts of social interactions, teamwork skills, or leadership skills required for successful performance on the job.

Integrity Tests

There are a number of tests designed to assess integrity, dependability, honesty, etc. Some of these are overt measures, asking questions directly about counterproductive behaviors; others are "covert", relying on the assessment of personality traits that relate to such behaviors (primarily, conscientiousness). These tests have been the subject of considerable controversy, but research over the last 10–15 years has consistently supported the usefulness of both the overt and covert measures. Sackett and his colleagues have conducted several reviews of research on the reliability, validity, and usefulness of integrity tests (Sackett & Decker, 1979; Sackett & Harris, 1984, 1985; Sackett et al., 1989). Ones et al. (1993) and McDaniel and Jones (1988) have subjected some of the same studies to meta-analysis (a statistical method designed to quantitatively summarize the outcomes of multiple validity studies).

O'Bannon et al. (1989) have also reviewed this research and, additionally, have given attention to a variety of practical issues that surround the administration and use of integrity tests (see also Murphy, 1993). Although each review raises different concerns, and most reviews lament the shortcomings of research on the validity of integrity tests, the general conclusion of the more recent reviews is positive. There is now a reasonable body of evidence showing that integrity tests have some validity for predicting a variety of criteria that are relevant to organizations. This research does not say that tests of this sort will eliminate theft or dishonesty at work, but it does suggest that individuals who receive poor scores on these tests tend to be higher risk employees in certain types of position. More recent research suggests that the traits which predict counter-productivity in one position can be positive indicators for another position where, for example, a degree of "expediency" may be necessary for success in the job (Tett, 1998; Robertson et al., in press).

Work Samples and Simulations

It has long been argued that predictions of future behavior that are based on samples of present behavior are likely to be more accurate than predictions that are based on measures of specific skills, ability, or knowledge (Wernimont & Campbell, 1968). Reviews by Asher and Sciarrino (1974) and Reilly and Chao (1982) provide at least partial support for this argument. This research suggests that one way to predict a person's future performance is to obtain a sample of their current work.

Work-sample tests range from those that involve relative simple tasks, such as a five-minute typing sample, to those involving complex samples of performance, such as those obtained using flight simulators. There are two common features to all work-sample tests that should be examined in evaluating these tests. First, every work-sample test puts the applicant in a situation that is in some essential way similar to a work situation and measures performance on tasks reasonably similar to those that make up the job itself. Second, every work sample differs in important ways from the job in which it will be used. Even when the tasks are identical to those required on the job, it is reasonable to expect that examinees who are trying to impress their prospective employers will show higher levels of motivation in work-sample tests than they will on the job. Thus, it is most reasonable to regard a work sample as a measure of maximal performance rather than a measure of typical performance. This is an important distinction, because measures of maximal performance are not necessarily correlated with measures of typical performance (Dubois et al., 1993; Sackett et al., 1988).

A work-sample test is most likely to be successful if the tasks that comprise the job are well-understood, can be done by a person working alone, and can be done with minimal job-specific training. For example, work samples for computer programming jobs might involve asking applicants to write the code needed to carry out specific tasks or functions. Work samples have been used most often in jobs that are not highly complex (e.g. clerical jobs, semi-skilled manufacturing jobs), but this technique also can be adapted and applied in managerial and professional jobs, as described in the section that follows.

Thornton and Cleveland (1990) reviewed the use of simulation methods in management development. All work samples involve simulating some aspects of the job, but such simulations differ considerably in their complexity and their fidelity. For example, complex business games, in which individuals assume various roles and make numerous decisions over periods of hours or even days with regard to a simulated business problem, are popular for both assessing and developing managerial competencies. Although at an operational level such games are a far cry from the leaderless group discussion, at a conceptual level they represent the same strategy for measurement; that is, observing behavior in a setting that reflects some aspect of the job itself. Thornton and Cleveland's review suggests that a wide range of methods for simulating key portions of the job performed by managers and professionals hold potential for predicting future success in these roles.

Assessment Centres

The assessment centre is not, as its name might imply, a place, nor is it a single, unified method of predicting job performance. Rather, an assessment centre is a structured combination of assessment techniques that is used to provide a wide-ranging, holistic assessment of each participant. This technique is most likely to be used in making managerial selection and promotion decisions, although assessment centres are also employed for many other jobs.

The assessment centre as it exists today is a lineal descendant of the multiple assessment procedures used by German and British psychologists in World War II and adopted by the American Office of Strategic Services (OSS) as aids in selecting agents and operatives (OSS, 1948). By the early 1970s, over 1000 companies had experimented with this method, prompting Hinrichs (1978) to refer to the assessment centre as one of the more phenomenal success stories of applied psychology. Although the assessment centres used in different organizations differ widely in terms of content and organization, there are several features that nearly all assessment centres share in common and that are distinctive to this approach (Bray et al., 1974; Bray & Grant, 1966; Finkle, 1976). They include the following:

1. *Assessment in groups.* In an assessment centre, small groups of participants are assessed simultaneously. Since group activities and peer evaluations are an integral part of most assessment centres, it would be impossible to use this technique to its fullest advantage in assessing a single individual.
2. *Assessment by groups.* The assessment team may be made up of managers, psychologists, consultants, or some mix of these three groups. Each participant's behaviour is observed and evaluated by a number of different assessors, and the final ratings represent the assessment team's consensus regarding the individual being evaluated.
3. *The use of multiple methods.* Assessment centre activities might include ability tests, personality tests, situational tests, interviews, peer evaluations, and performance tests. The central assumption of this method is that each test has its strengths and weaknesses and that a combination of diverse tests is necessary to capitalize on the strengths of each individual test.

4. *The use of situational tests.* Although the specific tests used vary from organization to organization, nearly every assessment centre uses some type of work-sample or situational test. Both the in-basket and the leaderless group discussion tests are popular, as are other role-playing exercises.
5. *Assessment along multiple dimensions.* The end result of an assessment centre is a consensus rating along each of several dimensions. For example, candidates going through an assessment centre at AT&T are rated on 25 dimensions, including organizational planning, resistance to stress, energy, and self-objectivity (Thornton & Byham, 1982). Each exercise in the assessment centre typically provides information relevant to one or more dimensions, and ratings of a specific dimension (e.g. energy) might reflect data obtained from several different exercises.

Empirical evaluations of assessment centres have generally been favourable (Borman, 1982; Finkle, 1976; Gaugler et al., 1987; Hinrichs, 1978; Howard, 1974; Huck, 1973; Thornton, 1992). Assessment centre ratings have been shown to provide valid predictions of future performance, even when there is a long lag between the assessment centre and the subsequent evaluation of employee performance and success. For example, the AT&T Management Progress Study documented the validity of assessment centre ratings, taken at the beginning of managers' careers, for predicting career progress decades later. In addition, assessment centres appear to be fair and relatively unbiased methods of making selection and promotion decisions.

VALIDITY OF STRUCTURED ASSESSMENT METHODS

There have been literally thousands of studies examining the relationship between scores on tests, interviews, and other methods of assessment and measures of job performance, work effectiveness, and other organizationally-relevant criteria (e.g. awards, patents, turnover). The results of these studies provide a clear picture of what methods work well and which work poorly as predictors of future performance and effectiveness.

The availability of paper-and-pencil tests, interviews, biographical information blanks, work samples, and assessment centres as alternative methods of predicting job performance leads to the question of which method is best. Reilly and Chao's (1982) review, though somewhat dated, provides an excellent starting point for this comparative assessment. They examined research on alternatives to standard ability tests and focused on eight alternative methods of predicting future job performance: biodata, interviews, peer evaluations, self-assessments, reference checks, academic performance, expert judgments, and objective tests. They evaluated each technique in terms of its criterion-related validity, practicality, and likelihood of providing unbiased predictions of future performance. Their review suggests that only biodata and peer evaluations show levels of validity that are in any way comparable to the validity of paper-and-pencil tests. They also suggest that none of the alternatives shows comparable levels of validity with less adverse impact against minority applicants than standardized

Table 4.1   Estimates of the validity of widely-used tests and assessments[1]

	Job performance	Performance in training[2]
Cognitive ability tests	0.51[a]	0.56
Work samples	0.54	–
Integrity tests	0.41	0.38
Conscientiousness measures	0.31	0.30
Structured interviews	0.51	0.35[3]
Assessment Centres	0.37	–
Reference checks	0.26	0.23
Job experience (years)	0.18	0.01
Years of education	0.10	0.20
Graphology	0.02	–

[1] The results presented here represent the average correlation between scores on tests, work samples, etc. and measures of job performance and performance in training.

[2] Too few studies of the validity of work samples, assessment centres and graphology as predictors of training performance exist to provide credible estimates of these validities.

[3] Combined structured/unstructured.

Source: Schmidt & Hunter (1999).

cognitive ability tests, and that when the issue of practicality is considered, paper-and-pencil tests are by far the best single selection device. A report by the National Academy of Sciences (Wigdor & Garner, 1982) reached a similar conclusion, that in employment testing there are no known alternatives to standard ability tests that are equally informative, equally fair, and of equal technical merit (see also Hartigan & Wigdor, 1989; Hunter, 1986; Hunter & Hunter, 1984).

Schmidt and Hunter (1999) summarize the practical and theoretical implications of 85 years of research on the validity and utility of selection tests. Their meta-analysis examines the validity of 19 selection procedures for predicting job performance and training. Table 4.1 summarizes some of their key findings.

The results presented suggest that structured interviews, work samples, and cognitive ability tests are all highly valid predictors of future performance and of success in training (validity coefficients of 0.30 or larger are usually interpreted as indicating a moderately strong relationship between the test and performance, and coefficients of 0.50 or larger are usually interpreted as indicating a strong relationship; Murphy & Myors, 1998). These results also suggest that assessment centres, personality inventories (particularly those that provide a measure of the trait, conscientiousness) and integrity tests provide useful predictors of performance in the job and in training. However, some widely-used methods of assessment do not appear to be very effective. For example, reference checks show some validity, but they are less valid and more costly than many alternatives (e.g. standardized tests). Candidates with more years of experience or more years of education are often favoured by recruiters and hiring managers (although this is not always the case in the IT industry), but there is actually very little relationship between experience or education and job performance or performance in training. Finally, graphology (handwriting analysis) is widely used in France and Israel and is being aggressively promoted in the US as a tool for assessing job candidates. Graphologists' ratings turn out to have virtually no relationship to peoples' subsequent job performance. Organizations that use this method in personnel selection might be better served by simply flipping a coin.

In particular, it is now widely accepted that:

1. Professionally developed ability tests, structured interviews, work samples, assessment centres and other structured assessment techniques are likely to provide valid predictions of future performance across a wide range of jobs, settings, etc.
2. The level of validity for a particular test can vary as a function of characteristics of the job (e.g. complexity) or the organizations, but validities are often quite consistent across settings.
3. It is possible to identify abilities and broad dimensions of personality that are related to performance in virtually all jobs.

(For reviews of research supporting these points, see: Hartigan & Wigdor, 1989; Hunter & Hunter, 1984; Reilly & Chao, 1982; Schmidt & Hunter, 1999; Schmitt et al., 1984; Wigdor & Garner, 1982. For illustrative applications of VG methods, see Callender & Osburn, 1981; Schmidt et al., 1979). Schmidt and Hunter (1999) reviewed 85 years of research on the validity and utility of selection methods. They concluded that cognitive ability tests, work samples, measures of conscientiousness and integrity, structured interviews, job knowledge tests, biographical data measures and assessment centres all showed consistent evidence of validity as predictors of job performance.

MULTIVARIATE PERSPECTIVES

Schmidt and Hunter (1999) and others (e.g. Murphy & Shiarella, 1998) note that organizations rarely use a single test as a basis for making decisions. Schmidt and Hunters' review suggests that using combinations of tests can lead to high degrees of accuracy in predicting job performance. For example, combining general mental ability tests with a work-sample test could yield a validity as high as 0.63. The same validity might be attained by combining a structured interview and an ability test. Ability tests combined with integrity tests might do even better (an estimated validity of 0.65).

As noted earlier, much of what we know about the validity of selection devices is based on analyses of univariate relationships between tests and criterion measures. However, personnel selection is always a multivariate process, involving multiple X variables *and* multiple Y variables. Organizations typically use more than one selection measure or test when hiring (Boudreau et al., 1994; Gatewood & Field, 1994; Hakstian et al., 1991a,b; Jones & Wright, 1992; Milkovich & Boudreau, 1994). Assessment methods (e.g. tests, interviews) that tap multiple domains (e.g. cognitive ability, personality) are the norm in most selection systems. More important, there is growing recognition of the fact that the domain of job performance is complex and multi-dimensional (Astin, 1964; Borman et al., 1997; Campbell, 1990; Conway, 1996; Murphy, 1989, 1996). The different facets that underlie the construct "job performance" may in some cases be only weakly interrelated, and different organizational policies for emphasizing one facet or another when defining "job performance" could lead to substantially different conclusions about the validity of selection tests.

Using a combination of cognitive ability measures and measures of personality traits to predict various facets of job performance can yield higher validities than those obtained when ability or personality measures are used alone. There are two reasons for this.

1. As noted above, both classes of measures show generalizable univariate validities.
2. General cognitive ability and conscientiousness appear to be only weakly related (Ackerman et al., 1995; Barrick et al., 1994; Brand, 1994; Cattell & Butcher, 1968; Cattell & Kline, 1977; Dreger, 1968; Ones et al., 1993; Wolfe & Johnson, 1995).

This implies that a combination of measures from these two domains will capture variance that is not adequately captured by even the best measures of ability or personality considered alone. It also implies that the exact way in which you combine predictors could have a substantial impact on the validity of a selection battery that includes ability and personality measures.

THE UTILITY OF SELECTION TESTS

Introduction

In research on personnel and human resource management, the term "utility analysis" is used to refer to the application of analytic methods to forecast and evaluate the effects of some intervention, test, training programme, or the like. Modern methods of utility assessment typically involve three general steps: (1) predict the outcomes of some decision or policy (e.g. adopting a particular test), (2) attach value to those outcomes, and (3) compare predicted changes in value with the costs involved in implementing the decision. Virtually all utility assessment methods currently in use can be thought of as elaborations of forecasting models developed by Taylor and Russell (1939) and by Brogden (1949). Taylor–Russell models were developed to deal with dichotomous criteria (e.g. whether or not employees would be "successful"), whereas Brogden's model was used to forecast continuous criteria, such as future performance levels.

Dichotomous-criterion models have a long and distinguished history (Cronbach & Gleser, 1965), and they have proved useful for evaluating a wide range of problems. However, there are two weaknesses that limit dichotomous-criterion models. First, these models often force one to artificially dichotomize criteria that are inherently continuous. For example, individuals seem to vary substantially in their job performance (Campbell et al., 1993), and treating performance as either "satisfactory" or "unsatisfactory" implies the loss of potentially important information. Second, although methods for attaching values to the outcomes predicted under dichotomous-criterion models (e.g. successful vs. un-successful performance) have been available for over 30 years (Cronbach & Gleser, 1965), these methods are seldom implemented. Most applications of dichotomous-criterion utility models have limited themselves to forecasting, and have not incorporated a systematic assessment of the costs or benefits of particular courses of action.

Brogden's model used linear regression to forecast criterion scores (y) on the basis of some predictor or intervention (x). In its most basic form, the utility equation states:

$$\text{Predicted value} = (r_{xy} * Z_x * SD_y) - C \qquad (4.1)$$

where r_{xy} refers to the validity of the intervention, or the relationship between the intervention and the criterion, Z_x refers to the "score" that individual receives on that intervention (e.g. test score, whether or not individual receives a treat-ment), SD_y refers to the variability of the criterion, and C refers to the cost, per person, of implementing the intervention. If both SD_y and costs are expressed in dollars, this equation yields the predicted value, per person, of implementing that intervention.

Boudreau (1991) reviews the increasing complexity and sophistication of util-ity models that have built on the equation shown above. Adjustments have been proposed to take into account a variety of financial parameters (Cascio, 1993), to include a wider range of costs (e.g. recruiting costs; Law & Myors, 1993; Martin & Raju, 1992) and a more realistic assessment of benefits (e.g. relatively lower per-formance and higher turnover during probationary periods; De Corte, 1994), to appropriately take into account range restriction (Raju et al., 1995) and to reflect uncertainties in the forecasting process (e.g. rejected job offers; Murphy, 1986). Most discussions of utility analysis have focused on selection testing, but Klaas and McClendon (1996) demonstrated the application of these techniques in evaluating pay policies.

Links to Organizational Performance

Several studies have attempted to apply concepts from traditional utility anal-ysis to estimate the impact of selection and other interventions on organiza-tional performance. Pritchard (1990) describes organization-level utility analy-ses, which provide estimates of changes in organizational productivity under different conditions or with different interventions. Roth (1994) broadened this method further, presenting multi-attribute utility estimates. Becker and Huselid (1992) suggest that traditional utility models can be easily adapted to forecast organization-level criteria (e.g. net sales), and demonstrate such an application.

Perhaps the most ambitious attempt to project from research on the validity and utility of individual selection measures to a higher level was presented by Hunter and Hunter (1984). They estimated that the use of valid selection tests on a nationwide basis would lead to an increase in productivity worth

$15 billion per year (See Hunter and Schmidt, 1982, for similar applications of utility analysis in estimating national productivity). This estimate was criticized on technical grounds by Hartigan and Wigdor (1989), but the more critical issue is probably one of whether cross-level inferences this sweeping are even feasible. Schneider et al. (2000) note that it is difficult to draw clear links between increased individual performance and enhanced organizational effectiveness. It is likely that the links between individual performance and national productivity are even more complex and tenuous.

There is a broader stream of research that attempts to link the use of structured personnel selection and other human resource management (HRM) practices (e.g. training and development) to various organization-level criteria. For example, the use of effective methods of recruitment and selection, training, and compensation have all been linked to the financial health of organizations (Gerhart & Milkovich, 1992; Russell et al., 1985; Terpstra & Rozelle, 1993). Other studies have looked at the way combinations of HRM practices might influence organizational performance, and have suggested links between the package of HRM practices used in an organization and its effectiveness (DeNisi, 2000; Schneider et al., 2000).

Watson Wyatt (2000) reports a survey of 400 US and Canada based public-quoted companies, each with at least $100 million in revenues or market value. They derived a measure called the Human Capital Index (HCI) based on answers to questions about how the organizations carry out 30 key HR practices. They demonstrated a clear relationship between the HCI and shareholder value creation, both in terms of total returns to shareholders (e.g. 53% over five years for low HCI companies compared with 103% for high HCI ones) and Tobin's Q, a measure of ability to create value in excess of physical assets. Most notably for the current chapter, the area of HR practice associated with the largest increase in both total return for shareholders and Tobin's Q was "recruitment excellence". Overall, they found that a one SD increase in HCI was associated with a 10.1% increase in market value. The main factors associated with recruiting excellence were:

1. that recruiting was explicitly designed to support the organization's business plan
2. that the organization had established a reputation as being a desirable place to work
3. that the selection process resulted in new hires who were well-equipped to perform their duties.

However, as Huselid (1995) cautions, the causal link between HRM practices and organizational effectiveness is far from clear, and it is possible that the use of high-quality HRM practices is the *result* of organizational effectiveness rather than its cause. For example, Milkovich and Wigdor (1991) examined the links between characteristics of incentive pay systems and a wide range of individual and organizational criteria. On the whole, their report suggested that it was not the design of the system that influenced its success, but rather the financial strength of the organization. Organizations that put lots of money into incentive pay systems seemed to report success no matter how these systems were designed, whereas organizations that could devote only meagre resources to their incentive pay systems often met with failure. Attempts to discover clear causal models in such complex situations may well be doomed to failure. Recruitment and selection practices are reflections of an organization, and an organization's culture and ways of dealing with people. These, in turn, will affect the way in which people view that organization as a more or less desirable place to work. As proposed earlier, there may be a "virtuous circle" relating organizational effectiveness to good selection and recruitment practices rather than one being the cause of the other.

PROBLEMS IN LINKING TEST VALIDITY WITH ORGANIZATIONAL EFFECTIVENESS

Research on the validity and utility of selection tests often appears to be based on a series of assumptions that, if true, would support the notion that the use of valid selection tests would have a substantial impact on an organization's effectiveness. These include the assumptions that:

1. scores on selection tests are closely linked with broad constructs that determine performance and effectiveness in one's job, such as general intelligence or job-related personality characteristics
2. high levels of these abilities and skills lead to better job performance but do not lead to any undesirable outcomes (e.g. turnover, dissatisfaction)
3. selection decisions flow directly from scores on selection tests, and
4. the performance of an organization is equal to the average of the performance levels of individuals in that organization.

One reason why it is difficult to make valid inferences about organizational effectiveness on the basis of research on the validity and utility of selection tests is that all four of these assumptions are at least partially incorrect.

First, the links between the tests and assessments that are most widely used in personnel selection and broad job-related constructs such as general intelligence are often weak or indistinct (Binning & Barrett, 1989). There are some selection tests that do a very good job measuring well-defined, job-related constructs (e.g. standardized tests of cognitive abilities and skills). However, for many widely-used selection tests (e.g. biodata inventories, interviews, simulations, integrity tests, assessment centres), the question of why they work continues to be debated (Klimoski & Brickner, 1987; Murphy, 1993; Thornton & Cleveland, 1990). Academic research on selection tests has often discussed these as if they were virtual stand-ins for core constructs such as ability, conscientiousness, etc. (see Murphy & DeShon, in press, for a critique of this assumption), but this is clearly not the case. The most popular assessment techniques (i.e. interviews) almost certainly measure a range of characteristics and attributes, some of which are likely to be truly job-related (e.g. cognitive ability, interpersonal skills), and others of which are likely to be sources of irrelevant bias (e.g. physical attractiveness).

The question of why tests and other assessments "work" (i.e. provide reasonably accurate predictions of future success) is absolutely critical to the processes of drawing inferences from these tests to broader criteria such as organizational effectiveness. For example, interviews appear to "work", in the sense that they do predict future performance and success in the organization. There are two possible explanations for why they work, and these might have fundamentally different implications for the organizations that use them. One possibility is that they work because they are valid measures of human attributes relevant to success in a wide variety of roles. The other is that they work because interviewers share the same biases and prejudices as managers, and that people seen by interviewers as "fitting in" will also be seen by their managers as the "right sort of people". Clearly, the question of why interviews work makes a great deal of difference to organizations, but it has not been examined in sufficient depth. Herriot and Anderson (1997) have criticized personnel selection research for its myopic focus on predictive validity. A more critical examination of alternate theories to explain the "success" of some selection tools and the "failure" of others is clearly needed.

We also need to re-examine the "criterion-problem". What is it that we should be trying to predict with selection measures? Traditionally, the focus has been on individual "job performance"—generally as measured by supervisor ratings. Organizational effectiveness depends on many factors that may not be captured in our traditional validation paradigms. Such factors include prosocial behaviours, team working, and acting to facilitate the work of others. Smith (1994) proposed a model that distinguishes between: "universals", those attributes that affect success or failure in any job; "occupationals", those attributes relating to particular occupational skills needs; and "relationals", those attributes concerned with the nature of relationships within an organization. Most of the research reviewed above has focused on the first of these and has largely ignored the other two areas.

Second, the assumption that personnel selection results in finding candidates who are better than others in terms of their likely level of performance, but who do not differ in any other ways from those who do not do well on selection tests, is difficult to accept. The individual differences that influence scores on selection tests are also likely to influence a wide range of work-related behaviours and outcomes. For example, it is likely that individuals who are selected on the basis of high levels of skill and experience will function differently in work teams than their less skilled and experienced counterparts. Unfortunately, it is difficult to tell whether they will be more effective, less effective, or whether this effectiveness will be moderated by characteristics of the teams and the task. Selection research has focused narrowly on the implications of tests and assessments for predicting task performance, but has not to date considered the broader issue of how those who are selected differ from those rejected in a wider range of behaviours or experiences.

It is possible that selecting the "best" applicants will not always lead to the best outcomes. Several theories of work motivation suggest that mismatches between a person's expectations and his or her experiences at work can be a powerful source of dissatisfaction (Kanfer, 1990). This suggests that hiring a candidate with very high levels of ability, skill, or other job-related qualifications might not always lead to positive work outcomes. People whose qualifications far exceed the demands of the job might become bored, dissatisfied, etc. A number of studies have examined the hypothesis that under-utilization of abilities, skills and qualifications can lead to decreased satisfaction and increased turnover (e.g. Geurts et al., 1999; King & Hautaluoma, 1977; Linberg, 1999). While empirical support for this hypothesis is far from uniform, some data do suggest that the "best" applicants can sometimes become dissatisfied and disconnected with jobs that offer few challenges.

One critical weakness in studies that attempt to draw inferences about organizational productivity and effectiveness on the basis of research on the validity and utility of selection tests is that the practice of personnel selection bears little resemblance to the assumptions that underlie these studies. First, studies of the validity and utility of selection tests are virtually always concerned with the relationship between a single test score and some criterion measure. Murphy and Shiarella (1998) note that selection decisions are rarely based on a single test score, but rather are typically multivariate in nature. Their analyses suggest that when the right sorts of tests and assessments are combined, it is possible to obtain multivariate validities that exceed typical univariate estimates. On the other hand, if the selection or weighting of tests is sub-optimal, operational validities may be considerably lower than those suggested by univariate validation research.

Studies of the validity and utility of tests are often based on the assumption that test scores are used in a straightforward way in selection—i.e. that applicants are ranked on the basis of their test scores, and that selection is based on a top-down principle. Top-down selection is well known to be statistically optimal, but it does not appear to be the norm. Organizations often use some form of test score adjustment or banding to group applicants (Cascio et al., 1991; Sackett & Wilk, 1994), and often use criteria other than test scores for selecting among groups. Other organizations use tests for screening purposes only, and make final selection decisions on a basis other than test scores. As Schmidt et al. (1984) note, use of these alternatives to top-down selection usually entails some loss in utility, and this loss can be substantial. Because utility studies typically assume that selection practices will be statistically optimal (i.e. top-down selection based solely on test scores), they will usually provided unrealistic estimates of the contribution of selection tests to individual productivity. This, in turn, is likely to lead to biased estimates of the effects of these tests on organizational productivity.

Most studies of selection test validity assume that selection decisions are a one-way affair. For example, Murphy (1986) notes that utility analyses typically assume that all job offers are accepted and that candidates do not withdraw consideration before organizations make accept–reject decisions. This is clearly not true; Murphy's (1986) analyses suggest that rejected job offers could reduce the actual value of selection by a substantial amount, when compared to the estimates obtained from most studies of validity and utility. Relatively few studies (an exception being Bretz & Judge, 1998, who looked at negative job information and self-selection decisions) have examined the factors that initially attract encourage good applicants to apply for a position and then remain in the selection process rather than withdraw. Gatewood et al. (1993) showed that applicants' perceptions of an organization are related to their intentions to pursue contact with that organization. Negative perceptions of the organization have also been shown to play a role in determining applicant withdrawal from the selection process (Ryan et al., 2000).

Withdrawal from the applicant pool can reduce the quality, not just the number, of those remaining in the pool (Barber & Roehling, 1993). Just as initial attraction of good applicants is important, so also is maintaining those applicants' interest in the job throughout the selection process to job offer and acceptance. This is one area where both the nature of the selection process and the speed to hire can have important consequences. Many employers are now turning to web-based recruitment and selection because it provides a much faster time-to-hire than traditional methods, as well as providing applicants with easier access (Bartram, 2001).

The paragraphs presented above have laid out a number of reasons to question the accuracy of forecasts of the effects of selection tests on individual productivity. However, even if these estimates turned out to be reasonably accurate, there would still be good reasons to question the leap from individual productivity forecasts to forecasts of organizational effectiveness. DeNisi (2000) notes that performance at a higher level is likely to be related to, but not be a simple sum or average of, performance at lower levels. Similarly, Herriot and Anderson (1997) question the hypothesis that the links between individual and organizational productivity and effectiveness are either close or uniform across settings. In particular, they note that the links between the behaviour of individuals in organizations and the performance of the organization as a whole is likely to be moderated by broad cultural factors. Schneider et al. (2000) suggest that these links may be influenced by organizational cultures. It is also likely that these links will be influenced by the structure of organizations (e.g. highly decentralized organizations will probably show different individual–organizational links than highly bureaucratic ones), by the way organizations are managed, and even by the nature of the products and services an organization provides.

In the US and elsewhere, there has been a longstanding rift between personnel psychologists, who are largely concerned with individual differences, and organizational psychologists, who are largely concerned with social systems. The linkage between personnel selection and organizational effectiveness is one that cannot be adequately understood from the myopic perspectives of either personnel psychology or organizational psychology, but rather must be attacked from both fronts. In other areas, such as performance appraisal and management, substantial progress has been made by combining the insights to be gained from multiple levels of analysis. There is every reason to believe that the same will occur as research on personnel selection moves from a narrow individual focus, in which links to organizational effectiveness are simply assumed, to a broader focus that examines the range of effects that good personnel selection is likely to have on organizations (DeNisi, 2000; Murphy & Cleveland, 1995; Schneider et al., 2000).

That there is a "virtuous circle" relating applicant attraction, good recruitment and selection practice, and organizational effectiveness has been well-demonstrated. What we do not yet understand is the nature of that relationship. Insofar as the success of an organization is dependent on the qualities of the people it employs, we need a better understanding of the organizational aspects of recruitment and selection processes on the one hand, and a better understanding of how individual performance contributes to organizational effectiveness on the other.

REFERENCES

Ackerman, P.L., Kanfer, R. & Goff, M. (1995). Cognitive and noncognitive determinants and consequences of complex skill acquisition. *Journal of Experimental Psychology: Applied*, **1**, 270–304.

Ahlburg, D.A. (1992). Predicting the job performance of managers: what do the experts know? *International Journal of Forecasting*, **7**, 467–472.

Arvey, R.D. & Campion, J.E. (1982). The employment interview: a summary and review of recent research. *Personnel Psychology*, **35**, 281–322.

Asher, J.J. & Sciarrino, J.A. (1974). Realistic work sample tests: a review. *Personnel Psychology*, **27**, 519–553.

Astin, A. (1964). Criterion-centered research. *Educational and Psychological Measurement*, **24**, 807–822.

Barber, A.E. & Roehling, M.V. (1993). Job postings and the decision to interview: a verbal protocol analysis. *Journal of Applied Psychology*, **78**, 845–856.

Barrick, M.R. & Mount, M.K. (1991). The Big Five personality dimensions and job performance: a meta-analysis. *Personnel Psychology*, **44**, 1–26.

Barrick, M.R., Mount, M.K. & Strauss, J.P. (1994). Antecedents of involuntary turnover due to a reduction in force. *Personnel Psychology*, **47**, 515–535.

Bartram, D. (2001). Internet recruitment and selection: kissing frogs to find princes. *International Journal of Selection and Assessment*, **8**, 261–274.

Bartram, D., Lindley, P.A., Foster, J. & Marshall, L. (1995). The selection of young people by small businesses. *British Journal of Occupational and Organizational Psychology*, **68**, 339–358.

Becker, B.E. & Huselid, M.A. (1992). Direct estimates of SD_y and the implications for utility analysis. *Journal of Applied Psychology*, **77**, 227–234.

Binning, J.F. & Barrett, G.V. (1989). Validity of personnel decisions: a conceptual analysis of the inferential and evidential bases. *Journal of Applied Psychology*, **74**, 478–494.

Borman, W.C. (1982). Validity of behavioral assessment for predicting military recruiter performance. *Journal of Applied Psychology*, **67**, 3–9.

Borman, W.C., Hanson, M. & Hedge, J. (1997). Personnel selection. *Annual Review of Psychology*, **48**, 299–337.

Boudreau, J.W. (1991). Utility analysis for decisions in human resource management. In M. Dunnette & L. Hough (Eds), *Handbook of Industrial and Organizational Psychology*, 2nd edn, Vol. **2**, pp. 621–745. Palo Alto, CA: Consulting Psychologists Press.

Boudreau, J.W., Sturman, M.C. & Judge, T.A. (1994). Utility analysis: what are the black boxes, and do they affect decisions? In N. Anderson & P. Herriot (Eds), *Assessment and Selection in Organizations: Methods and Practice for Recruitment and Appraisal*, pp. 77–96. New York: John Wiley.

Brand, C.R. (1994). Open to experience—closed to intelligence: why the "Big Five" are really the "Comprehensive Six". *European Journal of Personality*, **8**, 299–310.

Bray, D.W. & Grant, D.L. (1966). The assessment center in the measurement of potential for business management of potential for business management. *Psychological Monographs*, **80** (whole number 17).

Bray, D.W., Campbell, R.J. & Grant, D.L. (1974). *Formative Years in Business: A Long-term AT&T Study of Managerial Lives.* New York: John Wiley.

Bretz, R.D. & Judge, T.A. (1998). Realistic job previews: a test of the adverse self-selection hypothesis. *Journal of Applied Psychology*, **83**, 330–337.

Brogden, H.E. (1949). When testing pays off. *Personnel Psychology*, **2**, 171–183.

Callender, J.C. & Osburn, H.G. (1981). Testing the constancy of validity with computer-generated sampling distributions of the multiplicative model variance estimate: results for petroleum industry validation research. *Journal of Applied Psychology*, **66**, 274–281.

Campbell, J.P. (1990). Modeling the performance prediction problem in industrial and organizational psychology. In M.D. Dunnette & L.M. Hough (Eds), *Handbook of Industrial and Organizational Psychology*, Vol. **1**, pp. 687–732. Palo Alto, CA: Consulting Psychologists Press.

Campbell, J.P., McCloy, R.A., Oppler, S.H. & Sager, C.E. (1993). A theory of performance. In N. Schmitt & W. Borman (Eds), *Personnel Selection in Organizations*, pp. 35–70. San Francisco: Jossey Bass.

Campion, M.A., Palmer, D.K. & Campion, J.E. (1997). A review of structure in the selection interview. *Personnel Psychology*, **50**, 655–702.

Campion, M.A., Pursell, E.D. & Brown, B.K. (1988). Structured interviewing: raising the psychometric properties of the employment interview. *Personnel Psychology*, **41**, 25–42.

Carlson, K.D., Scullen, S.E., Schmidt, F.L., Rothstein, H. & Erwin, F. (1999). Generalizable biographical data validity can be achieved without multi-organizational development and keying. *Personnel Psychology*, **52**, 731–755.

Cascio, W.F. (1976). Turnover, biographical data, and fair employment practice. *Journal of Applied Psychology*, **61**, 576–580.

Cascio, W.F. (1993). Assessing the utility of selection decisions: theoretical and practical considerations. In N. Schmitt & W. C. Borman (Eds), *Personnel Selection in Organizations*, pp. 310–340. San Francisco: Jossey Bass.

Cascio, W., Outtz, J, Zedeck, S. & Goldstein, I.L. (1991). Statistical implications of six methods of test score use in personnel selection. *Human Performance*, **4**, 233–264.

Cattell, R.B. & Butcher, H.J. (1968). *The Prediction of Achievement and Creativity.* Indianapolis: Bobbs-Merrill.

Cattell, R.B. & Kline, P. (1977). *The Scientific Analysis of Personality and Motivation.* London: Academic Press.

Committee on Techniques for the Enhancement of Human Performance (1999). *The Changing Nature of Work: Implications for Occupational Analysis.* Washington, DC: National Academy Press.

Conway, J.M. (1996). Additional evidence for the task-contextual performance distinction. *Human Performance*, **9**, 309–330.

Cronbach, L.J. & Gleser, G.C. (1965). *Psychological Tests and Personnel Decisions*, 2nd edn. Urbana: University of Illinois Press.

De Corte, W. (1994). Utility analysis for the one-cohort selection–retention decision with a probationary period. *Journal of Applied Psychology*, **79**, 402–411.

DiMilia, L., Smith, P.A. & Brown, D.F. (1994). Management selection in Australia: a comparison with British and French findings. *International Journal of Selection and Assessment*, **2**, 80–90.

DeNisi, A.S. (2000). Performance appraisal and performance management: a multi-level analysis. In K. Klein and S. Kozlowski (Eds), *Multilevel Theory, Research, and Methods in Organizations*, pp. 121–156. San Francisco: Jossey-Bass.

Dreger, R.M. (1968). General temperament and personality factors related to intellectual performance. *Journal of Genetic Psychology*, **113**, 275–293.

DuBois, C., Sackett, P.R., Zedeck, S. & Fogli, L. (1993). Further exploration of typical and maximum performance criteria: definitional issues, prediction, and white–black differences. *Journal of Applied Psychology*, **78**, 205–211.

Finkle, R.B. (1976). Managerial assessment centers. In M. Dunnette (Ed.), *Handbook of Industrial and Organizational Psychology.* Chicago: Rand McNally.

Gaugler, B.B., Rosenthal, D.B., Thornton, G.C. & Bentson, C. (1987). Meta-analysis of assessment center validity. *Journal of Applied Psychology*, **72**, 493–511.

Gatewood, R.D. & Field, H.S. (1994). *Human Resource Selection*, 3rd edn. Hinsdale, IL: Dryden Press.

Gatewood, R.D., Gowan, M.A. & Lautenschlager, G.J. (1993). Corporate image, recruitment image, and initial job decision. *Academy of Management Journal*, **36**, 414–427.

Gerhart, B. & Milkovich, T. (1992). Organizational differences in managerial compensation and financial performance. *Academy of Management Journal*, **33**, 663–691.

Geurts, S.A., Schaufeli, W.B. & Rutte, C.G. (1999). Absenteeism, turnover intention and inequity in the employment relationship. *Work and Stress*, **13**, 253–267.

Gottfredson, L. (1986). Societal consequences of the g factor in employment. *Journal of Vocational Behavior*, **29**, 379–410.

Gottfredson, L. (1988). Reconsidering fairness: a matter of social and ethical priorities. *Journal of Vocational Behavior*, **33** (3), 293–319.

Gowing, M.K. & Slivinski, L.W. (1994). A review of North American selection procedures: Canada and the United States of America. *International Journal of Selection and Assessment*, **2**, 103–114.

Guion, R.M. & Gottier, R.F. (1965). Validity of personality measures in personnel selection. *Personnel Psychology*, **18**, 135–164.

Hakstian, A.R., Woolley, R.M., Woolley, L.K. & Kryger, B.R. (1991a). Management selection by multiple-domain assessment: I. Concurrent validity. *Educational and Psychological Measurement*, **51**, 883–898.

Hakstian, A.R., Woolley, R.M., Woolley, L.K. & Kryger, B.R. (1991b). Management selection by multiple-domain assessment: II. Utility to the organization. *Educational and Psychological Measurement*, **51**, 899–911.

Hartigan, J.A. & Wigdor, A.K. (1989). *Fairness in Employment Testing: Validity Generalization, Minority Issues and the General Aptitude Test Battery*. Washington, DC: National Academy Press.

Herriot, P. & Anderson, N. (1997). Selecting for change: how will personnel selection psychology survive? In N. Anderson and P. Herriot (Eds), *International Handbook of Selection and Assessment*. Chichester: John Wiley.

Hinrichs, J.R. (1978). An eight-year follow-up of a management assessment center. *Journal of Applied Psychology*, **63**, 596–601.

Hough, L.M., Eaton, N.K., Dunnette, M.D., Kamp, J.D. & McCloy, R.A. (1990). Criterion-related validities of personality constructs and the effect of response distortion on those validities. *Journal of Applied Psychology*, **75**, 581–595.

Howard, A. (1974). An assessment of assessment centers. *Academy of Management Journal*, **17**, 115–134.

Howard, A. (1995). *The Changing Nature of Work*. San Francisco: Jossey-Bass.

Huck, J.R. (1973). Assessment centers: a review of the external and internal validities. *Personnel Psychology*, **26**, 191–193.

Hunter, J.E. (1986). Cognitive ability, cognitive aptitudes, job knowledge, and job performance. *Journal of Vocational Behavior*, **29**, 340–362.

Hunter, J.E. & Hirsh, H.R. (1987). Applications of meta-analysis. In C.L. Cooper & I.T. Robertson (Eds), *International Review of Industrial and Organizational Psychology*, pp. 321–357. Chichester: John Wiley.

Hunter, J.E. & Hunter, R.F. (1984). The validity and utility of alternative predictors of job performance. *Psychological Bulletin*, **96**, 72–98.

Hunter, J.E. & Schmidt, F.L. (1982). Fitting people to jobs: the impact of personnel selection on national productivity. In M. Dunnette & E. Fleishman (Eds), *Human Performance and Productivity: Human Capability Assessment*. Hillsdale, NJ: Erlbaum.

Huselid, M.A. (1995). The impact of human resources management practices on turnover, productivity, and corporate financial performance. *Academy of Management Journal*, **38**, 635–672.

Ilgen, D.R. & Pulakos, E.D. (1999). *The Changing Nature of Performance*. San Francisco: Jossey-Bass.

Janz, T. (1982). Initial comparisons of patterned behavior description interviews versus unstructured interviews. *Journal of Applied Psychology*, **67**, 577–582.

Jensen, A. (1980). *Bias in Mental Testing*. New York: Free Press.

Jones, G.R. & Wright, P.M. (1992). An economic approach to conceptualizing the utility of human resource management practices. In G. Ferris & K. Rowland (Eds), *Research in Human Resources Management*, Vol. **10**, pp. 31–72. Greenwich, CT: JAI Press.

Kanfer, R. (1990). Motivation theory and industrial and organizational psychology. In M. Dunnette & L. Hough (Eds), *Handbook of Industrial and Organizational Psychology*, 2nd edn, Vol. **1**, pp. 39–74. Palo Alto, CA: Consulting Psychologists Press.

King, W.L. & Hautaluoma, J.E. (1977). Comparison of job satisfaction, life satisfaction, and performance of overeducated and other workers. *Journal of Social Psychology*, **127**, 421–433.

Klaas, B.S. & McClendon, J.A. (1996). To lead, lag, or match: estimating the financial impact of pay level policies. *Personnel Psychology*, **49**, 121–141.

Klimoski, R. & Brickner, M. (1987). Why do assessment centers work? The puzzle of assessment center validity. *Personnel Psychology*, **40**, 243–260.

Landy, F.J. & Trumbo, D.A. (1980). *Psychology of Work Behavior*, revised edn. Homewood, IL: Dorsey Press.

Landy, F.J., Shankster, L.J. & Kohler, S.S. (1994). Personnel selection and placement. *Annual Review of Psychology*, **45**, 261–296.

Latham, G.P., Saari, L.M., Pursell, E.D. & Campion, M.A. (1980). The situational interview. *Journal of Applied Psychology*, **65**, 422–427.

Law, K.S. & Myors, B. (1993). Cutoff scores that maximize the total utility of a selection program: comment on Martin and Raju's (1992) procedure. *Journal of Applied Psychology*, **78**, 736–740.

Linberg, K.R. (1999). Job satisfaction among software developers. *Dissertation Abstracts International Section A: Humanities & Social Sciences*, Vol. **60** (6-A), 2125.

Mael, F.A. (1991). A conceptual rationale for the domain of attributes of biodata items. *Personnel Psychology*, **44**, 763–792.

Martin, S.L. & Raju, N.S. (1992). Determining cutoff scores that optimize utility: a recognition of recruiting costs. *Journal of Applied Psychology*, **77**, 15–23.

McHenry, J.J., Hough, L.M., Toquam, J.L., Hanson, M.A. & Ashworth, S. (1990). Project A validity results: the relationship between predictor and criterion domains. *Personnel Psychology*, **43**, 335–355.

McDaniel, M.A. & Jones, J.W. (1988). Predicting employee theft: a quantitative review of the validity of a standardized measure of dishonesty. *Journal of Business and Psychology*, **2**, 327–345.

McDaniel, M.A., Whetzel, D.L., Schmidt, F.L. & Maurer, S.D. (1994). The validity of employment interviews: a comprehensive review and meta-analysis. *Journal of Applied Psychology*, **79**, 599–616.

Milkovich, G.T. & Boudreau, J.W. (1994). *Human Resource Management*, 7th edn. Homewood, IL: Richard D. Irwin.

Milkovich, G.T. & Wigdor, A.K. (1991). *Pay for Performance*. Washington, DC: National Academy Press.

Miner, M.G. & Miner, J.B. (1978). *Employee Selection Within the Law*. Washington, DC: Bureau of National Affairs.

Motowidlo, S.J., Dunnette, M.D., Carter, G.W., Tippins, N., Werner, S., Griffiths, J.R. & Vaughan, M.J. (1992). Studies of the behavioral interview. *Journal of Applied Psychology*, **77**, 571–587.

Mumford, M.D., Uhlman, C.E. & Kilcullen, R.N. (1992). The structure of life history: implications for the construct validity of background data scales. *Human Performance*, **5**, 109–137.

Murphy, K. (1986). When your top choice turns you down: effects of rejected offers on selection test utility. *Psychological Bulletin*, **99**, 133–138.

Murphy, K.R. (1989). Dimensions of job performance. In R. Dillon & J. Pelligrino (Eds), *Testing: Applied and Theoretical Perspectives*, pp. 218–247. New York: Praeger.

Murphy, K.R. (1993). *Honesty in the Workplace*. Pacific Grove, CA: Brooks/Cole.

Murphy, K.R. (1996). Individual differences and behavior in organizations: much more than g. In Murphy, K. (Ed.), *Individual Differences and Behavior in Organizations*, pp. 3–30. San Francisco: Jossey-Bass.

Murphy, K. & Cleveland, J. (1995). *Understanding Performance Appraisal: Social, Organizational and Goal-oriented Perspectives*. Newbury Park, CA: Sage.

Murphy, K.R. & Davidshofer, C.O. (1998). Psychological testing: principles and Applications, 4th edn. Englewood Cliffs, NJ, Prentice-Hall.

Murphy, K.R. & DeShon, R. (2000). Inter-rater correlations do not estimate the reliability of job performance ratings. *Personnel Psychology*, **53**, 873–900.

Murphy, K.R. & Myors, B. (1998). *Statistical Power Analysis: A Simple and General Model for Traditional and Modern Hypothesis Tests*. Mahwah, NJ: Erlbaum.

Murphy, K.R. & Shiarella, A. (1997). Implications of the multidimensional nature of job performance for the validity of selection tests: multivariate frameworks for studying test validity. *Personnel Psychology*, **50**, 823–854.

Murphy, K.R. & Shiarella, A. (1998). Implications of the multidimensional nature of job performance for the validity of selection tests: multivariate frameworks for studying test validity: Errata. *Personnel Psychology*, **51**, 822.

Nathan, B.R. & Alexander, R.A. (1988). A comparison of criteria for test validation: a meta-analytic investigation. *Personnel Psychology*, **41**, 517–535.

Neisser, U., Boodoo, G., Bouchard, T.J., Boykin, A.W., Brody, N., Ceci, S. Halpern, D.F., Loehlin, J.C., Perloff, R., Sternberg, R.J. & Urbina, S. (1996). Intelligence: knowns and unknowns. *American Psychologist*, **51**, 77–101.

O'Bannon, R.M., Goldinger, L.A. & Appleby, J.D. (1989). *Honesty and Integrity Testing: A Practical Guide*. Atlanta: Applied Information Resources.

Ones, D.S., Viswesvaran, C. & Schmidt, F.L. (1993). Comprehensive meta-analysis of integrity test validities: findings and implications for personnel selection and theories of job performance. *Journal of Applied Psychology*, **78**, 679–703.

Orpen, C. (1985). Patterned behavior description interviews versus unstructured interviews: a comparative validity study. *Journal of Applied Psychology*, **70**, 774–776.

OSS (1948). *Assessment of Men: Selection of Personnel for the Office of Strategic Services*. New York: Rinehart.

Owens, W.A. (1976). Background data. In M. Dunnette (Ed.), *Handbook of Industrial and Organization Psychology*. Chicago: Rand McNally.

Owens, W.A. & Schoenfeldt, L.F. (1979). Toward a classification of persons. *Journal of Applied Psychology*, **65**, 569–607.

Pritchard, R.D. (1990). *Measuring and Improving Organizational Productivity*. New York: Praeger.

Raju, N.S., Burke, M.J., Normand, J. & Lezotte, D.V. (1993). What would be if what is wasn't? Rejoinder to Judiesch, Schmidt, and Hunter (1993). *Journal of Applied Psychology*, **78**, 912–916.

Raju, N.S., Burke, M.J. & Maurer, T.J. (1995). A note on direct range restriction corrections in utility analysis. *Personnel Psychology*, **48**, 143–149.

Ree, M.J. & Earles, J.A. (1994). The ubiquitous productiveness of 'g'. In M.G. Rumsey, C.B. Walker & J.H. Harris (Eds), *Personnel Selection and Classification*, pp. 127–136. Hillsdale, NJ: Erlbaum.

Reilly, R.R. & Chao, G.T. (1982). Validity and fairness of some alternate employee selection procedures. *Personnel Psychology*, **35**, 1–67.

Robertson I., Baron, H., Gibbons, P., MacIver, R. & Nyfield, G. (2000). Conscientiousness and managerial performance. *Journal of Occupational and Organizational Psychology*, **73**, 171–180.

Rosse, J.G., Stecher, M.D., Miller, J.L. & Levin, R.A. (1998). The impact of response distortion on preemployment personality testing and hiring decisions. *Journal of Applied Psychology*, **83**, 634–644.

Roth, P.L. (1994). Multi-attribute utility analysis using the ProMES approach. *Journal of Business and Psychology*, **9**, 69–80.

Roth, P.L., Pritchard, R.D., Stout, J.D. & Brown, S.H. (1994). Estimating the impact of variable costs on SD_y in complex situations. *Journal of Business and Psychology*, **8**, 437–454.

Russell, J.S., Terborg, J.R. & Powers, M.L. (1985). Organizational performance and organizational-level training and support. *Personnel Psychology*, **38**, 849–863.

Ryan, A.M., Sacco, J.M., McFarland, L.A. & Kriska, S.F. (2000). Applicant self-selection: correlates of withdrawal from a multiple-hurdle process. *Journal of Applied Psychology*, **85**, 163–179.

Sackett, P.R. & Decker, P.J. (1979). Detection of deception in the employment context: a review and critique. *Personnel Psychology*, **32**, 487–506.

Sackett, P.R. & Harris, M.M. (1984). Honesty testing for personnel selection: a review and critique. *Personnel Psychology*, **37**, 221–245.

Sackett, P.R. & Harris, M.M. (1985). Honesty testing for personnel selection: a review and critique. In H.J. Bernardin & D.A. Bownas (Eds), *Personality Assessment in Organizations*. New York: Praeger.

Sackett, P.R. & Wilk, S.L. (1994). Within-group norming and other forms of score adjustment in psychological testing. *American Psychologist*, **49**, 929–954.

Sackett, P.R., Zedeck, S. & Fogli, L. (1988). Relations between measure of typical and maximal job performance. *Journal of Applied Psychology*, **73**, 482–486.

Sackett, P. R., Burris, L.R. & Callahan, C. (1989). Integrity testing for personnel selection: an update. *Personnel Psychology*, **42**, 491–529.

Schmidt, F.L. & Hunter, J.E. (1999). The validity and utility of selection methods in personnel psychology: practical and theoretical implications of 85 years of research findings. *Psychological Bulletin*, **124**, 262–274.

Schmidt, F.L., Hunter, J.E., Pearlman, K. & Shane, G.S. (1979). Further tests of the Schmidt–Hunter Bayesian validity generalization procedure. *Personnel Psychology*, **32**, 257–281.

Schmidt, F.L., Mack, M.J. & Hunter, J.E. (1984). Selection utility in the occupation of U.S. Park Ranger for three modes of test use. *Journal of Applied Psychology*, **69**, 490–497.

Schmidt, F.L., Hunter, J.E. & Outerbridge, A.N. (1986). Impact of job experience and ability on job knowledge, work sample, performance, and supervisory ratings of job performance. *Journal of Applied Psychology*, **71**, 432–439.

Schmidt, F.L., Ones, D.S. & Hunter, J.E. (1992). Personnel selection. *Annual Review of Psychology*, **43**, 627–670.

Schmitt, N., Gooding, R.Z., Noe, R.A. & Kirsch, M. (1984). Meta-analysis of validity studies published between 1964 and 1982 and the investigation of study characteristics. *Personnel Psychology*, **37**, 407–422.

Schneider, B., Smith, D.B. & Sipe, W.P. (2000). Personnel selection psychology. In K. Klein & S. Kozlowski (Eds), *Multilevel Theory, Research, and Methods in Organizations*, pp. 91–120. San Francisco: Jossey-Bass.

Schuler, H., Frier, D. & Kauffmann, M. (1993). *Personalauswahl, im europaischen Vergleich*. Gottingen: Verlaf fur Angewandte Psychologie.

Shackleton, V. & Newell, S. (1994). European management selection methods: a comparison of five countries. *International Journal of Selection and Assessment*, **2**, 91–102.

Sharf, J. (1994). The impact of legal and equal employment issues on personal history inquiries. In G. Stokes, M. Mumford & W. Owens (Eds), *Biodata Handbook*, pp. 351–390. Palo Alto: Consulting Psychologists Press.

Smith, M. (1994). A theory of the validity of predictor in selection. *Journal of Occupational and Organizational Psychology*, **67**, 13–32.

Stokes, G.S., Mumford, M.D. & Owens, W.A. (Eds) (1994). *Biodata Handbook*. Palo Alto, CA: Consulting Psychologists Press.

Taylor, H.C. & Russell, J.T. (1939). The relationship of validity coefficients to the practical effectiveness of tests in selection. *Journal of Applied Psychology*, **23**, 565–578.

Terpstra, D.E. & Rozelle, E.J. (1993). The relationship of staffing practices to organizational-level measures of performance. *Personnel Psychology*, **46**, 27–48.

Tett, R.P. (1998). Is conscientiousness always positively related to job performance? www.siop.org/TIPJuly98/tett.htm.

Tett, R.P., Jackson, D.N. & Rothstein, M. (1991). Personality measures as predictors of job performance: a meta-analytic review. *Personnel Psychology*, **44**, 703–745.

Thornton, G.C. (1992). *Assessment Centers in Human Resource Management*. Reading, MA: Addison-Wesley.

Thornton, G.C. & Byham, W.C. (1982). *Assessment Centers and Managerial Performance*. New York: Academic Press.

Thornton, G.C. & Cleveland, J.N. (1990). Developing managerial talent through simulation. *American Psychologist*, **45**, 190–199.

Watson Wyatt (2000). *The Human Capital Index: Linking Human Capital and Shareholder Value*. Bethesda, MD: Watson Wyatt Worldwide.

Wernimont, P.F. & Campbell, J.P. (1968). Signs, samples and criteria. *Journal of Applied Psychology*, **52**, 372–376.

Wiesner, W.H. & Cronshaw, S.F. (1988). A meta-analytic investigation of the impact of interview format and degree of structure on the validity of the interview. *Journal of Occupational Psychology*, **61**, 275–290.

Wigdor, A.K. & Garner, W.R. (1982). *Ability Testing: Uses, Consequences, and Controversies. Part I: Report of the Committee*. Washington, DC: National Academy Press.

Wolfe, R.N. & Johnson, S.D. (1995). Personality as a predictor of college performance. *Educational and Psychological Measurement*, **55**, 177–185.

CHAPTER 5

Training and Organizational Effectiveness

Phyllis Tharenou
Monarsh University, Australia

and

Eugene Burke
SHL Group plc, UK

INTRODUCTION

That the link between training investment and organizational effectiveness could be called into doubt might seem at odds to common sense. After all, we have all undergone training in some guise to acquire the knowledge and skills that we use in our daily working lives. Yet, on entering the twenty-first century, the links between training and organizational effectiveness are not perhaps as well understood as we might assume.

To evaluate the relationship between training and organizational effectiveness, measures of effectiveness will be classified using three types of outcome:

- HR outcomes (the more traditional perspective used in measuring the impact of training) focusing on the effect of training on changes in employee knowledge, skill and other behaviours
- production and service outcomes focusing on the impact of training on the quantity and quality of output
- investor outcomes focusing on the impact of training on returns from capital and stock market value of organizations.

The evidence provided by published research will show that the relationship between training and HR, production and service outcomes is direct and can be substantial, but that the impact of training may not be immediate and may be subject to time lags of 2–4 years. The relationship between training and investor outcomes is found to be contingent on and subject to interactions with organizational characteristics such as business direction and culture. Variations in the evidence offered by research owing to the type of measure used (hard versus

Organizational Effectiveness: The Role of Psychology
Edited by I.T. Robertson, M. Callinan and D. Bartram. © 2002 John Wiley & Sons, Ltd.

soft) and study design (cross-sectional versus longitudinal) will be discussed, and used to propose conditions under which the impact of training on organizational effectiveness can be enhanced.

Overall, the evidence will suggest that the impact of training on employee behaviours is in the region of a half standard deviation ($\delta = 0.5$) resulting in increases in productivity of between 15% and 20%, and is associated with higher stock market valuations of publicly quoted companies. We will give suggestions for what organizations can do to maximize returns from training investment, in particular the need to seat training programmes within an organizational strategy and the targeting of training on specific pay-offs framed by such strategy.

WHY ASK WHETHER TRAINING DOES IMPROVE ORGANIZATIONAL EFFECTIVENESS?

How would we perform our daily jobs if we were not trained to do so? The answer to this question may seem obvious—that is, we couldn't. Yet the pay-off from training investment is far from being taken as read in today's organizations. Importantly, employers are sceptical about whether training does pay off financially and, reflecting this scepticism, training is often one of the first human resource (HR) budget lines to be trimmed back or cut when the going gets tough commercially (Hubbard, 1997; Kirkpatrick, 1998; Polesky, 1998).

In seeming contradiction to this doubt in the payback from training investment is the growing awareness of the need for continuous learning to maintain competitive advantage in an increasingly global business environment (Polesky, 1998). Advances in technology and the change to knowledge work both place a high premium on skills that, in turn, would seem to argue for investment in training programmes (Ashton & Felstead, 1995; Gallie & White, 1993). This apparent contradiction (doubt in payback from training versus concerns over gaining competitive edge in world markets) has led governments in several countries to introduce legislation in an attempt to encourage or, indeed, coerce employers to train their workforces, and to introduce government funded training programmes (Ashton & Felstead, 1995; Noble, 1997).

However, there is a discernible variation in the views given by academics, advisors and governments round the world. Training and development appears to be less in Australia, Europe and North America than in Japan (with Japanese companies operating in North America investing more than their home grown counterparts) or in newly industrialized countries such as Brazil, Korea, Mexico and Taiwan (Ashton & Felstead, 1995; MacDuffie & Kochan, 1995; Pfeffer, 1998). This suggests that, to maintain the competitive edge in the global economy, investment in training and processes that support effective transfer of training into the workplace needs to be increased within the more established economies (Berwald, 1998; Tharenou, 1997). Furthermore, strategic approaches to training interventions do not appear to have been adopted worldwide. In contrast to scholars in the US where support for a more strategic approach has grown over the past decade, UK scholars have tended to conclude that training is not linked to strategic HR management practices (Heyes & Stuart, 1996; Rainbird, 1995;

Tregaskis, 1997). It does therefore seem timely to review the evidence of the link between training and organizational effectiveness and to explore what that evidence says about whether investment in training does pay off, and, if it does, how that pay-off can be maximized.

A FRAMEWORK FOR REVIEWING THE EVIDENCE

Clearly, a crucial question that needs to be answered is: what is the organizational impact to be expected from training investment (or, conversely, from lack of training investment)? Put bluntly, does training improve organizational effectiveness or not? To answer this question, some clarity is required as to what constitutes training (as opposed to other learning or development activities) and what constitutes organizational effectiveness.

For the purpose of this review, we adopt the definition of training as *the planned acquisition of skills, concepts and attitudes undertaken to improve a current organizational outcome*—as opposed to, say, activities intended to enhance longer-term personal and professional growth (Fitzgerald, 1992; Noe & Wilk, 1993).

For organizational effectiveness, we adapt the categories proposed by Dyer and Reeves (1995) as the basis for classifying outcome measures through which organizational effectiveness could be evaluated; that is, the intent to achieve objectives under the headings:

- *HR outcomes* such as the reduction of absence and turnover or improving employee skills
- *production and service outcomes* in the form of improvements in the quantity and quality of organizational output
- *investment outcomes* such as return in investment (ROI), return on equity (ROE) and return on assets (ROA), as well as shareholder returns and stock value.

This threefold framework has the benefit of being compatible with contemporary models for business strategy such as Kaplan and Norton's (1993) balanced scorecard, as well as allowing other outcomes to be included such as employee learning (an HR outcome), business operations (such as cycle time which would constitute a further example of a production and service outcome) as well as customer satisfaction (another production and service outcome). It also has the advantage of identifying key stakeholders in the valuation of organizational effectiveness; namely employees, customers and investors (as would be described in the business context as the value chain).

Of course, organizational effectiveness can be measured at different levels and within different time frames. To account for this, we classify evidence from published studies into individual and organizational levels in terms of the outcome measures reported. We also seek to classify and compare results from cross-sectional (e.g. one-shot surveys or studies using experimental versus control group designs) and longitudinal research designs (e.g. studies tracking individuals or organizational over time). In effect, this gives us a 3 (type of outcome category) by 2 (level of measurement) by 2 (cross-sectional versus longitudinal methodology) classification within which we could evaluate the trends apparent from published evidence of the impact of training on organizational effectiveness.

THE PUBLISHED EVIDENCE

HR Outcomes

In addition to those measures stated earlier, criteria explored in studies of HR outcomes are as diverse as withdrawal from and disruption of work activities, the frequency of accidents and strikes, as well as self-awareness and the inter-personal skills of managers. The majority of studies reporting HR outcome data have been cross-sectional in design and measured at the individual level.

The evidence from meta-analyses reported between the early 1980s and late 1990s show inconsistent results from training interventions. Guzzo et al. (1985) included training as one of 11 interventions evaluated across 98 US productivity experiments. While limited to only a subset of the studies evaluated (seven and eight respectively), training was found to have no impact on withdrawal rates (absenteeism and turnover) or disruption (accidents and strikes). This follows the results found in an earlier study reported by Katzell and Guzzo (1983). In contrast, Burke and Day's (1986) meta-analysis found substantial effect sizes for the impact of training on HR outcomes.[1] They found that managerial training increased the learning of objectively measured principles, facts, attitudes and skills ($\delta = 0.38$). Of the different types of training content, motivation/values ($\delta = 0.85$) and human relations training ($\delta = 0.41$) had the greatest effects. Man-agerial training also enhanced manager's job behaviour as reported by trainees, peers and supervisors ($\delta = 0.49$). Across the various HR outcomes evaluated, the results suggest that managers who receive training are around a half a stan-dard deviation higher than managers who do not receive equivalent training in managerial and interpersonal skills.

Part of the explanation for these contradictory results would appear to lie in the extent to which training programmes are skills-based and task-specific in content. Morrow et al. (1997) conducted a meta-analysis of the impact on job performance of 18 training programmes in a US Fortune 500 pharmaceuti-cal company. Training was found to enhance job behaviours and performance, but general managerial training was found to have less impact ($\delta = 0.31$) than sales/technical training ($\delta = 0.64$), and several managerial training courses had negative cost benefits due to their high costs. Consistent with Morrow et al.'s findings, Gattiker (1995) reported stronger effects for specific skills training than general training and development activities on job performance as reported from a survey of small to medium enterprises (SMEs) in Alberta, Canada (an 87% re-sponse rate was achieved in this survey). Change in performance reported by supervisors as attributable to training was greater for skills-specific than for general training programmes ($\delta = 0.27$ and 0.08 respectively).

---

[1] Using Cohen's (19) metrics, effect sizes involving mean comparisons between groups can be classified into small (0.3), medium (0.5) and large (0.8), where the effect size is measured in standard deviations.

These results suggest that while training programmes have been shown to impact positively on employee learning and job performance, they are most likely to have a significant impact on HR outcomes when they are delivered within a job-specific and skills-focused context. The evidence we have identified also suggests that training programmes are less likely to impact on withdrawal from and disruption in the workplace, suggesting that these outcomes need to be tackled by other HR and line management interventions.

Production and Service Outcomes

The studies that we classify under this category of organizational effectiveness are mixed as to the level of measurement (individual versus organizational) and the research design used (cross-sectional versus longitudinal).

Whereas Guzzo et al.'s study provided no support for the link between training and HR outcomes, their study does give strong evidence of the link between training and production and service outcomes. Of the 11 interventions they evaluated, training had the most powerful impact on output measures (quantity, quality and cost reduction) than any other intervention (including goal setting). In 74 studies, they obtained a δ of 0.74, suggesting that employees receiving training were almost a standard deviation higher in productivity than employees who were not receiving training.

Bartel (1994) assessed the impact of formal training programmes on net sales per employee by analysing data from 155 businesses that had either introduced a formal training programme before or after 1983. Other interventions such as job design, performance appraisal and quality improvement programmes were controlled for, as were differences in terms of the age, unionization and technological profiles of the businesses involved in the study. Businesses who were operating below their expected labour productivity levels in 1983 were those that most implemented new employee training programmes after 1983. They were also the businesses that showed the largest increases in productivity in the period 1983 to 1986. Productivity gains of 8.6% were directly attributable to the impact of the new training programmes, whereas other HR interventions reported by the business showed no direct effects.

In a French study, D'Arcimoles (1997) assessed the effects of HR policies including training on the productivity and economic performance of industrial firms using both cross-sectional data (61 companies), and longitudinal data (42 companies), collected between 1982 and 1989. He found significant relationships between the amount of investment in training and company's return on human capital and levels of productivity. However, in some cases the effects were delayed by as much as 3–4 years.

In contrast to the impacts on the top line shown by the last two studies, Holzer et al. (1993) showed impacts from training on the bottom line. Comparing US manufacturing firms using a state-financed training grant programme (66) with firms not in the program (91) and tracking these firms between 1986 and 1990, they found that training reduced scrap rates by 13%—a saving of between $30 000 and $50 000 each year (these were firms employing fewer than 500 employees).

Other factors such as worker participation practices, incentive payments and grievance procedures were all controlled for to isolate the direct impact on training. However, the training investment was not found to have an impact on sales.

Further evidence of the impact on the bottom line is offered by Lyau and Pucel (1995) in a study of Taiwanese auto parts manufacturers. While they also found that the level of investment in training (as measured by the direct and total costs of training) was not related to sales per worker when taken at gross value, they did find a relationship when the cost of materials was removed— i.e. when measured at margin. They estimated the value added by each worker through training equated to $430 in value-added labour productivity for every additional $28 in training investment when costs were accounted for.

While they do not offer evidence in the traditional statistical sense, two cross-sectional studies do offer further evidence of the potential impact of training on organizational and financial outcomes. Bassi and Van Buren (1998) assessed the training practices and expenditure of 540 US companies and members of the American Association for Training and Development (ASTD). They assessed whether each organization's performance was better, worse or no different in 1996 than in 1995 and compared their performance to other organizations in the same market sector (the companies included in the study covered a range of market sectors). Leading-edge firms (classified as 32 of the 540) were those who spent more on training and trained a greater proportion of employees than other companies. Leading-edge companies were also reported as having improved sales and profitability between 1995 and 1996 and were rated higher in the quality of their products and services than their market peers.

Bassi and McMurrer (1998) surveyed 40 publicly traded ASTD members. They compared companies in the top half of the distribution of training expenditure per employee (average of $900 per employee) to the bottom half of the distribution (average of $275 per employee). Those in the top half had higher net sales and annual gross profit per employee ($168 000 versus $121 000, a ratio of 1.39 : 1), and a higher capital-to-book ratio. Those who invested more in training were reported as valued more highly on Wall Street than those who invested less.

The evidence provided thus far would suggest a clear relationship between training investment and organizational outcomes in the form of productivity and profitability. However, as noted in the introduction to this section, studies under this category of organizational effectiveness comprised a mix of cross-sectional and longitudinal research designs, and the evidence provided thus far in this section has been drawn from longitudinal studies. Cross-sectional studies of organizational outcomes such as profits and margins are less favourable in the evidence they provide of the impact of training programmes.

Longitudinal studies consistently show that the investment in training, training grants and the introduction of formal training programmes by manufacturing and industrial companies increases organizational productivity and output (e.g. Bartel, 1994; D'Arcimoles, 1997; Holzer et al., 1993; Ichniowski, et al., 1997)— productivity gains in the region of 15–20% over a period of two to four years. In contrast, cross-sectional studies offer both positive evidence (Harel & Tzafrir, 1999; Russell, et al., 1985) and negative evidence (Delery & Doty, 1996; Koch & McGrath, 1996; Martell & Carroll, 1995) of training effects.

For example, Meschi and Metais (1998) surveyed 102 French HR and training managers of small to medium companies. The survey included a range of measures such as the percentage of payroll devoted to professional training along with perceived impact of training activities. No relationship was found between training investment and the economic performance of the companies included in this study. In contrast, Delaney and Huselid (1996) found positive relationships between training and perceived organizational performance over the three years prior to the study date. Furthermore, the impact of training was found to be independent of other HR practices. Harel and Tzafrir (1999) obtained similar results for a survey of 76 Israeli companies (employee selection programmes were also found to relate to perceived market performance alongside training investment in this study).

Why the apparent contradiction within cross-sectional studies and between cross-sectional studies and longitudinal ones? One important factor to be considered is the time lag that may be inherent between the introduction of a training programme and impacts on productivity and profits. As noted earlier, the time delays between a programme being introduced and measurable impact may be 2–4 years, though the impact has been shown to persist beyond that time frame. Another is the difference in the measures used, notably between hard indicators—productivity, cost and revenue (cash flow or turnover) data that are characteristic of longitudinal studies—and soft indicators, the perceptions of company managers of training programmes and organizational performance that are characteristic of cross-sectional studies. Data on the perceived impact of training programmes is not uncommon in training research (i.e. participants ratings of a training event), and is a factor that will be returned to later in this chapter for its implications regarding the scepticism often expressed as to the value added from training programmes mentioned at the outset of this chapter.

Investment Outcomes

Many readers will be familiar with the use of utility analyses to evaluate the monetary return from an intervention such as selection or training (Cascio, 1993). However, while utility approaches have been used to evaluate and communicate the potential cost benefits of training programmes (Wexley & Latham, 1991), utility estimates have also been shown to lower managers' support for an intervention (Latham & Whyte, 1994). This may relate to the relative unfamiliarity of managers with utility models and concepts, and others have argued for more direct and familiar financial indices of the impact of training. Phillips (1996a) recommended that return-on-investment (ROI) be used either (a) as a benefit-to-cost ratio (i.e. dividing the total benefits by the cost), or (b) by subtracting costs from the total benefits and then dividing by the costs to create a net ROI ratio. Typically the benefits are lagged in that savings or costs occur in the year after training is completed. Phillips also pointed out that ROI measurement is more effective when applied to a single programme linked to a direct pay-off and when the effects of other factors are directly controlled by the use of control groups. Other suggestions for appropriate data and study designs are given in subsequent articles by Phillips (1996b,c). The basic steps recommended by Phillips in calculating ROI are:

1. Collect evaluation data on measurable results.
2. Isolate the effects of training from other factors.
3. Convert the results to monetary benefits.
4. Total the costs of training.
5. Compute ROI or net ROI ratios.

Mention has already been made of studies touching on investment outcomes. Examples include the studies by Bassi and McMurrer (1998) who reported that companies with a higher investment in training were valued higher on Wall Street than their market peers with a lower investment in training. However, while the argument has been put that more direct evaluations using indices such as ROI, return-on-assets (ROA) and return-on-equity (ROE)—the latter two indices using similar computational approaches to ROI—should be more meaningful to managers, policy makers and investors, studies using these indices have provided less positive evidence of the links between training and investor outcomes.

Morrow et al. (1997) report mean ROIs of 45% and 418% respectively for managerial and sales/technical training programmes in the US. Mathieu and Leonard (1987) reported an average ROI of \$34 627 in the first year from a supervisor-training programme conducted for a US state bank. Barling et al. (1996) reported that the impact of transformational leadership training of managers resulted in increased personal loan sales when compared to previous sales for the 20 branches involved in the training programme.

In contrast, Delery and Doty (1996) found that training was not related to ROA and ROE measures of performance across 1050 US banks whereas appraisal and profit sharing policies were. Wright et al. (1999) found that training was negatively related to managers' ratings of profit margin, annualized profit growth and annual sales growth for 38 US refineries. Wiley (1991) found in over 200 retail stores that training emphasis was negatively related to store income.

Akin to the results from studies reporting production and service outcomes, the results for investment outcomes also appear paradoxical. However, as with production and service outcomes, part of the explanation lies in the use of cross-sectional (as in the Wright et al., 1999, study) versus longitudinal designs (the latter allowing for the time lag required for training impacts to become evident). Other studies also suggest that the link between training and investment outcomes is more indirect than with other categories of outcome. That is, the impact on investment outcomes is dependent on the impact on employee skills and behaviours, and also through the broader impact of training on organizational structures and processes.

Wong et al. (1997) assessed the links between managerial training supported by government funding and business growth (as measured by turnover) across 49 UK SMEs with 25 to 500 employees. Outcomes for these companies were compared with those for 89 companies matched by size, product and location who did not receive the government support. Survey data collected prior to the

training programme showed no relationships between the amount of managerial training and business growth. Twenty-four companies completed evaluations of the training six months after the programmes ended. Interviews showed
that the training programme was not seen to have improved financial performance, but the programme was seen to have improved internal processes such as
communication, co-operation, managing change and planning, and to have improved customer care and product quality (i.e. to have impacted on HR, product
and service outcomes).

Newkirk-Moore and Bracker (1998) evaluated whether training in strategic
planning was linked to measures such as ROA and ROE across 152 US community banks. Bank presidents and CEOs assessed their bank's commitment to
strategic planning by reporting attendance at different educational activities, the
level of employee sent to training and the frequency of training activities. The
banks included in the study were then classified into three groups: no formal
commitment to strategic planning (54%), a prescriptive commitment (9%) and a
strategic commitment (37%). Over and above the relationship between strategic
planning and investor outcomes, the frequency of sending managers on strategic planning training programmes was linked to ROE. That is, sending senior
managers to strategic planning training on a regular basis *in conjunction with*
a bank's enhanced commitment to strategic planning was related to a greater
return on stockholder's equity.

Bracker and Cohen (1992) found that training and development of entrepreneurs had no direct relationship with financial outcomes in 73 small elec-
tronics firms. However, when these firms were classified into structured planners
versus unstructured planners, investment in strategic planning training programmes for those entrepreneurs in structured planner firms was associated
with greater sales growth over a five-year period than for entrepreneurs who
did not receive training in strategic planning. As such, and while limited in their
number, the last two studies do suggest that the links between training provision
and investment outcomes are dependent on *interactions* with the strategic and
structural features of organizations, and that this link is a mediated rather than
a direct one.

RECONCILING THE EVIDENCE: FACTORS CONTRIBUTING
TO INCONSISTENCIES IN RESEARCH RESULTS

The 3 × 2 × 2 or twelve-cell framework outlined as the basis for this review
serves to explore those features that appear to contribute to variations, and indeed conflicts, in the evidence from published studies—in particular, the type of
measures and the type of research designs used. Figure 5.1 provides a summary
of findings using the twelve-cell framework which also serves to map out the
direction that research on training and organizational effectiveness has taken
over the last two decades.

Clearly, variations in results due to study design and measurements used
do suggest a need within training research for recommendations as to appropriate methodologies for evaluating the relationship between training and

	Individual level		Organizational level	
	Cross-sectional studies	Longitudinal studies	Cross-sectional studies	Longitudinal studies
Human resource outcomes	• No impact on turnover, disruption or absenteeism • Higher impact on job-specific knowledge, skills and attitudes • Higher impact for company-specific rather than generalized programmes	• Positive impacts on communication, cooperation and planning		
Production and service outcomes	• Contradictory evidence of perceptions of training impact on productivity and sales	• Higher productivity, sales (net of costs) and lower production costs (i.e. wastage) • Improvements in customer care and product quality		• Higher productivity for organizations with higher training investments • Rated higher in product quality • Effects can be delayed by up to four years
Investment outcomes			• Positive evidence found for the impact of training in US banks • Null or negative evidence found for investment measures (e.g. ROE and ROA) in banks, refineries and retail stores • Interaction found with business strategy	• Higher net sales, gross profits and capital-to-book ratio • Rated higher in value by stock market analysts • Interaction found with commitment to structured planning

Figure 5.1 Summary matrix of research into the links between training and organizational effectiveness

organizational effectiveness. For example, when using subjective or soft measures (as in cross-sectional studies) into production and service as well as investor outcomes, research needs to account for organizational factors such as how well espoused the link between training and organizational strategy is, and how clearly and widely organizational performance (such as productivity, revenue and profit data) is communicated to, and understood by, those asked to share their perceptions of training impact. Also, external factors such as market conditions and business/political cycles should be taken into account wherever feasible. Indeed, as well as the challenge in designing adequate studies to identify both direct and indirect links and interactions, a significant challenge is the issue of communication and the way in which training evaluations are translated into metrics that are meaningful within a specific organizational context.

ANSWERING THE QUESTION: DOES TRAINING IMPROVE ORGANIZATIONAL EFFECTIVENESS?

The evidence from our review suggests that training does improve organizational effectiveness in the following ways:

- Targeted skills and role/business (contextually) focused training increases HR outcomes in the form of job behaviours related to production and service outcomes.
- Contingent on business direction and conditions, the impact of training on HR, production and service outcomes *may* transfer to investment outcomes as measured by ROI and ROE indices, and as *perceived* by stock market valuations (which would be consistent with the increased interest in human capital and employee value-added indices among financial circles).

This interpretation is supported by the findings that training is related to investment outcomes in organizations that are capital intensive (Koch & McGrath, 1996) and when there is commitment to strategic planning (Bracker & Cohen, 1992; Newkirk-Moore & Bracker, 1998). This suggests a model as shown in Figure 5.2 in which direct effects of training are shown for HR, production and service outcomes, and an indirect relationship is shown for the effect of training *interacting* with organizational factors such as strategy and culture.

This view of the relationship between training and organizational effectiveness is also consistent with the notion of high-performance work systems (HPWS) in which several practices such as work design, continuous improvement, decision-making and information sharing are allied to complimentary HR practices such as selection, extensive training, performance management and incentivized compensation (Gephart & Van Buren, 1996; Pfeffer, 1998). The essence of HPWS is the horizontal integration of HR practices to ensure that they are complimentary in their effect, and the vertical integration of HR practices with business strategy.

Some have commented that, while training is part of HPWS (Huselid, 1995; Huselid & Becker, 1995), it does not appear to have to be part of HPWS to enhance

Organizational characteristics

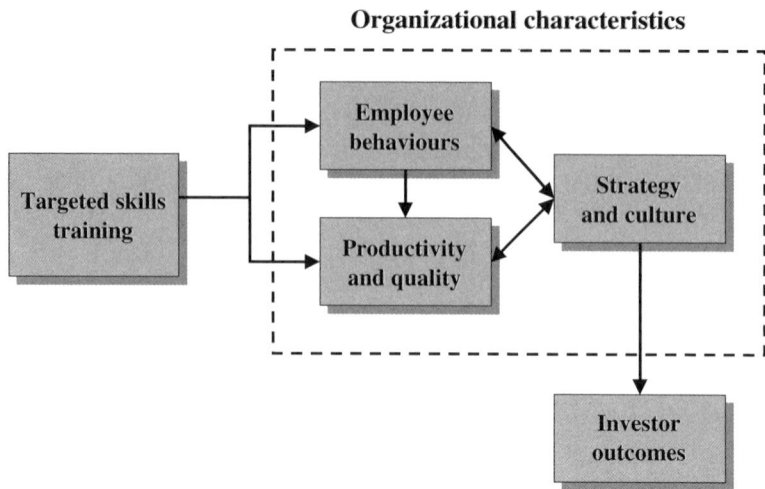

Figure 5.2   Direct and indirect effects of training on organizational effectiveness

organizational effectiveness (Delaney & Huselid, 1996; Ichniowski et al., 1997). Indeed, the direct contributions of training to certain categories of organizational effectiveness have been consistently noted in this review (as summarized in Figure 5.1 and as pictured in Figure 5.2). Perhaps the key point here is the *overall* or *cumulative* impact of HR practices within which training facilitates transfer of skills, knowledge and behaviours that enable organizations to address strategic objectives. The interest in managing the overall return from HR practices naturally leads to an interest in those conditions that serve to enhance or inhibit the impact of HR practices such as training on organizational effectiveness, among which will be the organizational culture or climate.

Rouiller and Goldstein (1993) defined training climate as the perceived cues and consequences that act to support or inhibit transfer of skills into the workplace. Situational cues within the workplace remind employees of their training and provide the opportunity to use new skills. These cues include goal cues, social cues such as the behaviour and influence processes shown by supervisors and peers, task cues such as the design of jobs and roles, as well as self-control cues.

Tracey et al. (1995) defined a continuous learning culture as the perceived need for employees to participate in ongoing knowledge and skills development. In such a culture, learning is an important part of everyday working life and is recognized as an essential responsibility of every employee's job or role, with this expectation supported by the nature of the social interactions and working relationships that take place within the organization and business unit.

The relationship of training to the implementation of organizational strategy and the development of organizational culture may also be reciprocal. While training enables the acquisition of skills that may improve performance on the job, training may also increase employee commitment and motivation that also serves to encourage increases in discretionary effort (MacDuffie, 1995). As such, while also providing necessary technical skills and knowledge, the effect of training targeted on meeting organizational needs supported by a learning culture may result in a greater amplified effect on organizational effectiveness. Spitzer (1999) provides an example of this amplified effect. Customer service representatives are provided with customer service training that improves their problem-solving skills. They return to their jobs better equipped to diagnose customers' problems and to solve them more quickly (a HR outcome). Customer satisfaction improves (a product and service outcome) and sales increase (contributing to an investment outcome through higher turnover or cash flow), while product returns and replacements are reduced (another product and service outcome) thereby reducing costs (again contributing to an investment outcome by improving margins or the bottom line). Consequently, overall, corporate profits increase and an investment outcome measure of organizational effectiveness has been enhanced (this example follows directly from the results as summarized in Figure 5.1).

Pfeffer (1998) has proposed that training is an essential ingredient of seven interrelated practices at the core of a committed workforce, namely: employment security; selective hiring of new personnel; self-managed teams and decentralization of decision-making; comparatively high compensation contingent on organizational performance; extensive training; reduced status distinctions and barriers; and extensive sharing of financial and performance information throughout the organization. Pfeffer comments that more training is provided by organizations with a commitment orientation rather than control-orientated management systems. (Pfeffer found that training in steel mills relying on commitment was 75% higher than mills relying on control. MacDuffie and Kochan (1995), reported training as higher in flexible and lean production systems as compared to mass production systems.) Pfeffer's proposition is that training is essential where organizations rely on front-line personnel with the skills and initiative to identify and resolve problems, to initiate changes in work methods and to take responsibility for quality.

The relationship hypothesized between training and investment outcomes (i.e. that it is mediated by culture and strategy) also helps to explain the lack of evidence from research seeking to directly test this relationship, as well as the negative impact of utility arguments on managers' perceptions of training proposals (e.g. Carson et al., 1998). Saks and Belcourt (1998) found that trainers' perceptions of how much learning from training activities improved organizational performance were related to their perceptions of the organization's market performance. This suggests that perceptions of training effectiveness are framed by organizational cues and again emphasizes the importance of organizational climate on perceptions of training effectiveness.

To summarize, then, training does indeed improve organizational effectiveness, but the extent of that effect will depend on the nature of the outcome measure taken, and on the organizational context within which that measurement is made. For each of the outcome categories used in this review, our review suggests the following levels of impact on organizational effectiveness:

- *HR outcomes.* There is little or no impact on certain types of outcome such as absenteeism and turnover, but some evidence of positive and moderate to high effects on job-related skills and organizationally focused training programmes—particularly on problem solving, diagnostic and planning skills with effect sizes (δ's) in the region of 0.5 (half a standard deviation).

- *Product and service outcomes.* Evidence gathered from cross-sectional studies based on executive's, supervisor's or trainer's perceptions is null or negative, but longitudinal studies show impacts on productivity, product quality and customer services. Evidence also shows that impact may be lagged by between two and four years.
- *Investment outcomes.* Evidence suggests that the relationship is mediated by organizational characteristics and the size of impact on other outcomes (i.e. HR, production and service). There is some evidence from longitudinal studies of impacts on investor and market analyst indices of company value.

The evidence we have identified on the impact of training can also be used to explore the potential impact of trimming back on or not investing in training. Taking the effect size identified for HR outcomes of $\delta = 0.5$, this can readily be translated into a benchmark figure. Such an effect size for the impact of a training programme would state that those receiving the programme would, on average, stand at half a standard deviation above those who did not receive the programme. This would represent moving an average employee within a given job or role from the 50th percentile in skills and knowledge to the 70th percentile (supposing of course that factors of ability, motivation and other individual differences have already been catered for through effective selection systems, and that the training programme is tied to effective transfer mechanisms as described above). In human capital terms, not investing in training (and allied HR practices) may therefore mean the difference between employee resources approaching the upper quartile or remaining in the middle or lower quartile. The potential consequences for organizational effectiveness are self-evident. Most importantly—and owing to the lagged effect of training on organizational effectiveness—not investing today has potentially serious implications for an organization's competitive advantage tomorrow.

WHAT SHOULD ORGANIZATIONS DO TO MAKE TRAINING MORE EFFECTIVE?

What can this review contribute to our understanding of how to enhance the organizational value of training programmes? Rather than describe the design of content and processes within a training programme, we will focus on the policy considerations that our review suggests organizations (whether in the private or public sectors) ought to consider in seating training programmes within HR practices tied to strategic objectives. This follows from the recommendations by those such as Barney and Wright (1998), Baron and Kreps (1999) and Hesketh and Ivancic (2000).

To begin with, training must be seen as part of a change management programme. In addition to effecting changes in individual employee behaviours that we will assume are directed at production and service outcomes, the introduction of training programmes will necessarily create changes to employee

perceptions and expectations. As such, the success or failure of a training intervention will depend on how well the change represented by a training intervention is managed. A key factor in this respect will be whether trainers are
personally credible to introduce change. Haccoun and Saks (1998) have argued
that trainers may not have the clout to directly effect change at an organizational
level, but, without some organizational support to their credibility, their potential to influence change through their training interventions will be undermined.

The use of change management principles will be even more important when
training is to be used to enhance outcomes at the organizational (rather than
individual) level. Wong et al. (1997) contrasted firms in which managerial training resulted in improvements in the organization of the firm and its external image with those firms in which these improvements were not achieved. What they
found was that the management of change differed between these two groups of
firms. Firms that improved had greater CEO commitment and leadership of the
change within which training was undertaken, as well as greater senior management support, team involvement, linking of training to business objectives
and the strategic plan, and the use of more highly skilled consultancy support.

Johns (1998) argued that the introduction of HR practices such as training
are akin to the introduction of innovations. The tendency in organizations is for
managers to see training as an administrative rather than a technical innovation.
Administrative innovations (such as recruitment, training and reward systems)
are widely seen as operating on the social system of an organization and as
matters of organizational style, whereas technical innovations are seen to directly
impact on product and services. Judgments and decisions regarding technical
innovations will therefore be based on different assumptions and perceptions
than judgments and decisions regarding administrative innovations, and Johns
recommends that trainers need to be aware of and capitalize on institutional and
political forces in implementing training programmes.

We have already noted the potential of training in strategic planning to support organizational strategy. Martocchio and Baldwin (1997) have argued that
strategic organizational training is an opportunity for organizations to transmit
competencies to employees that contribute, in aggregate, to organizational competitiveness. In their model, the nature of the training required will depend on
how turbulent the environment is that faces the organization. As environmental
turbulence increases, training should be focused on imminent business needs
and on business development. As environmental turbulence reduces and the environment is more stable, then training's role is primarily maintaining the skills
and knowledge of employees. Based on their model, Martocchio and Baldwin
recommend that organizations identify the key issues growing out of strategic
objectives and then use those issues as the starting point for defining training
initiatives.

Barney and Wright's (1998) suggestions to HR functions take these ideas a step
further. To add value, they recommend eliminating and consolidating training
programmes unrelated to the business of the organization, and then determining
which programmes to keep internal to the organization and which to outsource.
Those programmes that add rare knowledge, skills, abilities and attitudes should
be retained as internal and tailored to business needs. Those programmes that

are more general in nature and less unique to the organization should be considered for outsourcing. This approach also serves to restrict access to valuable organizational skills that can be exploited by other competing organizations.

Earlier, in relation to HPWS, the need to integrate training with other HR practices (horizontal) as well as with organizational strategy (vertical) was raised. Baron and Kreps (1999) have argued for consistency in the ways in which recruitment, training, promotion and compensation policies bear on a single employee. Organizations that choose to invest heavily in training their employees should gain value by carefully screening applicants. When on-the-job training (OJT) accumulates over a period of years, practices that reward seniority (and thus reduce turnover among employees with longer tenure) will add further value. When more senior workers use informal training with their junior colleagues, seniority-based rewards help by putting senior workers at no disadvantage when they share their knowledge.

The positive effects on production and service outcomes found from this review can occur only if training transfers to the job. Haccoun and Saks (1998) advocate that successful transfer of training depends on three factors:

1. *Individual differences of trainees*. Qualities that help transfer of training include ability, motivation to learn, self-efficacy and perceived control. Motivation to learn directs attention during the training experience while self-efficacy and perceived control increase the transfer of training to the job, both effects being conditional on the abilities of the trainee in relation to the nature and level of the skills to be acquired through training.
2. *Developing transfer skills*. The design of training should facilitate the transfer of training to the job. Training design should include principle and rules, opportunities for practice using identical elements to those in the job context, multiple examples and feedback. Haccoun and Saks advocate transfer enhancement practices (TEPs) that trainers add to existing programmes to enhance transfer. TEPs include goal-setting, relapse prevention and self-management techniques. TEPs require trainers to conceptually separate the substantive content of a training programme from the parameters that facilitate learning and transfer. From their known review, Haccoun and Saks concluded that self-management and relapse-prevention techniques are more effective than goal setting which may not be appropriate at the early stages of learning complex tasks. Both self-management and relapse-prevention techniques help individuals to identify environmental constraints on skills usage and to develop strategies for overcoming constraints. TEPs also help prevent skill relapse by teaching employees coping strategies for overcoming anticipated obstacles before they return to the workplace.
3. *The work environment*. Clearly, the work environment needs to support transfer, both in terms of the general organizational context and the specific job/work group. Mention has already been made of the characteristics of a training climate and a continuous learning culture. At the job level, supervisor and colleague support for the use of skills and the opportunity to use learned skills needs to occur. Hesketh and Ivancic (2000) recommend that trainers advise management on how to promote an organizational culture that

values ongoing training. The employee's supervisor and co-workers need to be informed of the goals of the training programme so that they can recognize and encourage attempts to transfer trained skills. Post-training support such as pre-planned opportunities for employee practice is an example of a practical way in which environmental support can be included in the overall training programme. Across an organization, such principles can be endorsed by appraisal and reward systems in which support for, and opportunities to practice, skills are encouraged.

In short and by way of a conclusion, the link between training and organizational effectiveness is enhanced when training programmes flow from organizational strategy and are targeted on the specific needs of an organization; when support for transfer of training into the workplace is endorsed and rewarded; when training programmes are allied with other HR practices that promote single-employee consistency, and that ensure that training is consistent with recruitment and reward practices; when training is seen as a change management process in which stakeholders are identified and involved, and in which the trainers are equipped to be credible in tackling change management issues; when the metrics through which training is evaluated and communicated are targeted on tangible outcomes that benefit the organization, and are meaningful to key stakeholders in the business; and when the return on training investment is seen as an investment today that will achieve the organization's strategy for tomorrow.

REFERENCES

Ashton, D. & Felstead, A. (1995). Training and development. In J. Storey (Ed.), *Human Resource Management*, pp. 234–253. London: Routledge.

Barling, J., Weber, T. & Kelloway, E.K. (1996). Effects of transformational leadership training on attitudinal and financial outcomes. *Journal of Applied Psychology*, **81**, 827–832.

Barney, J.B. & Wright, P.M. (1998). On becoming a strategic partner. *Human Resource Management*, **37**, 31–46.

Bartel, A.P. (1994). Productivity gains from the implementation of employee training programs. *Industrial Relations*, **33**, 411–425.

Baron, J.N. & Kreps, D.M. (1999). Consistent human resource practices. *California Management Review*, **41**, 29–53.

Bassi, L.J. & McMurrer, D.P. (1998). Training investment can mean financial performance. *Training and Development*, May, 40–42.

Bassi, L.J. & Van Buren, M.E. (1998). State of the industry report. *Training and Development*, January, 21–43.

Berwald, M.C. (1998). The challenge of profound transformation for industrial and organizational psychologists. *Canadian Psychology*, **39** (1–2), 158–163.

Bracker, J.S. & Cohen, D.J. (1992). The impact of training and development activities on small technology oriented entrepreneurial performance. *Journal of Small Business Strategy*, 1–14.

Burke, M.J. & Day, R.R. (1986). A cumulative study of the effectiveness of managerial training. *Journal of Applied Psychology*, **71**, 232–245.

Cascio, W.F. (1993). Assessing the utility of selection decisions: theoretical and practical considerations. In N. Schmitt & W.C. Borman (Eds), *Personnel Selection in Organizations*, pp. 310–340. San Francisco: Jossey-Bass.

Carson, K.P., Becker, J.S. & Henderson, J.A. (1998). Is utility really futile? A failure to replicate and an extension. *Journal of Applied Psychology*, **83**, 84–96.

D'Arcimoles, C.H. (1997). Human resource policies and company performance: a quantitative approach using longitudinal data. *Organization Studies*, **18**, 857–874.

Delery, J.E. & Doty, D.H. (1996). Modes of theorizing in strategic human resource management. *Academy of Management Journal*, **39**, 802–835.

Delaney, J.T. & Huselid, M.A. (1996). The impact of human resource management practices on perceptions of organizational performance. *Academy of Management Journal*, **39**, 949–969.

Dyer, L. & Reeves, T. (1995). Human resource strategies and firm performance. *International Journal of Human Resource Management*, **6**, 656–670.

Fitzgerald, W. (1992). Training versus development. *Training and Development*, **46**, 81–83.

Gallie, D. & White, M. (1993). *Employee Commitment and the Skills Revolution*. London: Policy Studies Institute.

Gattiker, U.E. (1995). Firm and taxpayer returns from training of semiskilled employees. *Academy of Management Journal*, **38**, 1152–1173.

Gephart, M.A. & Van Buren, M.E. (1996). The power of high performance work systems. *Training and Development*, **50**, 20–36.

Guzzo, R.A., Jette, R.D. & Katzell, R.A. (1985). The effects of psychologically based intervention programs on worker productivity. *Personnel Psychology*, **38**, 275–292.

Haccoun, R.R. & Saks, A.M. (1998). Training in the 21st century: some lessons from the last one. *Canadian Psychology*, **39** (1–2), 33–51.

Harel G.H. & Tzafrir, S.S. (1999). The effect of human resource management practices on the perceptions of organizational and market performance in the firm. *Human Resource Management*, **38**, 185–200.

Hesketh, B. & Ivancic, K. (2000). Training for transfer: new directions from I/O and cognitive psychology. In J. Langan-Fox (Ed.), *Human Performance and the Workplace*. Melbourne: Australian Psychological Society.

Heyes, J. & Stuart, M. (1996). Does training matter? *Human Resource Management Journal*, **6**, 7–21.

Holzer, H.J., Block, R.N., Cheatham, M. & Knott, J.H. (1993). Are training subsidies for firms effective? *Industrial and Labor Relations Review*, **46**, 625–636.

Hubbard, A. (1997). Analyzing training's effectiveness. *Mortgage Banking*, August, 77.

Huselid, M.A. (1995). The impact of human resource management practices on turnover, productivity, and corporate financial performance. *Academy of Management Journal*, **38**, 635–672.

Huselid, M.A. & Becker, B.E. (1995). Methodological issues in cross-sectional and panel estimates of the HR–firm performance link. *Industrial Relations*, **35**, 400–422.

Ichniowski, C., Shaw, K. & Prennushi, G. (1997). The effects of human resource management practices on productivity. *American Economic Review*, **87**, 291–313.

Johns, G. (1998). The nature of work, the context of organizational behavior, and the application of industrial–organizational psychology. *Canadian Psychology*, **39**, 149–157.

Kaplan, R.S. & Norton, D.P. (1993). Putting the balanced scorecard to work. *Harvard Business Review*, **71** (5), 134–147.

Katzell, R.A. & Guzzo, R.A. (1983). Psychological approaches to productivity improvement. *American Psychologist*, **4**, 468–472.

Kirkpatrick, D.L. (1998). *Evaluating Training Programs*. San Francisco: Berrett-Koehler.

Koch, M.J. & McGrath, R.G. (1996). Improving labor productivity: human resource management policies do matter. *Strategic Management Journal*, **17**, 335–354.

Latham, G.P. & Whyte, G. (1994). The futility of utility analysis. *Personnel Psychology*, **47**, 31–46.

Lyau, N-M. & Pucel, D.J. (1995). Economic return on training investment at the organization level. *Performance Improvement Quarterly*, **8** (3), 68–79.

MacDuffie, J.P. (1995). Human resource bundles and manufacturing performance. *Industrial and Labor Relations Review*, **48**, 197–221.

MacDuffie, J.P. & Kochan, T.A. (1995). Do U.S. firms invest less in human resources? Training in the world auto industry. *Industrial Relations*, **34**, 145–165.

Martell, K. & Carroll, S.J. (1995). Which executive human resource management practices for the top management team are associated with higher firm performance? *Human Resource Management*, **34**, 497–512.

Martocchio, J.J. & Baldwin, T.T. (1997). The evolution of strategic organizational training. *Research in Personnel and Human Resources Management*, **15**, 1–46.

Mathieu, J.E. & Leonard, R.L. (1987). An application of utility concepts to a supervisor skills training program. *Academy of Management Journal*, **30**, 316–335.

Meschi, P.X. & Metais, E. (1998). A socio-economic study of companies through their training policies: the French context. *Management International Review*, **38** (1), 25–48.

Morrow, C.C., Jarrett, M.Q. & Rupinski, M.T. (1997). An investigation of the effect and economic utility of corporate-wide training. *Personnel Psychology*, **50**, 91–119.

Newkirk-Moore, S. & Bracker, J.S. (1998). Strategic management training and commitment to planning. *International Journal of Training and Development*, **2**, 82–90.

Noble, C. (1997). International comparisons of training policies. *Human Resource Management Journal*, **7**, 5–18.

Noe, R.A. & Wilk, S.A. (1993). Investigation of the factors that influence employees' participation in development activities. *Journal of Applied Psychology*, **78**, 291–302.

Pfeffer, J. (1998). Seven practices of successful organizations. *California Management Review*, **40**, 96–124.

Phillips, J.J. (1996a). Was it the training? *Training and Development*, March, 42–47.

Phillips, J.J. (1996b). ROI: the search. *Training and Development*, February, 42–47.

Phillips, J.J. (1996c). How much is the training worth? *Training and Development*, April, 20–24.

Polesky, G.G. (1998). Ensuring cost effectiveness in support of training. *International Journal of Technology Management*, **16** (1/2/3), 256–266.

Rainbird, H. (1995). The changing role of the training function. *Human Resource Management Journal*, **5**, 72–90.

Rouiller, J.Z. & Goldstein, I.L. (1993). The relationship between organizational transfer climate and positive transfer of training. *Human Resource Development Quarterly*, **4**, 377–390.

Russell, J.S., Terborg, J.R. & Powers, M.L. (1985). Organizational performance and organizational level training and support. *Personnel Psychology*, **38**, 849–863.

Saks, A.M. & Belcourt M. (1998). Training activities and the transfer of training. Paper presented to the US Academy of Management Meetings, San Diego, California.

Spitzer, D.R. (1999). Embracing evaluation. *Training*, June, 42–47.

Tharenou, P. (1997). Determinants of participation in training and development. In C.L. Cooper & D.M. Rousseau (Eds), *Trends in Organizational Behavior*. New York: John Wiley.

Tracey, J.B., Tannenbaum, S.I. & Kavanagh, M.J. (1995). Applying trained skills on the job. *Journal of Applied Psychology*, **80**, 239–252.

Tregaskis, O. (1997). The role of national context and HR strategy in shaping training and development practice in French and U.K. companies. *Organization Studies*, **18**, 839–856.

Wexley, K.N. & Latham, G.P. (1991). *Developing and Training Human Resources in Organizations*. New York: HarperCollins.

Wong, C., Marshall, J.N., Alderman, & Thwaites, A. (1997). Management training in small and medium-sized enterprises: methodological and conceptual issues. *International Journal of Human Resource Management*, **8**, 44–65.

Wright, P.M., McCormick, B., Sherman, W.S. & McMahan, G.C. (1999). The role of human resource practices in petro-chemical refinery performance. *International Journal of Human Resource Management*, **10**, 551–571.

Wiley, J.W. (1991). Customer satisfaction. *Human Resource Planning*, **14**, 117–127.

CHAPTER 6

Performance Management and Organizational Effectiveness

Richard Williams
Assessment and Consultancy Unit, Home Office, UK
and
Clive Fletcher
Goldsmiths' College, UK

INTRODUCTION

If the rhetoric of practitioner-orientated literature is to be believed then performance management ought *par excellence* be the means by which individual performance is managed so as to contribute to organizational effectiveness. However, as is so often the case we find that there is a gap between rhetoric and reality. This is not to say that performance management does not make a contribution to organizational effectiveness, but the linkage is far from straightforward. One of the difficulties, as Chapter 1 by Sparrow and West indicates, is that there is little agreement as to the nature of organizational effectiveness. Another difficulty is that there is no single entity that is performance management: we will briefly outline the main types of model. We also will examine what is meant by performance (at the individual level) and consider the core work-psychology based interventions directed at the employee. We also will refer briefly to the emerging body of evidence on the impact of human resource management on organizational effectiveness.

THE NATURE OF PERFORMANCE MANAGEMENT

A scan of the literature over the past decade or so points to three principal models of performance management:

The views expressed in this chapter are those of the authors and do not necessarily reflect those of the Home Office.

Organizational Effectiveness: The Role of Psychology
Edited by I.T. Robertson, M. Callinan and D. Bartram. © 2002 John Wiley & Sons, Ltd.

- performance management as a system for managing organizational performance
- performance management as a system for managing employee performance
- performance management as a system for integrating the management of organizational and employee performance.

Performance Management as a System for Managing Organizational Performance

A good illustration of this view is found in Rogers (1990) writing about corporate, organization-wide systems of performance management in UK local government:

> The characteristics of such systems are that they are corporate systems which include the following processes as part of an annual integrated cycle of management:
> (1) setting corporate policy and resource aims and guidelines
> (2) specifying, within the framework provided by (1) above, a detailed set of plans, budgets, objectives, targets and standards of performance
> (3) regularly and systematically reviewing the performance of all services.

This is a model of performance management that we continue to see widely practised in the public sector, and in recent years it has been reinforced by UK central government initiatives to promote "Best Value", an outcome-orientated philosophy that emphasizes a customer focus and continuous improvement in service delivery. However, it is far from being confined to the public sector. For example, in one of the Chartered Institute of Personnel and Development's books on performance management (Lawson, 1995) we find a specification of the components of effective performance management, as set out in Table 6.1.

Table 6.1 Components of effective performance management

Effective performance management means:
- articulating your company's vision
- establishing key results, objectives and measures at key business unit level
- identifying business process objectives and the key indicators of performance for those processes
- identifying and installing effective departmental measures
- monitoring and controlling four key performance measures
  — quality
  — delivery
  — cycle time
  — waste
- managing the continuous improvement of performance in those key areas—"benchmarking" your performance against the best
- being prepared to aim for "breakthrough" improvements in performance when this is required by a significant shortfall in your performance measured against the performance of your major competitors.

Source: Lawson (1995).

What is depicted here is far from being new but perhaps is more familiar as strategic/business planning, operations management and such like. In other words, the emphasis here is on the determination of the organization's strategy and the implementation of that strategy through structure, technology, business systems and procedures, etc. Employees are *not* the primary focus, although they will be affected by changes in technology, structure, operating systems, etc.

Performance Management as a System for Managing Employee Performance

There are many variants of this model: what they have in common is that they typically represent performance management as a cycle. One illustration is found in Torrington and Hall (1995) who present performance management as a three-step process: planning, supporting, and reviewing performance. For Heisler et al. (1988) there are four elements—directing, energizing, controlling, and rewarding; and Schneier et al. (1987) give us five—planning, managing, reviewing, rewarding, and developing. A theme in much of this writing is the idea that manager and managed should have a shared view of what is expected of the employee; involvement and participation of a direct kind typically are advocated as the means by which this shared view is brought about. Supporting performance is seen as a responsibility of the line manager who also has a particular part to play in reviewing performance. Here again we have an activity that often is presented as being shared between manager and managed; that is, performance review is a joint activity in which the responsibility rests with the job holder as much as with the manager. Moreover, review is seen as an ongoing activity rather than as something that happens just once or twice a year. What we have here, in effect, is a development of performance appraisal.

Performance Management as a System for Integrating the Management of Organizational and Employee Performance

In simple terms this model may be regarded as a combination of the first two. But there are variations on the basic theme, essentially reflecting the extent to which there is an emphasis on organizational as compared to employee performance. Thus, certain of the integrative models place their emphasis more on managing organizational performance. For example, Rogers (1990) puts forward an elaboration of his corporate model which adds the management of employee performance:

> . . . corporate systems . . . include the following processes as part of an annual integrated cycle of management:
> (1) setting corporate policy and resource aims and guidelines
> (2) specifying, within the framework provided by (1) above, a detailed set of plans, budgets, objectives, targets and standards of performance
> (3) regularly and systematically reviewing the performance of all services.

... systems which integrate the procedures for managing organizational performance with those for managing the performance of individuals ... have
the following additional characteristics:
(4) procedures and systems for planning, monitoring and appraising the
    performance of individuals which are integrated with those for managing
    organizational performance.

Some, though not all ... have a fifth characteristic:
(5) systems, such as performance related pay, for rewarding individual
    achievements.

In those integrative models which adopt more of an employee focus, the
organizational context is, to varying extents, taken as a given. For example,
Ainsworth and Smith (1993) assume that:

- the important corporate issues of "mission" and the setting of corporate goals
  have been addressed and resolved
- objectives for the sub-sections of the organization (the departments, divisions
  or business units) have been set within the key results areas, and that the senior
  management group has identified just where the competitive advantage and
  value added dimensions of the business lie
- all of this has been communicated to and understood by those involved.

Rather more elaborate variations on this theme are shown in Table 6.2. Although they are intended to enhance organizational performance, what charac-
terizes these models is their emphasis on employee-focused interventions.

Though we find this variation in the literature, the weight of opinion amongst
British writers seems to view performance management as an essentially
employee-centred set of interventions. The main aim is to harness the contribution of individual employee performance to organizational performance. Thus,
at the heart of performance management we find a cycle of activity which includes policies and procedures for some or all of the following aspects of individual performance:

- directing/planning
- managing/supporting
- reviewing/appraising
- developing/rewarding.

The consensus position recognizes also that these activities take place within
a given organizational context, two facets of which are afforded particular
emphasis:

- the organization's mission, objectives, and business plan
- communication about that mission etc.

All this seems very reasonable, sensible and rational. We decide where the
organization is heading and what it is trying to do, we communicate that to all
our employees, and we have systems for planning the work of individuals so that
their efforts can be appropriately directed. Easier said than done, of course; and
when we look at the survey evidence about performance management practice it

Table 6.2 Integrative models of performance management

A "textbook" performance management system (Bevan & Thompson, 1991)	Main building blocks of performance management (Fletcher, 1993, 1994)	Requirements of the performance management process (Lockett, 1992)
The organization has a shared vision of its objectives, or a mission statement, which it communicates to all its employees	The development of the organization's mission statement and objectives	A clear statement of the organization's mission—i.e. what the organization needs to do to compete and survive in its current business environment
The organization sets individual performance management targets which are related both to operating unit and wider organizational objectives	Associated with this, the development of the business plan (business being interpreted in the broadest sense of the word)	A mechanism to enable the performance of individuals within the organization to be aligned with that mission statement and a way of adjusting performance requirements to meet new challenges which may arise
It conducts a regular, formal review of progress towards these targets	Enhancing communications within the organization, so that employees are not only aware of the objectives and the business plan, but can contribute to their formulation	A set of human resource management policies which support the organization's strategic aims and which give the individual incentive to work towards their own personal objectives. This involves creating an environment where high performance is actively encouraged and human resource policies are in tune with corporate goals
It uses the review process to identify training, development and reward outcomes	Clarifying individual responsibilities and accountabilities (which means, amongst other things, having job descriptions, clear role definitions, and so on, and being willing to be held accountable)	A clear statement of the organization's future goals—their vision and the direction in which they intend to move
It evaluates the effectiveness of the whole process and its contribution to overall organizational performance to allow changes and improvements to be made.	Defining and measuring individual performance (with the emphasis on being measured against one's own objectives rather than being compared with others)	A process which enables the critical capability factors within the organization to be developed as part of the performance management process. This is particularly relevant with regard to the development of people—their competence, skills and knowledge need to be a critical part of the development of capability
	Implementing appropriate reward strategies	
	Developing staff to further improve performance, and their career progression, in the future.	

seems that it doesn't always happen—performance management of the holistic, comprehensive and integrative kind that is advocated in much of the literature is rare (Williams, 2002). The dominant approach to managing employee performance still rests on appraisal, probably supplemented with appraisal-related pay. To this extent, then, the reality of contemporary performance management practice probably is best seen as "a logical progression in the history of the development of appraisal systems" (Lundy & Cowling, 1996). In keeping with this, and the scope of this volume, it is an employee-centred perspective that we take in this chapter.

THE NATURE OF PERFORMANCE

Before we can properly examine performance management interventions we need to consider what is meant by employee performance. There are two main perspectives: outputs/results and behaviours.

The former view is very evident in much of the practitioner-orientated literature on performance management; for example: "Basically, it means outcomes, results" (Ainsworth & Smith, 1993). We find the same idea in some of the academic literature as well:

> . . . performance can and should be measured in terms of outcomes or results produced. Performance is defined as: The *record of outcomes* produced on a *specified job function* or activity during a *specified time period* . . . Performance on the job as a whole would be equal to the sum (or average) of performance on the critical or essential job functions.
> (Bernardin et al., 1995b)

Prominent in much of the contemporary writing is the notion that employee performance should be defined in behavioural terms, for example:

> A performance consists of a *performer* engaging in *behaviour* in a *situation* to achieve *results*.
> (Mohrman et al., 1989)

> The performance domain is defined . . . as the set of behaviours that are relevant to the goals of the organization or the organizational unit in which a person works.
> (Murphy, 1990)

> Performance is . . . defined as synonymous with behaviour. It is something that people actually do and can be observed. By definition, it includes only those actions or behaviours that are relevant to the organization's goals and that can be scaled (measured) in terms of each individual's proficiency (that is, level of contribution). . . . Performance is *not* the consequence or result of action, it is the action itself . . . performance consists of goal-relevant actions that are under the control of the individual . . .
> (Campbell et al., 1993).

According to these definitions then, performance is *not* output or results. Central to the argument that we should not regard performance as task accomplishment or goal achievement is the fact that for many jobs results are not necessarily the product of what individual employees do—there may be other contributory factors that are nothing to do with the person doing the job (Cardy & Dobbins, 1994; Murphy & Cleveland, 1995). Moreover, workers do not have equal opportunity to perform, nor is everything that people do whilst at work necessarily task-related (Murphy, 1989). There also are the points that an over-concentration on outputs ignores important processual and interpersonal factors, and undue focus on outputs may misdirect employees as to what is required.

Thus, we have two different views of performance: results/outputs and behaviours. Defining performance as both, particularly at the same time, would seem to be unhelpful. One of the reasons for this is that to do so confounds the relationship between behaviours and outputs. Typically (e.g. Cardy & Dobbins, 1994; Waldman, 1994), behaviour is regarded as one of the *causes* of output, with output being one of the means by which the *effectiveness* of performance (that is, behaviour) may be judged. In other words we make judgements about the effectiveness of employees with reference to what they accomplish—the results they achieve, the output they produce. An illustration of this is provided by Campbell et al. (1993): "*Effectiveness* refers to the evaluation of the results of performance." And Ilgen and Schneider (1991) write in similar terms: "Performance is what the person or system does. Performance measurement is the quantification of what was done, and performance evaluation is the attachment of a judgement of the value or quality of the quantified performance measurement." All three are, of course, needed in performance management: the necessary first step is the expression of performance requirements.

In everyday practice, however, the term performance tends to be used in a loose way to embrace both outputs and behaviour. This may be a convenient shorthand; but from a practical point of view it is likely to be more useful to be precise about what is meant. Managing performance as outputs may require different interventions from the management of performance as behaviours. For example, the production of output may well involve many factors beyond the individual's control, such as the design of the work system.

PERFORMANCE IS BEHAVIOUR, BUT IS ALL BEHAVIOUR PERFORMANCE?

What is implied in these behavioural views (and in some cases is explicit) is the idea that, whilst performance is behaviour, not all behaviour is performance— only behaviour that is goal-relevant counts as performance. However, some writers have drawn a distinction between the aspects of jobs that are formally required and expected and those expectations which arise, perhaps as part of the *psychological contract*, in a more informal way. Thus, Borman and Motowidlo (1993) distinguish between *task performance* (i.e. activities that contribute to the technical core of the organization, e.g. selling policies in an insurance company) and *contextual performance* (which supports the broader social/psychological environment of the organization). Some examples of what they mean by the latter are given in Table 6.3.

Table 6.3 Examples of contextual performance and organizational spontaneity

---

Contextual performance
Borman & Motowidlo (1993)
- Volunteering to carry out task activities that are not formally a part of the job.
- Persisting with extra enthusiasm or effort when necessary to complete own task activities successfully
- Helping and co-operating with others
- Following organizational rules and procedures even when personally inconvenient
- Endorsing, supporting, and defending organizational objectives

Organizational spontaneity
George & Brief (1992)
- Helping co-workers
- Protecting the organization
- Making constructive suggestions
- Developing oneself
- Spreading goodwill

This class of behaviours has also been referred to as *organizational citizenship behaviour* (e.g. Bateman & Organ, 1983), *prosocial organizational behaviour* (Brief & Motowidlo, 1986), *organizational spontaneity* (George & Brief, 1992), or *extra-role behaviours* (Van Dyne et al., 1995). As Murphy (1999) notes, these terms are not interchangeable and the last is broader in scope than the others. However, there are elements of similarity as illustrated by the examples of organizational spontaneity. (See Motowidlo and Schmit (1999) for a fuller explication of points of similarity).

What is important to recognize about contextual performance is that, though these behaviours are to the benefit of the organization, they are not always a formal part of the job and to that extent they are much more heavily volitional or discretionary than are formally prescribed behaviours (Van Dyne et al., 1995). Of course, we might hope that all employees would help and co-operate with others, endorse the organization's objectives, and so on, but the point being made here is that these sorts of behaviours are not normally expressed as a formal job requirement. That said, the shift in emphasis towards quality and customer-orientated service may mean that for many jobs such behaviours are more explicitly expected these days (Bowen & Waldman, 1999; Waldman, 1994). Indeed, some North American research (MacKenzie et al., 1991, 1993) indicates that managers of sales personnel attach great weight to organizational citizenship behaviours (OCBs) when making performance evaluations. They examined such OCBs as altruism (voluntarily helping others), civic virtue (e.g. attending meetings that aren't formally required as part of the job) and conscientiousness, and concluded that "a salesperson's overall performance evaluation was determined more by his or her citizenship behaviour—including altruistic acts . . . and conscientiousness—than by his or her actual sales success". Motowidlo and Schmit (1999) note other studies showing that contextual performance influences supervisor ratings of overall performance and some studies show an association between contextual performance and indicators of organizational effectiveness.

This discussion of extra-role behaviours indicates one of the difficulties with the performance-as-behaviour view, namely mapping the behavioural domain. One attempt to do this has been made by Campbell (Campbell, 1990; Campbell et al., 1993, 1996) in his theory of performance. He presents a factor model of the components of performance and speculates that job performance can be described in terms of eight general factors, as shown in Table 6.4, with each factor containing a number of sub-factors.

Table 6.4   A taxonomy of major performance components

1. *Job-specific task proficiency.*   The first factor reflects the degree to which the individual can perform the core substantive or technical tasks that are central to the job. They are the job-specific performance behaviours that distinguish the substantive content of one job from another. . . .
2. *Non-job-specific task proficiency.*   This factor reflects the situation that in virtually every organization, but perhaps not all, individuals are required to perform tasks or execute performance behaviours that are not specific to their particular job. . . .
3. *Written and oral communication task proficiency.*   Many jobs in the workforce require the individual to make formal oral or written presentations to audiences that may vary from one to tens of thousands. For those jobs the proficiency with which one can write or speak, independent of the correctness of the subject matter, is a critical component of performance.
4. *Demonstrating effort.*   The fourth factor is meant to be a direct reflection of the consistency of an individual's effort day by day, the frequency with which people will expend extra effort when required, and the willingness to keep working under adverse conditions. It is a reflection of the degree to which individuals commit themselves to all job tasks, work at a high level of intensity, and keep working when it is cold, wet, or late.
5. *Maintaining personal discipline.*   The fifth component is characterized by the degree to which negative behaviour such as alcohol and substance abuse at work, law or rules infractions, and excessive absenteeism are avoided.
6. *Facilitating peer and team performance.*   Factor six is defined as the degree to which the individual supports his or her peers, helps them with job problems, and acts as a de facto trainer. It also encompasses how well an individual facilitates group functioning by being a good model, keeping the group goal-directed, and reinforcing participation by other group members. . . .
7. *Supervision/leadership.*   Proficiency in the supervisory component includes all the behaviours directed at influencing the performance of subordinates through face-to-face interpersonal interaction and influence. Supervisors set goals for subordinates, they teach them more effective methods, they model the appropriate behaviours, and they reward or punish in appropriate ways. The distinction between this factor and the previous one is a distinction between peer leadership and supervisory leadership. Although modeling, goal setting, coaching, and providing reinforcement are elements in both factors, the belief here is that peer versus supervisor leadership implies significantly different determinants.
8. *Management/administration.*   The eighth and last factor is intended to include the major elements in management that are distinct from direct supervision. It includes the performance behaviours directed at articulating goals for the unit or enterprise, organizing people and resources to work on them, monitoring progress, helping to solve problems or overcome crises that stand in the way of goal accomplishment, controlling expenditures, obtaining additional resources, and representing the unit in dealing with other units.

Source: Campbell et al. (1993).

Campbell argues that "three of the factors—core task proficiency, demonstrated effort, and maintenance of personal discipline—are major performance components of *every* job", although the others vary in the extent to which they apply to different jobs. The model remains speculative because, as yet, specific empirical tests are rare. However, Campbell suggests that other behavioural models can be accommodated within this framework—forms of organizational spontaneity and OCBs fit within various of the factors, for example (although they would, of course, cease to be voluntary behaviours if formally required). Also, much of the research on job behaviour can be related to the model.

ANTECEDENTS AND DETERMINANTS

So, we can see this model as a step forward in helping to map the behavioural domain of performance. Campbell's model represents a step forward in another respect, also; that is, in trying to set out a fuller understanding of the determinants of performance.

Early ideas about performance presented it as some function of a person's ability and their motivation. Campbell has considerably expanded this basic proposition. Each factor of performance is seen as a function of three determinants:

- declarative knowledge—knowledge of facts and things (what)
- procedural knowledge and skill—knowing how to
- motivation—in line with contemporary thinking this is seen as *choice behaviour*:
  (1) choice to expend effort
  (2) choice of level of effort to expend
  (3) choice to persist in the expenditure of that level of effort.

So, what is being proposed here is that the *direct* cause of what people do (their performance) is some function of knowledge, skill and motivation. The precise combination is unknown as the effects of personal factors are difficult to disentangle (Viswesvaran & Ones, 2000). Now this is rather different from much traditional thinking which has seen individual difference variables—intelligence, personality—as direct causes of behaviour. Campbell sees these as one class of *antecedents*; that is, they underlie knowledge and skill.

In passing, let us briefly note that this language is very reminiscent of at least some of the language of *competencies*, particularly the conceptualization that we associate with the McBer consultancy firm:

> Competencies can be motives, traits, self-concepts, attitudes or values, content knowledge, or cognitive or behavioural skills—any individual characteristic that can be measured or counted reliably and that can be shown to differentiate significantly between superior and average performers, or between effective and ineffective performers.
> (Hooghiemstra, 1992)

Woodruffe (1991) objects to the McBer definition on the grounds that it "seems to cover pretty well anything...". Indeed so, and mixing up traits, attitudes, thought processes, and behaviours would seem to be unhelpful, but it is in keeping with the Warr and Conner (1992) interpretation of competencies as "syndromes" or "important combinations" of characteristics. None the less, Woodruffe (1992) prefers a behavioural definition: " . . . a dimension of overt, manifest behaviour that allows a person to perform competently". All this is very confusing, and at the very least there is conceptual overlap in this area, perhaps even some conceptual redundancy, the status of competencies being particularly uncertain (Sparrow, 1994, 1996).

Other classes of antecedent include the individual's prior learning experience (e.g. their education, the training they have received) and aspects of the work context. Though Campbell is relatively silent on the nature and impact of work contextual factors, their importance has been explored by other writers. As one might expect the early models which sought to incorporate situational/contextual factors were somewhat rudimentary. Blumberg and Pringle (1982), for example, recognized the importance of ability and motivation (although rather broadened their scope by using the terms *capacity to perform* and *willingness to perform*) but added *opportunity to perform* as a third determinant. They gave as examples of opportunity factors: "tools, equipment, materials, and supplies; working conditions; actions of co-workers; leader behaviour; mentorism; organizational policies, rules, and procedures; information; time; pay". They saw such factors as either *enabling* or *constraining*. In similar vein, Guzzo and Gannett (1988) write of facilitators (driving performance towards the maximally attainable level) and inhibitors (restricting performance towards the minimally acceptable level).

Other behavioural scientists (e.g. Cardy & Dobbins, 1994; Waldman, 1994) have drawn on total quality management (TQM) ideas and have presented models of employee work performance which incorporate person and situational factors. The Cardy–Dobbins model is of particular interest because it seeks to incorporate both the output view of performance as well as the behavioural one. However, it does not capture interactions amongst the various determinants; these are better brought out by Waldman who takes a behavioural view of performance and draws on total quality management ideas (see also Bowen & Waldman, 1999).

Taking all of these ideas together enables a fuller model of performance. It recognizes that both output and behaviour are important, but that they have different determinants, as illustrated in Figure 6.1.

Person Factors

Though Cardy and Dobbins see person factors as having a direct effect on job-relevant behaviours, Campbell, as indicated above, takes a two-tier approach to the treatment of person factors—knowledge, skill and motivation are seen as the direct determinants of job-relevant behaviour, and other characteristics of the person (such as personality traits) are seen as underlying antecedents of those determinants. The importance of personal factors for performance management lies in the fact that they are what employees bring to the job and they may be capable of being enhanced or inhibited.

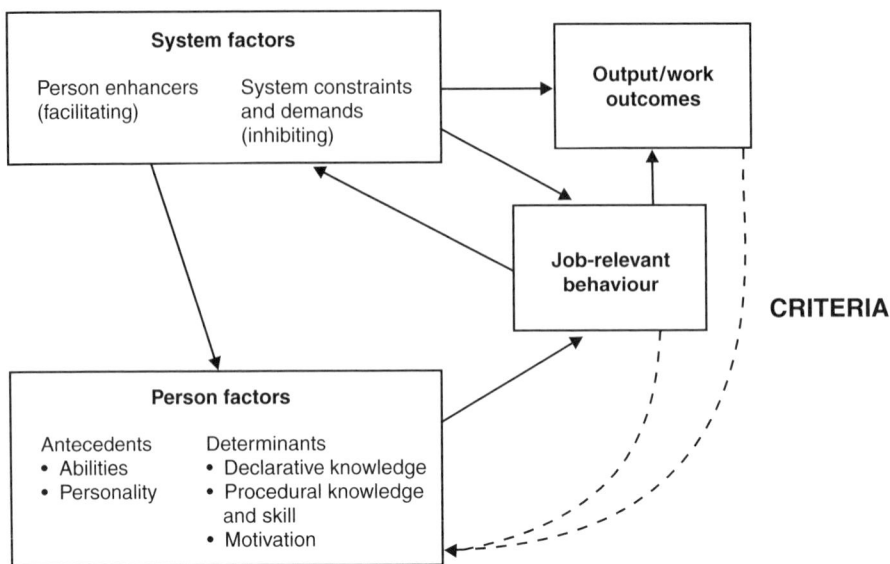

Figure 6.1 Determinants of job performance: person and system factors. Reproduced by permission from R.S. Williams (2002). Managing Employee Performance: Design and Implementation in Organisations. London: Thomson Learning

System Factors

What are system factors? Waldman (1994) takes a broad view, regarding them as existing at "multiple levels within an organization"—system-wide, department, work unit, team, etc. But as with the performance construct, mapping the domain or boundaries of system factors remains a difficulty. Schneider and Hough (1995) note this difficulty in offering what they refer to as an "heuristic catalogue" of situational factors, which they do not claim to be comprehensive, but which clearly illustrates that the domain of system factors is very broad. An abbreviated version of their list (showing only extra-individual factors) is given in Table 6.5.

What influence do system factors have? Though some research (e.g. Peters O'Connor, 1980) has focused on the constraining effect that system factors may have, the prevailing view today (e.g. Guzzo & Gannett, 1988; Waldman, 1994) recognizes that there may be either facilitating/enhancing/enabling effects or inhibiting ones. Thus, following Waldman the category "system factors" includes *person enhancers* and *system constraints and demands*.

Constraining and Inhibiting Factors

Under this heading we have "characteristics of technological and work processes, as well as organizational policies, structure, and culture" (Waldman, 1994). More specific examples of factors identified as constraints would include those investigated by Peters and O'Connor (1980) for example, such as tools and equipment, time availability, and the work environment. Evidence pertaining

Table 6.5   Potential situational (or system) factors

Task characteristics
- Consistency of task
- Stage of skill acquisition with respect to task
- Amount of task structure
- Time on task
- Amount of time pressure to complete task
- Skill variety, task identity, task significance, autonomy, and feedback

Goal characteristics
- Specificity
- Complexity
- Difficulty
- Rewards associated with goal attainment
- Conflict with other goals
- Performance versus mastery goal

Characteristics of physical environment
- Ambient conditions (e.g. light, noise, heat)
- Time of day
- Danger of bodily harm
- Workplace layout (e.g. open plan office versus non-open plan office; amount of privacy at workstation)
- Work locus (home versus office)

Characteristics of work role
- Role ambiguity
- Role overload
- Role conflict

Characteristics of social environment
- Personality of co-workers (supervisors, subordinates, and peers)
- Management style of immediate supervisor (e.g. autocratic versus democratic)
- Cohesiveness of work group
- Amount of social support from co-workers, friends and family
- Work primarily in groups versus work primarily independently

Characteristics of organization
- Organizational values
- Organizational reward systems
- Level of employee ownership in organization
- Amount of organizational instability (e.g. rapid changes in leadership; downsizing; growth)
- Nature of administrative policies and procedures (e.g. level of bureaucracy)
- Organizational structure (e.g. matrix versus hierarchical)

---

to certain of the last of these has been reviewed by Baron (1994). Many of the findings are unsurprising. For example, conditions that are too noisy, too hot or too cold have been shown to have deleterious effects; level of illumination, air quality, crowding are illustrations of other such environmental factors.

Baron sees these factors as having an indirect effect on performance (and other outcomes, such as work attitudes). Environmental factors are presented as having their impact "on a wide range of mediating mechanisms and processes occurring within individuals". Summarizing Kane (1993), Bacharach and

Bamberger (1995) note that "constraints may have a negative impact on the performance of particular job functions by making it more difficult for individuals to take maximum advantage of their job-related knowledge, skills and abilities, and by reducing their overall level of task effort".

The idea that aspects of the situation may have a constraining effect on aspects of the person is far from new. Mischel (1977), for example, argued that "strong" situations have a constraining effect in that they inhibit the expression of individual differences—in other words, in "strong" situations people tend to behave in a similar way regardless of their different personalities, or a particular individual will behave in a required way because the situation demands it rather than because it is his or her "natural" predisposition. More recently, Adler (1996) has taken up this theme in his exploration of the linkages amongst personality and work behaviour.

Facilitating and Enhancing Factors

Waldman (1994) refers to certain system factors as "person enhancers" which "affect performance indirectly by first influencing aspects of the individual. . . . Person enhancers are proposed to involve aspects of HR systems, leadership processes, and job design that may develop and motivate individuals." Campbell and his colleagues take a similar view and regard system factors as antecedents which have an indirect effect on performance (behaviour) by first changing the employee's declarative knowledge, procedural knowledge and skill, and/or motivation. In other words, person enhancers may have multiple effects—that is, they simultaneously affect several person factors. For example, goals, goal-setting and feedback have motivational and informational (that is, knowledge-related) effects.

Direct or Indirect Effects

Thus far system factors have been presented as having indirect effects on work behaviour; that is, person factors are seen as mediators—constraints and facilitators alike are seen as operating in this way. However, the way in which constraints operate remains a matter of some debate. On the one hand, Campbell and colleagues take the view that constraints have an indirect effect on work behaviour—they influence motivation first. Against this Guzzo and Gannett contend that inhibitors may also have direct effects: "Barriers to performance such as shortages of tools and too little time can make it physically impossible to complete tasks effectively." So, individuals may have both the motivation and the requisite knowledge and skill, but are constrained by some aspect of the work system from doing what is expected of them—as when rain stops play, for example.

When we turn to the work-system perspective on performance we also find the argument that system factors may have a more direct effect. Thus, as noted earlier, we find claims (in particular in certain of the early quality management literature) that system factors account for as much as 95% of the variation in work output. Yet, as various commentators (e.g. Cardy, 1998; Masterson & Taylor, 1996) note, there is little hard evidence to support these claims; rather, they are more of an assumption than an established fact (Cardy & Dobbins, 1994). Though we might wish to dispute how much of work output is attributable to system factors as compared to employees' behaviour, there is no doubting the direct effect of the former, and Hesketh & Neal (1999) recently have argued that technology (broadly defined) "can be both a determinant and an antecedent of performance". For example, the quality of output produced by tool-makers will partly be a function of the machine in use, not just the facility with which it is operated by the worker. And in sales jobs the number of units sold will be subject to the influence of buyer behaviour, the price and other attributes of what is being sold, etc. All this, of course, merely echoes the arguments put forward earlier for not regarding output as performance.

Distinct Entities or Opposites

Another matter of some dispute is whether facilitators and inhibitors should be regarded as distinct entities or as opposites. If we take the "opposites" perspective, a deficit in a system factor would be seen as a constraint whereas sufficient presence of the same factor would be taken as facilitating. Guzzo and Gannett (1988) prefer the "distinct entities" perspective. So, for example, the absence of needed tools is likely to be a constraint, restricting performance towards the minimally acceptable level. But having the required tools doesn't guarantee maximum performance—this still is dependent on the worker's knowledge, skill and motivation. Facilitators, on the other hand, are those situational factors which enhance performance.

But this issue is far from resolved. Surely it is possible for certain system factors, albeit manifested in different ways, to have both facilitating and constraining effects? Job design and supervisory behaviour are two illustrations. Though there are supervisory behaviours which are supportive and performance enhancing in their effect, there are other behaviours which may be damaging in their effect; for example, negative feedback. Thus, the distinction between enhancing and constraining factors may not be so clear-cut as is sometimes presented. Moreover, the impact of system factors on person factors (and vice versa) is further complicated by interactions amongst them.

PERSON–SYSTEM INTERACTION

Earlier we considered how system factors impinge upon aspects of the person and so affect his or her performance. However, not only can the system affect the person, but the person can affect the system. This partly is a matter of perception. For example, though system factors sometimes are seen as constraints (whether direct or indirect in their effect) it is possible, suggest Guzzo and Gannett, for them to be seen as "a challenge", that is as "an obstacle to be overcome". This, then, points to the element of choice which may be found within jobs. Stewart (e.g. 1991) draws attention to this in the context of managerial jobs (and certain others) in her identification of demands, constraints and choices: " . . . there is a core of work, *demands*, that anyone in the job will have to do; these demands are the tasks that cannot be ignored or delegated if the job holder is to survive in the job". Constraints " . . . are the factors that limit what the job holder can do: they include resource limitations and people's attitudes". Choices are the areas of opportunity within a job—what the manager decides she or he will do.

To some extent all three aspects of managerial jobs are partly a matter of perception—managers need to perceive themselves as having choice over what they do. In the same vein, Stewart refers to job holders "exaggerating the work that they must do" (demands) and "exaggerating the constraints", both of which may be forms of impression management (Rosenfeld et al., 1995). But the scope for the individual performer to influence their job varies also according to its design, in particular to the extent of autonomy allowed. Waldman (1994) sees this, and hierarchical level, as factors moderating the relationship between person and system factors. Thus, managerial jobs, for example are likely to offer greater scope for the incumbent to decide how to go about the job and, quite possibly, for deciding what the job is.

Moreover, those at the higher levels are able not only to influence the nature of their own jobs but also the design of other jobs within the work system. Though system factors may have a direct impact on the behaviour and output of those working within the system, the system itself is a product of managerial choices and decisions. It is for this reason that Deming (1986) and other authorities in the quality management field see managers as having the responsibility for improving work systems so as to remove performance problems. This seems to be an implicit recognition of the importance of person factors over system factors, at least for certain jobs.

In view of the reciprocal relationship between system and person factors we might suppose that the "person factors" and "system factors" boxes in Figure 6.1 ought to be connected. Though system factors have a direct impact on person factors, the effect of the latter on the former is indirect in that it operates through behaviour.

The idea of reciprocal and interacting influences is a theme which is found widely in the literature (e.g. Schneider, 1987; Davis-Blake & Pfeffer, 1989; Chatman, 1989; Edwards, 1991). Over and above the examples already mentioned, Kanfer (1995) notes:

> . . . motivation and performance exert reciprocal influences on one another. Not only does motivation affect performance, but performance can affect motivation. Knowledge of how one has performed or is progressing on a task may weaken or strengthen subsequent task motivation depending on performance level, attributions about the cause of performance, and motivational conditions.

Kanfer here is referring to the place of feedback in employee performance. Though this is a system factor, Figure 6.1 includes feedback loops leading from outcomes and behaviours to person factors so as to make more explicit the importance of feedback.

PERSON *AND* SYSTEM

There is no doubt that both person *and* system factors influence work behaviours and outputs. What is far from clear is how much of the variation in performance (whether defined as outputs or job-behaviours) is attributable to the one set or the other. If we subscribe to Deming's (1986) thinking our position would be that most workers (certainly those on the shop floor, that is the direct producers or service deliverers) within an organization function or operate at about the same level and that variation in what they produce is accounted for mostly by system factors that are outside the individual's control. However, this has not been confirmed empirically (Cardy & Dobbins, 1994). Moreover, some (e.g. Stone & Eddy, 1996) have argued that system accounts of performance have under-estimated the importance of person factors, almost (others have argued—e.g. Masterson & Taylor, 1996) to the point of ignoring the role of the individual. But, employees are not passive within the work system—they react (positively or negatively) to the ways in which they are treated.

Very often many system factors will be seen as fixed (and may in reality be so) and outside the control of the individual performer or his or her line manager, and as such they may be regarded as being outside the boundaries of a performance management system. For example, once a work system has been designed it may well be difficult to change and in consequence it may have to be taken as given. Equipment may be difficult to replace or modify. And there invariably are resource limitations of one sort or another. However, the only point being made here is that these sorts of factors may have a very direct impact on performance. But how much is not clear. What seems most likely is that the extent of variation attributable to system/person factors varies from job to job (Cardy & Dobbins, 1994). Key factors here would seem to be hierarchical level and the amount of autonomy that is allowed by the job (Waldman, 1994). At higher levels and in jobs offering greater autonomy personal factors may actually be more important than aspects of the system.

THE IMPACT OF PERFORMANCE MANAGEMENT INTERVENTIONS

One implication of the model outlined above is that performance management interventions need to be focused not just on the worker but on the work system/context also. However, as we noted earlier, performance management more commonly is seen as person-centred: though we will reflect this here in our consideration of work-psychology based interventions, we will pay some attention to those concerned with the work system more broadly.

As a starting point, of particular interest is the meta-analytic work of Guzzo and his colleagues (Katzell & Guzzo, 1983; Guzzo et al., 1985; Guzzo, 1988). This examined the impact of various work-psychology based interventions on performance (variously defined, although they actually used the term *productivity*), and identified the following as generally having positive effects: training, socio-technical interventions, goal setting, work redesign, supervisory methods, and appraisal and feedback. Certain of those listed—particularly goal setting and feedback—remain very much at the heart of employee-centred approached to performance management, and these have been the subject of more recent meta-analyses and other reviews.

Goal-setting is much advocated in the literature, particularly that which is practice orientated (e.g. Ainsworth & Smith, 1993; Armstrong, 1994, 1995; Costello, 1994; LGMB, 1993; Lockett, 1992; Moores, 1994), and it has a strong theoretical underpinning. What typically is proposed is a cascading process, very reminiscent of management by objectives (MbO) and this cascading process commonly is seen as the means by which individual goals and objectives are aligned with organizational goals. Lower level goals, according to the theory of performance management, ought to be consistent with those set at the top—Rummler & Brache (1995) refer to this as a "performance logic"—but such goal consistency cannot be assumed. In setting goals members of departments, work teams, and so on may set goals consistent with their interests as they see them. To the extent that consistency between individual and higher level goals is not achieved, then the goal setting process may be sub-optimal in contributing to organizational effectiveness.

Ensuring consistency of goals thus becomes one of the main challenges for performance management systems—a participative and involving approach may help to bring this about. Rodgers and Hunter (1991), for example, make out the case for participation in their meta-analytic review of management by objectives (MbO). In their view, both theory and research evidence support the positive productivity effects of MbO's three components (participation, goal-setting, and feedback).

Though a role for employee participation has been much advocated in the performance management literature, the evidence for its performance enhancing effects is a matter of some debate. An important meta-analytic review by Wagner (1994) concluded that participation does have positive effects on performance (and satisfaction) but concluded that the magnitude of these effects was so slight as to be of limited practical significance. However, Ledford and Lawler (1994) noted the narrowness of Wagner's definition of participation and argued that negligible positive effects were an inevitable consequence: "Limited participation has limited effects." Elsewhere, Lawler (e.g. 1991) has advocated a broader conceptualization of participation as "high involvement"—essentially an organization-wide strategy.

So far as goals are concerned, one of the most robust of research findings in the behavioural sciences is that goal-setting has a beneficial effect on employees' work performance (Locke & Latham, 1990). Positive findings have been reported from real-life studies in the workplace and from experimental studies in the laboratory. Studies have been carried out on a range of jobs and into quality as well as quantity goals. The main findings of the research are that:

- Difficult, challenging goals lead to higher performance than do easy goals, *provided that* the job holder accepts and is committed to the goals. In simple terms, the harder the goal, the higher the performance (given goal acceptance).

• Specific goals lead to higher performance than do vague, general 'do your best goals' or than no goals at all.

However, this is not to say that goal-setting is some kind of panacea. As Mitchell et al. (2000) recently have noted, goals "work better on simple tasks and after a task is well learned". Also, goal-setting does not necessarily work alone: as well as goal commitment (particularly important for difficult goals), there must be feedback for goals to have their positive effects (Locke & Latham, 1990).

The thorough meta-analytic review of feedback interventions by Kluger and DeNisi (1996) supported the linkage as between goals and feedback. More generally, they found that feedback does improve performance but they also found considerable variation to the extent that reduced performance may also result. The earlier quote from Kanfer (1995) referred to the possibly deleterious effects of feedback—in other words, feedback may be constructive or destructive (Baron, 1988; London, 1995, 1997), a facilitator or an inhibitor.

However, the provision of feedback has taken a considerable leap forward in the form of the increasingly-used multi-source, multi-level feedback systems (often called 360-degree feedback in its broadest form). These have been mainly used for developmental purposes but a growing number of organizations are linking them to performance management through appraisal. To some extent, the research on the impact of 360-degree feedback echoes Kluger and DeNisi's wider consideration of feedback processes, in that it shows somewhat mixed results. Initially, the focus of research on such systems was on changes in ratings over successive feedback episodes; i.e. do managers improve where they need to as indicated by feedback, so attracting more positive ratings on subsequent occasions, and do they show greater self awareness as indicated by increased congruence between self and other ratings? Atwater et al. (1995) did find that ratings of managers improved over successive feedback episodes, and both they and others (London & Wohlers, 1991; Hazucha et al., 1993; Smither et al., 1995; Walker & Smither, 1999) report greater correlation of self ratings with colleagues' ratings over time. However, demonstrating that ratings become more positive over time does not prove that performance has improved; better ratings could stem from a number of other sources, including impression management (London & Smither, 1995; Fletcher & Baldry, 1999). There is very little research published so far linking use of multi-source feedback to performance improvements. Bernadin et al. (1995a) report no change in volume of store sales following use of feedback with 48 managerial staff in a retail organization, and no change in ratings from customers. Baldry and Fletcher (2000) report a mixed pattern of relationships between feedback and subsequent performance appraisal assessments, with significant correlations observed between self (0.25) and boss (0.50) feedback process ratings and appraisal ratings.

In similar vein, the effects of financial rewards (performance-related pay is a key element in performance management in many organizations) are not uniformly positive. This was noted in the meta-analytic review by Guzzo et al. (1985): of all the work-psychology based interventions they examined this was the one where they found the greatest variability in effects. And in a later review Heneman (1992) concludes: "The results to date on the relationship between merit pay and subsequent motivation and performance are not encouraging." This may be because particular systems that have been implemented may have been poorly designed and operated in practice. However, it may be that performance-related pay (PRP) fails because it does not meet the requirements that psychological theory (e.g. expectancy theory) suggests—in other words, at least some applications of PRP will have been doomed from the outset.

Even at its most basic, performance management is not a single intervention. However, we know relatively little about the impact of interventions in combination. According to Guzzo and Gannett (1988) there is at least suggestive evidence that the use of multiple interventions has positive impact over and above those achieved by single interventions. For example, embedding a mechanism such as performance appraisal in a wider approach to selection and development makes it more effective and less of an annual ritual that appears to exist in a vacuum. The research evidence shows that such integrated HR and performance management policies do make an impact on employee attitudes and organizational commitment (Caldwell et al., 1990; Kinicki et al., 1992; Fletcher & Williams, 1996), which in turn can impact organizational performance (Ostroff, 1992; Patterson et al., 1998).

It remains the case that there is little research on the effect of multiple interventions, although the recent human resource management literature on "high performance" employment systems is of some relevance here. The first point we should note about this literature is that there are somewhat different views as to what constitute "high performance" practices. For example, Becker and Gerhart (1996) note that there is disagreement about variable pay and internal promotions. That said, this growing body of literature does indicate that there is a positive association between a range of human resource management practices and various measures (objective and perceptual) of organizational performance (e.g. Becker & Gerhart, 1996; Delaney & Huselid, 1996). Such findings are encouraging but they bring with them the implication that performance management should be seen more in the broad terms set out earlier rather than as a narrow set of interventions focused on the individual.

REFERENCES

Adler, S. (1996). Personality and work behaviour: exploring the linkages. *Applied Psychology*, **45** (3), 207–224.

Ainsworth, M. & Smith, N. (1993). *Making It Happen: Managing Performance at Work.* Sydney: Prentice Hall.

Armstrong, M. (1994). *Performance Management*. London: Kogan Page.

Armstrong, M. (1995). *A Handbook of Personnel Management Practice*, 5th edn. London: Kogan Page.

Atwater, L., Roush, P. & Fischthal, A. (1995). The influence of upward feedback on self-ratings and follower ratings of leadership. *Personnel Psychology*, **48**, 1, 35–59.

Bacharach, S.B. & Bamberger, P. (1995). Beyond situational constraints: job resources inadequacy and individual performance at work. *Human Resource Management Review*, **5** (2), 79–102.

Baldry, C. & Fletcher, C. (2000). The impact of multiple source feedback on management development: findings from a longitudinal study. *Proceedings of the British Psychological Society Occupational Psychology Conference, Brighton*, pp. 104–108. Leicester: British Psychological Society.

Baron, R.A. (1988). Negative effects of destructive criticism: impact on conflict, self-efficacy, and task performance. *Journal of Applied Psychology*, **73**, 199–207.

Baron, R.A. (1994). The physical environment of work settings. *Research in Organizational Behaviour*, **16**, 1–46.

Bateman, T.S. & Organ, D.W. (1983). Job satisfaction and the good soldier: the relationship between affect and employee "citizenship". *Academy of Management Journal*, **26**, 587–595.

Becker, B. & Gerhart, B. (1996). The impact of human resource management on organizational performance: progress and prospects. *Academy of Management Journal*, **39**, 779–801.

Bernardin, H.J., Hagan, C. & Kane, J.S. (1995a). The effects of a 360-degree appraisal system on managerial performance: no matter how cynical I get I can't keep up. In W.W. Tornow (Chair), *Upward Feedback. The Ups and Downs of It*. Syposium conducted at the Tenth Annual Conference of the Society for Industrial and Organizational Psychology, Orlando, FL.

Bernardin, H.J., Kane, J.S., Ross, S., Spina, J.D. & Johnson, D.L. (1995b). Performance appraisal design, development, and implementation. In G.R. Ferris, S.D. Rosen & D.T. Barnum (Eds), *Handbook of Human Resource Management*. Cambridge, MA: Blackwell.

Bevan, S. & Thompson, M. (1991). Performance management at the crossroads. *Personnel Management*, November, 36–39.

Blumberg, M. & Pringle, C.C. (1982). The missing opportunity in organizational research: some implications for a theory of work performance. *Academy of Management Review*, **7**, 560–569.

Borman, W.C. & Motowidlo, S.J. (1993). Expanding the criterion domain to include elements of contextual performance. In N. Schmitt, W.C. Borman & Associates (Eds), *Personnel Selection in Organizations*. San Francisco: Jossey-Bass.

Bowen, D.E. & Waldman, D.A. (1999). Customer-driven employee performance. In D.R. Ilgen & E.D. Pulakos (Eds), *The Changing Nature of Performance*. San Francisco: Jossey-Bass.

Brief, A.P. & Motowidlo, S.J. (1986). Prosocial organizational behaviour. *Academy of Management Review*, **11**, 710–725.

Caldwell, D.F., Chatman, J.A. & O'Reilly, C.A. (1990). Building organizational commitment: a multifirm study. *Journal of Occupational Psychology*, **63**, 245–261.

Campbell, J.P. (1990). Modeling the performance prediction problem in industrial and organizational psychology. In M.D. Dunnette & L.M. Hough (Eds), *Handbook of Industrial and Organizational Psychology*. Palo Alto, CA: Consulting Psychologists Press.

Campbell, J.P., McCloy, R.A., Oppler, S.H. & Sager, C.E. (1993). A theory of performance. In N. Schmitt, W.C. Borman and Associates (Eds), *Personnel Selection in Organizations*. San Francisco: Jossey-Bass.

Campbell, J.P., Gasser, M.B. & Oswald, F.L. (1996). The substantive nature of job performance variability. In K. Murphy (Ed.), *Individual Differences and Behaviour in Organizations*. San Francisco: Jossey-Bass.

Cardy, R.L. (1998). Performance appraisal in a quality context: a new look at an old problem. In J.W. Smither (Ed.), *Performance Appraisal: State of the Art in Practice*. San Francisco: Jossey-Bass.

Cardy, R.L. & Dobbins, G.H. (1994). *Performance Appraisal: Alternative Perspectives*. Cincinnati: South-Western.

Chatman, J.A. (1989). Improving interactional organizational research: a model of person–organization fit. *Academy of Management Review*, **14** (3), 333–349.

Costello, S.J. (1994). *Effective Performance Management*. New York: Irwin.

Davis-Blake, A. & Pfeffer, J. (1989). Just a mirage: the search for dispositional effects in organizational research. *Academy of Management Review*, **14** (3), 385–400.

Delaney, J.T. & Huselid, M.A. (1996). The impact of human resource management practices on perceptions of organizational performance. *Academy of Management Journal*, **39**, 949–969.

Deming, W.E. (1986). *Out of the Crisis*. Cambridge, MA: MIT Press.

Edwards, J.R. (1991). Person-job fit: a conceptual integration, literature review, and methodological critique. In C.L. Cooper & I.T. Robertson (Eds), *International Review of Industrial and Organizational Psychology*, Vol. **6**. Chichester: John Wiley.

Fletcher, C. (1993). *Appraisal: Routes to Improved Performance*. London: Institute of Personnel Management.

Fletcher, C. (1994). Performance appraisal in context: organizational changes and their impact on practice. In N. Anderson & P. Herriot (Eds), *Assessment and Selection in Organizations*. Chichester: John Wiley.

Fletcher, C. & Williams, R. (1996). Performance management, job satisfaction and organisational commitment. *British Journal of Management*, **7**, 169–179.

Fletcher, C. & Baldry, C. (1999). Multi-source feedback systems: a research perspective. In C.L. Cooper. & I.T. Robertson (Eds), *International Review of Organizational and Industrial Psychology*, Vol. **14**. Chichester: John Wiley.

George, J.M. & Brief, A.P. (1992). Feeling good—doing good: a conceptual analysis of the mood at work/organizational spontaneity relationship. *Psychological Bulletin*, **112**, 310–329.

Guzzo, R.A. (1988). Productivity research: reviewing psychological and economic perspectives. In J.P. Campbell, R.J. Campbell & Associates (Eds), *Productivity in Organizations*. San Francisco: Jossey-Bass.

Guzzo, R.A. & Gannett, B.A. (1988). The nature of facilitators and inhibitors of effective task performance. In F.D. Schoorman and B. Schneider (Eds), *Facilitating Work Effectiveness*. Lexington, MA: Lexington Books.

Guzzo, R.E., Jette, R.D. & Katzell, R.A. (1985). The effects of psychologically based intervention programmes on worker productivity: a meta-analysis. *Personnel Psychology*, **38**, 275–291.

Hazucha, J.F., Hezlett, S.A. & Schneider, R.J. (1993). The impact of 360-degree feedback on management skills development. *Human Resource Management*, **32**, 325–351.

Heisler, W.J., Jones, W.D. & Benham, P.O. (1988). *Managing Human Resources Issues*. San Francisco: Jossey-Bass.

Heneman, R.L. (1992). *Merit Pay: Linking Pay Increases to Performance Ratings*. Reading, MA: Addison-Wesley.

Hesketh, B. & Neal, A. (1999). Technology and performance. In D.R. Ilgen & E.D. Pulakos (Eds), *The Changing Nature of Performance*. San Francisco: Jossey-Bass.

Hooghiemstra, T. (1992). Integrated management of human resources. In A. Mitrani, M. Dalziel & D. Fitt (Eds), *Competency Based Human Resource Management*. London: Kogan Page.

Ilgen, D.R. & Schneider, J. (1991). Performance measurement: a multi-discipline view. In C.L. Cooper & I.T. Robertson (Eds), *International Review of Industrial and Organizational Psychology*. Chichester: John Wiley.

Kane, K. (1993). Situational constraints and performance: an overview. *Human Resource Management Review*, **3** (2), 83–103.

Kanfer, R. (1995). Motivation and performance. In N. Nicholson (Ed.), *Blackwell Encyclopedic Dictionary of Organizational Behaviour*. Oxford: Blackwell.

Katzell, R.A. & Guzzo, R.A. (1983). Psychological approaches to productivity improvement. *American Psychologist*, **38**, 468–472.

Kinicki, A.J., Carson, K.P. & Bohlander, G.W. (1992). Relationship between an organization's actual human resource efforts and employee attitudes. *Group and Organization Management*, **17**, 135–152.

Kluger, A.N. & DeNisi, A. (1996). The effects of feedback interventions on performance: a historical review, a meta-analysis, and a preliminary feedback intervention theory. *Psychological Bulletin*, **119** (2), 254–284.

Lawler, E.E. (1991). Participative management strategies. In J.W. Jones, B.D. Steffy & D.W. Bray (Eds), *Applying Psychology in Business*. Lexington, MA: Lexington Books.

Lawson, P. (1995). Performance management: an overview. In M. Walters (Ed.), *The Performance Management Handbook*. London: Institute of Personnel and Development.

Ledford, G.E. & Lawler, E.E. (1994). Dialogue. Research on employee participation. Beating a dead horse? *Academy of Management Review*, **19**, 633–636.

LGMB (1993) *People and Performance*. Luton, UK: Local Government Management Board.

Locke, E.A. & Latham, G.P. (1990). *A Theory of Goal Setting and Task Performance*. Englewood Cliffs, NJ: Prentice Hall.

Lockett, J. (1992). *Effective Performance Management*. London: Kogan Page.

London, M. (1995). Giving feedback: source-centered antecedents and consequences of constructive and destructive feedback. *Human Resource Management Review*, **5** (3), 159–188.

London, M. (1997). *Job Feedback*. Mahwah, NJ: Erlbaum.

London, M. & Wohlers, A.J. (1991). Agreement between subordinate and self-ratings in upward feedback. *Personnel Psychology*, **44** (2), 375–390.

London, M. & Smither, J.W. (1995). Can multi-source feedback change perceptions of goal accomplishment, self-evaluations and performance related outcomes? Theory-based applications and directions for research. *Personnel Psychology*, **48**, 803–839.

Lundy, O. & Cowling, A. (1996). *Strategic Human Resource Management*. London: Routledge.

MacKenzie, S.B., Podsakoff, P.M. & Fetter, R. (1991). Organizational citizenship behaviour and objective productivity as determinants of managerial evaluations of salespersons' performance. *Organizational Behaviour and Human Decision Processes*, **50** (1), 1–28.

MacKenzie, S.B., Podsakoff, P.M. & Fetter, R. (1993). The impact of organizational citizenship behaviour on evaluations of salesperson performance. *Journal of Marketing*, **57**, 70–80.

Masterson, S.S. & Taylor, M.S. (1996). Total quality management and performance appraisal: an integrative perspective. *Journal of Quality Management*, **1**, 67–89.

Mitchell, T.R., Thompson, K.R. & George-Falvy, J. (2000). Goal setting: theory and practice. In C.L. Cooper & E.A. Locke (Eds), *Industrial and Organisational Psychology: Linking Theory with Practice*. Oxford: Blackwell.

Mischel, W. (1977). The interaction of person and situation. In D. Magnusson & N.S. Endler (Eds), *Personality at the Crossroads*. Hillsdale, NJ: Erlbaum.

Mohrman, A.M., Resnick-West, S.M. & Lawler, E.E. (1989). *Designing Performance Appraisal Systems*. San Francisco: Jossey-Bass.

Moores, R. (1994). *Managing for High Performance*. London: Industrial Society.

Motowidlo, S.J. & Schmit, M.J. (1999). Performance assessment in unique jobs. In D.R. Ilgen & E.D. Pulakos (Eds), *The Changing Nature of Performance*. San Francisco: Jossey-Bass.

Murphy, K.R. (1989). Dimensions of job performance. In R.F. Dillon & J.W. Pellegrino (Eds), *Testing: Theoretical and Applied Perspectives*. New York: Praeger.

Murphy, K. R. (1990). Job performance and productivity. In K.R. Murphy & F.E. Saal (Eds), *Psychology in Organizations*. Hillsdale, NJ: Erlbaum.

Murphy, K.R. (1999). The challenge of staffing a postindustrial workplace. In D.R. Ilgen & E.D. Pulakos (Eds), *The Changing Nature of Performance*. San Francisco: Jossey-Bass.

Murphy, K.R. & Cleveland, J.N. (1995). *Understanding Performance Appraisal*. Thousand Oaks, CA: Sage.

Ostroff, C. (1992). The relationship between satisfaction, attitudes and performance: an organizational level analysis. *Journal of Applied Psychology*, **77**, 963–974.

Patterson, M., West, M., Lawthom, R. & Nickell, S. (1998). *Issues in People Management*. IPD Report No. 22, Institute of Personnel & Development, London.

Peters, L.H. & O'Connor, E.J. (1980). Situational constraints and work outcomes: the influence of a frequently overlooked construct. *Academy of Management Review*, **5**, 391–397.

Rodgers, R. & Hunter, J.E. (1991). Impact of management by objectives on organizational productivity. *Journal of Applied Psychology Monograph Series*, **76** (2), 322–336.

Rogers, S. (1990). *Performance Management in Local Government*. Harlow, Essex: Longman.

Rosenfeld, P., Giacalone, R.A. & Riordan, C.A. (1995). *Impression Management in Organizations*. London: Routledge.

Rummler, G.A. & Brache, A.P. (1995). *Improving Performance*, 2nd. edn. San Francisco: Jossey-Bass.

Schneider, B. (1987). The people make the place. *Personnel Psychology*, **40**, 437–453.

Schneider, R.J. & Hough, L.M. (1995). Personality and industrial/organizational psychology. In C.L. Cooper & I.T. Robertson (Eds), *International Review of Industrial and Organizational Psychology*. Chichester: John Wiley.

Schneier, C.E., Beatty, R.W. & Baird, L.S. (1987). Introduction. In *The Performance Management Sourcebook*. Amherst, MA: Human Resource Development Press.

Smither, J.W., London, M., Vasilopoulos, M.L., Reilly, M.R., Millsap, R.E., Salvemini, N. (1995). An examination of the effects of an upward feedback program over time. *Personnel Psychology*, **48** (1), 1–34.

Sparrow, P.R. (1994). Organizational competencies: creating a strategic behavioural framework for selection and assessment. In N. Anderson & P. Herriot (Eds), *Assessment and Selection in Organizations. First Update and Supplement*. Chichester: John Wiley.

Sparrow, P.R. (1996). Too good to be true. *People Management*, 22–27 December.

Stewart, R. (1991). *Managing Today and Tomorrow*. Basingstoke: Macmillan.

Stone, D.L. & Eddy, E.R. (1996). A model of individual and organizational factors affecting quality-related outcomes. *Journal of Quality Management*, **1** (1), 21–48.

Torrington, D. & Hall, L. (1995). *Personnel Management: HRM in Action*, 3rd edn. Hemel Hempstead: Prentice-Hall.

Van Dyne, L., Cummings, L.L. & Parks, J.M. (1995). Extra-role behaviours. *Research in Organizational Behaviour*, **17**, 215–285.

Viswesvaran, C. & Ones, D.S. (2000). Perspectives on models of job performance. *International Journal of Selection and Assessment*, **8** (4), 216–226.

Wagner, J.A. (1994). Participation's effects on performance and satisfaction: a reconsideration of research evidence. *Academy of Management Review*, **19**, 312–330.

Waldman, D.A. (1994). The contributions of total quality management to a theory of work performance. *Academy of Management Review*, **19** (3), 510–536.

Walker, A.G. & Smither, J.W. (1999). A five year study of upward feedback: what managers do with their results matters. *Personnel Psychology*, **52**, 393–423.

Warr, P. & Conner, M. (1992). Job competence and cognition. *Research in Organizational Behaviour*, **14**, 91–127.

Williams, R.S. (2002). Managing Employee Performance: Design and Implementation in Organizations. London: Thomson Learning.

Woodruffe, C. (1991). Competent by any other name. *Personnel Management*, September, 30–33.

Woodruffe, C. (1992). What is meant by a competency? In R. Boam & P. Sparrow (Eds), *Designing and Achieving Competency*. Maidenhead: McGraw-Hill.

CHAPTER 7

Maintaining and Enhancing Motivation as a Contribution to Organizational Effectiveness

John Arnold
Business School, Loughborough University, UK
and
Wouter Schoonman
Instituut voor Best Practice, Netherlands

INTRODUCTION

Motivation concerns the forces which initiate, direct and sustain behaviour, and which also determine the intensity of that behaviour (Pinder, 1998). It can be considered an extremely broad topic in psychology, not only because of the scope of this definition, but also because there is a huge variety of behaviours to which the notion of motivation can be applied. For some behaviours, such as eating and drinking, motivation can be considered partly and perhaps primarily physiological. For other areas, including behaviour at work, the role of physiological factors is likely to be much more limited. Nevertheless, ideas from many different areas of psychology can be and have been used to analyse motivation at work. This is appropriate because people do not leave parts of their minds or bodies at home when they go to work.

In this chapter we aim to examine the extent to which recent and not so recent ideas in the psychology of motivation can be applied to the effectiveness of organizations in the early twenty-first century. We contend that there are some well-established principles that help to explain individual performance at work, but that two factors limit the utility of those principles. The first is the changing nature of work and work organizations, and the way some individuals respond to those changes. The second concerns the fact that much motivation theory

Organizational Effectiveness: The Role of Psychology
Edited by I.T. Robertson, M. Callinan and D. Bartram. © 2002 John Wiley & Sons, Ltd.

and research focuses upon individual task behaviour, with little reference to the person as a whole, nor to the co-ordination of different individuals' efforts in order to achieve the multiple organizational goals described in Chapter 1.

We continue in the next section by providing a very brief outline of various theories of work motivation. A detailed analysis is well beyond the scope of this chapter, and in any case many readers will already be fairly familiar with them. More in-depth coverage can be found in Pinder (1998) or Robertson et al. (1992). In the following section we discuss some aspects of working life in to-day's organizations, with a particular emphasis on their possible implications for motivation and its role in achieving organizational effectiveness. Then we review the capacity of motivation theories to address those changing aspects of working life. We note the increasing theoretical and research interest in the role of the self and identity in motivation, and devote a section to a brief re-view of these and a practical example of how one aspect of identity—personal values—can be assessed at work.

THEORIES OF MOTIVATION AT WORK

Theories of motivation have developed substantially over the last hundred years or so. In the early days, Frederick Taylor's Scientific Management operated as if human nature was to do as little work as possible. So people required control, threat of punishment, simple tasks and purely monetary rewards. This very me-chanical view of the person at work was challenged in the middle part of the twentieth century by those who recognized that people at work were fundamen-tally social beings who wished to interact with others and could be influenced by them. There was also a general recognition that people brought a variety of needs with them to work. Hollway (1991) amongst others has argued that al-though this can be considered a more enlightened view than that of Taylorism, it was often used to support the position of management relative to employees through notions of enlightened self-interest: treating people better would lead to better (or more) work.

Several theories of human needs were developed around the 1940s to 1960s. Some, like the well-known offering from Maslow (1943), were based on human-ist ideas about personal growth and an optimistic view of people as striving to fulfil their potential (sometimes referred to as self-actualization). Others fo-cused on one or a small number of needs that were believed to have particular significance—for example McClelland's (1961) work on need for achievement. Others again such as Murray (1938) tried to identify a comprehensive set of hu-man needs. The growth-orientated theories provided much of the inspiration for theory and research which advocated motivation through stimulating work which offered skill use, discretion and responsibility, and feedback on their per-formance (Herzberg, 1966; Hackman & Oldham, 1976). Systematic documented attempts to enrich work in this way have been relatively few in number, and many more sociologically-minded theorists have stressed issues of power and control that block or limit their use (Braverman, 1974).

Need theories can basically be categorized as content theories; that is, they attempt to describe and analyse *what* motivates people. Some other theories are much more process-orientated; that is, they focus on *how* motivation operates. These tend to have a cognitive orientation where the emphasis is upon people's thought processes, either conscious or unconscious. The most often cited example is Vroom's (1964) expectancy theory. This is designed to predict and explain how a person selects a course of action from a number of alternatives. Three elements are thought to affect the decision. The first is termed *valence*—the person considers what rewards might accrue if a particular course of action is successfully undertaken, and how much he or she values those rewards. The second is *instrumentality*, which is the perceived likelihood that successful completion of the course of action will lead to those rewards. The last is *expectancy*. This is a person's assessment of the probability that they are capable of successfully undertaking the course of action. Vroom proposed that motivational force is a product of these three elements, but subsequent research has shown that additive models are at least as predictive (Schwab et al., 1979).

Probably the most successful theory in increasing work performance is goal-setting (Locke & Latham, 1990). This too is a cognitively-orientated process theory. The fundamental idea is that people's behaviour is dictated by their intentions to achieve goals which are of personal significance. Difficult (but not impossible) and specific (as opposed to vague) goals are the best sort because they focus a person's attention and stimulate him or her to develop appropriate behavioural strategies. All this assumes that the person accepts the goal and feels committed to it. This is more likely if he or she has had a hand in setting it. A large and continuing stream of research has developed on goal-setting, and a number of refinements and developments have emerged. These include the use of goals with groups as opposed to individuals, the circumstances in which performance-based goals may not be helpful, and the role of individual difference variables such as personality and ability in the goal-setting process (Ambrose & Kulik, 1999). We will return to some of these later.

Another line of thinking in work motivation is based on notions of fairness and justice. An early formulation is Adams' (1965) equity theory. This proposes that we regulate the direction, effort and persistence of our behaviour by comparing what we contribute to our work and the rewards we get from it with our perception of the contributions and rewards experienced by other people who are significant to us. More recent work examines broader notions of justice (Greenberg, 1987). It is proposed that people seek distributive justice (that is, rewards fairly distributed) and procedural justice (that is, fair and impartial procedures for allocating rewards). If we perceive that our rewards relative to our contributions are poor compared with others, we will be motivated to achieve a more equitable comparison. We might do this by seeking more rewards, contributing less, revising our perceptions of the value of the contributions and rewards of ourselves in comparison to others, or by changing the person or group we compare ourselves with. The most interesting situation concerns where we perceive we are over-rewarded. Do we happily accept this, or do we do something about it? Equity theory has received some research support (Ambrose & Kulik, 1999) but cannot be considered to offer a comprehensive view of motivation at work. However, as we will see later, notions of fairness do crop up a lot.

In recent years individual difference constructs have become more prominent in several theories. One source of this is developments in personality theory, coupled with recognition that it is difficult to establish motivational laws that apply to everyone. Another is the expansion of self theories, including social cognition (e.g. Bandura, 1986) and social identity (Tajfel & Turner, 1985). These recognize the role of our conceptions of ourselves in our choices of courses of action, and in evaluations of our behaviour and performance. Leonard et al. (1999) attempt to draw together various strands of work in motivation and propose five different motivational orientations:

1. *Intrinsic process.* People engage willingly only in activities they consider fun.
2. *Extrinsic/instrumental motivation.* People focus on the achievement of goals for the tangible rewards this will bring.
3. *External self-concept.* People draw their sense of self from their social position, so motivation rests primarily on being associated with group or organizational success, and the recognition from others that follows.
4. *Internal self-concept.* Again, these people need to be able to associate with success, but only they need to recognize the association—social affirmation is not required.
5. *Goal internalizaton.* Goals are important to the extent that they reflect values of importance to the individual.

To what extent can these theories and concepts contribute to our understanding of organizational effectiveness? We now turn to that issue.

MOTIVATION AND ORGANIZATIONAL EFFECTIVENESS IN A CHANGING WORLD

As noted earlier, motivation concerns all three of direction, effort and persistence. In reality, the extent to which people are motivated is usually inferred from data about the quantity or (more rarely) the quality of their work output. This is in spite of the fact that researchers all acknowledge the obvious point that work performance depends partly on factors other than motivation. Worse, the quantitative or qualitative output usually refers to quite a narrow task or a small set of closely interrelated tasks. This means that the direction of a person's behaviour is not really addressed by the research. It is assumed that what the person does reflects what they and everyone else agree they should be doing. How many of us in work have the luxury of such clarity and consensus? The long-lived popularity of the constructs of role ambiguity and role conflict in work and organizational psychology (e.g. Ivancevich & Matteson, 1980) demonstrates just how often there is ambiguity and disagreement about what a person should be doing in his or her work. This signals a need for motivation theory and research to "get real" in a number of ways. We now turn to a more detailed analysis of that point.

It is clear from Chapter 1 of this book that motivation is a secondary organizational goal. It is a means to some other ends. The direction element of motivation—what people choose to do—is therefore crucial. Furthermore, it is crucial at two levels. The first level concerns the choices an individual makes (or decisions that are imposed upon him or her) about what work tasks to do, and when. The second level concerns the extent to which the work activities engaged in by different individuals in an organization complement each other and thus help towards the achievement of multiple organizational goals. Staff who are willing to exert a lot of effort and to persist in doing so are clearly an asset, but much of their value is lost if their activities are not co-ordinated.

It is likely that employees are more concerned than they once were to achieve results and to be seen to do so. Many are in the position (or believe so) that this is the only way in which any degree of job security can be achieved. In this respect at least, reward may be more contingent upon behaviour now than was once the case. The popularity of performance-related pay schemes may serve to strengthen further this connection, despite their dubious effectiveness and their capacity to induce cynicism amongst employees (Herriot & Pemberton, 1995).

The potentially large number and wide variety of organizational goals described in Chapter 1 has motivational dangers. Individuals need to know which of the goals are central to their role, which are peripheral, and which irrelevant. Even when a particular organizational goal is irrelevant to an individual's role, he or she needs to know key things to *avoid* doing (e.g. buying from a supplier whose employment policies in the developing world have not been checked). It must also be borne in mind that individuals are likely to find some organizational goals more consistent with their own values (and therefore more rewarding) than others. We return to this point later in the chapter.

An individual's role may include significant contributions to more than one organizational goal. In this case there is plenty of scope for goal conflict. As noted in Chapter 1, in some circumstances different organizational goals may themselves be in conflict. Clarity is required about which are the goals to which the person should give priority. These may differ from the organization's overall priorities. That is, some individuals' roles will inevitably concern goals which are either less important than some others for the organization, or which are as important but less in the limelight. People in these types of roles may well require very explicit affirmation and reward if their motivation is to be maintained.

Especially where roles tend to focus on only one organizational goal it is important that each individual values the efforts of others in the same organization who are required to contribute to the achievement of different goals. People's social identities can often impede this, as they seek to maintain positive self images partly through comparison with outgroups (Ashforth & Mael, 1989). Also, especially in large organizations, or where many people are contributing to a particular organizational goal, individuals may feel that their personal contribution will not make much difference to the overall outcome, or at least not be seen to do so. They may therefore reduce their effort—this is referred to as social loafing. Social psychological research has shown that there are ways of making individual contributions more visible which can reduce social loafing (Kerr & Brunn, 1983). The trends towards individualized contracts, goal-setting and performance management in the workplace may serve to make individual contributions more readily identifiable.

Even so, it may often be difficult for individuals to see how their personal contribution, however identifiable, can make much of a difference one way or the other to the achievement of organizational goals. Some goals are likely to seem quite far removed from individuals. They may be quite diffuse—that is, poorly defined. It may be difficult for a person to see connections between their specific behaviours in day-to-day work and the achievement of (for example) organizational profitability. Thus whilst employees may be happy to bask in the reflected glory of organizational success because this bolsters their self-identity, they may need other incentives to motivate them day by day. These could include extrinsic rewards or expression of internalized values, or the opportunity simply to do something one enjoys (Leonard et al., 1999).

Many of the potential tensions between individual and organization also apply to the relationship between individual and work group. The strength of trends in the workplace towards teamworking and short-term projects in groups with shifting membership can be exaggerated. However, they seem to be real enough (McCann & Buckner, 1994). This style of work makes considerable demands on some individuals, but can lead to considerable learning and growth. Just as with whole organizations, groups may have multiple goals, potentially conflicting goals, tensions with the goals of individual group members, or ambiguities concerning the relationships between the specific behaviours or individuals and the general group goals. As we will see shortly, work and organizational psychologists have conducted some research which addresses these individual versus group issues.

The direction component of motivation can play a particularly evident role in work behaviour when individuals are recruited on the basis of the overall fit between their competencies, values or other personal attributes and the strategic direction of the organization, as opposed to their suitability for a particular job. This seems to be becoming more common (though not yet the norm) and arises from a recognition that roles within organizations need to be fluid in order to capitalize upon the pace of change (Lawler, 1994). Individuals in this position are in what Weick (1996) amongst others has termed a weak situation—that is, one with relatively few constraints and consequently considerable personal autonomy. The opportunity to define one's goals and methods is not always an unmixed blessing. It requires some skill from individuals and co-ordination from organizations. In the absence of either or both of these, there is the danger of talented and highly motivated individuals pursuing incompatible or unattainable goals, or duplicating the same ones. Not that the more traditional use of tightly defined job descriptions necessarily gets round this. That makes it look as if all necessary functions are being carried out, but whether that is really the case depends on the skills and (dare one say) motivation of the incumbents. The restrictions of roles mean that individuals whose motivation is not harnessed tend to do a bare minimum. Where roles are less clearly defined, there is usually plenty of motivation and activity but not necessarily much co-ordination.

Some authors have argued that it is possible to make a virtue out of the necessities of unstable labour markets and rapid change. In such circumstances it is possible, in fact desirable, to pursue a so-called boundaryless career (Arthur & Rousseau, 1996). Individuals pursuing such a career are by no means immune from labour markets, but are able to ride the waves of change through accumulation of competencies and experiences, a wide range of contacts, personal flexibility, willingness to try new things, and sheer opportunism. There is some substance to counter-arguments that relatively few people are in a position to operate like this, and that in any case many labour markets do not really support boundaryless careers (Gunz et al., 2000). Nevertheless, the reality for some people of this kind of career does have implications for motivation in today's organizations. A so-called careerist orientation (Feldman & Weitz, 1991) where individuals pursue their own goals, possibly at the expense of those of the organization, may become more common. A more general point is that motivation may become more often driven by personal values and less often by organizational reward systems.

That tendency may have been accelerated by the extensive organizational restructuring and downsizing of the 1980s and 1990s. During that period many people found that their job was less secure than they had imagined, and that their employing organization was unable or unwilling to honour their loyalty over a period of perhaps many years. They thought they had a relationship of trust and reciprocity with their employer—a so-called relational psychological contract (Rousseau, 1995). On the basis of "once bitten twice shy", many individuals are now said to be much more hesitant about committing themselves in this way. They prefer (or are resigned to) a so-called transactional psychological contract. Here the deal with the employer is much more like an economic transaction than a lasting relationship (Herriot et al., 1998). Many employers also prefer this, since in some respects it reduces their commitment to employees. But it can be argued that some employers still seek deep commitment from employees without offering the same in return (Hirsh & Jackson, 1996). They may seek to motivate staff through appeals to loyalty, the company mission and notions of "we're all in this together". However, staff are cynical about that since they know full well that they can be cast adrift at any time.

Employees' motivation in these circumstances often looks quite instrumental because they may seek maximum financial rewards and development of skills which maintain or enhance their employability. But what they do with their money and the kinds of employment they seek often reflects their personal goals and values in quite a deep way. Meanwhile there are still plenty of people in organizations who feel that their employer has reneged on its commitments. They may respond to this with attempts to "get even" through revenge or passive resistance or to "get safe" by keeping their heads down and avoiding risk (Herriot & Pemberton, 1995). They are likely to be highly sensitized to possible violations of their rights by their employer and highly conscious of comparisons with other people who might be getting a better deal than they are (Robinson & Morrison, 2000).

WHAT DO MOTIVATION THEORIES SAY ABOUT LIFE IN TODAY'S WORK ORGANIZATIONS?

Expectancy and Goal-setting

As noted earlier in this chapter, two of the most influential motivation theories are expectancy and goal-setting. Both of these say some important things about motivation in organizations. Formulated originally as a theory of choice (i.e. direction) of behaviour, expectancy theory alerts us to some of the psycho-logical processes that may be involved when a person attempts to choose which of multiple and/or conflicting goals they will pursue at any given moment. It also helps to clarify why motivation may be particularly problematic at this time in economic and social history. In terms of valence, some organizational goals will be more attractive than others to any individual employee. Part of that valence is likely to depend upon the importance an individual attaches to the achievement of each organizational goal, not only because of tangible rewards it brings, but also because of the extent to which the goal reflects his or her personal values concerning what is good and right.

The concept of instrumentality is also helpful. Individuals may struggle to see how their behaviour can be instrumental in the achievement of broad orga-nizational goals. They take some convincing that their behaviour can reliably affect some outcomes in uncertain times, when the continued health or even existence of their employing organization cannot be taken for granted. This is another reason why individuals' goals need to be clearly defined with obvious and short-term connections between specific behaviours and goal achievement. Even then, this may not help if the goals are not attractive in themselves or if the rewards attached to them are not valued by the individual.

The level of expectancy may also be an issue. Van Eerde and Thierry's (1996) meta-analysis suggests that the expectancy component of the theory is at least as significant as the other two in accounting for variance in outcome variables. But it cannot be taken for granted that people feel a sense of expectancy, particularly perhaps at this present time. Individuals may lack confidence in their capacity to execute key work behaviours successfully, especially when they are required to undertake a wide range of responsibilities involving interaction with a wide range of people and with a fast pace of change which requires frequent learning and re-learning. In extreme cases people can be immobilized by this. Sensitivity is therefore required in managing them when they apparently do not respond to performance incentives. Support, within reasonable limits, to assist individuals develop a sense of expectancy or self-efficacy may well be required in preference to punishment or a revised set of incentives.

What can goal-setting theory contribute to our understanding of motivation? As noted earlier, goal-setting is often touted as a (or even the) motivation the-ory that works because it describes how behaviour is initiated and sustained, and the processes by which this occurs. At one time it was suggested that pro-ponents of the theory concentrated on individuals' goals and performance, at the expense of the group level of analysis (Austin & Bobko, 1985). Subsequent work has shown that goal-setting often works for groups as well as individuals (O'Leary-Kelly et al., 1994). However, the effect tends to be smaller in real-life groups than in laboratory studies. This perhaps suggests that the interpersonal dynamics and/or the conflicts between individual and collective goals in extant groups can override the potential performance benefits of group goal-setting. This is clearly an important caution in an era when groups and teams are assum-ing increasing significance at work. Research with real-life groups by Crown and Rosse (1995) has shown that if individual goals are consistent with group goals, then the group's performance can exceed that obtained with no goals, individual goals or (crucially) group goals only. Although the task was an artificial one carried out in a laboratory, it was carefully designed to be non-summative—that is, the group's overall performance was not simply the sum of the accomplishments of individuals. In that sense it was realistic. One can imagine that considerable care and creativity is often required to devise individual goals which do not compromise group ones, but if it can be done, the pay-off in terms of performance is likely to be considerable.

Feedback on performance level has frequently been found to be an important mediator of the impact of goal-setting. Unfortunately, in many tasks it is not self-evident how well one has done, and therefore feedback from others is required. Yet with people's experience of increasing workloads, there is often little encouragement to take the time to review the performance of others and give them feedback. Even the nature of the goals themselves can be problematic. There is good evidence that when people are learning new and complex tasks it is best to avoid goals based on performance at the task because they appear to inhibit learning (Kanfer & Ackerman, 1989). It is better to set goals (if they are to be set at all) that concern learning the parameters of the task. This, once accomplished, sets a firmer foundation for effective task performance. This is a significant point in the many workplaces that are experienced as highly pressured by those who inhabit them, with requirements for frequent learning of new skills, and a strong emphasis on short-term results. In such environments, a heavy reliance on performance goals may well be counter-productive even though very alluring.

The impact of goal-setting on performance appears negligible unless commitment to goal achievement is high (Klein et al., 1999). So the issue becomes, what factors affect commitment? As Klein et al. observe, commitment is uniformly high when goals are self-set. Their meta-analytic findings also suggest that participation in goal-setting (that is, having some influence on the goals set or at least the opportunity to accept or reject them) can increase goal commitment. It also seems that self-efficacy has an impact on goal commitment where the goal is difficult. People who lack belief in their capacity to complete goal-relevant tasks successfully are not willing to take on the goal (Wofford et al., 1992). There is evidence that the overall self-efficacy of a group affects the goals its members set for themselves, and also group performance (Durham et al., 1997). This may partly explain why laboratory-based goal-setting is more often successful in increasing performance than goal-setting with groups which have a history and a future.

All this suggests that senior managers need to be extremely careful in trying to engender commitment based purely on appeals to how goal-achievement will benefit the organization. Employees are less likely than they once were to trust the organization, or indeed to care unduly about its fate as long as they remain employable. It is also important not to impose goals without consultation. And whilst it is important to avoid the trap of responding to someone's low self-efficacy by setting insufficiently challenging goals, it is again clear that their belief in themselves does matter.

Conflict between goals also matters. This has most commonly been investigated in the context of quality versus quantity (e.g. Locke et al., 1994). When it is difficult to achieve two or more goals simultaneously, or when individuals receive conflicting instructions about what goal to prioritise, then performance on at least one goal tends to suffer. This re-emphasizes the need for individuals to be clear about which of the organization's goals they are contributing to in their role. Related to this, one future challenge for goal-setting theory is a clearer analysis of the process of motivation. The outcome variable is most commonly performance, and it is often not clear what aspects of behavioural choice, effort and persistence are responsible for any improvements in performance observed. Another challenge (shared by some other motivation theories and some other domains of work and organizational psychology) is to incorporate more personality and self-concept variables as potential moderators or mediators of goal-setting effects (Ambrose & Kulik, 1999). This has begun with self-efficacy, and also with the distinction between different personal goal orientations (Farr et al., 1993). It could usefully be extended, perhaps to personality variables such as conscientiousness.

Other Theories

Hackman and Oldham's (1980) Job Characteristics Theory (JCT) postulates that motivation is a function of psychological states which are induced by the extent to which a person experiences skill variety, task identity, task significance, feedback and autonomy in his or her work. There is moderate research support for this general framework, though less for some of its more specific predictions. Some similar points to those already made are highlighted by JCT, though from a rather different angle and with different language.

To experience an absence of task identity may also be to experience goal conflict. An absence of skill variety may not only detract from the intrinsic motivation of the person's present job, it may also inhibit his or her employability for future roles. Work is likely to be experienced as significant if it has obvious connections with organizational goals, though as noted earlier it would be naïve to expect everyone to feel a strong sense of personal commitment to those. Some employees experience more autonomy than they once did, if only because their bosses are too busy to observe them closely! Attempts to empower employees in medium and lower status roles in organization have been common in recent years. Although they appear often to be more rhetoric than reality, empowerment programmes can lead to greater autonomy, at least in how and when job tasks are carried out even if the overall goals of the job remain the same (Handy, 1995). However, empowerment does not happen in a social vacuum. The history of relationships in the organization, and employees' attributions of the motives for the introduction of empowerment, may render changes like increased autonomy irrelevant or even damaging ("they're making me take on more responsibility without any more pay"). The importance of feedback and the difficulty, on occasions, of providing it, has already been discussed.

It is easy to see the relevance of key concepts in justice theories to motivation in today's organizations. Downsized and decentralized organizations may place quite low emphasis on the use of consistent and documented procedures in their human resource management. Such procedures tend to be labelled bureaucratic and inefficient, and therefore to be avoided, especially when the pressure is on for rapid results (Templer & Cawsey, 1999). There may well be some advantages to this, but one drawback is the likelihood of increasing perceptions of procedural and distributive injustice. Some individuals may seem to receive disproportionately favourable outcomes by methods perceived as secretive, biased or sketchy. It is probably impossible to eradicate all perceptions of unfairness, not least because in complex organizations there is such a wide range of people, events, rewards and performance criteria available for individuals to draw upon in forming impressions and conclusions. But given that perceptions of unfairness are likely to attack motivation at a number of different levels (for example, the extent to which people will commit to difficult goals, and the extent to which they perceive their behaviour as instrumental in leading to valued outcomes), it is worth taking steps to minimize it.

Equity theory too may help in the conceptualization of some motivational issues at work, especially for those people in work organizations who feel that they used to have a better deal some years ago than they do now. Equity theory posits that we compare the ratio of what we put into our work with what we get out of it with the ratio for other people. This can perhaps be extended to comparisons with oneself at some time in the past, although if things are perceived to have become worse for everyone, that might take the sting out of the deterioration. The trouble with equity theory is that it is almost infinitely flexible. As noted earlier, people can change the person or persons with whom they compare themselves, or change the values they place on the inputs or outcomes of self or other comparison. It is hard to escape the conclusion that a person uses comparisons to validate his or her existing feelings and opinions about work rather than to form them. In an era with more individualized contracts it is perhaps relatively difficult to evaluate the inputs and outcomes of others in the same workplace. On the other hand, those who engage in a boundaryless career are likely to have extensive networks of contacts, and thus plenty of comparison outside their current employer to choose from. Herriot and Pemberton (1995) note that employees feel a great sense of inequity when they compare the pay rises and pay-offs of their top executives with their own. It seems that such discrepancies continue, in spite of strongly expressed concern about them, at least in the UK.

There is something rather joyless about many of these theories. Little reference is made to the possibility that people may gain enjoyment from simply doing their tasks, even though this notion of intrinsic motivation is hardly new. The images of people striving to achieve goals, or calculating probabilities, or comparing themselves with others all seem earnest almost to the point of obsessiveness. Cognitive evaluation theory (Deci & Ryan, 1980) suggests that extrinsic rewards can actually undermine intrinsic motivation when those rewards are perceived as being intended to control. There is some dispute about this, and it seems that financial rewards on the whole encourage performance rather than undermine it (Jenkins et al., 1998). Nevertheless, the evidence for the undermining effect of extrinsic rewards in the circumstances specified by Deci and Ryan does seem compelling (Deci et al., 1999). It raises the possibility that management policies like performance-related pay and paper-based quality control systems may actually make employees less inclined to perform to high standards, because those systems are often perceived as promoting values that employees don't approve of.

MOTIVATION FOR EXTRA-ROLE ACTIVITIES

Ambrose and Kulik (1999) note that much research on motivation no longer carries that label. Instead, it refers to a specific topic area such as management or leadership, and discusses motivational issues either as a central focus or a subsidiary one. In other words, the concept of motivation is applied to phenomena other than overall job or task performance.

Certain of those topic areas have particular relevance for present purposes. Chapter 1 points out that the current and future competencies of employees in an organization are crucial. Therefore individuals' motivation to acquire wider and/or deeper competencies has considerable significance. Probably most people would say that they wish to develop their competencies, but in highly pressured workplaces the acid test is whether they find the time and other resources to do so when the emphasis is on short-term performance and day-to-day deadlines. Some elements of this find their way into analyses of career management by individuals (e.g. Noe, 1996) and the motivation to engage in training has received some sporadic attention in the literature (see Tharenou, 1997, for a review). There seems to be plenty of psychological, demographic and organizational predictors of participation in training and development, but relatively little theorizing about them.

Another significant area is organizational citizenship behaviour (OCB). This is defined as co-operative behaviour that has positive consequences for the organization but is not required or formally rewarded (Van Dyne et al., 2000). OCBs most often take the form of helping others with their responsibilities. Research on OCB increased in volume through the 1990s. This probably reflects concern in organizations that employees should "go the extra mile" to help ensure organizational success in increasingly competitive markets, and also play a constructive role in teams. Not surprisingly, there are some signs that the extent to which a person engages in OCBs is influenced by his or her satisfaction with the organization and perceptions of distributive and procedural justice (Organ, 1990). However, there is an increasing sense that dispositional variables also play a major role—that is, some people are simply more disposed towards engaging in "good citizen" behaviours than others. These dispositional variables seem to include both personality characteristics and values (McNeely & Meglino, 1994). This may indicate that management interventions have only a limited impact on the OCBs of employees, but even so, it might be appropriate to reward them if they really are valued. One suspects that in many organizations good citizenship is in fact reflected in promotion and pay decisions, but this is not obvious because citizenship behaviours are not stated as criteria for those decisions.

THE SELF IN MOTIVATION

Reference to the self has been made repeatedly in this chapter. Care must be taken to avoid the concept of the self being invoked in an over-generalized way to "explain" variance unaccounted for by situational variables or experimental manipulations. The self has long been considered to consist of two connected concepts—the "I" which acts upon the world in order to achieve goals, and the "me" which is the set of descriptions the person believes can be applied to him or her. The "I" and the "me" are of course connected: for example often the "I" initiates action which reflects the nature of the "me".

There have been occasional calls to include the self more explicitly in theories of work motivation (e.g. Handy, 1976). On the whole this has been reflected by the inclusion of individual difference measures (for example of personality, needs or motives) in motivation research. This continues to the present day (see, for example, Kanfer and Ackerman's (2000) description of the nature and measurement of six motivational traits), but gradually the conceptualizing of individual difference variables has moved away from traditional notions of needs and towards theoretical perspectives offered by social cognition. Self-efficacy is the most obvious example of this. It has been shown to have an apparently direct effect on task performance as well as moderating effects on the impact of motivational interventions (Stajkovic & Luthans, 1998). Self-efficacy can perhaps be considered an aspect of the "me" which influences the goals, plans and behavioural strategies initiated by the "I".

How does this kind of influence work? In part it works through processes described in existing motivation theories. For example, a person with a low sense of self-efficacy for a particular task will have little expectancy that he or she can complete it successfully. But some other self-processes step outside what is explicitly covered in the established theories of motivation. Many theorists of the self suggest that we are motivated to validate our self-concept, and therefore we behave in ways which, deliberately or unconsciously, are likely to confirm our views of self (Leonard et al., 1999). Interestingly, there has been some suggestion that this is true even when a person has a very negative self-concept (Korman, 1970). Apparently we would rather have the comfort of confirming an existing negative view of self than the confusion of having our low expectations of self disconfirmed. However, this rather pessimistic view has been challenged by those who consider that human behaviour is motivated more by striving towards the ideal self than by confirmation of the existing self (Bandura, 1991). Either way, concepts of self are viewed as a key reference point a person uses in deciding what course(s) of action to pursue, how long to pursue them, and how much effort to exert.

There has been much discussion of whether a person has one self or many, and if many, how the different selves relate to each other. For example, an individual might view him or herself as assertive and dominant at work, but as meek and submissive when with relatives. Sociologists in particular tend to take the view that each person possesses multiple selves, and that the selves tend to be specific to different life roles, and perhaps even to different situations. Another view is that there is one general self-concept, certain aspects of which become more or less salient in any given role or situation. Social psychologists have invoked the notions of social identity and social categorization in their analyses of how self-concept is expressed in terms of membership of certain social groups and the possession of characteristics of that group which contrast with other groups (see, for example, Turner, 1999). Experimental studies have shown that it is possible to influence the self-concept and attitudes a person reports by manipulating the salience of certain group memberships. This is said in turn to influence the collective goals and interests that a person is motivated to achieve (Van Knippenberg, 2000). In some circumstances no particular group memberships are salient. It is then that the most individualized aspects of the self-concept come to the fore— that is, those aspects of the self that depend least on group memberships. The person is then most likely to respond to individualized rewards and concepts such as self-development and self-actualization. Even so, it may be that a person is not very confident about who he or she is and seeks validation from other people (Leonard et al., 1999).

All this does not necessarily mean that in order to influence work motivation it is necessary to work directly on a person's self-concept. People's experiences over time can influence the way they see themselves, particularly their competencies and interests. Also, knowledge of how individuals see themselves can help to clarify which rewards they will value most, and which tasks they are likely to be willing to tackle in a committed manner. This does imply a quite deep and personal knowledge of individuals. The boundaryless career perspective suggests that salient group identities may concern workgroup or profession rather than the employing organizations as a whole. Even more likely, there will be an increasing emphasis on aspects of self-concept that reflect one's individuality rather than group identity. Leonard et al. (1999) assert that there are three elements of this personal self-concept: traits, competencies and values. The last of these probably provides the most stable and influential reference point people use to guide their behaviour; especially in the absence of clear and stable social norms. It may well be that the extent to which an organization appears to reflect a person's own values has a key impact on his or her motivation to remain involved in it. We now turn to an empirical study of values in the work setting in order to illustrate and investigate this issue.

VALUES, SATISFACTION AND COMMITMENT: A CASE STUDY

In this case study a multinational IT company was faced with a problem. Every year this company hires a few thousand graduates. In the current labour market the recruitment, selection and training of these "young professionals" is an expensive process. After their initial training, these young professionals are hired by clients of the company to participate in IT projects, often carried out at the client's premises. The turnover in this group of freshly recruited people was about 15%, a figure considered to be too high by the IT company. Every young professional leaving the company within a year implied a loss of some Dfl 50 000 (or £14 000). It was decided to take a closer look at values, here seen as one of the operationalizations of motivation.

Values are considered important drivers and motivators of human behaviour. A value can be thought of as a concept or idea that is important to an individual which leads to certain behaviours. Attention to values increased greatly during the 1960s (see, for example, Allport et al., 1960). In the 1970s, Rokeach (1973) was the leading thinker in this field. In the late 1980s and 90s the work of Schwartz—building on Rokeach—seems to be the most comprehensive effort to map out the nature of human values. Schwartz (1992) and his colleagues have built the Universal Model of Human Values and validated this model in 44 countries, showing the role of values in different cultures. The works of Trompenaars (1993) and Hofstede (1998) on cultures, and Schein (1996) on career anchors, focus on the role values play in the work place. Within the working environment, the importance of values seems to be increasingly recognized (Meglino & Ravlin, 1998; Van Vianen, 2000).

For this study, an instrument—called values @ work—derived from the SHL model of values was used. As in the Schwartz model on which it is based, the SHL model consists of a circumplex with two bipolar axes (see Figure 7.1).

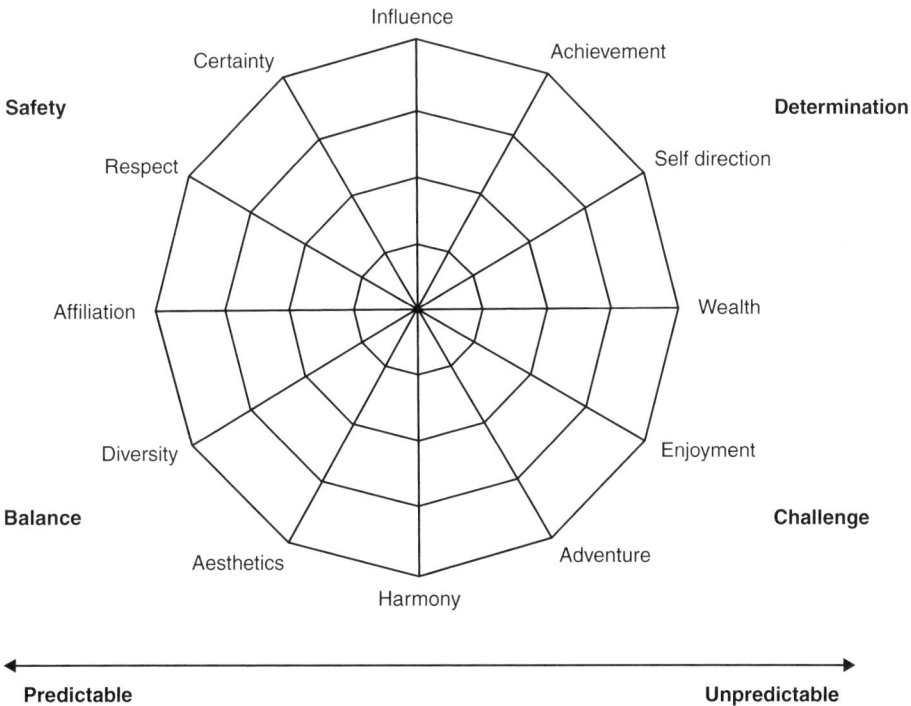

Figure 7.1 The SHL model of values @ work. © 2000 SHL Group plc. Reproduced by permission

Table 7.1 Value cluster definitions

Value cluster	The importance and the need of:
Influence	Exercising influence on processes and people Wanting to take decisions, having final responsibility, possessing power over people
Achievement	Delivering recognizable achievements and excelling in this regard Experiencing success, being respected and having a solid reputation
Self-direction	Determining direction by oneself, choosing one's own goals, taking the fate in own hands Experiencing freedom, being independent, organizing one's own work
Wealth	Being strongly rewarded in financial terms, making as much money as possible Material rewards in general, having a yearly pay rise, having no worries about money
Enjoyment	Having pleasant experiences, enjoying those joyful things that can come with work Having a nice working environment and having fun at work
Adventure	Experiencing many different things, a lot of variety, doing interesting things Venturing into the unknown, having new experiences
Harmony	Being internally balanced, acting ethically and respecting the natural environment Understanding the world, gathering knowledge and wisdom, supporting justice
Aesthetics	Enjoying beautiful things, appreciating design and developing a good taste Engaging with artistic people and developing own artistic talents further
Diversity	Understanding other cultures, learn from and adapt to these cultures Being sensitive and accepting with regard to other cultures and customs
Affiliation	Helping others, engaging in an open and honest way with others and being patient with others Having friendly relationships and being trusted
Respect	Supporting traditional ways of acting, doing what is expected and work according to agreed standards Keeping up with regular values and customs and engage in a decent way with other people
Certainty	Being sure about the job and the future, having well-defined tasks and knowing what is expected Running small risks and respecting those placed above.

Source: SHL Group plc. Reproduced by permission.

The four poles of the dimensions, as well as the clusters, are described in Tables 7.1 and 7.2.

In the values @ work instrument the items are administered twice. The candidate first has to rate the importance of each item in the Ideal case. After that,

Table 7.2 Higher-order factor definitions

Determination	Achieving, having influence, Self-determination, changing things
Challenge	Having fun, doing new, challenging things on your own behalf
Balance	Being internally balanced, appreciating differences, enjoying the beauty of life
Safety	Engaging with other people in a predictable, respectful and pleasant way

Source: SHL Group plc. Reproduced by permission.

the same items have to be rated with the current work situation in mind (the Actual). In the Ideal administration a "relaxed Q-sort" format is used, implying certain restrictions on the number of items that can be rated as very important, important, and so on. The administration of the Actual situation uses a standard Likert format.

The model and the measurement arising from it offer the opportunity to identify in some detail the bases of motivation at work for individuals, and also the extent to which their current work provides (at quite an abstract level) what they are looking for. At least three interesting issues follow. They may be the subject of future research and development. First, to what extent can observable features of jobs and reward systems be linked to specific values? Answers to this question will help make a crucial connection between the surface and underlying aspects of motivation, and perhaps help to address the lack of correspondence between needs and tangible behaviour and rewards for which the old needs theories were criticized. Second, over time to what extent do individuals change their values in line with what their work offers and/or influence the nature of their work so that it offers more of what they value? Work on socialization (e.g. Schaubroeck et al., 1998) suggests both are likely. Third, does a good match between the person and their work predict outcomes like satisfaction, motivation and performance? Holland's (1997) model of vocational choice is sometimes criticized for its neglect of values (Arnold, 1997), so here may be an opportunity to test their importance. Kalliath et al. (1999) also report some promising initial findings on this.

Lau (2000) carried out the research in this case study. Lau administered both the values @ work instrument (independent variables) as well as four other outcome measures (dependent variables)—organizational commitment, continuance commitment, job satisfaction and job withdrawal—to a sample of over 300 young professionals in the multinational ICT company. His findings are summarized below.

Organizational commitment was found to be significantly negatively correlated with the Total Item measure of P–O values fit ($r = -0.29$) and the higher order values cluster of *Determination* ($r = -0.29$). This suggests that as individuals perceive the Organization preference for values to exceed their own (P < O), they are more likely to report higher levels of organizational commitment, both generally and more specifically with regards to *Determination* values.

When continuance commitment was correlated with the values-fit measures the only significant relationship found was with the values cluster of

Safety ($r = 0.25$). This positive relationship was interesting as it highlights the differences in the way the two conceptualizations of commitment interact with measures of values fit. It seems that as the individual preference for *Safety* values exceeds that of the Organization (P > O) continuance commitment increases— that is to say, as the individual places greater importance upon values of *Safety*, he or she is more likely to stay in the job because of a feeling of little choice based upon the sacrifices and external opportunities.

Job satisfaction showed the most correlations with the measures of values fit of the four dependent variables examined. It was negatively correlated overall with Total Item fit ($r = -0.34$) as well as with the values clusters of *Determination* ($r = -0.34$) and *Challenge* ($r = -0.31$). Similarly to organizational commitment, reported job satisfaction levels were higher as perceived Organization preference of values exceeded those of the individual (P < O).

Job withdrawal showed a weak but positive and significant correlation with Total Item fit ($r = 0.23$) and the much stronger positive and significant correlation with the values cluster of *Determination* ($r = 0.42$). These findings show that reported levels of job withdrawal intentions are higher as individual values preference exceeds those of the organization (P > O). This is particularly the case with regard to *Determination* values.

These findings suggest two main conclusions. First, in a general sense people are attracted by organizations which appear to endorse a range of values, but particularly (at least for this sample) values concerning personal agency. Second, to some extent, a match between person and organization is less important than the absolute extent to which the organization endorses values. Perhaps, then, professional employees in the early twenty-first century are motivated not so much by a cosy values fit, but by a challenging organization that offers scope for full expression of self-identity, including personal values.

CONCLUSIONS

Several theories of work motivation have been around for many years. They are described, appropriately, by Ambrose and Kulik (1999) as "old friends". They are certainly old, and they are friends not only because of their familiarity but also because most of them say something useful about the work performance of individuals. Further, they include concepts that can help us understand some of the potential consequences for motivation of changes in the workplace that have happened over the last two decades.

On the other hand, there is increasing realization that motivation theories tend to pay insufficient attention to the self, which includes a sense of one's own personality traits, competencies and values. Recent developments of established theories and formulations of new ones have started to rectify that. In an era of supposedly boundaryless careers (Arthur & Rousseau, 1996) driven by individuals, it is particularly important to reflect the self more fully in motivation theories. Preferably this should be done in an integrated holistic way (Leonard et al., 1999) rather than using isolated constructs such as self-efficacy, helpful though these are. It may well require the use of self constructs as major drivers of motivation rather than as moderators of other factors. One novel aspect of this could be an extension of equity theory to include comparison of self now with self in the past, as well as with other people. Such a comparison is certainly implied in some work on the psychological contract, but rarely pursued in depth.

There is also a need to look more closely at the direction component of motivation—that is, what it is that a person is motivated to do. The achievement of organizational effectiveness requires more than individuals who work hard at set tasks. For one thing, roles and tasks are often not clearly defined, and are subject to rapid change. Many people have considerable choice about exactly what they do at work, and how they do it. Motivation theory and research needs to pay more attention to how people make these choices. In spite of the existence of expectancy theory which seeks to explain choice of course of action, most motivation research has focused on how hard and persistently people exert effort once the task has been defined.

The achievement of organizational objectives also requires co-ordination of individuals' efforts so that all organizational goals receive appropriate attention. Within groups, it requires skilful use of specific and challenging individual and group goals which complement each other rather than compete. It also needs individuals who are orientated towards teams, not just themselves. Yet it may well be mistaken to treat such an orientation as an individual difference variable. It may depend much more upon which aspects of a person's identity are evoked at work. If employees' ties to organizations really are loosening, it may be that quite individual aspects of identity (as opposed to collective aspects such as company membership) drive behaviour at work. Or perhaps professional and functional/departmental identities are most salient. More research is needed to investigate how elements of identity become salient at work, and the impact of this on choice of behaviour, effort and persistence.

The failure of motivation theories to address adequately the "what" element of motivation has been one reason why research on behaviour that is not purely task performance (but which nevertheless contributes to organizational effectiveness) has developed relatively independently of the motivation literature. Examples are organizational commitment and organizational citizenship behaviour. Another area that has received some attention, but needs more, is the motivation to acquire new knowledge and skills. Effective work performance usually requires knowledge as well as motivation, and the nature of the knowledge required may change rapidly. If motivation theory is to strengthen its contribution to organizational effectiveness, a key challenge will be to export more constructs and practical techniques to fields not traditionally labelled "motivation".

ACKNOWLEDGEMENTS

Thanks to Lisa Jones for her help in preparing this chapter. Simon Lau is thanked for his contribution to the values @ work material. Tables 7.1 and 7.2 and Figure 7.1 are reproduced by kind permission of SHL Group plc, who retain all rights and title to these materials.

REFERENCES

Adams, J.S. (1965). Inequity in social exchange. In L. Berkowitz (Ed.), *Advances in Experimental Social Psychology*, Vol. 2. New York: Academic Press.

Allport, G.W., Vernon, P.E. & Lindzey, G. (1960). *A Study of Values*. Boston: Houghton Mifflin.

Ambrose, M.L. & Kulick, C.T. (1999). Old friends, new faces: motivation research in the 1990s. *Journal of Management*, **25**, 231–292.

Arnold, J. (1997). *Managing Careers into the 21st Century*. London: Paul Chapman Publishing.

Arthur, M.B. & Rousseau, D.M. (Eds) (1996). *The Boundaryless Career: A New Employment Principle for a New Organizational Era*. Oxford: Oxford University Press.

Ashforth, B.E. & Mael, F. (1989). Social identity theory and the organization. *Academy of Management Review*, **14**, 20–39.

Austin, J.T. & Bobko, P. (1985). Goal-setting theory: unexplored areas and future research needs. *Journal of Occupational Psychology*, **58**, 289–308.

Bandura, A. (1986). *Social Foundations of Thought and Action: A Social Cognitive Theory*. Englewood Cliffs, NJ: Prentice Hall.

Bandura, A. (1991). Social cognitive theory of self regulation. *Organizational Behavior and Human Decision Processes*, **51**, 248–287.

Braverman, J. (1974). *Labor and Monopoly Capital*. New York: Monthly Review Press.

Crown, D.F. & Rosse, J.G. (1995). Yours, mine, and ours: facilitating group productivity through the integration of individual and group goals. *Organizational Behavior and Human Decision Processes*, **64**, 138–195.

Deci, E.L. & Ryan, R.M. (1980). The empirical exploration of intrinsic motivational processes. In L. Berkowitz (Ed.), *Advances in Experimental Social Psychology*, Vol. 13, pp. 39–80. New York: Academic Press.

Deci, E.L., Koestner, R. & Ryan, R.M. (1999). A meta-analytic review of experiments examining the effects of extrinsic rewards on intrinsic motivation. *Psychological Bulletin*, **125**, 627–668.

Durham, C.C., Knight, D. & Locke, E.A. (1997). Effects of leader role, team-set goal difficulty, efficacy, and tactics on team effectiveness. *Organizational Behavior and Human Decision Processes*, **72**, 203–231.

Farr, J.L., Hofman, D.A. & Ringenbach, K.L. (1993). Goal orientation and action control theory: implications for industrial and organizational psychology. In I.T. Robertson & C.L. Cooper (Eds), *International Review of Industrial and Organizational Psychology*, Vol. 8, Chichester: John Wiley.

Feldman, D.C. & Weitz, B.A. (1991). From the invisible hand to the gladhand: understanding a careerist orientation to work. *Human Resource Management*, **30**, 237–257.

Greenberg, J. (1987). A taxonomy of organizational justice theories. *Academy of Management Review*, **12**, 9–22.

Gunz, H., Evans, M. & Jalland, M. (2000). Career boundaries in a "boundaryless" world. In M. Peiperl, M. Arthur, R. Goffee & T. Morris (Eds), *Career Frontiers*. Oxford: Oxford University Press.

Hackman, J.R. & Oldham, G.R. (1976). Motivation through design of work: test of a theory. *Organizational Behavior and Human Performance*, **16**, 250–279.

Hackman, J.R. & Oldham, G.R. (1980). *Work Redesign*. Reading, MA: Addison-Wesley.

Handy, C.B. (1976). *Understanding Organizations*. Harmondsworth, UK: Penguin.

Handy, C. (1995). Trust and the virtual organization—how do you manage people who you do not see? *Harvard Business Review*, May–June, 40–50.

Herriot, P. & Pemberton, C. (1995). *New Deals*. Chichester: John Wiley.

Herriot, P., Hirsh, W. & Reilly, P. (1998). *Trust and Transition*. Chichester: John Wiley.

Herzberg, F. (1966). *Work and the Nature of Man*. Cleveland, OH: World Publishing.

Hirsh, W. & Jackson, C. (1996). *Strategies for Career Development: Promise, Practice and Pretence*. Brighton: Institute for Employment Studies.

Hofstede, G. (1998). Attitudes, values and organizational culture: disentangling the concepts. *Organizational Studies*, **19**, 477–493.

Holland, J.L. (1997). *Making Vocational Choices: A Theory of Vocational Personalities and Work Environments*, 3rd edn. Eaglewood Cliffs, NJ :Prentice Hall.

Hollway, W. (1991). *Work Psychology and Organizational Behavior*. London: Sage.

Ivancevich, J.M. & Matteson, M.T. (1980). *Stress and Work*. Glenview, IL: Scott, Foresman and Co.

Jenkins, G.D., Mitra, A., Gupta, N. & Shaw, J.D. (1998). Are financial incentives related to performance? A meta-analytic review of empirical research. *Journal of Applied Psychology*, **83**, 777–787.

Kalliath, T.J., Bluedorn, A.C. & Strube, M.J. (1999). A test of value congruence effects. *Journal of Organizational Behavior*, **20**, 1175–1198.

Kanfer, R. & Ackerman, P.L. (1989). Motivation and cognitive abilities: an integrative/aptitude-treatment interaction approach to skill acquisition. *Journal of Applied Psychology*, **74**, 657–690.

Kanfer, R. & Ackerman, P.L. (2000). Individual differences in work motivation: further explorations of a trait framework. *Applied Psychology: An International Review*, **49**, 470–482.

Kerr, N.L. & Brunn, S.E. (1983). Dispensibility of member effort and group motivation losses: free-rider effects. *Journal of Personality and Social Psychology*, **44**, 78–94.

Klein, K.J., Wesson, M.J., Hollenbeck, J.R. & Alge, B.J. (1999). Goal commitment and goal-setting process: conceptual clarification and empirical synthesis. *Journal of Applied Psychology*, **84**, 885–896.

Korman, A.K. (1970). Toward a hypothesis of work behavior. *Journal of Applied Psychology*, **56**, 31–41.

Lau, S.K.H. (2000). *The Measurement of Work Values: A Field Test of the Values Fit Process and its Relationship to Individual Outcomes*. MSc dissertation, University of Manchester.

Lawler, E.E. (1994). From job-based to competency-based organizations. *Journal of Organizational Behavior*, **15**, 3–15.

Leonard, N.H, Beauvais, L.L. & Scholl, R.W. (1999). Work motivation: the incorporation of self-concept-based processes. *Human Relations*, **42**, 970–998.

Locke, E.A. & Latham, G.P. (1990*). A Theory of Goal-Setting and Task Performance*. Englewood Cliffs, NJ: Prentice Hall.

Locke, E.A., Smith, K.G., Erez, M., Chah, D-O. & Schaffer, A. (1994). The effects of intra-individual goal conflict on performance. *Journal of Management*, **20**, 67–91.

Maslow, A.H. (1943). A theory of motivation. *Psychological Review*, **50**, 370–396.

McCann, J.E. & Buckner, M. (1994). Redesigning work: motivations, challenges and practices in 181 companies. *Human Resource Planning*, **17**, 23–41.

McClelland, D.C. (1961). *The Achieving Society*. Princeton, NJ: Van Nostrand.

McNeely, B.L. & Meglino, B.M. (1994). The role of dispositional and situational antecedents in prosocial organizational behavior: an examination of the intended beneficiaries of prosocial behavior. *Journal of Applied Psychology*, **79**, 836–844.

Meglino, B.M. & Ravlin, E.C. (1998). Individual values in organizations: concepts, controversies, and research. *Journal of Management*, **24**, 351–390.

Murray, H.J. (1938). *Explorations in Personality*. Oxford: Oxford University Press.

Noe, R.A. (1996). Is career management related to employee development and performance? *Journal of Organizational Behavior*, **17**, 119–133.

O'Leary-Kelly, A.M., Martocchio, J.J. & Frink, D. D. (1994). A review of the influence of group goals on group performance. *Academy of Management Journal*, **37**, 1285–1301.

Organ, D.W. (1990). The motivational basis of organizational citizenship behavior. *Research in Organizational Behavior*, **12**, 43–72.

Pinder, C.C. (1998). *Work Motivation in Organizational Behavior*. Upper Saddle River, NJ: Prentice Hall.

Robertson, I.T., Smith, M. & Cooper, D. (1992). *Motivation: Strategies, Theory and Practice*, 2nd edn. London: Institute of Personnel and Development.

Robinson, S.L. & Morrison, E.W. (2000). The development of psychological contract breach and violation: a longitudinal study. *Journal of Organizational Behavior*, **21**, 525–546.

Rokeach, M. (1973). *The Nature of Human Values*. New York: Free Press.

Rousseau, D.M. (1995). *Psychological Contracts in Organizations*. London: Sage.

Schaubroeck, J., Ganster, D.C. & Jones, J.R. (1998). Organization and occupation influences in the attraction – selection – attrition process. *Journal of Applied Psychology*, **83**, 869–891.

Schwab, D.P., Olian-Gottlieb, J.D. & Heneman, H.G. (1979). Between-subjects expectancy theory research: a statistical review of studies predicting effort and performance. *Psychological Bulletin*, **86**, 139–147.

Schein, E.H. (1996). Career anchors revisited: implications for career development in the 21st century. *Academy of Management Executive*, **10**, 80–88.

Schwartz, S.H. (1992). Universals in the content and structure of values: theoretical advances and empirical tests in 20 countries. In M. Zanna (Ed.), *Advances in Experimental Social Psychology*, Vol. **25**, pp. 1–65. Orlando: Academic Press.

SHL (2000). Values@work. Technical Manual Version 2.0. Utrecht, Netherlands: SHL Group plc.

Stajkovic, A.D. & Luthans, F. (1998). Self-efficacy and work-related performance: a meta-analysis. *Psychological Bulletin*, **124**, 240–261.

Tajfel, H. & Turner, J.C. (1985). The social identity theory of intergroup behaviour. In S. Worchel & W.G. Austin (Eds), *Psychology of Intergroup Relations*, 2nd edn. Chicago, IL:Nelson-Hall.

Templer, A.J. & Cawsey, T. (1999). Rethinking career development in an era of portfolio careers. *Career Development International*, **4**, 70–76.

Tharenou, P. (1997). Organizational, job, and personal predictors of employee participation in training and development. *Applied Psychology: An International Review*, **46**, 111–134.

Trompenaars, F. (1993). *Riding the Waves of Culture*. London: Brealey.

Turner, J.C. (1999). Some current themes in research on social identity and self-categorization theories. In N. Ellemers, R. Spears & B. Doosje (Eds), *Social Identity: Context, Commitment, Content*, pp. 6–34. Oxford: Blackwell.

Van Dyne, L., Vandewalle, D., Kostova, T., Latham, M.E. & Cummings, L.L. (2000). Collectivism, propensity to trust and self-esteem as predictors of organizational citizenship in a non-work setting. *Journal of Organizational Behavior*, **21**, 3–23.

Van Eerde, W. & Thierry, H. (1996). Vroom's expectancy models and work-related criteria: a meta-analysis. *Journal of Applied Psychology*, **81**, 575–586.

Van Knippenberg, D. (2000). Work motivation and performance: a social identity perspective. *Applied Psychology: An International Review*, **49**, 357–371.

Van Vianen, A.E.M. (2000). Person–organization fit: the match between newcomers' and recruiters' preferences for organizational cultures. *Personnel Psychology*, **53**, 113–149.

Vroom, V.J. (1964). *Work and Motivation*. Chichester: John Wiley.

Weick, K.E. (1996). Enactment and the boundaryless career: organizing as we work. In M.B. Arthur & D. Rousseau (Eds), *The Boundaryless Career: A New Employment Principle for a New Organizational Era*. Oxford: Oxford University Press.

Wofford, J.C., Goodwin, V.L. & Premack, S. (1992). Meta-analysis of the antecedents of personal goal level and of the antecedents and consequences of goal commitment. *Journal of Management*, **18**, 595–615.

CHAPTER 8

Culture and Organizational Effectiveness

Susan Cartwright
Manchester School of Management, UK
and
Helen Baron
SHL Group plc, UK

INTRODUCTION

Traditionally, the application of psychology in the workplace has tended to focus at the individual (micro) level, rather than at a more macro organizational level of analysis which emphasizes the outcome of collective behaviour and endeavour. However, increasingly, many researchers have adopted the perspective that organizational membership can best be defined and understood as a cultural relationship (Rafaeli, 1997). The culture of an organization acts as a kind of social glue which binds individuals together and performs two types of function: internal integration and external adaptation. The task of leadership in and of organizations is conceptualized as the management of shared meaning or ambiguity (Pfeiffer, 1978).

Within the context of the organizational effectiveness model (Lawler & Ledford, 1997), an organization is considered to be effective when there is a good fit among its strategy, competencies, capabilities and environment. According to Beehr (1995), the attainment of the desired strategic outcomes depends upon the success of the organization at five strategic tasks: cohesion, co-ordination, commitment, communication and the development of a workforce with appropriate competencies. Organizational culture and culture management are seen as important strategic tools in accomplishing these essential strategic tasks (Schuler, 1997). For organizations are unlikely to be effective if their culture is out of step with changes that are taking place in the environment, structure, and work practices (Burnes, 1996). For example, research on the failure of re-engineering projects has highlighted the role of culture in determining the success of major change initiatives (Scott-Morgan, 1994). The implication that

Organizational Effectiveness: The Role of Psychology
Edited by I.T. Robertson, M. Callinan and D. Bartram. © 2002 John Wiley & Sons, Ltd.

organizational culture is a variable which can be manipulated to meet requirements and to improve organizational effectiveness is not without its critics and
has been the subject of much debate. Meek (1988) adopts the "purist" view,
that culture is something an organization "is" and has challenged the cultural
pragmatists who regard culture as something an organization "has". Inherent
in this view is the notion that organizational cultures change and evolve over
time and that the process of change cannot be accelerated by managerial change
programmes. On the other hand, the work of Cummings and Huse (1989) has
documented a number of successful cultural change initiatives. Central to the
success of such programmes has been the following elements: clear strategic
vision, top management commitment, symbolic leadership, supporting changes
in structure, procedures and management style and some change in organizational membership.

It is not the intention to continue this theoretical debate in this chapter, but
rather to accept that culture differentiates organizations, that it influences behaviour and so contributes to organizational effectiveness. In considering any
change, managers need to consider the importance of that change to the future
of the organization alongside the risk of its failing due to cultural resistance
(Schwartz & Davis, 1981). The aim of this chapter is twofold. It discusses the
theoretical concept of organizational culture, its manifestations and typologies
integrated with case study examples which illustrate the way in which cultural
analysis has usefully informed management thinking and change practices.

THE CONCEPT OF ORGANIZATIONAL CULTURE

The notion that organizations are mini societies and can be considered as having a culture has its theoretical origins in sociology and anthropology where the
concept is fundamental to the understanding of any society or societal group.
Culture is considered a powerful, enduring and pervasive influence on human
behaviour. Through the socialization process within a culture, individuals learn
the priorities and values of that society and the acceptable and unacceptable
ways of thinking and behaving expected of members of that society. It is through
culture that societies confer and communicate identity and maintain regular-
ity and social order. In this respect, corporate culture has been described as
a form of labour control (Willmott, 1993). Managerial interest in the concept
or organizational culture first became fashionable in the early 1980s, following
the publication of a number of best selling books (Peters & Waterman, 1982;
Deal & Kennedy, 1982) which linked cultural strength with organizational performance. Prior to this, earlier work in the 1960s had tended to focus on the
role of organizational structure, technology and design in determining organizational effectiveness (Woodward, 1965; Lawrence & Lorsch, 1967; Burns & Stalker,
1961).

There are many definitions of organizational culture within the literature. All
tend to reflect the classic sociological/anthropological definition (Tylor, 1871)
as concerning the internalization of a set of beliefs, assumptions values which
shape behaviour:

- Culture is taken to be the shared attitudes, values, beliefs and customs of members of a social unit or organization (Martin, 1985).
- Organizational culture is shared meanings, patterns of belief, symbols, rituals and myths that evolve across time and that function as social glue (Smircich, 1985).
- A pattern of basic assumptions—invented, discovered or developed by a given group as it learns to cope with its problems of external adaptation and internal integration—has worked well enough to be considered valid and therefore to be taught to new members as the correct way to perceive, think and feel in relation to those problems (Schein, 1985).

Most large organizations have mission statements which articulate the direction of the business and the values they wish to promote and maintain in their dealings with suppliers, customers, employees and the wider community. Organizations such as the Co-operative Bank and the Body Shop are well known for their strong ethical stance and their commitment to environmental issues. In the case of the Co-operative Bank, ethical values directly influence their investment policies, whereas the values of the Body Shop are reflected in its approach to product testing and packaging.

Whilst values are considered to be a sufficient basis for action (Bougon et al., 1977), in that values are what we act to keep, the essence of organizational culture is even more deeply rooted. Culture is not merely a set of shared values but a set of basic assumptions and beliefs which operate in an often unconscious "taken for granted" way (Schein, 1985) and frame reality. For example, inherent in the culture of the Body Shop is a deep-seated belief that (wo)man has a duty to actively protect the planet on which (s)he lives. Schein suggests that culture has a number of elements which exist at four different levels of awareness (see Figure 8.1).

As well as being a powerful determinant of individual and group behaviour (Buono et al., 1985) culture has visibility and "feelability" (Schein, 1985) of which one is often more conscious when moving from one culture to another—what is

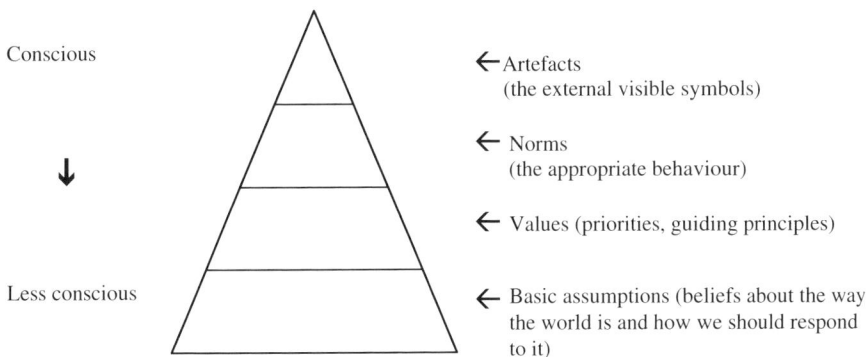

Figure 8.1 Schein's four levels of culture awareness. Reproduced with permission from Schein (1985)

termed "culture shock". Denison (1990) emphasizes that cultures can provide a positive public face for the organization.

Culture is determined by a variety of factors, including history and ownership, size, technology, type of business activity and goals, the external environment and its people, particularly its founders and business leaders.

According to Schein (1985), organizational culture manifests itself in a variety of ways which include:

- climate and physical environment
- the way in which people interact, the language they use, even the way in which they dress
- the way in which work is organized and conducted (e.g. production line assembly versus cellular team arrangements)
- the organization's self image and the dominant values it espouses often through its mission statements, company and product literature
- the way in which it treats its employees and responds to its customers
- the rules for playing the organizational game (e.g. the types of behaviour associated with being a good employee or effective manager).

CULTURE AND EFFECTIVENESS

Organizational culture, and the potential conflict between different sub-cultures within an organizational context, affects the way in which a company conducts its business in the widest sense. This includes the market strategy it adopts, the type and quality of service it offers its customers (Harrison, 1987), its HRM systems and practices (Holt & Kabanoff, 1995) and the kind of psychological environment it creates for its employees (Cartwright & Cooper, 1996, 2000). Furthermore, the significant growth in mergers, acquisitions and strategic alliances, both domestically and internationally, has emphasized the challenges faced by organizations in adapting and integrating with other corporate and national cultures.

ORGANIZATIONAL PERFORMANCE

In their study of 62 of America's consistently high performing companies of the 1970s and 80s, Peters and Waterman (1982) presented a set of attributes which characterized corporate excellence. In particular, they emphasized that organizations with strong, yet flexible cultures were likely to out-perform those with weaker, fragmented or rigid cultures. Intuitively, their argument suggesting a simple causal relationship between cultural strength and performance was a persuasive one, particularly from a practitioner perspective. A strong and clearly articulated culture provides a means of focusing and directing the efforts and activities of organizational members on a common organizational purpose (Watson, 1986). Strong cultures eliminate the necessity to provide employees with detailed instructions or to engage in lengthy discussions as to how to approach particular issues and problems, so enhancing the capability of an organization to effectively pursue its strategic objectives (Sathe, 1983).

Over time the performance of many of the excellent companies identified by Peters and Waterman has declined dramatically and the methodological shortcomings of the research have been heavily criticized (Wilson, 1992). Subsequent research has found a positive correlation between cultural strength and short-term performance, but a weak, and in some cases, negative correlation with longer-term performance (Denison, 1990). This is not surprising given the changing environments in which organizations operate. The cohesiveness engendered by strong cultures can lead to "group think" and an insularity which makes organizations become "prisoners" of their own culture to the extent that they fail to recognize or are unable to change quickly enough. Organizational cultures in providing stability and predictability for its members are inherently resistant to change.

Forces against change can be both at the organizational level (e.g. leaders, tried and tested recipes for success, lack of resources) and at the individual level (e.g. habit, security in the past and fear of failure).

When organizations recognize the need to change, an assessment of the cultural forces which may inhibit that change is essential to ensure that there is cultural and strategic alignment. A change in organizational leadership is often a significant driver and catalyst for strategic and cultural change. Senior management teams play an important role in both shaping and maintaining the culture of an organization. It is reasonable to expect their personal and corporate values may be closely linked. As senior managers have the positional power to promote or sabotage change initiatives, it is important that any proposed changes associated with a change in leadership gain the personal acceptance and commitment of all the new leader's senior colleagues if they are to have any chance of being successful. As the case study below illustrates, the personal values and motivations of individuals at the most senior level in an organization may be inconsistent with the proposed changes in strategic direction and need to be confronted.

Case Study 1: Change and its Cultural Implications

A small, but successful, medical supplies company was a comfortable and friendly place with a very stable workforce; it was not unusual to find people who had been with the organization for 20 years or longer. The management team also fitted this pattern, although Tom had recently taken over as MD, from his long-serving predecessor.

It was Tom who initiated the development review. Since his arrival he had been impressed by the strengths of his management team. They showed real commitment to the business, had a good mix of skills and worked together hard and well. However, he felt that with the developments in the health service, the market for their products was changing, and the company needed to be ready to adapt to new circumstances. He felt the team needed to adopt a more active and sophisticated approach to management to be able to meet the challenges of the future. He hoped the review would show them how to do this.

The process included completing a number of psychometric assessments including a measure looking at the underlying motivations of each manager (Motivation Questionnaire, SHL, 1992). The results were fed back to each individual and, a little later, a consultant mediated a joint session between each member of the management team and the MD.

The MQ profiles revealed the sources of energy of the team. They were all quite strongly motivated by Commercial Outlook. They liked seeing how their work benefited the business, and this, together with their above-average scores on Personal Principles, was the source of their great commitment to the company. However, in other respects energies were moderate and more typical of lower levels than senior managers. Although striving to meet objectives would energize the group, they were not motivated by competition and there was a tendency to give in relatively easily in the face of a more difficult challenge. Only one was particularly motivated by opportunities to exercise power and influence. There was also a rather low tolerance of work encroaching on to private life. Although they worked hard at their jobs, these were not workaholics!

John, perhaps the most able of the group, was typical of this pattern. In charge of finance he had little need for power or control. He did not have much personal ambition and resisted Tom's suggestions that he change his style. Although often the first in the team to diagnose a problem and suggest a solution, he made little effort to persuade others to adopt it. He had a very low need for affiliation and would return to work alone on his figures rather than trying to influence policy in what he perceived was the right direction. He had a high need for Material Reward and for Ease and Security. Therefore he avoided taking risks, particularly if these could affect his financial security.

The review helped the MD to understand his team much better. Their motivational structures were perfectly attuned to the stable quality of the business up to now. He realized that the changes that he was trying to introduce were going to be difficult for the team, although other evidence from the review showed they had the capacity to cope with it. The pro-activity and assertiveness he was trying to generate did not come naturally and they would not respond to being played off, one against another. He would need to support them in learning these new ways of working together. However, the profiles had also shown the key to energizing the group. Their will for the commercial success of the enterprise would be a real source of motivation in meeting the challenges of the future.

The Need for Cultural Compatibility

On a much wider scale, a growing body of research has emphasized the importance of the goodness of both the strategic and the cultural fit between organizations which decide to work together. Studies have linked the poor economic performance and negative behavioural outcomes of merged and acquired organizations to cultural incompatibility and the ensuing battles for cultural dominance of one partner over another (Business Institute of Management, 1986; Hunt, 1988; Cartwright & Cooper, 1996). Furthermore, research evidence has found that the pattern of international M&A activity reflects the preferences of decision-makers to select organizational partners in countries which they perceive have similar business cultures to their own (Cartwright et al., 1997).

ONE CULTURE OR MANY?

Current thinking increasingly recognizes the limitations in the culture–excellence approach of treating culture as a homogeneous integrated entity. Organizations are characterized by multiple cultures. Individuals are members of many societal groups, aside from work groups, and may identify with others on the basis of gender, ethnic background, religion etc. Such cultural identities may potentially be carried into organizational settings and may influence the cultural context of an organization. In addition, workplace identity may be derived from membership of a particular profession, team, department or division.

Fedor and Werther (1995) suggest that organizational culture can be studied from three perspectives: integration, differentiation and fragmentation. The integration perspective focuses on the consistencies within a culture; whereas differentiation and fragmentation are concerned with identifying the inconsistencies and ambiguities within a culture and its sub-cultures. More recently Sackman (1997) has proposed that culture may be both integrated and differentiated through the framework of cultural knowledge. She draws the distinction between directory knowledge (the how things are done) as emphasizing the integrated and shared aspects of the culture, and dictionary knowledge (the different labels people use to denominate things and events) as emphasizing the difference between sub-cultures. Within any organization there is likely to be a cultural consensus as to values, priorities and behaviours, and, at the same time some degree of conflict between competing sub-cultures. Furthermore, that balance will vary between organizations and within the same organization at different points in time.

Differences between managerial and shop-floor cultures have been widely observed and researched (Laurila, 1997) as well as differences associated with the length of tenure; i.e. old timers and newcomers (Cartwright & Cooper, 1996). Schein (1985) highlights the potential discrepancy between the publicly espoused culture of an organization, promoted by corporate literature and senior management, and the reality of organizational life; i.e. the actual culture in use.

Professional cultures can also exert a powerful influence on attitudes and behaviours. Doctors and nurses, whilst working in a common organizational setting tend to adopt pro-social behaviours towards members of their own professional group, thus creating and reinforcing cultural divisions between the two groups (Hernes, 1997). A study of the five leading UK pharmaceutical companies (Cartwright et al., 1997) found evidence of a strong and similar R&D culture operating in and across all the companies. This R&D culture was characterized as being high on the debate of ideas but low on risk taking.

As the case study below illustrates, cultural perceptions can vary considerably in different parts or divisions of the same organization.

Case Study 2: Kream Consolidated Dairies

Kream Consolidated Dairies is a large organization which collects and processes raw milk and distributes dairy products. Over 300 members of staff from five divisions completed the Corporate Culture Questionnaire (SHL, 1995) to provide a profile of the organization as part of a consultancy intervention.

The profile of the organization is shown in Figure 8.2. Overall, the organization's culture is not an unusual one with scores not far from the average for other organizations on any of the dimensions studied. This is not in itself a positive or a negative result. The evaluation of a culture depends on whether it is effective in promoting the achievement of organizational goals.

When the senior managers were polled on their view of an ideal culture for Kream, it became apparent that they would have liked to see higher scores on many of the scales—thus they were not satisfied with the culture as described. For instance, management wanted to have a higher level of *Communication effectiveness*; staff in the different divisions rated this as poor to moderate. Shift workers particularly rated it as low. Clearly organizational messages were not permeating well beyond the centre and hardly reached those who were not desk based—despite the perception in headquarters that much effort was expended in communication to others. New methods of communication needed to be found to keep all staff informed of organizational goals and initiatives.

While perhaps it is understandable that perceptions of communication effectiveness might differ, and those who communicate overestimate the extent to which their messages are reaching the desired audience, other dimensions of culture might be expected to be open to more objective assessment.

However, a similar difference in scores between divisions was found in *Degree of formalization*. Corporate headquarters rated this as very low and suggested that slightly more formality of working methods would be a good thing. However, the divisions rated formalization as high or very high. One explanation may be that the divisions are more aware of the strict health and safety regime under which they work than are corporate people who have less contact with the actual products. This finding also suggests that corporate headquarters is cut off from the production divisions and may have difficulty understanding the day to day reality of most people in the organization. Further, initiatives from head office to formalize procedures even more could be seen as very burdensome by those outside rather than a welcome reduction in ambiguity. The culture survey helped head office to understand more about the other parts of the organization.

It was not only corporate headquarters that had a different view of the organization from the other divisions. Sometimes the divisions differed from each other. For instance, *Employee influence on decisions* was high at corporate headquarters and moderate in all divisions except one—those who worked directly with the farmers. They felt they had little opportunity to influence decision-making, and particularly changes that they wanted on behalf of the dairy farmers were constantly ignored. Together with the lack of communication effectiveness, this suggests that corporate headquarters needed to invest more energy in explaining company policy to the divisions.

Overall the survey provided many indications of issues that needed to be addressed if the organization was to work together to achieve its aims.

CULTURE AND THE INDIVIDUAL

There is no ideal culture which is suitable for all organizations. The most appropriate culture will depend upon the nature of the organization and its history as well as its corporate vision and strategic plan. The desired culture and values of an organization should be reflected in the core competencies expected of members of the organization. Not only should competencies reflect the values of the culture, they should also be strongly linked to reward structures and mechanisms which reinforce the desired behaviours.

Organizational effectiveness is often reduced by competing values and reward systems. For example, some years ago we encountered an off-shore oil company which was constantly re-stating its commitment to the promotion of safety culture and the ongoing improvement of its work practices. Yet, it had a reward system which paid bonuses to work teams related to the continuous number of days they worked over a three-month period without an accident. This had the effect of suppressing the reporting of accidents or "near miss" incidents. Employees, rather than drawing attention to potential hazards and unsafe practices, actively ignored them and, in some cases, deliberately covered up workplace injuries team members may have suffered. Similarly, it is not uncommon for organizations who would like to move to a more "team-based culture" to have in place appraisal systems which evaluate and reward employees on individually based dimensions like "ability to work independently" rather than on criteria which reflects their contribution to collective effort and the sharing of information and responsibility with others.

Job satisfaction is influenced by a variety of individual, social, cultural, organizational and environmental factors (Wooliams & Mosely 1999). However, some studies have found that particular types of organizational cultures, notably those which foster autonomy and allow for the exercise of freedom in the work environment, are potentially more satisfying and motivating environments in which to work (O'Reilly et al., 1991; Cartwright & Cooper, 1996; Wooliams & Mosely, 1999). Denison (1990) examined organizational performance over a five-year period, based on return on investment, and concluded that organizations which had a participative culture significantly outperformeded their competitors between year 2 and year 5.

Individuals will seek to join organizations with values which are congruent with their own and leave those where there is a misfit between the two. Schweiger and DeNisi (1981) argued that it is important for organizations to provide potential entrants with a realistic preview of their culture to avoid the problem of unmet expectations. Through a process of trial and error learning, over time organizations work to develop recruitment and selection systems which enable

Summary Kream Culture Profile

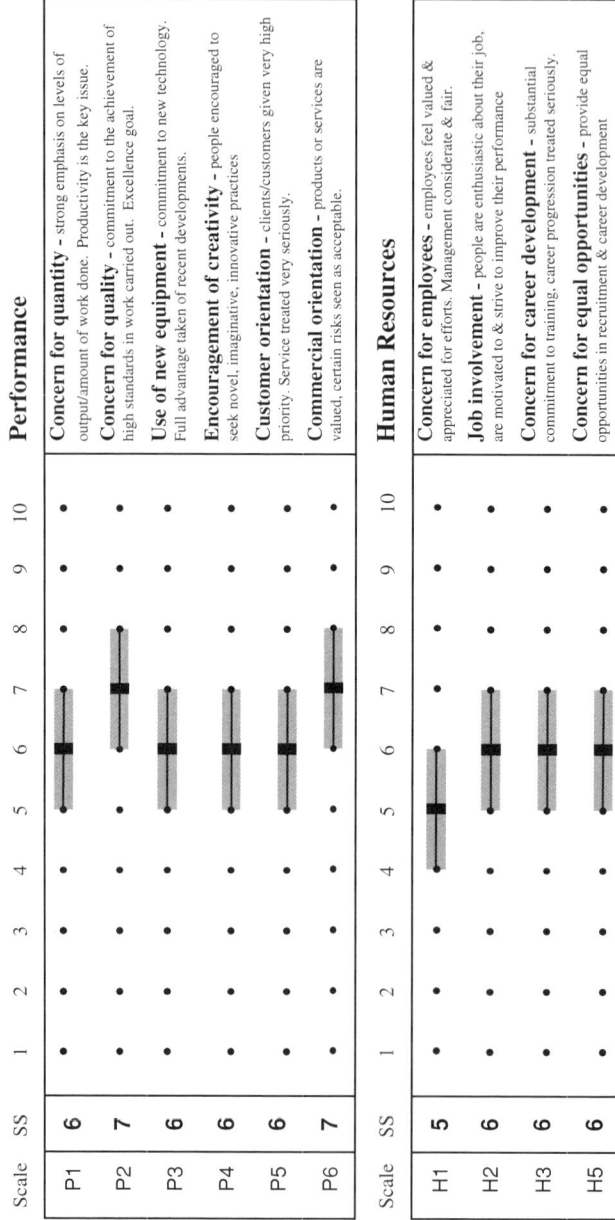

Performance

Scale	SS	1	2	3	4	5	6	7	8	9	10	
P1	6	•	•	•	•	•	●	•	•	•	•	**Concern for quantity** - strong emphasis on levels of output/amount of work done. Productivity is the key issue.
P2	7	•	•	•	•	•	•	●	•	•	•	**Concern for quality** - commitment to the achievement of high standards in work carried out. Excellence goal.
P3	6	•	•	•	•	•	●	•	•	•	•	**Use of new equipment** - commitment to new technology. Full advantage taken of recent developments.
P4	6	•	•	•	•	•	●	•	•	•	•	**Encouragement of creativity** - people encouraged to seek novel, imaginative, innovative practices
P5	6	•	•	•	•	•	●	•	•	•	•	**Customer orientation** - clients/customers given very high priority. Service treated very seriously.
P6	7	•	•	•	•	•	•	●	•	•	•	**Commercial orientation** - products or services are valued, certain risks seen as acceptable.

Human Resources

Scale	SS	1	2	3	4	5	6	7	8	9	10	
H1	5	•	•	•	•	●	•	•	•	•	•	**Concern for employees** - employees feel valued & appreciated for efforts. Management considerate & fair.
H2	6	•	•	•	•	•	●	•	•	•	•	**Job involvement** - people are enthusiastic about their job, are motivated to & strive to improve their performance
H3	6	•	•	•	•	•	●	•	•	•	•	**Concern for career development** - substantial commitment to training, career progression treated seriously.
H5	6	•	•	•	•	•	●	•	•	•	•	**Concern for equal opportunities** - provide equal opportunities in recruitment & career development

Figure 8.2 The completed Culture Questionnaire for Kream Consolidated Dairies. © 1995 SHL Group plc. Reproduced by permission

Decision Making

Degree of formalisation - very systematised, bureaucratic & structured, clear sets of rules & regulations.

Employee influence on decisions - staff have autonomy in planning & doing their job & decision making

Decision making effectiveness - appropriate decisions are made with due speed rather than delayed.

Concern for the longer term - committed to anticipating future demands, constraints, & possibilities.

Rate of change - Systems, procedures or working methods are frequently updated. Restructuring common.

Environmental concern - committed to ecological issues, environment considered in decisions made.

Concern for Safety - Attention is paid to safety, both of customers and the workforce

Scale	SS	1	2	3	4	5	6	7	8	9	10
D1	8							7			
D2	5					5					
D3	4				4						
D4	5					5					
D5	7							7			
D6	7							7			
D7	6						6				

Relationships

Vertical group relations - good relationships between management & staff. Few destructive conflicts.

Lateral group relations - units co-operate & not compete, effective collaboration toward organisational goals

Interpersonal co-operation - individuals support each other constructively, conflicts resolved easily.

Communication effectiveness - quality, quantity & speed of communication are of high standard.

Awareness of organisational goals - key objectives & strategic goals have been well disseminated.

Scale	SS	1	2	3	4	5	6	7	8	9	10
R1	4				4						
R2	4				4						
R3	5					5					
R4	5					5					
R5	6						6				

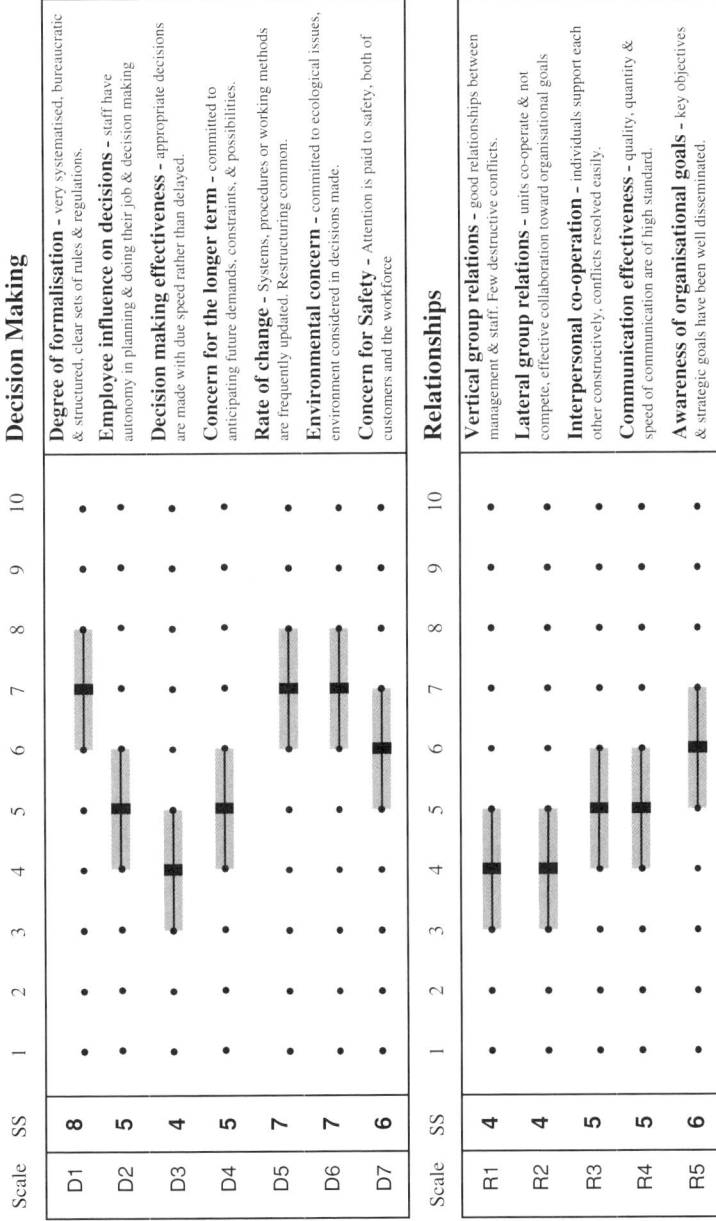

Norm: Composite Group of 24 Organisations: Average scores are between 5 and 6.

Figure 8.2 (continued)

them to identify those individuals who fit the organization and resemble current organizational membership. The tendency for organizations to become more homogenous in terms of their culture and demography is consistent with the selection–attraction–attrition (SAA) model (Schneider, 1987) and theories of interpersonal attraction (Pfeiffer, 1978). It is a powerful means of ensuring that there is a high level of cultural agreement within the organization. Whereas high levels of cultural agreement amongst members supports co-ordination and employee motivation, in the longer term it can cause strategic myopia and a lack of flexibility (Koene et al., 1997).

Major change in any organization will bring about some conflict between the existing values of the individual and that of the new culture. According to Cummings and Huse (1989), one of the most effective ways of achieving cultural change is to change the organizational membership and the process of recruitment and induction. This approach to change has been described as the tactics of the machine gun, and if taken to the extreme can destroy the accumulated value and wisdom within an organization. A more conciliatory approach, suggested by Schein (1985), is to analyse the beliefs, values and assumptions of those who are seen as the guardians and promoters of the existing culture and the implications of the change for their own behaviour. This approach is reflected in the team building activities which were undertaken in the newly formed business units, following the break-up of British Rail. This process is described in the case study below.

Case Study 3: Team Building in the Newly Formed "Infrastructure Services"

Rail services in the UK were privatized in the mid 1990s and a number of private companies were formed. One of these was an infrastructure maintenance company. There were many challenges facing this organization and its newly designated board of directors. It needed to maintain the provision of service within a very different structure, manage a large operation and many staff, as well as moving from a public sector to a profit oriented culture. The board of this new organization needed to work as a team to meet these challenges, yet in many cases they had not even met their colleagues before being appointed.

As part of a programme to get to know each other and to start to formulate the strategy for the new organization, each director underwent a psychometric assessment looking at personality style and underlying motivations. The group were not sure enough of each other to share the results openly, but each received feedback on themselves, with some indication of how their style might be perceived by others.

While it is relatively easy for a group of people to get to know each other's typical personal style in approaching people and tasks, it is underlying motivations and values that go to make a common culture for a team. We can see when someone is outgoing, has a structured approach, follows or flouts conventions etc. However, it is more difficult to know what drives a person to behave in a certain way.

The individual feedback that members received helped them to be more aware of their basic motivations, and how these might differ from those of others in the team. Overall the group showed a typical profile for senior directors of a large business organization—they liked exercising power and responsibility, had a commercial orientation in their values, and had little need for their own personal development. However, there were some strong trends that differed from other such groups—they had a strong need for flexibility in the way they worked and were likely to react against bureaucratic or highly structured processes; and they had a greater need for achievement, competition and material reward than other senior managers.

In many ways, these shared values and motivations would help the group in working together. Where everyone put commercial success as their first priority it would be easier to agree over actions and determine an appropriate strategy. However, in providing direction for the whole organization, they would need to think how their decisions and actions would be perceived and carried out by the workforce. Already disturbed by the changes in organizational structure, the workforce could be expected to view with suspicion their new directors. However, the legacy of the old public service ethos meant that, typically, commercial values might be rejected. Equally, the old procedural approach of the rail company would have tended to attract people who valued a more structured approach and would feel uncomfortable with the preference of the board for more flexible working practices.

In addition, although there was a great deal of commonality among the new board, there were areas where they differed. These were likely to be the source of future conflicts, if the group were not careful. Discussion of underlying differences in values can help to focus and diffuse conflict. For instance, there were some differences between the board members in their attitude to risk. In discussing a possible risky course of action, those who felt enlivened by an element of risk would be likely to be in favour, whereas those who valued security would tend to be against it. A conflict over whether to follow the course of action would be likely to ensue. If this were to focus only on whether the action would be successful it would be difficult to resolve. Often in this situation, each side has difficulty understanding the arguments of the other. The risk averse group would feel the other side were failing to understand how dangerous the action might be, and the risk takers would feel the more security minded had not understood the opportunity the action presented. Each side's evaluation of the action would be affected by their basic values yet the discussion might not touch on this area at all. This type of conflict is common where two different cultures meet. However, if the group were to share their different attitudes to risk taking, they would find it easier to understand the positions of the different parties, and thereby resolve the conflict in a more logical manner.

TYPOLOGIES OF ORGANIZATIONAL CULTURE

Some researchers who have attempted to conceptualize and represent differences between organizational cultures have found it useful to draw upon type theories. One of the most widely known is that of Harrison (1972) which links culture with organizational structure. According to Harrison, there are four broad types of culture: power, role, task/achievement and person/support.

Power cultures are usually found in small entrepreneurial companies. They are characterized by centralized decision-making and have the advantage of being able to react swiftly. Such cultures are often represented as a web structure. To their disadvantage, the lack of autonomy afforded to employees working in this type of culture often results in low morale and feelings of powerlessness. Power cultures often encounter major problems as the organization becomes bigger and more specialized.

Role cultures are probably still the most common form of organizational structure and typical of large organizations, particularly in the public sector. They are bureaucratic, mechanistic, with rigid structures and clear role boundaries. Decision-making is slow and problems are referred up to the next hierarchical level. To their advantage they are often experienced by employees as being fair and secure environments in which to work.

Task/achievement cultures are usually associated with project environments, as what is important is getting the job done (the task), rather than the prescribing of how it should be done (the process). Task cultures encourage team working and individual autonomy and value expertise. They can be very stimulating cultures in which to work but can also be very exhausting and demanding. Task cultures can face problems of "burn out". The lack of formal authority can also be a problem.

Person/support cultures are relatively rare in commercial organizations as they are associated with minimalist structure. Central to the person/support culture is the notion that the wishes and development of the individual are primary. Therefore such cultures are more likely to be found in community organizations such as the kibbutz or other types of co-operatives. However, commercial organizations can vary in the extent to which they incorporate elements of a person/support culture.

There are numerous other typologies in the literature. Kabanoff (1991, 1993) proposed a value-based typology utilizing three categories: élite, meritocratic leadership and collegial. Denison (1990) developed a four-fold categorization that links culture to strategic emphasis and environmental needs: an adaptability culture characterized by a strong external focus; a mission culture characterized by a shared vision; an involvement culture characterized by a high level of internal involvement and participation; and a consistency culture which emphasizes continuity and stability. Trompenaars (1997) similarly developed a four-type model which has strong parallels with the work of Harrison.

Hofstede (1991) advocated a dimensional approach whereby different cultures can be compared in terms of their relative position on a number of key dimensions or factors; e.g. orientation towards individualism vs. collectivism, power distance, masculinity vs. femininity, and the extent to which they seek to avoid risk. Hofstede's work was based on a study investigating the role of national culture and the type of business cultures which predominate in different countries. Subsequent research by Trompenaars (1997) has expanded this study and proposed a number of additional dimensions. The tension between the type and the dimensional (trait) approaches to organizational culture mirrors a similar tension within the personality literature.

ASSESSING ORGANIZATIONAL CULTURE

Research into organizational culture has adopted a variety of approaches. Commonly used methods of assessing culture include the analysis of archival information, organizational documentation and folklore; critical incident techniques; and questionnaire surveys. Smit (1997) used more novel methods involving the plotting of neural networks to understand team cultures. Cartwright (1998) incorporated projective techniques to communicate differences in corporate culture in a merger situation.

There are a number of available culture measures (for example, see Harrison & Stokes, 1990; Saville & Holdsworth, 1993; Tucker et al., 1990; Trompenaars, 1997, Cooke & Lafferty, 1989) which focus on behaviours and, to a lesser extent, values. The Corporate Culture Questionnaire (CCQ), published by Saville and Holdsworth (1993), consists of 23 scales which cluster around four cultural domains: performance, human resources, decision-making and relationships. Questionnaire measures have the advantage of being a more cost-effective and less labour-intensive means of collecting data from large samples. They also enable systematic comparisons to be made both between and within organizations and can provide a useful baseline measure against which to monitor change. The findings of a recent correlation and factor-analytic study of four major self-report measures (Xenikou & Furnham, 1996) indicated considerable overlap and inter-correlations between subscales both within and between measures, thus confirming their validity.

However, the psychometric properties of many instruments still remain to be proven. Cartwright (1997) points out, compared with qualitative methods, questionnaire measures address a more confined domain of cultural enquiry which may not necessarily capture cultural priorities. The emerging consensus amongst researchers is that certain methods of cultural enquiry may be more appropriate for studying and explaining different aspects and levels of culture in an organization and are best used in combination (Rousseau, 1990).

FUTURE ISSUES

According to Ouchi (1993), organizational effectiveness and performance can be predicted by the degree to which organizations develop human assets that are unique to a particular organization—what is termed "human asset specificity". This perspective emphasizes that competitive advantage is not only linked to employee training and development but also depends upon the organization's ability to make employees feel a sufficient sense of attachment to the organization to want to work hard for and remain in that organization. As individuals are increasingly recruited to perform organizational roles rather than jobs, key competencies such as flexibility, problem solving, self-management and continuous learning have achieved prominence. Developing the kind of organizational culture which both attracts and retains individuals with those skills and competencies, rather than exercising them elsewhere, becomes crucial.

Given the changing nature of work and work organization, businesses in the future will find it increasingly difficult to co-ordinate the activities and efforts of the workforce and maintain a cohesive and inclusive culture. Increasing diversity in the composition of the workforce together with increased globalization have given rise to a new organizational form—"the multi-cultural organization" (Cox & Tung, 1997). This is an organizational form which is characterized by increased cultural heterogeneity among stakeholder groups, particularly employees, customers and suppliers. Multi-culturalism presents organizational challenges at the macro-level in terms of structural, cultural and informal integration. Valuing people and handling dissent will assume a greater priority. Multi-culturalism also has implications at the individual level in that the ability to lead diverse groups becomes an important managerial competence.

At the same time, changes in employment patterns indicate that the number of people working full time, on a permanent basis, in conventional organizational settings will continue to fall (Feldman, 1997). As organizations have faced rapid change in the profile of needed skills, they have increasingly become tempted to buy rather than develop new skills within the existing workforce (Lawler & Ledford, 1997). The rise in the contingent workforce has profound implications for individuals who are pursuing careers outside traditional organizational boundaries. There are also significant organizational and psychological implications in terms of the relational contract between employer and employee and the expectations one party has of the other. For if individuals are expected to be more self-motivated and self-reliant in their acquisition of skills and knowledge, then their relationship with their employer is unlikely to extend beyond being a transactional one. The shift of responsibility for training and development from organization to the individual may result in short-term financial gains but lead to losses in the longer term. In the context of organizational culture, differences in worker status can cause tensions and conflict between subcultures.

Technological advances continue to influence organizational design. The concept of the "virtual organization" and distance working challenges traditional definitions of what an organization is. Social relationships between organizational members become much loser in these new forms of organizational design, which will threaten the sense of community and shared culture that has dominated management literature for such a long time as being a desirable and effective organizational attribute. In the future, how will organizations engage the affective commitment of their workforce? For if individuals are working for several employers, are on short-term contracts, or based in locations remote from the organization, to what extent will they be willing, or have the opportunity to, acculturate and identify with the organization?

The future presents a significant cultural challenge for organizations in terms of maintaining internal integration and will bring more sharply into focus the emotional rather than the structural aspect of organization. Consequently, the role of psychology and strategic OB will, as Schuler (1997) has predicted, increase in prominence as a means of helping organizations manage these new realities effectively in a number of ways. By understanding and analysing the salient characteristics of its culture and the assumptions and beliefs that underpin it, an organization will be more able to:

- identify cultural values and behaviours which may facilitate or inhibit change within the organization
- identify factors which may contribute to making the organizational culture unattractive to new recruits and certain employee groups, e.g. women, ethnic minorities
- identify conflicting values and behaviours within or between different subcultures in an organization which may reduce organizational effectiveness
- understand the problem of cultural integration when entering into mergers, acquisitions, strategic alliances and collaborative working arrangements with other organizations.

Organizational psychologists have a valuable role to play in facilitating cultural awareness and understanding. Because of the "taken for granted" way in which culture operates, it is very difficult—indeed some would argue impossible (Schein, 1985)—for those inside a culture to be able to objectively analyse and describe that culture and fairly compare it with others. As Trompenaars (1997) observes, cultural ethnocentricity produces a tendency for people to automatically equate something different with something wrong; i.e. "their way is clearly different from ours, so it cannot be right". An organizational psychologist possesses the skills and techniques to objectively conduct a cultural assessment and challenge its appropriateness for current circumstances or future change. Organizational psychologists can usefully work with organizations to suggest actions which can be taken to promote cultural change. Typically these are likely to involve the following:

- ensuring that reward and appraisal systems are aligned with the new behaviours that the organization wishes to promote
- introducing changes in the physical environment and methods of work organization which discourage habitual behaviours
- identifying new training needs
- reducing individuals' perception of risk and fear of failure and so encouraging experimentation with new ideologies and working practices
- identifying key performance indicators and developing mechanisms for monitoring change
- introducing a wide-scale consultative process to engage and involve employees in the change process
- introducing "new blood" into the organization.

Whilst instruments and methodologies exist which can be used to conduct some form of diagnostic cultural audit of an organization to ensure that this is aligned with its strategic objectives, specific measures which assess the degree of person–culture match in the context of the selection and assessment literature are less well developed. However, cultural knowledge gained from an informed assessment of an organization's culture can be used to help companies present a realistic cultural preview to job applicants, to enable them to decide whether their expectations and needs are likely to be met, and as a result whether they will "fit" into the organizational culture.

CONCLUSIONS

In terms of organizational effectiveness, the challenge for organizations is to develop and maintain a culture which is adaptive, yet highly consistent and responsive to internal and external needs and demands—and, at the same time, is in alignment with the company's strategic goals and objectives. This is a complex and difficult task given the diverse range of stakeholder interests which an organization has to satisfy and to keep in balance.

External adaptation may often detrimentally affect internal integration. New ways of working and organizational structures may require considerable cultural change and individual adjustment. We have already seen how adaptation to the customer demand for more flexibility in the purchase of goods and services has forced organizations to change their traditional working patterns and methods of organization—Sunday trading, 24-hour tele-banking and internet shopping being obvious examples of organizational adaptation to consumer demand. However, considerable internal adaptation has also been required of employees to meet these demands in terms of their implicit/explicit employment contracts, working practices and culture. The necessity to work long and/or unsociable hours, and to adhere to demanding performance and service agreements, may increase customer satisfaction but results in an internal culture which places excessive stress on the employees and adversely impacts on their non-work life.

Given the dynamic nature of the external and internal environments in which organizations continue to operate, organizations need to regularly assess the type of culture that they currently have and the extent to which this is appropriate to the future demands and needs of various stakeholders. Increasing cultural awareness and the conduct of some form of culture audit can greatly inform the way in which managers implement, manage and anticipate change.

ACKNOWLEDGEMENTS

Figure 8.2 is reproduced by kind permission of SHL Group plc, who retain all rights and title to this material.

REFERENCES

Beehr, T.A. (1995). *Psychological Stress in the Workplace*. London: Routledge.
Bougon, M., Weick, K. & Binkhurst, D. (1977). Cognition in organizations. *Administrative Science Quarterly*, **22**.

Buono, A.F., Bowditch, J.L. & Lewis, J.W. (1985). When cultures collide: the anatomy of a merger. *Human Relations*, **38**, 477–500.

Burns, T. & Stalker, G.M. (1961). The management of *Innovation*. London: Tavistock.

Burnes, B. (1996). *Managing Change*, 2nd edn. London: FT Pitman Publishing.

Cartwright, S. (1997). Organizational partnerships. In C.L. Cooper & S.E. Jackson (Eds), *Creating Tomorrow's Organizations*. Chichester: John Wiley.

Cartwright, S. (1998). Cultural compatibility in mergers and acquisitions. *Journal of Professional HRM*, **13**, 10–16.

Cartwright, S. & Cooper, C.L. (1996). *Mergers, Acquisitions and Strategic Alliances: Integrating People and Cultures*. Oxford: Butterworth–Heinemann.

Cartwright, S. & Cooper, C.L. (2000). *HR Know How in Mergers and Acquisitions*. London: IPD.

Cartwright, S., Cooper, C.L. & Jordan, J. (1997). Managerial preferences in international mergers and acquisition partners. In D. Hussey (Ed.), *The Strategic Challenge*. Chichester: John Wiley.

Cooke, R.A. & Lafferty, J.C. (1989). *Organizational Culture Inventory*. Plymouth, MI: Human Synergistics.

Cox, T. & Tung, R.L. (1997). The multi-cultural organization revisited. In C.L. Cooper & S.E. Jackson (Eds), *Creating Tomorrow's Organizations*. Chichester: John Wiley.

Cummings, T.G. & Huse, E.F. (1989). *Organisation Development and Change*. St Paul, MN: West.

Deal, T.E. & Kennedy, A. (1982). *Corporate Cultures*. Reading, MA: Addison-Wesley.

Denison, D. (1990). *Corporate Culture and Effectiveness*. New York: John Wiley.

Fedor, K.J. & Werther, W.B. (1995). Making sense of cultural factors in international alliances. *Organizational Dynamics*, **23** (4), 33–47.

Feldman, D. (1997). Career issues facing contingent and self-employed workers: prospects and problems for the 21st Century. In C.L. Cooper & S.E. Jackson (Eds), *Creating Tomorrow's Organizations*. Chichester: John Wiley.

Harrison, R. (1987). *Organizational Culture and Quality of Service*. London: Association for Management Education and Development.

Harrison, R. (1972). Understanding your organisation's character. *Harvard Business Review*, (50) May/June, 119–228.

Harrison, R. & Stokes, H. (1990). *Diagnosing your Organization's Culture*. Berkeley, CA: Harrison & Associates.

Hernes, H. (1997). Cross cutting identifications in organizations. In S.A. Sackman (Ed.), *Cultural Complexity in Organizations*. Thousand Oaks, CA: Sage.

Hofstede, G. (1991). *Cultures and Organizations*. London: McGraw-Hill.

Holt, J. & Kabanoff, B. (1995). The relationship between organizational value systems and HRM systems. Paper presented at the Inaugral Conference of Industrial and Organizational Psychology, Sydney, July.

Hunt, J. (1988). Managing the successful acquisition: a people question. *London Business School Journal*, summer, 2–15.

Kabanoff, B. (1991). Equity, equality, power and conflict. *Academy of Management Review*, **16**, 416–441.

Kabanoff, B. (1993). An exploration of espoused culture in Australian organizations. *Asia Pacific Journal of Human Resources*, **31**, 1–29.

Koene, B.A., Boone, A.J.J. & Soeters, J.L. (1997). Organizational factors influencing homogeneity and heterogeneity of organizational cultures. In S.A. Sackman (Ed.), *Cultural Complexity in Organizations*. Thousand Oaks, CA: Sage.

Laurila, J. (1997). Discontinuous technological change as a trigger for temporary reconciliation of managerial subcultures. In S.A. Sackman (Ed.), *Cultural Complexity in Organizations*. Thousand Oaks, CA: Sage.

Lawler, E. & Ledford, G.R. (1997). New approaches to organizing. In C.L. Cooper & S.E. Jackson (Eds), *Creating Tomorrow's Organization*. Chichester: John Wiley.

Lawrence, P.R. & Lorsch, J.W. (1967). *Organization and Environment*. Boston, MA: Harvard Business School.

Martin, J. (1985). Culture collisions in mergers and acquisitions. In P.J. Frost, L.F. Moore, M.R. Louis et al. (Eds), *Organizational Culture*. Beverly Hills: Sage.

Meek, V.L. (1988). Organizational culture: origins and weaknesses. *Organization Studies*, **9**, 453–473.

O'Reilly, C.A., Chatman, J. & Caldwell, D.F. (1991). People and organizational culture: a profile comparison approach to assessing person–organization fit. *Academy of Management Journal*, **34**, 487–516.

Ouchi, W.G. (1993). Competitive advantage. Paper presented at Michigan Business School; cited in Denison (1990).

Peters, T.J. & Waterman, R.H. (1982). *In Search of Excellence: Lessons from America's Best Run Companies*. London: Harper & Row.

Pfeiffer, J. (1978). *Organizational Design*. Arlington Heights, IL: AHM Publishing.

Rafaeli, A. (1997). What is an organization? Who are the members? In C.L. Cooper & S.E. Jackson (Eds), *Creating Tomorrow's Organizations*. Chichester: John Wiley.

Rousseau, D.M. (1990). Assessing organizational culture: the case for multiple methods. In B. Schneider (Ed.), *Organizational Climate and Culture*. San Francisco: Jossey-Bass.

Sackman, S.A. (1997). *Cultural Complexity in Organizations*. Thousand Oaks, CA: Sage.

Sathe, V. (1983). Some action implications of corporate culture: a manager's guide to action. *Organizational Dynamics*, autumn, 4–23.

Saville & Holdsworth (1992). *Motivation Questionnaire*. Thames Ditton, Surrey, UK.

Saville & Holdsworth (1993). *Corporate Culture Questionnaire*. Thames Ditton, Surrey, UK.

Saville & Holdsworth (1995). *Culture Questionnaire*. Thames Ditton, Surrey, UK.

Schein, E.H. (1985). *Organizational Culture and Leadership*. San Francisco: Jossey-Bass.

Schneider, B. (1987). The people make the place. *Personnel Psychology*, **40**, 437–453.

Schuler, R.S. (1997). A strategic perspective for organizational behaviour. In C.L. Cooper & S.E. Jackson (Eds), *Creating Tomorrow's Organisations*. Chichester: John Wiley.

Schwartz, H. & Davis, S. (1981). Matching corporate culture and business strategy. *Organizational Dynamics*, **10**, 30–48.

Schweiger, D.M. & DeNisi, A. (1981). Communication with employees following a merger. *Academy of Management Journal*, **34**, 110–135.

Scott-Morgan, P. (1994). *The Unwritten Rules of the Game*. New York: McGraw-Hill.

SHL (1995). Kream Consolidated Dairies. Culture Questionnaire. Utrecht, Netherlands: SHL Group, plc.

Smircich, L. (1985). Is the concept of culture a paradigm for understanding organizations and ourselves? In P.J. Frost, L.F. Moore, M.R. Louis et al. (Eds), *Organizational Culture*. London: Sage.

Smit, I.T. (1997). Patterns of coping: a study of team cultures and health. Thesis, Utrecht University.

Trompenaars, F. (1997). *Riding the Waves of Culture*. London: Nicholas Brealey Publishing.

Tucker, R.W., McCoy, W.J. & Evans, L.C. (1990). Can questions objectively assess organizational culture? *Journal of Managerial Psychology*, **5** (4), 4–11.

Tylor, E. (1871). *Primitive Culture*, Vol. **1**. London: John Murray.

Watson, T.J. (1986). *Management Organization and Employment Strategy*. London: Routledge & Kegan Paul.

Willmott, H. (1993). Strength is ignorance; slavery is freedom: managing culture in modern organizations. *Journal of Management Studies*, **30**, 515–521.

Wilson, D. (1992). *A Strategy for Change*. Routledge: London.

Woodward, J. (1965). *Industrial Organization: Theory and Practice*. London: Oxford University Press.

Wooliams, P. & Mosely, T. (1999). Organization culture and job satisfaction. Culture in Business Paper 1, ABS 1996:6: Anglia Business School.

Xenikou, A. & Furnham, A. (1996). A correlation and factor analytic study of four questionnaire measures of organizational culture. *Human Relations*, **49**, 349–371.

CHAPTER 9

Leadership and Organizational Effectiveness

Beverly Alimo-Metcalfe
Nuffield Institute, University of Leeds, UK
and
Gill Nyfield
SHL Group plc, UK

THE COST OF POOR LEADERSHIP

A recent issue of *Fortune* magazine included a cover feature devoted to "Why CEOs Fail", including an article by Linda Grant and Richard Hagberg, with the self-explanatory title "Rambos in Pinstripes: Why So Many CEOs are Lousy Leaders".

Amongst the research evidence provided, it included valuable clues based on data collected from 511 US CEOs, as to why so many fail to inspire loyalty in their staff. From the measures used, which include personality instruments and evaluations from thousands of co-workers, the authors identified some of the most salient characteristics, which were: impatience, impulsivity, manipulation, dominance, self-importance, and over-criticism of others.

More specifically, in relation to leadership, Grant and Hagberg (1996) identify what they refer to as "the three pillars of leadership", which were: being the inspiring evangelist for a vision; managing implementation; and building relationships with subordinates. The "lousy" leaders failed because of their ego-centricity, lack of skill in developing talent, and creating an environment reminiscent of a battle ground, where an ethos of "survival of the fittest" pervades. It is clear that the building of relationships with their boards and employees, and the lack of attention to team-building, was another major cause of failure.

Fortunately the magazine also included a study of the eight characteristics of successful CEOs, which were:

- integrity, maturity and energy
- business acumen
- people acumen

Organizational Effectiveness: The Role of Psychology
Edited by I.T. Robertson, M. Callinan and D. Bartram. © 2002 John Wiley & Sons, Ltd.

- organizational acumen
- curiosity, intellectual capacity, and a global mindset
- superior judgement
- an insatiable appetite for accomplishment and results
- powerful motivation to grow and convert learning into practice.

The success of General Electric (GE), one of the world's most profitable organizations, and one of the most successful on the US stock exchange for several years, has, according to GE Board member Gertrude Michelson, been due not only to the legendary leadership of Jack Welch (who has been CEO since 1971), but because of GE's belief in the "institutional development of leadership". Its commitment is demonstrated by a spend of $800 million a year on training and leadership development, which is half its annual expenditure on R&D (*Fortune Archives*, 1998, Vol. 137, No. 4, p. 1).

John Kotter, one of the most distinguished writers and researchers in the field of management and leadership, has spent over 20 years studying executive leadership. He maintains that there is considerable variation in the styles adopted by successful business leaders, but believes that at a deeper level of content, there are three uniformities amongst them. These are, that they:

- help a group to establish some sensible direction
- are very successful at getting relevant partners aligned with, buying into, and believing in the direction they have set
- have "the ability to create conditions that energize and inspire people to get off their fannies" (*Fortune Archives*, op. cit., p. 5).

Beneath this somewhat earthy summary lies decades of intensive research into the nature of leadership.

CONTENT OF THE CHAPTER

In considering the subject of leadership and how psychological interventions have positively impacted on organizational effectiveness, the question is at one level tautological, since the subject of leadership is about researching a phenomenon which, by definition, implies a positive outcome on the behaviour of individuals and organizations. However, definitions of leadership have changed over time, as have the foci of leadership research, and the interventions of psychologists in applying research to organizational practices such as recruitment and selection, performance management, training and development.

This chapter will provide a brief history/overview of leadership research with respect to its definition, and the methodologies adopted, and the conclusions drawn. It will then look at some of the most recent studies which have focused on "the new leadership" paradigm and the benefits to organizations. Finally, it will discuss the implications of recent studies on psychological interventions in organizations.

A HISTORY OF LEADERSHIP RESEARCH

Psychologists, along with other social scientists, have long-held a fascination for studying what makes some people particularly effective in influencing the behaviour of other individuals, or groups, "to make things happen which would not otherwise occur or prevent things from happening that ordinarily would take place" (Rosenbach & Taylor, 1993, p. 1). Clearly, organizational psychologists are concerned with outcomes which increase organizational effectiveness. Such researchers have looked at leadership from a variety of perspectives, which include; *who leaders are*—namely, the identification of personal attributes which differentiate those perceived as leaders, or perceived as displaying leadership, from those who are not; also what leaders *do*, and *how* they do it. More recent research has focused attention on the *relationship* between leaders and followers, with some writers stressing the need to study followership. This is not only because all leaders are also followers, but also because modern notions of leadership place considerable emphasis on the power and importance of followers in ultimately enabling leadership to have greatest effect (e.g. Lee, 1993; DePree, 1993).

Most commentators regard the research efforts of the 1930s to 1950s as delineating the beginning of the formal study of leadership.

This era is often referred to as the "Great Man" or Trait approach, when there was a general assumption that what differentiates leaders from non-leaders, or followers, was their personality. That is, it was due to the possession of certain characteristics such as intelligence, energy, dominance, which are largely in-born, and thus are enduring, which suggested therefore that they predicted effectiveness in a variety of situations. However, two important reviews of the literature by Stodgill (1948) and Mann (1959) were widely interpreted as concluding that there were no consistent findings in relation to personality characteristics which differentiated leaders from non-leaders.

One of the major potential benefits anticipated by the early leadership researchers was that, if a consistent relationship was found between personality and appearing leader-like (i.e. being seen as emerging as a leader in a group with no formally appointed leader), then personality measures could help organizations improve their selection processes. Although, in principle, the idea was and still is undoubtedly appealing to organizations, it was soon recognized that no single personality, or other personal characteristic, such as intelligence, could consistently predict a leader emerging, or being accepted by members of a group. It is the combination of various characteristics, together with characteristics of the *situation*, which needs to be taken into account when attempting to select individuals for leadership roles.

Thus in the 1950s, the attention of psychologists investigating leadership switched from focusing on the personal characteristics of leaders, to the *behaviour* of individuals who influenced followers. Of the number of research studies in this area, the most famous were those undertaken by the researchers at the Ohio State University.

Studies at the Ohio State University (e.g. Fleishman, 1953; Fleishman & Harris, 1962) led these researchers to produce a model of leadership style based on a combination of two dimensions, which they referred to as "consideration" (i.e. concern for individuals), and "initiating structure" (e.g. activities such as planning, organizing, identifying specific tasks and objectives), and which, importantly, they maintained were independent of each other. Thus being high or low on one of the dimensions did not affect the degree to which a leader displayed behaviours on the other dimension. The consideration behaviours of a "leader" — i.e. Supervisor/Manager, someone who occupies a leadership role—were found to correlate positively with employee satisfaction, but negatively with the productivity of the manager's group (Stodgill, 1974).

One of the most popular practical outcomes of these style theories of leadership was the Managerial Grid (1964), developed by US psychologists Blake and Mouton, which provided a two-dimensional grid based on concern for people, and concern for results. It provided descriptions of the styles which characterized a variety of combinations on the grid. Despite the descriptions provided by Blake and Mouton for the four corners of the grid, they clearly advocated the position which represented a combination of high scores on both dimensions.

The main contribution of this period of leadership research was to emphasize the benefits of both major components of leadership style. However, the major omission of this research was the lack of consideration given to situational variables which affect the appropriateness of a particular style. The research did not provide answers to questions such as: Does the leader need the full commitment of his/her staff to achieve success in a particular activity? Is there only one way of successfully achieving the activity? Does the leader have all the information necessary for achieving success? Is there a time constraint on achieving an outcome? What authority does the manager have to get something achieved? etc. undoubtedly affect the effectiveness of a manager's approach to leading and influencing the behaviour of his/her staff.

This realization led to the development of a variety of new models of leadership, which dominated the late 1960s and 1970s and which came to be known as contingency theories of leadership. Examples of these theories include the classic model developed by Fiedler (1967), known as Fiedler's Contingency Model, which placed specific attention on three situational variables: the position power of the leader, the degree to which a task is structured, and the quality of leader–member relationships. Other models which became popular were House's Path Goal theory of leadership (House, 1971), and Vroom and Yetton's (1973) normative model of leadership behaviours which linked various options in leadership style to clear situational criteria.

The late 1970s and early 1980s marked a watershed in the history of leadership (Hunt, 1996) since the situational and contingency models, whilst providing guidelines for dealing with complexity, and greater efficiency, offered little advice as to how to approach leadership in an environment of continuous and significant change. Mintzberg (1982), in particular, produced a scathing critique of the irrelevance of leadership research to practising managers.

It was in this climate that the "new leadership" paradigm emerged (Bryman, 1992), which encompassed "visionary" (Sashkin, 1988), "charismatic" (House, 1977; Conger, 1989; Conger & Kanungo, 1988), or "transformational" models (Bass, 1985; Tichy & Devanna, 1986; see Bryman, 1992, for a review). Situational and contingency models which preceded the emergence of the new leadership are referred to as models of "traditional" (Hunt, 1996), or "transactional" (Bass, 1998a) leadership, or "management" (Kotter, 1990). They provide valuable information as to how to plan, organize, create order and structure, at times of relative stability, but are not sufficient in leading organizations through times of rapid change.

One of the first comparisons between models of transactional and transformational leadership was articulated not by a psychologist, but a political scientist—James McGregor Burns (1978)—who developed his model based on Weber's (1947) seminal work on charismatic leaders.

US psychologist and leadership scholar, Bernard Bass (1985), built on Burns' notions of leadership and corrected a fundamental error in Burns' theory; namely, Burns' assertion that transformational and transactional leadership are at opposite ends of a single continuum of leadership. On the basis of his later research, Bass (1990a,b) found the two approaches to be independent and complementary. Bass asserts that transactional leadership entails an exchange between leader and follower in which the leader rewards the follower for specific behaviours, and for performance that meets with the leader's wishes, and criticizes, sanctions or punishes non-conformity or lack of achievement. Rewards may be tangible, such as financial "perks" and incentives, or non-tangible, such as prestige. Such exchanges cater to the self-interest of followers (Bass, 1998a). Bass also argues that research comparing the effects of transactional and transformational leadership has shown that "generally transformational leadership is more effective and satisfying than transactional leadership alone although every leader does some of each. Context and contingencies are of some importance as a source of variance, but the fundamental phenomena transcend organizations and countries" (Bass, 1998b, p. 1).

Bass developed his model of transformational leadership based on data from interviews with 70 South African executives, in which he asked them if they had known transformational leaders, as described by Burns. From these data, he and his colleague Bruce Avolio developed an instrument which measures the full range of leadership modes, the Multi-factor Leadership Questionnaire (MLQ) (Bass & Avolio, 1990a,b). It measures the following dimensions of leadership:

- *Idealized influence*. Transformational leaders behave in ways that result in them being admired, respected and trusted, such that their followers wish to emulate them. They are extraordinarily capable, persistent, and determined.
- *Inspirational motivation*. Transformational leaders behave such that they motivate and inspire those around them by providing meaning, optimism and enthusiasm for a vision of a future state.
- *Intellectual stimulation*. Transformational leaders encourage followers to question assumptions, reframe problems, and approach old solutions in new ways, and to be creative and innovative. At times, their followers' ideas may differ from those of the leader, who may solicit or encourage such responses.
- *Individualized consideration*. Transformational leaders actively develop the potential of their followers by creating new opportunities for development,

coaching, mentoring, and paying attention to each follower's needs and de-
sires. They know their staff well, as a result of listening, communicating, and
"walking around" encouraging, rather than monitoring their efforts.

The two transactional components comprise:

• *Contingent reward.* Approved follower actions are rewarded; disapproved
  actions are punished or sanctioned.
• *Management by exception (active) and management by exception (passive).* These
  are corrective transactional dimensions. The former involves a monitoring of
  performance, and intervention when judged appropriate; the latter reflects
  correction only when problems emerge.

Laissez-faire is a style of leadership that is, in fact, an abrogation of leadership,
since there is an absence of any transaction. This style is deemed to be most
ineffective (e.g. Bass, 1998a, p. 7).
   More recent research by Bass and colleagues has led to a revision of the model
of transformational leadership, in which the two transactional components are
combined into one (Avolio et al., 1999).
   Over 20 years of research has been undertaken by psychologists adopting,
most commonly, the MLQ (Carless, 1998) to compare the effectiveness of transformational and transactional leadership styles, which has provided evidence
that the transformational style is generally more effective and satisfying than the
transactional alone (Bass, 1998a,b), and that followers' commitment is greater.
These studies have ranged from studies of the leadership style of secondary
school teachers, white collar workers, and supervisors of insurance company
employees to military personnel (e.g. Bass, 1998a). Other studies have shown a
negative relationship between a leader's transformational leadership style and
staff stress levels (Bass, 1998a).
   Whilst there are numerous studies which provide evidence of the superior-
ity of the transformational approach over the transactional, Bass (1998b) has
emphasized two important points; namely, that both are crucial for managerial and organizational effectiveness, and that both are generally evident at all
managerial levels in organizations.

LEADERSHIP AND ORGANIZATIONAL CULTURE

Psychologists in the field of leadership research have given their attention also
to the culture of organizations. Prominent US scholar, Ed Schein, referred to the
inextricable link between leadership and organizational culture, describing them
as "two sides of the same coin". This has been found to be particularly true for
the relationship between the leadership approach of the CEO and the culture of
his/her organization.
   Bass and Avolio see an inextricable link between leadership and organizational culture, stating "The organization's culture develops in large part from its
leadership while the culture of an organization can also affect the development

of its leadership" (Bass & Avolio, 1993, p. 113). They maintain that the process by which leaders influence culture is by the creation and reinforcement of organizational norms and behaviour. In human resource terms, Bass maintains that recruitment, selection and placement decisions are all influenced by the prevalent values and norms.

In an organization which is moderately to highly transformational, there is likely to be a strong sense of belonging and mutual trust; values, vision and fulfilment will be frequently discussed. Such an organization is more likely to be innovative and to be able to adapt to changing circumstances, and to encourage empowerment and autonomy. Leaders who create or build such cultures are likely to have a strong sense of purpose and a clear vision, and to take responsibility for developing and valuing staff contributions, whilst encouraging questioning of the status quo.

Organizations which are highly transactional, and also low in transformational, will be characterized by rules, regulations, rigid structure, explicit contracts, and controls. They are likely to foster self-interest at the expense of co-operation and collaboration amongst staff; goals are probably short-term, and staff will feel they have little opportunity to use their discretion and are more likely to feel controlled, and perhaps exploited. Individuals in leadership positions who create or reinforce such organizations reflect the transactional behaviours of contingent rewards, or sanctions, in return for staff performance. Alternatively, they may adopt a management-by-exception style, and are likely to maintain organizational status quo, discouraging creative thinking and challenges to traditional ways of operating. Their staff will consequently feel disempowered, under-valued, and more stressed (Bass, 1998a).

In the typology of organizations provided by Bass & Avolio (1993), nine types of organizations are described, which include not only those organizations cited above, but also those which represent variations of combinations of scores of the two dimensions.

To support the validity of their research, Bass (1998a) cites a study which investigated the relationship between transformational and transactional organizational culture and quality improvement. Given that organizations need to become more adaptable, the organizational typology created by Bass and Avolio must surely be judged to be of considerable importance.

Bass and Avolio (1993), and Bass (1998a) in his recent book, also provide suggestions as to how organizations may work towards becoming more adaptive by creating a more transformational culture, or indeed—as may also be appropriate—stronger functional transactional characteristics.

TRANSFORMATIONAL/TRANSACTIONAL LEADERSHIP AND ORGANIZATION LIFE CYCLES

A frequently asked question by those interested in the complementary roles of transformational and transactional leadership, is whether different organizations require different balances in these modes of leadership. A second, and related, question is whether the same balance between the two leadership approaches is required at various stages of an organization's development. Organizational psychologists have attempted to provide some guidance in this area.

In relation to the first question, Kotter (1990) provided a valuable two-dimensional model representing the importance of the degree of complexity, and the degree of change being experienced by an organization, in determining the balance needed between the two leadership approaches.

The link between leadership, organizational life cycle stages of Birth, Growth, Maturity, and Death or Revitalization, and organizational effectiveness, has been explored by several researchers. US leadership scholar Jerry Hunt and colleagues have made a particular contribution to understanding the importance of the various components of transformational and transactional leadership behaviours, at different stages of organizational growth (Hunt et al., 1988; Hunt, 1996). Their model has important implications for OD strategy, as well as for the chief executive's leadership activities.

LEADERSHIP STYLE AND THE SUCCESS OF ORGANIZATIONAL MERGERS

Psychologists have investigated the relationship between leadership style and post-merger outcome measures of staff satisfaction with the merger, in an attempt to provide guidelines for good practice.

One such study was undertaken by Covin et al. (1997) of a Fortune 100 company that had recently experienced a merger. It included a group of employees from the acquired organization, plus a group of employees from the acquiring organization. The researchers employed an instrument specifically designed for the study, which was based on a combination of elements of the MLQ, and the Leader Behavior Description Questionnaire (Stodgill, 1963), to measure leadership style. Their findings revealed that the greatest absolute difference in leadership scores for the high and low post-merger-satisfaction groups, was the degree of perceived transformational leadership behaviour adopted by the leaders. They also found, as they had expected, that the leadership profiles associated with merger satisfaction for acquiring and acquired-firm employees differed. For the acquired-firm employees, transformational leadership was the strongest predictor, followed by reward power and coercive power. For employees with the acquiring firms, reward power was the strongest predictor of post-merger satisfaction. However, differences also emerged across managerial, union clerical, and clerks and secretarial employee groups.

Covin and co-workers draw attention to the findings of Schweiger and DeNisi (1991), that negative effects of mergers not only do not disappear with time, but they become more serious. Thus, organizations need to be aware of the fact that the style of leadership adopted is most critical in the early stages of a merger process. Further, they add that the use of coercive power has a significant and negative correlation with post-merger satisfaction, which implies that the use of threats, manipulation and/or misinformation is deleterious to longer-term employee satisfaction.

These contributions of psychologists may have considerable importance. Not only is there little published research in relation to evidence-based good practice in handling mergers and acquisitions, but also a recent study by West and Patterson (1998) found a significant relationship between employee satisfaction, and organizational productivity and profitability.

THE EFFECT ON PERFORMANCE OF LEADERS' EXPECTATIONS

Psychologists have for decades studied the effects of expectations of performance on performance outcomes. Otherwise known as the "Pygmalion effect", its significance in educational settings has been well-established. One such study by Rosenthal and Jacobson (1968), which showed that teachers' expectations of their pupils' performance can significantly effect the children's performance, was to become a classic.

Organizational psychologists have conducted similar research in relation to adults, and found the same powerful effects of managers' expectations on the performance of their staff (e.g. King, 1974). Livingstone (1988), in a *Harvard Business Review* article entitled "Pygmalion in management", cites numerous examples of the power of managers' expectations of the performance of their staff, including extracts from Bennis and Nanus's (1985) book *Leadership*, which was based on their interviews with 90 CEOs and top administrators in public sector organizations. Bennis and Nanus state:

> Our study of effective leaders strongly suggested that a key factor was . . .
> positive self-regard. . . . Positive self-regard seems to exert its force by creating in others a sense of confidence and high expectations, not very different from the fabled Pygmalion effect. [Unfortunately] managers often unintentionally communicate low expectations, they become "negative" Pygmalions who undermine the self-confidence of their employees and reduce their effectiveness. Managers must be extremely sensitive, therefore, to their own behavior and its impact on subordinates. They must guard against treating their employees in ways that lower their feelings of efficacy and self-esteem and are unproductive.

A more recent study of manager expectations was undertaken by Eden (1990) in relation to the effect on group performance; in this instance the subjects of the study were Israeli military platoons and platoon leaders. His findings revealed that the groups which were allocated a leader who, although he had never met his platoon members, was led by an experimenter to have high expectations of the group's potential, performed significantly higher than groups who were allocated leaders whose expectations were not influenced by the experimenters. This led Eden to conclude that managers' expectations of subordinates *as a group* can be raised and that the Pygmalion effect can be produced for whole work groups.

Given the prevalence of team working in organizations, and the potential cost of contrast effects when managers hold differentially high expectations of members of staff, these findings from the realm of organizational psychology provide invaluable guidance for individuals with team leadership responsibilities.

THE IMPORTANCE OF MANAGERIAL SELF-AWARENESS (MSA) TO EFFECTIVENESS AS A LEADER

A relatively new area of study in the field of organizational psychology, namely "managerial self awareness" (MSA), has shown great promise in elucidating a relatively elusive aspect of leadership.

The new paradigm of transformational leadership places considerable emphasis on the importance of direct reports' perceptions of leader effectiveness, and the impact of the leader's behaviour on direct reports' levels of job satisfaction, motivation, commitment, and performance.

The development and increasing popularity of 360°/multi-rater feedback (360°/MRF) processes in organizations over the last 15 years or so has no doubt been due in large part to the emergence of the "new leadership" models. The importance of self-awareness in relation to leadership has been argued by many psychologists, and is hardly surprising given that modern notions of transformational leadership have drawn attention to the need for managers to understand the impact of their behaviours on co-workers, particularly their subordinates.

Fortunately, there are now substantial data from 360°/MRF use, which have been analysed by organizational psychologists to illuminate the relationship between managers' self-ratings of leadership effectiveness, with the perceptions of their line manager and peers, and then to relate it to various outcome measures.

Studies have consistently found a negative relationship between the size of self–other agreements of leadership effectiveness ratings, and positive outcomes. That is, the smaller the disparity, the more beneficial the outcome. For example, Wexley et al. (1980) found that direct reports were more satisfied with the relationship they had with their line manager when there was a closer match between managers' self-ratings and the ratings of their direct reports. In addition, several studies have found that higher performers in the area of management and leadership are less likely to inflate their self-described leadership effectiveness than are low performers. For more detailed descriptions of the process of 360-degree feedback, and reviews of findings, see Alimo-Metcalfe (1998), Atwater and Yammarino (1997) and Fletcher and Baldry (1999).

These findings by organizational psychologists have helped to illuminate a relatively elusive aspect of leadership, but one that is receiving far greater attention from organizations wishing to improve their leadership selection and development processes. Whether managerial self-awareness (MSA) is a personality trait, or a skill which may be learned or improved, or a combination of the two, needs further investigation, but its crucial importance in leadership surely cannot be denied. Fletcher and Baldry (1999) make the case well:

> If one lacks it, then it is difficult to see how one can manage work relationships successfully, how one can contribute well as a team member, and how one can adapt one's behaviour to the circumstances and individuals. In organizations and job roles that are continually changing, it is surely impossible to learn and develop in the ways needed to cope with the capacity to seek and use feedback on one's behaviour.

How much more important must this be for those in leadership positions?

CAN LEADERSHIP BE DEVELOPED?

The question of whether leadership can be developed, or whether it is largely in-born, has exercised the minds of psychologists since the earliest days of leadership research. For some psychologists, such as Zaleznik (1993), there is little doubt as to the importance of personality, and early socialization.

Studies which have found a relationship between personality or cognitive measures and leadership, although contributing to our understanding of the phenomenon, rarely explain more than 20% of the variance in measures of leadership. Bass (1998a), who summarized the findings from research relating to the prediction of scores on the MLQ, states:

> ... validities of individual (personality) scales tend to be modest but in optimum combination correlate significantly higher. This suggests a pattern of personality traits where each trait may not be highly predictive of leadership potential by itself but can account in combination with other traits for as much as 35% of the criterion variance in some situations.

It is worth noting the last three words of the quote above, since we know that a multitude of situational variables, which can rarely be controlled for in studies, can have a powerful moderating effect on the results.

The role of heredity in relation to transformational leadership has received little attention, but Bass (1998b) cites the findings from a study by Vernon (1998) which compared the self-rating scores on the MLQ obtained by identical and non-identical twins. This suggested that 25–50% of the variance can be attributed to genetic factors. Nonetheless, as Bass noted, these figures still leave room for the potential contributions of development activities/interventions.

Arguably, the most promising contribution of organizational psychologists to leadership development has been their activities in the field of 360-degree/multi-rater feedback processes.

HOW EFFECTIVE IS THE USE OF 360°/MRF IN DEVELOPING TRANSFORMATIONAL LEADERSHIP?

Organizational psychologists are keen to apply research findings on leadership to practical programmes of development. Given the direct relationship between self-awareness and various outcome measures of leadership performance, it is not surprising that leadership development interventions have made considerable use of providing feedback from 360°/MRF processes. The popularity of its use in leadership programmes is indisputable (e.g. Bass, 1998a; Antonioni, 1996; Clifford & Bennett, 1997; Redman & Mathews, 1997), but what is the evidence that the use of 360°/MRF can affect positive changes in leadership behaviour? Recent studies by psychologists have looked at the effect of 360°/MRF in changing managers' self-perceptions of leadership effectiveness, the perceptions of their subordinates, and the performance of their work units/teams, and have provided evidence of its beneficial effects. For example, a study by Smither et al. (1995) found that managers who had initially been marked low to moderate by their subordinates—on behaviours which included aspects of leadership, such as supporting subordinates, coaching, and encouraging participation—six months after receiving the feedback were rated again and were seen to have improved. Moreover, the results could not have been attributed solely to regression to the mean. An important question is whether the improvement lasted. A follow-up study by some of the original researchers (Reilly et al., 1996) showed that the improvements in the mangers' performance had been sustained for a further two years. Two further studies which used the MLQ showed similar results (Atwater et al., 1995; Barling, et al., 1996).

The importance of support and development opportunities following the receipt of 360°/MRF has been stressed by various writers (e.g. Alimo-Metcalfe, 1998; Antonioni,1996; Church & Waclawski, 1998; London et al., 1990). The study by Barling et al. (1996) was a field experiment examining the effects of transformational leadership training and goal-setting, following feedback from subordinates of their MLQ ratings on the transformational dimensions. The authors conclude that "a training and goal-setting intervention is able to change leaders' transformational behaviors in the expected direction", and that "changing transformational leadership can exert some effects on financial performance" (p. 831).

It is interesting to note that the training interventions consisted of a one-day group session on the nature of transformational leadership, and the importance of goal-setting, plus "four individual booster sessions" (p. 827).

Bass (1998a) describes in detail the content of transformational leadership development interventions employed in various organizations, and provides examples of their effective outcomes.

PROMISING AREAS FOR FUTURE LEADERSHIP RESEARCH

Gender and Leadership

Several writers have documented the history of leadership research from the perspective of gender and concluded that there has been a distinct male gender bias with respect to the construction of leadership (e.g. Heilman, 1983; Jacobson & Jacques, 1990; Schein, 1994), and with respect to the interpretation of findings which have compared men's and women's approaches (e.g. Jacobson & Jacques, 1990). Prior to the 1970s there was little, if any, interest in the question of whether there are gender differences, since only men were studied.

Following equal opportunities legislation in the US and the UK in the early 1970s, women were entering previously male occupations, such as management, and gender differences in leadership styles were investigated. Few differences were found (e.g. Powell, 1993), and when found they were relatively minor; but they suggested that women were likely to be more participative and democratic in decision-making (e.g. Eagly, 1991), and more team-orientated (e.g. Ferrario, 1994). However, feminist writers, such as Carol Gilligan (1982), made the perceptive point that the differences were drawn as a result of women being compared to the male norm, as opposed to a real study of differences in which each gender is viewed in its own right.

It was only in the 1990s that major differences with respect to gender and leadership style began to emerge. Adopting the MLQ, US professor Judy Rosener (1990) published the findings from a survey of female and male executives' descriptions of their leadership approach. It revealed significant differences with respect to their stated leadership styles, with women scoring higher on the preference for transformational behaviours (apart from Intellectual Stimulation, which showed no significant differences). A possible reason for the lack of gender differences in previous research may have been the fact that leadership instruments designed prior to the MLQ had measured only transactional aspects of leadership (Alimo-Metcalfe, 1994; Bass et al., 1996; Eagly & Johnson, 1990).

Rosener's research attracted a great deal of interest, and criticism (*Harvard Business Review*, 1991, letters section). The main criticism, and a legitimate one, was that the data were of dubious validity, since they were based solely on self-report. However, two independent UK studies which investigated the constructs of leadership held by senior female and male senior managers in two major public sector organizations (Alimo-Metcalfe, 1995; Sparrow & Rigg, 1993) obtained data which supported Rosener's findings, with women in general identifying transformational components, and men in general identifying transactional ones.

Several studies have now looked at gender and leadership style as rated anonymously by co-workers of managers as part of 360-degree feedback. Such studies have consistently revealed that women are rated as significantly more transformational, in general, than men (e.g. Bass & Avolio, 1994; Bass et al., 1996; Druskat, 1994).

Alimo-Metcalfe (1994) has argued that the implications of these findings for organizations' managerial selection, assessment, and development processes are considerable, with respect to the sample from whom the criteria are elicited, the content and method of the assessment process, and the judgement of assessors.

Leadership and Social Distance

This is one of the least known areas of leadership research. A core, if not defining, component of US models of "the new leadership" paradigm (Bryman, 1992), is that of "charisma". Charisma is an attribution that followers make of certain individuals from observations of their behaviours (Willner, 1984), and is, arguably, influenced by the social distance between leader and follower. It has been a subject of interest to psychologists in the leadership field from at least the 1970s, with Katz and Kahn (1978) maintaining that social distance is an essential prerequisite of charismatic leadership. They have stated that since immediate bosses/supervisors are constantly under the scrutiny of their staff, they cannot escape being viewed as "very human and very fallible and their subordinates cannot build an aura of magic about them. . . . Day to day intimacy destroys illusions" (p. 546). Other writers, however, including Bass (1985), assert that charisma is a phenomenon of interpersonal relationships, and can thus be attributed to a supervisor with whom staff work closely on a regular basis, and can be evident in managers at any level in the organization.

Yagil (1998), in her study of the attributions by charisma of Israeli soldiers to their close and distant leaders (i.e. platoon and batallion commanders respectively), found that the proximity of distance between leader and follower was, in fact, an advantage. She provides several reasons for this, including the fact that close leaders can be more powerful as role models since they are in regular contact, and can hence reinforce such behaviours frequently, and in addition, their very fallibility may make them more attractive.

Israeli psychologist Shamir (1995) has argued that it is important to distinguish between the study of distant and close leaders when investigating the characteristics of charismatic leaders. In an exploratory study, Shamir found that whilst some similarities emerged, several significant differences were also found with respect to close and distant charismatic leaders.

> Distant charismatic leaders were more frequently characterized as having rhetorical skills, having an ideological orientation and a sense of mission, being persistent and consistent with respect to their mission, being courageous, and having social courage in the sense of expressing their opinions without fearing criticism or conforming to social pressures. Close charismatic leaders were more frequently characterized as being sociable, open and considerate of others, having a sense of humor, having a high level of expertise in their field, being highly dynamic and active, having an impressive physical appearance, being intelligent or wise, setting high performance standards for themselves and their followers, and being original or unconventional in their behavior. (p. 31)

The behaviours which Yagil identified as importantly related to attributes of charisma amongst close leaders were not interpersonal qualities, as found by Shamir, but extraordinary qualities. They included terms such as "brilliant" and "a hero".

In considering the value of such research, it is important to remember the prevalence of military data, and we need to ask whether these are the sort of attributes that would emerge from studies in non-military organizations. This has yet to be tested, along with the question of whether "charisma" is the appropriate starting point for understanding the nature of transformational leadership.

A UK STUDY OF TRANSFORMATIONAL LEADERSHIP

Over the last seventy plus years, US psychologists have provided an invaluable source of information about the nature of leadership, and their contributions still dominate the landscape. However, researchers have started to point out the absence of consideration of *the influence of context* in modern studies of transformational leadership (e.g. Yukl, 1999), not least of which is the influence of different cultures across the world. With the increased move to global-thinking in organizational effectiveness, there must be a need for studies to be undertaken outside the US, a point already made by US researchers (e.g. Hunt & Peterson, 1997).

For such research to add to our understanding of the nature of leadership, it can be argued that it is essential not to start with any existing notion of leadership, such as presuming it to relate to a defining component, such as charisma. It seems most appropriate to start with a qualitative methodology, rather than merely testing the validity of an existing instrument. This is also particularly important since leadership is a social influence process (Parry, 1998), and it is best judged by the observations of followers (e.g. Bass, 1990; Rost, 1993).

As stated above, it is also important to note that all major models of leadership have been based on studying men's notions of leadership.

The Study

Two UK psychologists recently undertook a major national study of the nature of leadership (Alimo-Metcalfe & Alban-Metcalfe, 2001). The first stage of this study was undertaken in two large public sector organizations (health and local government). It involved interviewing 160 female and male managers, at chief executive to middle level positions, in various organizations in these two public sectors, employing the Repertory Grid technique of eliciting constructs (Kelly, 1955). From the 2000 plus constructs of leadership elicited, a pilot instrument was developed and distributed to a random stratified sample of organizations, and to a random stratified sample of male and female managers at various levels within each organization. Each manager was asked to consider their current, or a previous boss, and to anonymously rate the extent to which they agreed with the items which described the behaviours of these managers, in relation to their leadership.

Factor analysis of the responses from each of the two major public sector organizations revealed nine and six factors respectively. The nine factors emerging were labelled as follows:

1. *Genuine concern for other's well-being and development:* displays a genuine interest in people as individuals; values their contributions; holds positive expectations of what individuals can achieve; develops other's potential.
2. *Political/stakeholder sensitivity and skills:* sensitive to the different agenda and needs of various internal and external stakeholders; involves stakeholders in developing a shared vision; is inspirational in transmitting the vision.
3. *Decisive, determined, self-confident:* is decisive when required to be; prepared to take difficult decisions; resilient to setbacks; can cope with the stress of leadership.
4. *Integrity, trusted, honest and open:* admits when is wrong; is trusted because is consistent in what s/he says and does; makes decisions on moral and ethical principles.
5. *Empowers—Delegates in ways that develop potential in others:* creates opportunities for individuals to use their potential; trusts staff to take decisions/ initiatives on important matters; delegates effectively because knows individual's potential.
6. *Inspirational networker, promoter and communicator:* has an extensive network of contacts in the external environment, and uses this to promote the

work/achievements of the organization/team to the outside world; is able to effectively communicate the vision of the organization/dept. to the internal and external stakeholders; is strongly committed to bringing stakeholders together to develop the joint vision, and the means of achieving it.

7. *Accessible and approachable:* accessible to staff at all levels; keeps in touch using face-to-face communication; creates a sense of "presence" rather than absence in the organization/department.

8. *Clarifies boundaries, keeps others informed, involves others in decisions:* makes clear the boundaries of responsibility; involves appropriate staff when making decisions; keeps people informed of what is going on in different parts of the organization.

9. *Encourages critical and strategic thinking:* encourages individuals to question traditional approaches to their jobs, and to think of wholly new approaches/solutions to problems; encourages strategic rather than short-term thinking.

Three Additional Training/Development Scales also emerged:

1. *Intellectual versatility:* has the capacity to deal with a wide range of complex issues; can deal effectively with ambiguity and uncertainty.

2. *Manages change sensitively and skilfully:* is sensitive to the impact of change on different parts of the organization/team; maintains a balance between the need for stability and the need for change; sensitive to the agenda of different stakeholders.

3. *Risk-taker, entre-intra-preneurial:* is prepared to take calculated risks to achieve important outcomes, and to empower others; adopts an entrepreneurial approach to developing the organization/department/service.

These scales form the basis of a new 360-degree feedback questionnaire, The Transformational Leadership Questionnaire (TLQ).

Discussion of Results

There is a great deal in common in the results from these two public sectors (Alban-Metcalfe & Alimo-Metcalfe, 2000a,b). The models of leadership which emerged reflect, in part, descriptions of transformational leadership previously described in the US literature, but there were some important differences between the US and the UK findings.

The first most important difference was that "charisma", which forms the major component in several US models (Bass, 1990, 1998a; Conger, 1989; Conger & Kanungo, 1988; House, 1977; Shamir et al., 1993) is far less conspicuous as a defining leadership quality in the UK model. The major component of the UK model is "Genuine concern for others' well-being and development", similar to Bass's fourth and least important transformational dimension, which he names "Individualized consideration", and is far more representative of "the servant as leader" model of Greenleaf (1970, 1996). Thereafter, emphasis on the UK model is on connectedness with stakeholders, internal and external to the organization, the development of leadership in others by empowerment and encouraging the questioning of approaches to one's job, and the way in which service is delivered. Whilst these latter characteristics are reflected in the Bass model, there is still a "heroic" core to his and other US models, which Yukl (1999) notes, but which is far less pronounced in the UK model.

Visioning in the UK model is defined by behaviours of engaging others in the process, as opposed to a single individual's actions.

It is not clear to what extent the differences in the UK versus US models are attributable to the difference in methodologies employed. In the UK, the research was initially qualitative, and it involved a significant proportion of females as well as males in the design of the leadership questionnaire piloted, and the sample on whom the final analyses were based. Yet another reason may be that the UK study was conducted in the public sector. The UK researchers are currently undertaking a new study in the UK private sector, which may help inform this.

The implications of this first major UK study of leadership, for UK organizations, are numerous, particularly in relation to selection, promotion, performance management, and development activities. The findings also make very clear that the typical transactional competencies identified by organizations in these processes are simply not sufficient in identifying transformational leadership. Finally, the research findings suggest that there may be cultural differences in the way in which leadership behaviour is construed, which begs the need for similar studies in different cultural contexts.

THE ROLE OF PERSONALITY IN MODERATING THE TRANSFORMATIONAL LEADERSHIP STYLE

Finally, in relation to the general leadership literature, the link between personality and leadership was the prime focus of research in the 1930s and 1940s, but as described earlier, was abandoned following reviews of the literature, which were interpreted as concluding no consistent link. However, more recently, organizational psychologists have shown a renewed interest in the relationship between personality and leadership style.

A particularly interesting research study was undertaken by Church and Waclawski (1995), that attempted to link the personality orientation of senior managers to the degree to which their staff felt "enabled". Church and Waclawski argue that the distinction between "empowerment" and "feeling enabled" is an important one, since the former focuses more on the actions of the manager who relinquishes some control, whereas the latter term focuses on the psychological state of the direct report, who experiences an enhanced state of "ownership and commitment to a project or task" (Church & Waclawski, 1995, p. 23). Thus, empowerment can be seen as an independent variable, with the possible outcome of enablement being experienced by a direct report as a dependent variable. It can reasonably be argued that managers with a predominantly transformational style are more likely to empower their staff.

Using two well-established personality measures, namely, the Myers Briggs Type Indicator (MBTI) and the Kirton Adaption Inventory (KAI), Church and Waclawski created four categories of managers which served to differentiate amongst subordinates' ratings of transformational vs. transactional leadership behaviours, for a given executive population (p. 26).

The psychologists compared the managers' self ratings of the extent to which they enabled their subordinates, and the frequency with which they adopted certain enabling behaviours, to the subordinates' ratings of their managers' use of enabling behaviours, and how enabled they felt as a result. They found that there were no significant differences between the subordinates of the different groups of managers, with respect to how enabled they felt, but a fascinating discovery was in the behaviours of enabling perceived to be adopted by the different managerial groups. For example, one group of managers, labelled the "motivators", were seen as more likely to: encourage risk-taking; maintain a challenging and motivating work environment; and to take time to celebrate accomplishments. Another group, labelled the "Inventors" were found to be "significantly better at innovating, setting direction, and establishing a sense of mission about their work, but only average at influencing followers by arousing their hopes, enthusiasm, and energy" (p. 41).

The way in which the group labelled "managers" appeared to foster strong feelings of enablement in their subordinates was through encouraging their staff "to take action and use novel ideas and approaches to solving problems" (p. 41).

The increased use of more work-orientated questionnaires, including the Occupational Personality Questionnaires developed by SHL (1984, 1999), has demonstrated that they can be effective in predicting overall management performance. In addition, specific personality scales also relate more strongly to management competencies such as leadership, analytical thinking, creativity, strategic thinking and the more administrative skills of organizing and planning. However, whilst overall aspects of leadership qualities are significantly predicted, the prediction of specific transformational leadership dimensions has still to be clearly shown.

The value of the research by these psychologists has been to illuminate understanding in organizations of the relationship between personality and the process of leadership. Similar research is needed in relation to other crucial components of leadership; for example, supporting the development of potential, encouraging leadership in others, engaging others in the vision process, challenging traditions, etc.

The next section looks at the practical applications of the findings from leadership research, to organizational recruitment, selection, and development activities.

WHAT IS HAPPENING IN PRACTICE?

In practice, the identification and development of leadership skills remains a key issue for many organizations around the world. There are reports of a "shortage" of effective leaders which places more emphasis on the need for organizations to:

• recruit new people with appropriate skills or potential
• identify potential already within the organization
• ensure appropriate development to enhance that potential.

Most organizations today select, assess and develop managers against a list of characteristics, often called "competencies". A typical list might include "leadership" as an entity by itself, or would have it as a "higher" order attribute, following on from a combination of competencies such as "developing others, influencing, relationship building and teamwork".

In reviewing many of these lists of competencies, it is not clear that all organizations have separated out "leadership" from "management", or transformational from transactional leadership. Management is more concerned with planning, organizing and controlling resources—the transactional style. Whilst good managers need to have these management skills, that alone will not make them highly effective leaders. They also need to have the transformational leadership skills to empower those around them to fulfill their objectives.

It is perhaps more debatable whether all effective transformational leaders also need to be good managers. It is doubtful that senior executives in large organizations reach that level without being perceived as having good "managerial" skills. More entrepreneurial organizations and smaller companies are more likely to have senior people who are strong leaders rather than managers, with often the founder being a classic case. Richard Branson, CEO of Virgin, appears typical—and he ensures he has strong managers around him to help bring his ideas to fruition.

Selection of Leaders

In reviewing the practices organizations undertake in relation to the selection and assessment of leaders, there is some indication that the emphasis is more on assessing the transactional rather than the transformational leadership style. This may well be because the former is easier to assess, but it has negative implications for ensuring we have our "leaders" for tomorrow.

The selection techniques tend to vary depending on the level at which the individual is being recruited. "Young potential leaders", selected straight from university or college, tend to be put through assessment centres where group exercises and personality questionnaires have been shown to be reasonable predictors of management effectiveness, and some aspects of leadership. In many cases the group exercise may be the main opportunity for candidates to show their transformational leadership potential.

Self-report personality questionnaires have also shown significant relationships with overall job performance, potential for promotion to senior management, and leadership skills, as described earlier in the chapter. The evidence for the validity of in-tray exercises in selecting leaders is less compelling. It tends to concentrate on the more managerial or administrative qualities of the role, rather than the interpersonal. These techniques are becoming more commonly used with more experienced managers, even up to the level of CEO. However, at this top level there is still a heavy reliance placed on the interview, and track record as a predictor of the leadership qualities required. Here, besides assessing their competence there is a strong emphasis on whether their style of work will fit in the new organization.

Other research which organizations are starting to use is related to the need to identify organizational values and culture, and to explore the match of an individual's values and motivators to those of the organization. This becomes more important as individual roles and jobs become less well defined, and where organizations are almost continually changing and adapting to meet new demands.

The evidence would indicate that there is some room for improvement in the practice of the assessment of transformational leadership qualities. However, in the meantime, the data are still strong enough to conclude that managers— whether young graduates, first line or experienced—selected through the use of these multi-method procedures, are more likely to have, or be able to develop, the kind of skills required of tomorrow's leaders.

Development

For those already within the organization, similar methodologies are required to identify potential for leadership to supplement existing appraisal/performance management systems. Whilst assessment centres are used to identify high-potential managers, the trend today is more for "development" centres. These employ similar techniques, but the emphasis is on development, with considerable feedback of results both during and after the centre, which can be used as a basis for future development. It is here, as well as in improving the performance management process, that organizations have adopted the latest research information and embraced 360-degree or multi-rater feedback. The nature and methodology of the MRF technique makes it less suitable for selection purposes.

As indicated earlier, the evidence indicates that the inclusion of 360-degree instruments in the process significantly enhances the quality of the information available. An individual's awareness of how others actually view their performance increases the willingness of the individual to embrace the feedback, and to be motivated to develop new skills and change/moderate some behaviours. The number of organizations taking up this technique is increasingly rapidly (e.g. Antonioni, 1996), with very positive results when the instrument is well-designed and carefully implemented (Alimo-Metcalfe, 1998). Many organizations have developed their own or tailored 360-degree instruments to map onto their own organizational competencies; but, so far, most of these are targeted at covering a range of management competencies, rather than be more specifically directed at leadership, as assessed in the MLQ and the TLQ.

Other more recent trends in development are towards results-orientated leadership development, which can be summarized as having three components:

- identifying activities important for success in the present and future and the underlying skills, competencies and values required
- assessment of the managers including their competencies, motivators and values, and identification of the "gaps" between what they have and the organizational needs
- work-related development activities to enhance the skills.

The early evidence indicates that this more targeted approach produces learning and results which more quickly and effectively affect the organization.

Implicit within this is less reliance on the more traditional methods for development. The value of training courses has been under question for some time, and they are best seen as appropriate for the acquisition of certain skills and knowledge. Even this function is now starting to be being replaced by "on-line" web-based learning facilities by which individuals can pick up and work through assignments at their own pace to suit their work patterns.

On the other hand, activity-based leadership development, whether conducted inside or outside the organization, has gained in popularity, and has the benefit of allowing managers to learn, experiment, and explore new ways of doing things, without too expensive repercussions for the individual, their colleagues, and their organizations. Activities are normally organized so that individuals receive immediate and direct feedback on what behaviours were related to successful outcomes and what their colleagues felt were, for example, supportive and empowering behaviours. They also importantly have the opportunity to observe, and even feel the effects of, how others go about trying to achieve similar objectives. However, work-related development is more focused and happens on the job, as it involves the manager learning whilst actually fulfilling her/his role. In identifying development needs, specific projects/tasks are identified where the competencies are required and the tasks are then completed under guidance of a "coach". This might be the boss or a colleague but importantly someone who is more adept at that particular activity. The coach can help agree learning objectives and then provide guidance and is able to give immediate feedback. As an example, a manager may have been identified as less strong in involving his/her team in projects, which results in them feeling less satisfied and not taking enough responsibility for the outcomes. A coach can help the manager think through how he or she can approach the new project differently, and what behaviours and actions are likely to be supportive and non-supportive. After agreeing the action-plan, the coach can provide a "sounding board" along the way and help objectively review the results at the end.

The use of mentors has also become more common, particularly for more senior managers; but the evidence indicates they are also very useful for managers at lower levels. The mentor can take a broader view of the role and how the individual approaches it, taking account of his or her strengths and weaknesses of leadership style, and help prioritize issues and relate what has been learnt to other situations. This can be particularly important if there are a number of coaches. Mentors can be from outside the organization, or from within, where they are typically more senior and in a different part of the organization.

The evidence is that these more work-related and flexible development activities will increase. Whilst organizations recognize that their people are one of their most important assets, and that managers/leaders need to learn and develop to continue to be effective, the resources available are increasingly more limited, so more cost effective ways are being sought. Managers are now expected to manage more of their own development, but often in more demanding situations, and where de-layering has increased the complexity of the job and increased the size of the steps between levels. It represents a real challenge to ensure that we have the leaders required to take forward the complex businesses of the new millennium.

CONCLUSIONS

In this chapter, we have sought to explain the significant contributions that psychologists, particularly occupational and organizational psychologists, have made to identifying factors which affect organizational effectiveness. The influence of leadership in organizations is ubiquitous. It affects fundamental aspects of an organization's success, ranging from the development of the organization's vision, creation of its culture, the nature of relationships between those who work within it, and the relationships with other organizations with whom it does business, or provides services. At the level of the individual, the nature and quality of the leadership has been shown to affect motivation, job satisfaction, identity, self-esteem and well-being, as well as individuals' performance. It must, therefore, be the subject of considerable importance, not only to academics, but also to practitioners in the field of leadership assessment and development, and of course, to those who are responsible for managing others.

The work of organizational psychologists has better informed us as to what constitutes effective leadership and its underlying behaviours. The best leaders are likely to have a combination of what we call today transformational and transactional qualities. However, it has also identified how complex leadership is, being situationally dependent, and affected by culture, in ways that we still have to fully understand. Undoubtedly, more research is required.

Research by psychologists has also emphasized the need for good leaders to help organizations to develop their people's potential to the highest levels, thereby meeting the increasing demands of stakeholders. The evidence suggests that effective leaders are neither just born nor made, so there needs to be a balance of good selection practices, plus the thoughtful continuous development of appropriate qualities. Also, most importantly, the involvement of multi-rater feedback may well prove to be a watershed in more successfully influencing an individual to actually change his or her behaviour in ways that improve outcomes.

Improved ways of identifying and measuring effective and ineffective leaders, in particular situations, will lead to a better understanding of how organizations should be structured. This will ultimately provide the data to help answer the question: How much impact does leadership have on the overall effectiveness of an organization? And, therefore, how much effort should we put into it?

REFERENCES

Alban-Metcalfe, R.J. & Alimo-Metcalfe, B. (2000a). An analysis of the convergent and discriminant validity of the Transformational Leadership Questionnaire. *International Journal of Selection and Assessment*, **8** (3), 158–175.

Alban-Metcalfe, R.J. & Alimo-Metcalfe, B. (2000b). The Transformational Leadership Questionnaire (TLQ-LGV): a convergent and discriminant validity study. *Leadership and Organisation Development Journal*, **21** (5), 280–296.

Alimo-Metcalfe, B. (1994). Gender bias in the selection and assessment of women in management. In M.J. Davidson & R. Burke (Eds), *Women in Management: Current Research Issues*. London: Paul Chapman.

Alimo-Metcalfe, B. (1995). An investigation of female and male constructs of leadership and empowerment. *Women in Management Review*, **10**, 3–8.

Alimo-Metcalfe, B. (1998). 360 degree feedback and leadership development. *International Journal of Selection and Assessment*, **6** (1), 35–44.

Alimo-Metcalfe, B. & Alban-Metcalfe, R.J. (2001). The development of a new transformational leadership questionnaire. *Journal of Occupational and Organizational Psychology*, **74**, 1–27.

Antonioni, D. (1996). Designing an effective 360-degree appraisal feedback process. *Organizational Dynamics*, **25** (2), 24–38.

Atwater, L.E. & Yammarino, F.J. (1997). Self–other rating agreement: a review and model. *Research in Personal and Human Resources Management*, **15**, 121–174.

Atwater, L., Roush, P. & Fischthal, A. (1995). The influence of upward feedback on self–follower ratings of leadership. *Personnel Psychology*, **48**, 35–59.

Avolio, B.J., Bass, B.M. & Jung, D.I. (1999). Re-examining the components of transformational and transactional leadership using the Multifactor Leadership Questionnaire. *Journal of Occupational and Organizational Psychology*, **72**, 441–462.

Barling, J., Weber, T. & Kelloway, E.K. (1996). Effects of transformational leadership training on attitudinal and financial outcomes: a field experiment. *Journal of Applied Psychology*, **81**, 827–832.

Bass, B.M. (1985). *Leadership and Performance Beyond Expectations*. New York: Free Press.

Bass, B.M. (1990). *Bass and Stodgill's Handbook of Leadership: Theory, Research, and Applications*, 3rd edn. New York: Free Press.

Bass, B.M. (1998a). *Transformational Leadership: Industrial, Military, and Educational Impact*. Mahwah, NJ: Lawrence Erlbaum.

Bass, B.M. (1998b). Current developments in transformational leadership: research and applications. Invited address to the American Psychological Association, San Francisco, August.

Bass, B.M. & Avolio, B.J. (1990a). *Multifactor Leadership Questionnaire*. Palo Alto, CA: Consulting Psychologists Press.

Bass, B.M. & Avolio, B.J. (1990b). *Transformational Leadership Development: Manual for the Multifactor Leadership Questionnaire*. Palo Alto, CA: Consulting Psychologists Press.

Bass, B.M. & Avolio, B.J. (1993). Transformational leadership and organisational culture. *Public Administration Quarterly*, **17**, 112–122.

Bass, B.M. & Avolio, B.J. (1994). Shatter the glass ceiling: women may make better managers. *Human Resource Management*, **33**, 549–560.

Bass, B.M., Avolio, B.J. & Atwater, L. (1996). The transformational and transactional leadership of men and women. *International Review of Applied Psychology*, **45**, 5–34.

Bennis, W. & Nanus, B. (1985) *Leaders*. New York: Harper & Row.

Blake, R.R. & Mouton, J.S. (1964). *The Managerial Grid*. Houston, TX: Gulf.

Bryman, A. (1992). *Charisma and Leadership in Organizations*. London: Sage.

Burns, J.M. (1978). *Leadership*. New York: Harper & Row.

Carless, S.A. (1998). Assessing the discriminant validity of transformational leader behaviour as measured by the MLQ. *Journal of Occupational and Organizational Psychology*, **71**, 353–358.

Church, A.H. & Waclawski, J. (1995). The effects of personality orientation and executive behaviour on subordinate perception of workgroup enablement. *International Journal of Organizational Analysis*, **3** (4), 20–51.

Church, A.H. & Waclawski, J. (1998) Making multi-rater feedback systems work. *Quality Progress*, **31** (4), 81–89.

Clifford, L. & Bennett, H. (1997). Best practice in 360 degree feedback. *Selection and Development Review*, **13** (2), 6–9.

Conger, J.A. (1989). *The Charismatic Leader: Behind the Mystique of Exceptional Leadership*. San Francisco, CA: Jossey-Bass.

Conger, J.A. & Kanungo, R.N. (1988). Behavioural dimensions of charismatic leadership. In J.A. Conger & R.N. Kanungo (Eds), *Charismatic Leadership: The Elusive Factor in Organizational Effectiveness*, pp. 78–97. San Francisco, CA: Jossey-Bass.

Covin, T.J., Kolenko, T.A., Sightler, K.W. & Tudor, R.K. (1997). Leadership style and post-merger satisfaction. *Journal of Management Development*, **16** (1), 22–33.

De Pree, M. (1993). Followership. In W.E. Rosenbach & R.L. Taylors (Eds), *Contemporary Issues in Leadership Research*. Oxford: Westview Press.

Druskat, V.U. (1994). Gender and leadership style: transformational and transactional leadership in the Roman Catholic Church. *Leadership Quarterly*, **5**, 99–119.

Eagly, A.H. (1991). Gender and leadership. Paper presented at the Annual Meeting of the American Psychological Association, San Francisco, CA.

Eagly, A.H. & Johnson, B.T. (1990). Gender and leadership style: a meta-analysis. *Psychological Bulletin*, **108**, 233–256.

Eden, P. (1990). Pygmalion without interpersonal contrast effects: whole group gain from raising manager expectations. *Journal of Applied Psychology*, **75**, 394–398.

Ferrario, M. (1994). Women as managerial leaders. In M.J. Davidson & R. Burke (Eds), *Women in Management: Current Research Issues*. London: Paul Chapman.

Fiedler, F.E. (1967). *A Theory of Leadership Effectiveness*. New York: McGraw-Hill.

Fleishman, E.A. (1953). The description of supervisory behaviour. *Journal of Applied Psychology*, **37** (1), 1–6.

Fleishman, E.A. & Harris, E.F. (1962). Patterns of leadership behaviour related to employee grievances and turnover. *Personal Psychology*, **15** (1), 43–56.

Fletcher, C. & Baldry, C. (1999). Multi-source feedback systems: a research perspective. In C.L. Cooper & I.T. Robertson (Eds), *International Review of Industrial and Organisational Psychology*, Vol. **14**, pp. 149–194. New York: John Wiley.

Gilligan, C. (1982). *In a Different Voice*. Cambridge, MA: Harvard University Press.

Grant, L. & Hagberg, R. (1996). 'Rambos in pinstripes: Why so many CEOs are lousy leaders'; cited in *Fortune Archives* (1999), Vol. **139**, No. 12, 21 June, p. 1.

Greenleaf, R.K. (1970). *The Servant as Leader*. San Francisco, CA: Jossey-Bass.

Greenleaf, R.K. (1996). *On Becoming a Servant Leader*. San Francisco, CA: Jossey-Bass.

Heilman, M.E. (1983). Sex bias in work settings: the lack-of-fit model. In B.M. Straw & L.L. Cummings (Eds), *Research in Organizational Behaviour*, Vol. **5**, Greenwich, CT: JAI Press.

House, R.J. (1971). A path goal theory of leadership effectiveness. *Administrative Science Quarterly*, **16** (3), 321–328.

House, R.J. (1977). A 1976 theory of charismatic leadership. In J.G. Hunt & L.L. Larson (Eds), *Leadership: The Cutting Edge*, pp. 189–207. Carbondale, IL: Southern Illinois University Press.

Hunt, J.G. (1996). *Leadership: A New Synthesis*. Newbury Park, CA: Sage.

Hunt, J.G., Baliga, B.R. & Peterson, M.F. (1988). Strategic apex leader scripts and an organizational life cycle approach to leadership and excellence. *Journal of Management Development*, **7** (5), 61–83.

Hunt, J.G. & Peterson, M.F. (1997). Two scholars' views of some nooks and crannies in cross-cultural leadership. *Leadership Quarterly*, **8**, 343–354.

Jacobson, S.W. & Jacques, R. (1990). Of knowers, knowing and the known: a gender framework for revisioning organizational and management scholarship. Presentation to the Academy of Management Annual Meeting, 10–12 August, San Francisco, CA.

Katz, D. & Kahn, R.L. (1978). *The Social Psychology of Organizations*, 2nd edn. New York: John Wiley.

Kelly, G.A. (1955). *Psychology of Personal Constructs*, Vols. **1** & **2**. New York: Norton.

King, A.S. (1974). Expectation effects in organization change. *Administrative Science Quarterly*, **19**, 221–230.

Kotter, J.P. (1990). *A Force for Change*. London: Free Press.

Lee, C. (1993). Followership: the essence of leadership. In W.E. Rosenbach & R.L. Taylor (Eds), *Contemporary Issues in Leadership Research*. Oxford: Westview Press.

Livingstone, J.S. (1988). Pygmalion in management. *Harvard Business Review*, Sept/Oct, 121–130.

London, M., Wohlers, A.J. & Gallagher, P. (1990). A feedback approach to management development. *Journal of Management Development*, **9** (6), 17–31.

Mann, R.D. (1959). A review of the relationships between personality and performance in small groups. *Psychological Bulletin*, **56** (4), 241–270.

Mintzberg, H. (1982). 'If you're not serving Bill and Barbara, then you're not serving leadership'. In J.G. Hunt, U. Sekaran & C.A. Schriesheim (Eds), *Leadership Beyond Establishment Views*. Carbondale, IL: Southern Illinois University Press.

Parry, K.W. (1998). Grounded theory and social processes: a new direction for leadership research. *Leadership Quarterly*, **9**, 85–105.

Powell, G. (1993). *Women and Men in Management*, 2nd edn. Newbury Park, CA: Sage.

Redman, T. & Mathews, B.P. (1997). What do recruiters want in a public sector manager? *Public Personnel Management*, **26** (2), 246–256.

Reilly, R.R., Smither, J.W. & Vasilopoulos, N.L. (1996). A longitudinal study of upward feedback. *Personnel Psychology*, **49**, 599–612.

Rosenbach, W.E. & Taylor, R.L. (Eds) (1993). *Contemporary Issues in Leadership*. Oxford: Westview Press.

Rosener, J. (1990). Ways women lead. *Harvard Business Review*, Nov/Dec, 119–125.

Rost, J.C. (1993). *Leadership for the Twenty-first Century*. Westport, CT: Praeger.

Rosenthal, R. & Jacobson, L. (1968). *Pygmalion in the Classroom: Teacher Expectation and Pupils' Intellectual Development*. New York: Holt, Rinehart & Winston.

Sashkin, M. (1988). The visionary leader. In J.A. Conger & R.N. Kanungo (Eds), *Charismatic Leadership: The Elusive Factor in Organizational Effectiveness*, pp. 122–160. San Francisco, CA: Jossey-Bass.

Schweiger, D. & DeNisi, A. (1991). Communication with employees following a merger: a longitudinal field experiment. *Academy of Management Journal*, **34** (1), 110–135.

Schein, V. (1994). Managerial sex typing: a persistent and pervasive barrier to women's opportunities. In M.J. Davidson & R.J. Burke (Eds), *Women in Management: Current Research Issues*. London: Paul Chapman.

Shamir, B. (1995). Social distance and charisma: theoretical notes and an exploratory study. *Leadership Quarterly*, **6**, 19–47.

Shamir, B., House, R.J. & Arthur, M.B. (1993). The motivational effects of charismatic leadership: a self-concept based theory. *Organization Science*, **4**, 577–594.

SHL (1984). *OPQ Manual and User's Guide*. SHL Group, Surrey, UK.

SHL (1999). *OPQ32 User's Guide and Technical Manual*. SHL Group, Surrey, UK.

Smither, J.W., London, M., Vasilopoulos, M.L., Reilly, M.R., Millsap, R.E. & Salvemini, N. (1995). An examination of the effects of an upward feedback program over time. *Personnel Psychology*, **48** (1), 1–34.

Sparrow, J. & Rigg, C. (1993). Job analysis: selecting for the masculine approach to management. *Selection and Development Review*, **9** (2), 5–8.

Stodgill, R.M. (1948). Personal factors associated with leadership: a survey of the literature. *Journal of Psychology*, **25**, 35–71.

Stodgill, R.M. (1963). *Manual for the Leader Behaviour Description Questionnaire*. Columbus, OH: Ohio State University.

Stodgill, R.M. (1974). *Handbook of Leadership: A Survey of Theory & Research*. New York: Free Press.

Tichy, N. & Devanna, M. (1986). *Transformational Leadership*. New York: John Wiley.

Vernon, T. (1998). Untitled reference. Society for Industrial and Organizational Psychology, Dallas, TX; cited in Bass (1998b).

Vroom, V.H. & Yetton, P.N. (1973). *Leadership and Decision Making*. Pittsburgh, PA: University of Pittsburgh Press.

Weber, M. (1947). *The Theory of Social and Economic Organizations*. (T. Parsons, trans.). New York: Free Press (original work published in 1924).

West, M. & Patterson, M. (1998). People power: the link between job satisfaction and productivity. *Centre Piece*, **3** (3), 2–5.

Wexley, K.N., Alexander, R., Greenwalk, J. & Couch, M. (1980). Attitudinal congruence and similarity as related to interpersonal evaluation in manager–subordinate dyads. *Academy of Management Journal*, **23**, 320–330.

Willner, A.R. (1984). *The Spellbinders: Charismatic Political Leadership*. New Haven, CT: Yale University Press.

Yagil, D. (1998). Charismatic leadership and organisational hierarchy: attributing charisma to close and distant leaders. *Leadership Quarterly*, **9** (2), 161–176.

Yukl, G. (1999). An evaluation of conceptual weakness in transformational and charismatic leadership theories. *Leadership Quarterly*, **10** (2), 285–307.

Zaleznik, A. (1993). Managers and leaders: are they different? In W.E. Rosenbach & R.L. Taylor (Eds), *Contemporary Issues in Leadership*, pp. 36–56. Oxford: Westview Press.

CHAPTER 10

Competency and Individual Performance: Modelling the World of Work

Rainer Kurz
SHL Group plc, UK
and
Dave Bartram
SHL Group plc, UK

INTRODUCTION

The Editors' Introduction outlined a comprehensive framework for investigating organizational effectiveness, and highlighted the fact that organizational performance accrues from the performance of individuals. It also presented the outline of a model of competency, and distinguished between competency, competency potential, competency requirements and outcomes. The present chapter builds on this, using empirical research and existing psychological taxonomies in order to develop a comprehensive framework for conceptualizing competency and performance in the work place. The emphasis is on developing a means of organizing the knowledge we have about people and their performance within organizations.

One goal of psychological science is to provide theories and tools to assess, predict and shape performance. While there is a long history of research in the behavioural sciences relating to performance at work, an overarching conceptual model is still somewhat lacking. Herriot and Anderson (1997) suggest that the traditional paradigm of personnel psychology is somewhat struggling to accommodate a number of developments in the international business environment and their effects on human resources management. They call for a wider theoretical framework for personnel psychology. Furnham (1995) has also lamented the paucity of literature at the interface between personality and occupational psychology, while presenting a broad research model for examining the relationship between personality and work.

Organizational Effectiveness: The Role of Psychology
Edited by I.T. Robertson, M. Callinan and D. Bartram. © 2002 John Wiley & Sons, Ltd.

To develop a model of performance at work, it is necessary to clarify the differences between behaviours, performances and outcomes. It is also important to consider the ways in which person and organizational variables interact to produce each of these. Individual effectiveness is as complex a construct as organizational effectiveness. Individuals display different modes of behaviour with different stakeholders, and stakeholders judge individual effectiveness using multiple criteria. Judgements of individual effectiveness, however, tend to be about extended sequences of behaviours rather than about discrete behavioural episodes. When we talk about "performance at work" we tend to imply a continuous process, an extended sequence of behaviours that have coherence for the actor and those acted upon. While behaviours can be described in isolation, performances can be thought of as choreographed sequences of behaviours that have a function and purpose.

Performance can be judged against performance criteria, while behaviours can only be described. Performances can generally be regarded or judged in terms of observable activities or the outcomes they are directed towards achieving: the actor or others perceive performances as more or less effective as a function of how successful they are in achieving their intended outcomes.

In this chapter we will endeavour to outline a model of performance at work that integrates academic theories and occupational assessment practices into a unifying framework that can be applied to competency-based human resources management. The chapter is divided into three parts.

1. The first part extends the exploration of competencies initiated in the Introduction and relates competency to the requirements made upon people for performance in the work place on the one hand, and to underlying psychological characteristics (competency potential) on the other.
2. The second part describes the need for an overarching 'World of Work' (WoW) performance model, which maps out a structure for working life behaviour, the psychological variables that underlie such behaviour, and the situational (organizational and social) contexts within which such behaviour occurs. This section describes the structural components of a model and develops taxonomies for four key segments of working life.
3. The final part of the chapter outlines how these concepts of behaviour, competency and performance relate to human resources management.

PART 1: COMPETENCY AT WORK

Competency-based Assessment

The competency approach to selection and assessment is one based on identifying, defining and measuring individual differences in terms of specific work-related constructs that are relevant to successful job performance. Over the last 25 years this approach has gained rapidly in popularity, due partly to the way in which the concepts and language used have currency within the world of human resources management.

The profiling of jobs in terms of competency requirements has increasingly replaced more traditional task-based job analysis, most noticeably in countries outside the United States. Competency profiling differs from job analysis in that the focus of the former is on the desirable and essential behaviours required to perform a job, while the latter focuses on the tasks, roles and responsibilities associated with a job. These are complementary ways of looking at the same thing, with the competency analysis providing a person specification and the job analysis a job description. The main advantage of the competency modelling approach has been its success in building the models that lay the foundations for organization-wide integrated human resources applications.

The problem with competency as a construct is that there is considerable confusion and disagreement about what competencies are and how they should be measured (Shippmann et al., 2000). Competency-based assessment has also suffered in the past from being used and developed by a wide range of practitioners many of whom had not had a psychologist's background of training in scientific method and measurement. However, Shippmann et al. (2000) note that there is evidence of increasing rigour in the competency approach and that it is now emerging as a complementary approach to job analysis.

What is Competency?

In the Editors' Introduction competencies were defined as "sets of behaviours that are instrumental in the delivery of desired results or outcomes". This behavioural view of competency needs to be contrasted with the earlier trait-based approach of Boyatzis (1982) in his seminal book *The Competent Manager*: "A job competency is an underlying characteristic of a person which results in an effective and/or superior performance of a job ... it may be a trait, motive, skill, aspect of one's self image or social role, or body of knowledge that he or she uses". Boyatzis' original definition is clear in identifying competency as an underlying characteristic (rather than a collection of behaviours), but is less clear on the relationship between competencies as constructs and psychological constructs such as motives, traits, skills and so on.

Warr and Connor (1992) noted in their discussion of approaches to job competence that Boyatzis' model of personal competencies is quite close to traditional person characteristics assessment models, while more recent competency oriented interventions place higher emphasis on establishing and describing the requirements of the job situation. Boam and Sparrow (1992) also take a trait-oriented view on competencies, while also recognizing the need to cater for role and career stream, or occupational, competencies.

Woodruffe (1992) states that "Competencies are indeed the same as aspects of personality such as traits and motives, but those terms are so poorly understood and agreed that to say that competencies are, for example, traits risks competencies inheriting the confusion that surrounds traits." He then goes on to move away from the trait-based definition and present one more in line with that of the present authors: "A competency is the set of behaviour patterns that the incumbent needs to bring to a position in order to perform its tasks and functions with competence." Woodruffe suggests excluding components of work performance such as technical skills, knowledge and abilities from the competencies definition.

It follows from the definition of competency presented here that competencies should be specified in "action" terms. That is, while "leadership" is not a competency, "providing leadership" is. Thus we need to be careful not to define competencies as things which people possess ("He has lots of leadership") but as behaviours that people exhibit ("He provides lots of leadership"). This clarification requires us to reconsider some of the constructs that are often considered to be "competencies" (e.g. energetic, persuasive), and classify them as antecedents or determinants of competency rather than competencies *per se*.

Behavioural Repertoires

In terms of the definition presented here and in the Editors' Introduction, competency relates to behavioural repertoires: the range and variety of behaviours we can perform, and outcomes we can achieve. A competency is not the behaviour or performance itself but the repertoire of capabilities, activities, processes and responses available that enable a range of work demands to be met more effectively by some people than by others. Such repertoires may be defined by reference to their relevance to the World of Work (or some other such context).

The analogy of a musician's repertoire is helpful in capturing this notion. A musician delivers performances that cover a range of styles and content, which may be judged as more or less good by listeners. These performances fall within the musician's repertoire and are a consequence of his or her competency as a musician. This competency is not the same thing as the performances, but it is what enables the performances to occur. The behaviours that the musician has to be skilled and adept at are also not the same thing as the performance. The performance is the choreographed stream of behaviours that will be judged overall as either "good" or "bad", "effective" or "ineffective", "successful" or "unsuccessful".

We can develop this analogy further by considering the differences between the person who has learnt by rote one piano piece and the person who has developed competence as a jazz musician and is able to extemporize around any melody or chord sequence. Both show relevant desired behaviours (i.e. competency as musicians), but the nature of these is very different. Using a single performance as evidence of competency might fail to differentiate between such people. The nature of the musician's competency lies not just in the individual performances, but also in his or her ability to generalize and to transfer knowledge and skills from one job task or role to another.

The Relationship Between Competencies and Other Psychological Constructs

A competency, then, is a construct that represents a constellation of the characteristics of the person that result in effective performance in his or her job.

The various uni-dimensional psychological characteristics that underpin competencies can be considered as components of these constellations. The constellations or clusters of characteristics that make up competencies may be extensive in the case of broad competencies or limited in the case of more specific ones. The main factor that distinguishes a competency from other weighted composites of psychological constructs is the fact that *a competency is defined in relation to its significance for performance at work*, rather than its content in purely psychological terms. It differs from constructs such as abilities or personality traits, which are uni-dimensional and defined as characteristics of the person, that "exist" and can be measured in isolation from a work context.

Models of Job Competency

Most of the work on defining models of job performance has focused on the managerial area. There are some exceptions, such as Hunt's (1996) work on entry level jobs in the service industries, and analyses of the competencies required for jobs in the military (e.g. the work of Campbell et al., 1990, on Project A). In relation to managerial competencies, Tett et al. (2000) reference 12 different models from the academic literature dating back to Flanagan (1951). They also note that while there is considerable overlap in terms of content between these various models, there are also marked differences in detail, description, definition, emphasis and level of aggregation. In addition to these are a range of generic practitioner models developed for use in occupational psychology consulting. These include such generic models as Lominger's Career Architect; PDI's PROFILOR; SHL's executive, manager, customer service and blue collar models; and various others.

The practice-based models tend to be more fully developed than the academic ones and contain a lot more detail in terms of instrumentation, behavioural anchors, associated development action points, and data on correlations with dispositional measures. The academic models, on the other hand, tend to focus on trying to identify a small number of general dimensions that can provide a comprehensive yet parsimonious account of the domain.

What is needed are approaches that combine the parsimony and structure of the academic models with the usability and practicality of those developed in the field.

Componential Models of Job Competency

The merging of the academic and practice-based approaches to competency models can be found in the hierarchical approach to model building. General high-level constructs can provide the basis for accounting for major portions of variance in performance, while more detailed dimensions are required for everyday use by practitioners. Even more finely grained constructs may be required for the detailed competency profiling of jobs.

Tett et al. (2000) developed a taxonomy of 53 competencies clustered under nine general areas. These 53 competencies were derived from the results of subject matter experts sorting 147 behavioural elements. The nine general areas were: traditional functions; task orientation; dependability; open-mindedness; emotional control; communication; developing self and others; occupational acumen; and concerns.

Borman and Brush (1993) propose a structure of 187 behaviours mapping on to 18 main dimensions, which in turn map to four very broad dimensions: leadership and supervision; interpersonal relations and communication; technical behaviours and mechanics of management; and useful behaviours and skills (such as job dedication). This structure has been supported by subsequent meta-analysis research (Conway, 1999).

A further example of this approach is seen in the job competency framework developed by Bartram et al. (2000). This also adopts a three-tier structure. This structure represents a "deep structure" that underlies the development of competency models, which are defined as specific "surface structures". Just as different utterances in spoken language can map on to a common underlying proposition, so differently described competencies within models can map on to a common underlying construct.

The bottom tier of the structure consists of a set of 110 component competencies. The deep structure defines the relationships between these components, their mapping on to a set of 20 competency dimensions (the middle tier) and their loadings on eight broad "competency factors" (the top tier).

The Bottom Tier: Component Competencies

The 110 component competencies were derived from extensive content analyses of both academic and practice-based competency models. This analysis covers managerial and non-managerial positions. As a consequence, the content of the components covers a wider domain than that addressed by Tett et al. in their work on managerial competencies.

The component competencies can be considered to be competencies broken down to the point where no competency is subsumed by any other competency. As such, the components represent the "building blocks" for creating specific sets of competencies. They are not necessarily uni-dimensional. In terms of level of aggregation, they lie between the behaviours described by Borman and Brush (1993) and Tett et al. (2000) and the 53 components identified by Tett et al. (2000).

The component building blocks are defined in relation to five levels of complexity by behavioural indicators and other information. These levels provide the basis for generating competency sets corresponding to different job layers within an organization (from manual worker to senior manager and director level).

The Middle Tier: Competency Dimensions

The 20 middle-level dimensions were derived from analyses of generic and client-specific competency models. They represent the competencies that have been frequently identified in job analyses and used for assessment and development centres over the last two decades. Figure 10.1 lists the 20 competency

8 Competency Factors	20 Competency Dimensions
1 LEADING & DECIDING	1.1 Deciding & Initiating Action
Need for Power & Control	1.2 Providing Leadership & Supervision
2 SUPPORTING & CO-OPERATING	2.1 Team Working & Supporting
Agreeableness	2.2 Serving Customers & Clients
3 INTERACTING & PRESENTING	3.1 Relating & Networking
Extraversion	3.2 Persuading & Influencing
	3.3 Communicating & Presenting
4 ANALYSING & INTERPRETING	4.1 Writing & Reporting
'g'	4.2 Applying Expertise & Technology
	4.3 Problem Solving
5 CREATING & CONCEPTUALISING	5.1 Learning & Researching
	5.2 Creating & Innovating
Openness	5.3 Forming Strategies & Concepts
6 ORGANISING & EXECUTING	6.1 Planning & Organising
Conscientiousness	6.2 Delivering Quality
	6.3 Complying & Persevering
7 ADAPTING & COPING	7.1 Adapting & Responding to Change
Emotional Stability	7.2 Coping with Pressures & Setbacks
8 ENTERPRISING & PERFORMING	8.1 Achieving Results & Developing Career
Need for Achievement	8.2 Enterprising & Commercial Thinking

Figure 10.1 Relationships between the top and middle tiers of the job competency framework deep structure. The underlying dispositional traits most strongly associated with each of the "Big Eight" factors are shown in italics. © SHL Group plc. Reproduced by permission

dimensions and shows how they relate to the top tier "Big Eight" competency factors (see below).

The Top Tier: Competency Factors—The "Big Eight"

Various analyses of competency data support the view that variance in competency measures can be accounted for by eight broad factors (one of which incorporates aspects of specialist knowledge and skills). These eight factors appear to reflect the psychological constructs that underlie competencies. Specifically the trait markers for the eight factors can be identified as:

- "g" or general reasoning ability
- the "Big Five" personality factors
- two factors relating to need for achievement and need for power or control.

This "Big Eight" structure has been replicated in a number of different data sets including analysis of the ratings of 54 competencies in the OPQ32 UK national standardization sample data (SHL, 1999), analysis of data from a large set of job applicant data collected over the Internet in the USA ($n = 26\,000$), and from analyses of data obtained from two generic 360-degree competency inventories. In addition to providing the highest level tier of the deep structure, this factorial structure also provides us with a valuable mechanism for mapping measures of disposition or attainment on to competencies. More recently, the first tranche of data from a longitudinal study being carried out with the SHL–UMIST Research Centre has provided further confirmation of the eight factor structure.

This analysis used data from the NEO (Costa & McRae, 1992), OPQ32 (SHL, 1999), the Motivation Questionnaire (SHL, 1992), measures of Values, measures of reasoning ability and ratings on the 20 competency dimensions and eight competency factors described in Figure 10.1.

It is worth reflecting on the extent to which these eight factors cover the main areas of individual differences that have been studied by psychologists over the past century. The general intellective factor, "g", was first "discovered" by Spearman (1904) and is one of the most visible products of psychology. While arguing about many areas of detail, most professionals would agree that differences in overall levels of performance at work are related to differences in intellectual ability (Ree & Earles, 1991; Ree et al., 1994; Carretta and Ree, 2000). Hunter and Hunter (1984) demonstrated that intellectual ability is the single most effective and generalizable predictor of performance.

The "Five-Factor Model" (e.g. Norman, 1963; Barrick and Mount 1991; Digman, 1990; Matthews, 1997) of personality traits provides the psychological basis for five corresponding constructs in the above job competency model. Extroversion underpins "Interacting and Presenting", Emotional Stability forms the basis for "Adapting and Coping", Conscientiousness underlies "Organizing and Executing", Openness to Experience largely determines "Creating and Conceptualizing", Agreeableness underpins "Supporting and Co-operating".

Achievement has, according to Cassidy and Lynn (1989), six components: work ethic, pursuit of excellence, status aspiration, competitiveness, acquisitiveness, and mastery. While some of these are part of the Conscientiousness FFM construct, their sum gives rise to a quite distinct, more dynamic and energetic behaviour pattern. This is captured within the "Enterprising and Performing" competency construct.

Decisiveness and ascendancy are often included in the "Extroversion" construct, but can be more directly related to Need for Power or Control, or the motivation to manage (Miner & Smith, 1982). The Leading and Deciding construct covers this ground.

The eight competency factors provide a parsimonious account of the 12 Supra-Competencies identified by Dulewicz (1989). "Managing staff" and "Assertiveness and decisiveness" combine into Leading and Deciding, "Persuasiveness" and "Oral communication" are accounted for by Interacting and Presenting. Enterprising and Performing covers the ground of "Energy and Initiative", "Achievement motivation" and "Business sense". "Strategic perspective", "Analysis and judgement", "Planning and organizing", "Interpersonal Sensitivity", and "Adaptability and resilience" map fairly obviously on to the remaining factors.

The Relationship Between Competence and Competency

The job competency model outlined above is not a model of competence. It is unfortunate that two very similar words have been used to describe two different constructs. We make a very clear distinction between these within the present model. Competence is about mastery in relation to specified goals or outcomes. The measurement of competence at work involves the assessment of performance in the workplace against some pre-defined set of occupational or work-related standards. These standards define the performance criteria associated with competence in the workplace. Statements of or about competence are, therefore, statements about an individual's standard of achievement in relation to some defined set of work standards or requirements.

Competence, in relation to occupational standards-based qualifications, has been defined as "the ability to apply knowledge, understanding and skills in performing to the standards required in employment. This includes solving problems and meeting changing demands" (Beaumont, 1996). This reflects the common notion that competence is about the application of knowledge and skills, judged in relation to some standard or set of performance standards.

Competence, therefore, relates to performance or outcomes, and involves the description of tasks, functions or objectives. Competencies, on the other hand, relate to the behaviours underpinning successful performance; what it is people do in order to meet their objectives; how they go about achieving the required outcomes; what enables their competent performance.

Standards of competence tend to be specified in terms of performance criteria that relate to outcomes. Methods of assessing competence may include workplace assessments, simulations and other techniques. The performance standards required tend to be set by a recognized authority or body responsible for awarding or accrediting occupational qualifications (e.g. the QCA accredits standards set by National Training Organizations in England; professional bodies define standards of competence for professional practice; and so on).

In essence, then:

- Competencies are "behavioural repertoires", while competence is a "state" of attainment.
- Competence is about achievement and is always backward-looking. A statement of competence is a statement about where a person is now, not where they might be in the future.
- Competencies can be used in a backward-looking (e.g. 360-degree feedback), concurrent (e.g. assessment centre) or forward-looking way (i.e. competency potential) to predict what they should be able to achieve.
- People demonstrate competence by applying their competencies in a goal-directed manner within a work setting.

Any framework that claims to deal with competence needs to provide a basis for the specification of statements of competence. It is important to understand, however, that a job competency model like the one being outlined here will not itself contain a specification of knowledge and skills. Competencies relate to *how* knowledge and skills are used in performance, and about *how* knowledge and skills are applied in the context of some particular set of job requirements.

Specifications of knowledge and skills do, however, form part of the definition of job and occupation competence (that is, the standards of performance that a person needs to achieve in work) and relate to domains within the WoW model described below.

A Taxonomy for Knowledge and Skills

While much is known about the acquisition of knowledge and skills from the training literature, frameworks for the description of knowledge and skills are less well developed. A considerable amount of research, however, has been carried out in the context of work on occupational standards (i.e. formal specifications of what constitutes competence in the workplace), on the problems of knowledge identification, specification and assessment (Mitchell & Bartram, 1994). Based on this work, the following four-dimensional taxonomy is suggested as a tool for conceptualizing occupational expertise.

The first dimension distinguishes between four broad types of expertise that are required in an occupation: what people need to "know, understand and be able to do".

- *"Knowing what": Data, facts and information*—using facts about things and processes; e.g. fact sheets, data.
- *"Knowing why": Theories, principles, models*—understanding the rationale, the reasons why. This is particularly important in problem solving and in professional practice where one's choice of methods and interpretation of information may be driven by the theoretical perspective that has been adopted.
- *"Knowing how": Methods, techniques, procedures*—applying techniques and procedures; e.g. how to analyse data, how to conduct an interview etc.
- *"Knowing when"*: Experience, exposure, practice—recognizing problems, timing of intervention, co-ordinating conflicting information and making timely judgements

Knowing "what" and "why" are reflected in the knowledge segment of the attainment domain, knowing "how" is reflected in the skills segment, and knowing "when" in the experience segment. The qualifications segment contains statements of competence, which represent the formal recognition of attainments that generally embody mixtures of all four "types of knowing". Academic qualifications tend to focus more on what and why, while practice qualification focus more on how and when.

The second dimension concerns the extent, scope or coverage of expertise. As for the three-tier job competency model described above, this can also be defined in a hierarchical manner. For defining expertise, however, it is useful to consider five levels.

- *Field expertise* can be defined as expertise that affects many aspects of competent performance across jobs within a wide employment sector (e.g. manufacturing, science, the arts and media, social and health care, commerce, administration).
- *Occupational expertise* is expertise that affects many aspects of competent performance across jobs within a specific occupation. It is also sometimes referred to as "over-arching" knowledge and skill, as it provides the conceptual structuring that ties together the various elements of competence in an occupation.
- *Functional or specialist expertise* is that which is of relevance to the performance of one function within an occupation (e.g. managing a psychological care service).

- *Task expertise* is that which is of relevance to one task, or category of tasks within a job.
- *Element expertise* relates to that needed for some discrete component or element of a task.

The third dimension considers the openness or accessibility of expertise and understanding. It may be:

- *Knowledge and skills that are open and public.* These are readily available, or skills, experiences or qualifications that anyone can acquire (e.g. having a driving licence, being able to use the Internet).
- *Knowledge and skills that are occupation-specific* and generally known only to those qualified individuals within an occupation or profession. This covers what we often refer to as "trade secrets" or "tricks of the trade". Professions (e.g. law and medicine) often encourage the creation of mystique around their occupation-specific areas of knowledge and skill in order to maximize other people's perception of their value as professionals.
- *Knowledge and skills that are organization-specific* and generally known only to those within the organization. This includes shared, rather than personal, knowledge of the organization's formal and informal structures and processes, working practices and commercial information relating to products and services.
- *Knowledge that is personal*, relating to an individual's particular job and his or her history of work experience. This includes personal local knowledge acquired through organizational socialization processes, tacit job knowledge (Wagner & Sternberg, 1985), and one's own particular way of knowing how to get things done in one's organization or work group.

The fourth dimension focuses on the distinction between *required* and *pre-requisite* expertise. Pre-requisite, or "enabling" expertise, is what a person needs to bring to a new situation. It includes the attainments (qualifications, experience, knowledge and skills) one assumes a trainee to have at the start of a training course, for example. This distinction is very important as competency potential includes not only dispositional attributes but also those aspects of a person's attainments that are pre-requisites for the development of competency in any new situation.

In assessing people for new positions it is important to distinguish between what one expects people to bring with them in terms of existing occupational expertise (their attainments), and what one expects them to be able to learn and develop once appointed (their potential).

Summary

Job competency models are developing towards more sophisticated structures based on empirical data. The work of Tett et al. (2000), Borman and Brush (1993) and Bartram et al. (2000) all support the need for hierarchical models, with a small number of broad factors at the top and large numbers of components or elements at the bottom.

Job competencies have been conceptualized in terms of behavioural repertoires that enable (or constrain) the range and quality of a person's work. On the one hand, an individual may operate according to a set of relatively inflexible rehearsed responses (e.g. an ability to operate machinery according to a set procedure). On the other hand, the person may have developed a more flexible set of meta-skills and plans (e.g. an understanding of the principles underlying the operation of various machines or systems, which will enable the person to fix problems and transfer skills to new situations and applications).

Competency can be considered to develop through the interactions between person characteristics (i.e. these determinants and their antecedents) on the one hand, and organizational characteristics ("system factors") on the other. These system factors may act to enhance or impose constraints and demands on opportunities for the demonstration and development of competency.

- Competency is defined in working life terms rather than dispositional or attainment terms.
- Competency is defined, operationally, by the performance repertoires or outcome states to which it refers.
- Competency definitions should be in action or outcome-oriented terms, while competence is defined in terms of attainments.

The bases of competency are uni-dimensional disposition and attainment attributes. A competency construct is, then, a multi-dimensional attribute complex that links dispositions and attainments to performance. The dispositional traits constitute what Campbell et al. (1993) refer to as "antecedents" in their model of work performance, while the attainments relate to what they call "determinants".

PART 2: MODELLING THE WORLD OF WORK

Broad Job Performance Models

Surprisingly little attention has been paid to the task of bringing together various models of job competency, and job performance under an overarching structure that ties together the influences of individual and organizational variables on performance and effectiveness.

Campbell (1990) and Campbell et al. (1993) developed a model of job performance that differentiates eight major dimensions: job-specific task proficiency, non-job-specific task proficiency, written and oral communication task proficiency, demonstrating effort, maintaining personal discipline, facilitating peer and team performance, supervision/leadership, and management/administration. In this model, task-specific proficiency relates to core tasks and skills required to perform one's job. These tend to be reflected in those job competencies judged as "essential" for job incumbents. Non-job-specific task proficiency, on the other hand, represents a whole range of other factors—desirable and incidental competencies.

This division between task and non-task performance is reflected in the tendency for working-life performance to be dichotomized into task and contextual performance (Borman & Motowildo, 1993). Contextual aspects of work performance are also referred to as Organizational Citizenship Behaviour (OCB: Smith et al., 1983).

A slightly different emphasis is noted by Van Dyne et al. (1995) who describe "extra-role" behaviours that contribute to organizational effectiveness. These would include: helping other workers, promoting the organization in public, developing oneself etc. Many of these competencies are actually contained within the job competency model described earlier. However, they may not be stressed as important by the organization when specifying the competencies required for a specific position. While it may be convenient to distinguish between task and non-task aspects of proficiency, it can also be misleading in that it may tend to de-emphasize the importance of the latter in determining overall individual effectiveness in performance at work (Conway, 1999).

Going beyond the notion of OCB-type competencies, Woodruffe (1992) and Boam and Sparrow (1992) call for additional types of competency to account for career stream, role and "core" competency. The latter is meant to reflect how business is carried out in a particular industrial sector, and leads to culture-based competencies that reflect the kind of behaviours, attitudes and values that are required in order to be successful.

Using a process of lexical analysis, Viswesvaran (1993, cited in Viswesvaran & Ones, 2000) identified ten dimensions as accounting for 486 job performance measure descriptions. These dimensions were overall job performance, job performance or productivity, effort, job knowledge, interpersonal competence, administrative competence, quality, communication competence, leadership, and compliance with rules. These dimensions provide a useful set of criteria for characterizing the various ways in which individuals can be judged to be "effective" at work.

The World of Work (WoW) structure proposed below endeavours to provide a framework within which this broad notion of individual effectiveness can be described and analysed.

Mapping the World of Work

Before describing the proposed structure, it will be useful to consider how the World of Work itself is structured. Pearlman (1980) discusses various approaches to modelling job families. A taxonomy is needed that will both reflect meaningful and practical clusters of occupations at the surface level and reflect what we know about empirical clustering of job-related dispositional and attainment variables at a deeper level. As such, this sort of taxonomy would provide the basis for making occupation–function relationship predictions, and provides a segmentation of job families that can be used to benchmark vacancies in an organization.

Holland (1959, 1985) developed over many years an elaborate theory of vocational choice. Central to this is a comprehensive model of person–environment match revolving around six vocational types (Realistic, Investigative, Artistic, Social, Enterprising, Conventional). The theory has attracted a high amount of academic attention with a lot of empirical support for the central typology (e.g. Spokane, 1985; Tranberg et al., 1993; Arnold et al., 1995). Others have argued for fewer than six types or dimensions:

- Prediger and Vansickle (1992) proposed two dimensions (data–ideas and people–things).
- Gottfredson (1986) differentiated four functional work areas (physical, bureaucratic, social and artistic).
- Ackerman and Heggestad (1997) provided evidence for four "trait complexes" (science–maths, clerical–conventional, social, and intellectual–cultural) that overlap but do not match Gottfredson's.

Arnold et al. (1995) predict that the Hexagon will remain prominent in career theory and practice. For many practitioner applications a more detailed breakdown is required, as seen from early applications of the model to the Strong–Campbell Interest Inventory to more recent applications in the Career Pathfinder interest inventory (SHL, 2000).

As the Holland occupation taxonomy can be mapped onto all these other approaches reviewed here, and as it has a high degree of use in practice, it is adopted here as the basis for differentiating occupation- and function-specific capabilities in the competency at work model.

The World of Work Model

The World of Work (WoW) model (Kurz, 1999a) has been developed over the last ten years in an effort to bring together and integrate research and application streams of occupational assessment. It attempts to provide a structured collection of taxonomies and concepts that outline an overarching, rationally derived framework for describing behaviour, competency and performance at work.

Robertson and Kinder (1993) provided a starting point for the WoW model by demonstrating through meta-analysis of 20 validation studies that both personality and aptitude scales have sizeable point-to-point correlations with relevant managerial performance dimensions. Kurz (1999b) developed expert system equations to predict competency dimensions from personality and aptitude scales, and found consistent validation evidence across nine studies. Gotoh (1999) successfully cross-validated these prediction equations with a Japanese sample. Kurz (2000) provides further evidence of consistent relationships between aptitudes and job competencies. Kurz and Morley (1996) and Kurz and Morris (1997) reported construct valid linkages between aptitudes and interest in job families.

Structure of the Model

Boyatzis (1982, p. 35) represented person characteristics, separated into a traits and motives sphere at the very centre of a radial map, followed by a social roles and self-image sphere and finally a skills sphere underlying behaviour. The environment is represented in his model by a cultural and organizational environment sphere at the outside, followed by a functional and situational demands sphere. He argues rightly that each of the components which relate to performance have some impact on each other.

The present model caters for broadly the same characteristics of people and environments, but offers a more finely grained structure as well as a topographical mapping that places related elements near each other. In the WoW model the radial map consists of five domains with four segments each (see Figure 10.2). Person–Environment models (Mischel & Shoda, 1995) lend themselves to a visual representation in circular form. Person characteristics are typically shown on the inside, environment characteristics on the outside with behaviour actions placed in between. In Figure 10.2, the two domains of person variables, "Disposition" and "Attainment", represent person characteristics and are a development of such well-established taxonomies as the seven-point plan

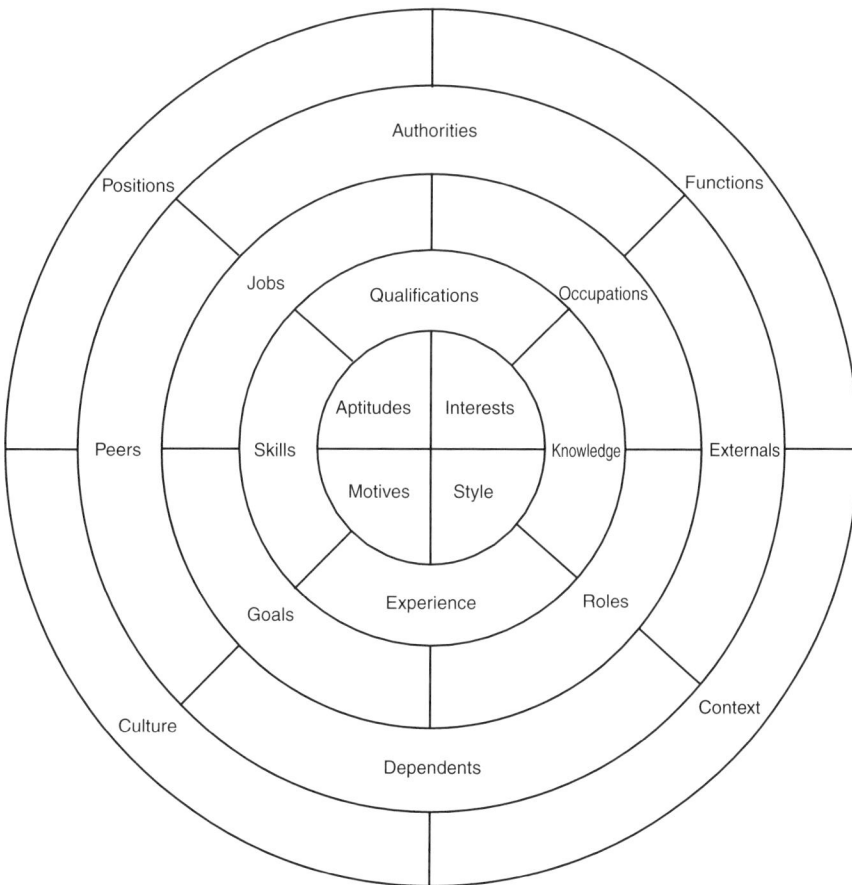

Figure 10.2 World of Work (WoW) model featuring five radial domains, from Disposition at the centre, through Attainment, Working Life, and Social relations to the Organization at the periphery. © SHL Group plc. Reproduced by permission

(Rodger, 1952). Two domains of environment variables, "Organization" and "Social Relations", represent organization characteristics. The fifth domain, "Working Life", is located at the interface of people and organization characteristics.

The structure will be described in terms of the five domains shown in Figure 10.2. Following this, four working-life taxonomies are developed.

The Disposition Domain

Dispositions are conceptualized in the model as underlying personal characteristics that are shaped slowly through developmental experiences, and lead a person to respond in typical ways. The disposition domain covers both ability and personality.

1. *Aptitudes* cover reasoning and learning abilities.
2. *Interests* cover patterns of preference related to vocational choices. The WoW model builds on the well-researched and widely applied work of Holland (1985) on "vocational types".
3. *Motives* cover underlying "needs" and "values", those aspects of disposition that energize and sustain behaviour at work. The theories in this field are rather diverse and lack a unifying framework. In its current form, however, the WoW model utilizes four clusters of motives (Energy and Dynamism, Synergy, Intrinsic, Extrinsic). These have been factor analytically derived from the 18 dimensions of the SHL Motivation Questionnaire (SHL, 1992).
4. *Style* covers typical cross-situational behavioural consistencies, or "personality". This segment covers the domain of the Five-Factor Model (FFM: see above).

The Attainment Domain

Attainments represent a person's achievements, thus reflecting the biography or working-life history of the person. The Attainment segments cover "Qualifications", "Skills", "Knowledge" and "Experience". These are key areas of interest for employers especially when assessing the suitability of work-experienced applicants for jobs, or when analysing training needs.

1. *Experience*. Surprisingly little has been written about work experience in the occupational psychology literature in spite of its relevance in organizational settings, especially selection. However, recently Tesluk and Jacobs (1998) have proposed a comprehensive model of the work experience construct that may stimulate more research in this area. In the WoW model experience is an important domain segment in its own right that covers the history of job-relevant experiences accumulated by an individual.
2. *Qualifications* include educational qualifications and job-relevant ones, e.g. professional licences and organization-specific training. Work-related (as opposed to academic) qualifications certify that competence has been

achieved at a particular point in time. Qualifications have high practical importance, as they are often requirements for individuals to perform in certain occupations.
3. *Knowledge* (as discussed above).
4. *Skills* (as discussed above).

The Organization Domain

This domain covers the organizational variables that may impact on people's performance at work. In terms of measurement, it is the domain that relates to job or position analysis and organizational profiling. (Visser et al. (1997) provide an overview of recent developments in this field.) Instruments, such as the Position Analysis Questionnaire (McCormick et al., 1977) and the Work Profiling System (SHL, 1995), assess task and context characteristics through structured questionnaires and can translate these into both human attribute and competency-based specifications. In the WoW model:

1. *Positions* represents the set of task behaviours a person has to carry out to do his or her job.
2. *Culture* refers to the prevailing belief systems in an organization that impact on job objectives and the evaluation of people's performance.
3. *Functions* refers to the duties and roles the organization expects the job incumbent to perform (e.g. manage production resources, develop people etc.).
4. *Context* refers to a range of situational characteristics of a position. These may be in terms of job level, location, division, community etc. As a category it also serves to represent external variables that may impact on the behaviour of organizations and their employees such as mergers, economic situation, society changes etc.

The Social Relations Domain

Organizational socialisation research primarily concerns the transition of newcomers into an organization, and has evolved as a discipline largely independent of other topics, such as selection (Anderson & Ostroff, 1997). In the WoW model a wider "Social Relations" domain is invoked to represent social structures and ongoing interaction processes in the workplace. They have a profound influence on an individual's behaviour, which in turn influences the behaviour of other people in the organization as well as outside.

The model defines four categories of social relationship in the workplace. These are defined in terms of power, control and responsibility relationships. In the workplace, individuals will each have relationships with:

1. *Authorities:* those in superior positions (e.g. line managers) who set directions and goal for them.
2. *Dependents:* those who they manage (either direct reports or those for whom they are the resource manager)

3. *Peers:* colleagues within the organization with whom one has an equal power–control position.
4. *Externals:* relevant people outside the organization (e.g. clients or suppliers) with whom they have to interact in order to carry out their job.

Figure 10.2 visually differentiates vertical relationships (above or below in the hierarchy) and lateral relationships (inside or outside the organization). Social relations are important for predicting and explaining people's behaviour, and even more so for explaining differences in (perceptions of) performance. Research into 360-degree feedback (Warr & Bourne, 1999) found that correlations between line-manager and self-assessments of performance rarely exceeded 0.35, even with highly reliable measurement tools. This result suggests that it may be illusive to search for an objective "true" measure of performance at work, as an individual's performance may legitimately be judged differently from the differing organizational perspectives of his or her manager, subordinates, colleagues or customers.

The Working Life Domain

The framework for examining organizational effectiveness outlined in the Editors' Introduction highlighted the pivotal role of the individual. The working-life domain provides a framework within which to describe, explain, predict and modify performance-related behaviours, outcomes, choices and states. It is located at the interface of "inside" (person) and "outside" (situational) variables, and is segmented into four categories.

1. *Job* variables relate to an individual's working life in relation to job requirements, and are concerned with observable job-related behaviours.
2. *Occupation* variables cover career choice and classification in terms of occupations and professions. This links closely with the organization domain definition of requirements in terms of function. That is, organizations select or train people to carry out particular profession- or occupation-specific functions that require the application of certain specialist knowledge and skills.
3. *Role* variables relate to more dynamic processes and states as reflected in dyadic, individual–team or wider individual–group relations. Such role expectations are shaped by the prevailing social relational context.
4. *Goal* variables relate primarily to emotional–affective states; for example, an individual's job satisfaction in relation to performance outcomes, or levels of stress induced by conflicts between personal values and the prevailing organizational culture. Adaptation, within the WoW model, is seen as closely related to goal-seeking, with the process of matching organizational and individual goals as being a key aspect of performance management.

These four categories provide a basis for conceptualizing working life issues, and for linking psychological characteristics of people with organizational and other contextual variables. The central working life domain is intended to provide a basis for conceptualizing important aspects of working life in a non-evaluative, descriptive way. To this end the four segments described are elaborated in the following ways.

- The "Job" segment caters for "general", directly observable activities and closely related aspects of working life. The corresponding job competency taxonomy is intended to be as far as possible generally applicable, and to this end is modelled largely on well-established intelligence, motivation and personality theory.
- The "Occupation" segment is designed to capture career choices and other aspects of vocational life largely based on Vocational Type theory. This also provides the starting point for capturing general job function expertise. Central to this segment is a taxonomy of vocational types and job families.
- The "Goal" segment aims to account for tangible goals and results or outcome criteria that are valued by a variety of stakeholders. The corresponding taxonomy is therefore largely based on motivational need theory.
- The "Role" segment represents socio-dynamic processes at work. Capitalizing on social group, dynamic and transactional theories a broad taxonomy of process interactions is adopted.

The following sub-sections outline some central links between the working life constructs and underlying disposition characteristics. Taxonomies are also outlined, for each of these four segments, that build on a range of well-established psychological theories.

The Job Competency Taxonomy

The three-tier job competency model outlined earlier provides a useful taxonomy for the job segment, as it captures the bulk of job tasks, components and behaviours. The "Big Eight" structure (Bartram et al., 2000) provides the basis for relating directly observable activities performed at the workplace to underlying psychological attributes. Furthermore, the three-tier competency framework provides the necessary building blocks for describing work behaviour. It also provides the basis for making predictions about performance from measures of competency potential. These predictions are developed from the data available about the relationships between measures of disposition and attainments at the competency factor, dimension and component levels.

Occupation Competencies and the Occupation Taxonomy

As noted above, the six vocational types identified by Holland (1985) provide a good starting point for delineating a model of occupation competency. In career guidance there is a need to assess an individual's suitability for various careers, and provide well-reasoned advice. Assessments of the individual and his or her circumstances needs to be related to highly structured, reliable and valid information about people and careers. A suitable occupation taxonomy can provide a representation of job families and occupations in the real world, and helps to keep track of and plan career changes.

From an organizational angle it can be observed that most organizations already use some administrative categories to classify different kind of jobs by occupational function (e.g. IT, sales, engineering, personnel, marketing, production). Especially employment related agencies and departments deal with a multitude of jobs across such categories on a daily basis. For placement and succession planning purposes psychologically meaningful occupation categories promise greater versatility and robustness in the match of people and vacancies.

Occupation competency concerns the effective application of occupational expertise and modes of behaviour. Each occupational field has its own sets of rules and requirements that regulate who is allowed to do what kind of work and how people should behave. These requirements apply universally to all individuals who want to work within that occupation. In most professions (e.g. medicine, accountancy and law) some of these expectations are defined in terms of qualification procedures and others in terms of codes of practice that are enforced through disciplinary procedures. In other occupations, while the qualification requirements for entry to the occupation may be explicit, other aspects of desired behaviour may be more implicit than explicit.

To identify what kinds of competency are required for people to perform well in different occupations requires research into types of people, and types of jobs. A model of occupation competencies should provide comprehensive coverage of occupations in the world of work, and spell out how each construct in the model relates to disposition and attainment complexes.

Goal Competencies and the Goals Taxonomy

The central focus for the "Goals" taxonomy is the categorization of aims, targets, goals, and corresponding business and personal results in terms of what people value. The motives segment in the disposition domain in the WoW model is central to this issue, but so far lacks an overarching consensus model.

- The Motivation Questionnaire (SHL, 1992) covers Energy and Dynamism, Synergy, Intrinsic and Extrinsic needs that are measured by eliciting to what extent certain work situations would be motivating or de-motivating; i.e. what situational outcomes people value.
- Schein (1990) covers similar ground through his set of eight Career Anchors. They represent deep underlying long-term needs that an individual wants to satisfy: Managerial competence; Technical/Functional competence; Autonomy/Independence; Security/Stability; Entrepreneurial creativity; Service/Dedication to a cause; Pure challenge; Life style integration. These represent a mix of abilities, motives, needs and values, and are clearly linked to what kind of outcomes (Promotion, Reward, Responsibility) are valued.

These two models can be combined with the four criteria of organizational effectiveness described in the Editors' Introduction to provide a goal taxonomy that helps to conceptualize business results and other outcome variables.

1. *Economic goals* relate to extrinsic Stability and Reward needs. Stability corresponds broadly to the career anchor of the same name, as well as status

and security needs identified in various motivational theories. Reward relates to career progression and material reward motives, and the Managerial Competence career anchor.

2. *Technology goals* form the basis for distinguishing intrinsic Mastery and Autonomy needs. Mastery incorporates needs for personal growth, interest and stimulation, and corresponds to the Technical/Functional competence career anchor. Autonomy satisfies the need for independence and flexibility, and relates to the career anchor of the same name.

3. *Commercial goals* form the basis of energy- and dynamism-related Productivity and Commerce constructs. Productivity covers goal-accomplishment and output delivery in response to day-to-day business operation, and is linked to "Pure Challenge" in the Schein model. Commerce covers commercial and client orientation, and thus relates to the Entrepreneurial creativity career anchor.

4. *Social goals* relate to Society and Harmony synergy needs. Individuals with a Service/Dedication to a cause career anchor tend to have strong personal principles, and a need for affiliation and helping people. Harmony corresponds somewhat to the Life style career anchor, but also incorporates need for recognition and open communications at the workplace.

Goal-setting theory (Locke, 1968) suggests that the goals of employees help to explain their motivation and job performance. Locke views motivation as goal-directed behaviour, and argues that goals that are clear and challenging will result in higher levels of employee motivation and performance than ambiguous and easy goals. Goal competency constructs can aid the process of defining and communicating goals, and assessing output results against the desired goals.

Goal competency relates to the capability for setting goals, managing and directing one's motivation and structuring behaviour and development activities towards goals. The goal-directed behaviours people exhibit in their working life need to be differentiated in relation to their underlying values and needs. As discussed earlier, these can be viewed in terms of the relationship of needs to four main areas for goal setting: economic, technological, commercial and social.

Role Competencies and the Roles Taxonomy

The behaviour and effectiveness of groups is not just simply a matter of adding up or averaging individual characteristics, but depends on psychodynamic processes. Power relationships, lengths of service in a group, clarity of goals etc. all interact in ways that have to be modelled at the intra-group level, and manifest themselves in certain outcome "states" of the relationships.

- Belbin (1981) developed a model consisting of eight team types (Co-ordinator, Shaper, Plant, Monitor–Evaluator, Resource investigator, Completer, Team worker, Implementer), and demonstrated that the actual composition of the group influences group effectiveness. The model rapidly became very popular, and also received considerable academic attention.

- Bass (1985) presented a transactional model of leadership styles (Directive, Delegative participative, Consultative and Negotiative) and sub-ordinate styles (Receptive, Self-reliant, Collaborative, Informative and Reciprocating sub-ordinate) that helps to clarify dynamic processes.
- Guest (1997) reviewed transactional, transformational and other situational models in the leadership area.

Any of these can provide avenues for exploring processes and outcomes in group situations. Similarly models of peer relationships (e.g. buying/selling; influencing/listening) can also provide useful angles for uncovering process dynamics.

Role competency is central in the analysis team interactions, and where organizations are interested in group activity that aims to increase productivity, coherence and identity, or reduce conflict, stress and strain. Key to this is the accurate assessment of team processes, as well as perceptions of their effectiveness. (Brannick et al. (1997) provide a detailed account of recent developments in the assessment and measurement of team performance.)

Team processes can be related to individual behaviours and characteristics, and to a department's and organization's goals. Dulewicz (1995, p. 82) defined a team role as "a pattern of behaviour characteristics of the way in which one team member interacts with another so as to facilitate the progress of the team as a whole". He also showed how Belbin's dimensions relate to boss ratings of competency, and dispositional personality dimensions.

Role competency captures the kind of behavioural repertoires required for the range of social roles an individual assumes at work—in both formal and informal groups. An individual needs to act and respond differently when communicating with his or her boss, peer, sub-ordinates or clients. Indeed picking the right kind of role scripts is probably central to how effective others judge one's work performance to be. Actual behaviours may at face value not appear effective in meeting some explicit organizational goal. However, the same behaviour sequence may meet exactly the role requirements of the situation as viewed by significant others in the immediate workplace. People have multiple roles and a range of behavioural repertoires available associated with those roles. Their ability to adapt their workplace behaviour to role expectations while still seeking to fulfil longer-term goals is a key issue in determining effectiveness.

Interactions Between the Five Domains of the WoW Model

Ways of categorizing working life performance are intended to capture and represent what actually happens at the workplace. They should cater for short-term behaviour–outcome sequences (e.g. a customer dialogue), as well as long-term sequences (e.g. career path of an individual). Some aspects of working life could serve as positive or negative indicators of effectiveness, and thus underscore "good" or "poor" performance. The segments of the five domains of the WoW model are of course highly interrelated, and interact dynamically.

Dispositions lead individuals to behave in particular ways, mediated by attainments, and moderated by the situation. The consequences of working life manifest themselves in certain outcomes. These in turn build up the port-folio of attainments, and in the long term also influence dispositions. Attain-ments therefore mediate the relationship between dispositions and working life.

Organization characteristics drive individuals to show certain behaviours (e.g. talk to a customers, analyse data) and outcomes (e.g. make a product, sell x amount of insurance policies). The situational requirements and possibilities may be represented quite differently in the minds of the individual, authority, subordinate, peer and client social relations. The relationship of organization characteristics with individual behaviours and outcomes is thus mediated by the perceptions and opinions of the relationships within the social relations domain. In turn an individual's behaviour and outcome may affect the organi-zation's characteristics, as moderated by the observer's own attitudes and ex-pectations. Social relations thus mediate the relationship between organization and working life.

PART 3: COMPETENCY IN HUMAN RESOURCES MANAGEMENT

The main operational aspects of HRM include recruitment, selection, develop-ment, career guidance and performance management, while the more strategic aspects include succession planning, compensation and organizational devel-opment. See Schuler and Jackson (1999) for a recent account of the latest devel-opments in strategic HRM.

Competency models should be relevant for all these applications across a whole organization. In practice, competency models tend to have been con-structed to meet only the needs of a specific aspect of HRM in a certain part of an organization. Linked to this, many of the models are of an *ad hoc* nature and vary widely in terms of quality and usability (Fletcher et al., 1998).

In the light of the definition of competencies presented in the Editors' Introduction, the development of the notion of job competency presented in the first part of this chapter and the elaboration of the other aspects of compe-tency (occupation, role and goal) defined in the WoW model, the broad view of competency can now be defined as "the effective response to work de-mands". This is achieved by the integration of job, occupation, goal and role competency.

1. *Job competency* is a "set of general behaviours, rooted in underlying disposi-tions, that are instrumental in the delivery of desired results or outcomes".
2. *Occupation competency* is a "set of function-specific behaviours that are closely linked to underlying attainments, and are pre-requisites for responding effectively to work demands and delivered products and services".
3. *Goal competency* is "the initiation, continuation and successful completion of goal-directed behaviours in response to organization demands".
4. *Role competency* is "a set of social setting-specific transaction process be-haviours that are instrumental in the delivery of results and outcomes that satisfy the demands made by social relationships within that setting".

As noted in the Introduction, "competency potential" encompasses the individual attributes that are necessary for someone to produce the desired behaviours and outcomes. Disposition and attainment characteristics give rise to competency potential. Individual differences in person characteristics determine competency potential strengths and weaknesses. These in turn are likely to manifest themselves in superior and inferior effectiveness respectively.

"Competency requirements" encompass the situational factors that determine what kind of behaviours and outcomes are desirable. Organization and social relation characteristics give rise to competency requirements. Environmental differences in organization and social relation characteristics lead to differences in competency requirements that manifest themselves in facilitators and barriers.

Figure 10.3 provides an elaboration of the competency model outlined in the Introduction. Competency potential and competency requirements jointly

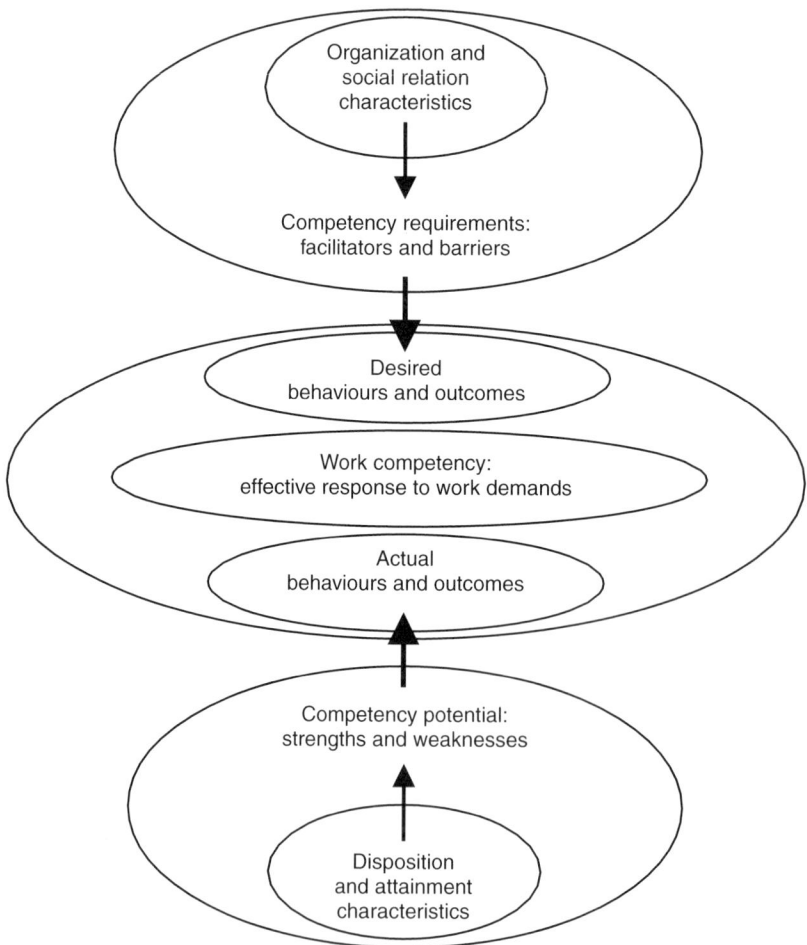

Figure 10.3 The central role of work competency in linking person and environment characteristics to effectiveness. Work competency is understood here to include job, occupation, role and goal competency types

determine behaviours that lead to certain outcomes. The competency construct (of effective response to work demands) explains how desirable behaviours are channelled through goal-directed performances to achieve the goals and outcomes set by the organization. Competency is, therefore, a construct at the interface of people and organization characteristics. To properly assess competency, it is necessary to clearly specify what is meant by an effective response to work demands. Desirable behaviours and desired outcomes have to be specified to serve as benchmarks against which actual behaviours and outcomes can be assessed. "Behaviour–outcome" sequences as such, and even more so the perceptions of effectiveness, feed back to the person and organization domains, and gradually change their characteristics.

CONCLUSION AND OUTLOOK

In this chapter we have argued the need for an overarching model to pull together the various micro-models and taxonomies relating to performance at work. We have presented a model of "Competency at work" that attempts to link the world of psychological assessment and effectiveness at work through the WoW framework. This in turn offers a broader perspective on competency-based approaches to human resources management (HRM) by providing a common "surface" language for both worlds, with firm links to "deep" underlying psychological constructs. In contrast, many of the competency models that have emerged over the last 20 years take either a purely behavioural or a purely dispositional position. What is more, the measurement instruments associated with them have often not been exposed to psychometric evaluation.

The framework for examining organizational effectiveness outlined in the Editors' Introduction highlighted the pivotal role of the individual. The competency at work framework developed here aims to aid the description, explanation, prediction and modification of individual performance and effectiveness. It should also facilitate the aggregation of data and information from the individual to the team, department and organizational level, and vice versa.

For the researcher, structures like the WoW model enable the development of point-to-point prediction equations that link psychometric dispositional measures to related competency dimensions. Such linkages can serve as *a priori* predictions for validation and research purposes (e.g. meta-analysis), and should be supported in empirical studies. In practice, such relationships will be modelled, tested and refined in a cyclical manner. Warr (1999) has provided a valuable advance to methodology in this area by developing a method for assessing the conceptual concordance between dispositional and competency constructs. This will aid theory-based modelling of predictor–criterion relations.

Various domains and their segments have been outlined, together with their top-level constructs. It should be recognized that each of these can be unpacked and expanded in a hierarchical manner. Some taxonomies have been suggested, such as: the Holland model for occupations; the Bartram et al. (2000) model for job competencies; the FFM model (Costa & McRae, 1992) for personality measures; and so on. Given limits of space in the present chapter, only some of this detail has been presented here. Further detailed elaborations of the domains and segments of the model are suggested in Kurz (2000).

The model has been developed primarily by integrating current theories and practices through heuristic and empirical modelling. While certain linkages between elements of the model have been already confirmed empirically, a lot of work remains to specify the vast majority of the relations in more detail, and validate those predictions.

ACKNOWLEDGEMENT

SHL Group plc materials have been reproduced in this chapter with the kind permission of SHL Group plc, who retain all rights and title to these materials.

REFERENCES

Ackermann, P.L. & Heggestad, E.D. (1997). Intelligence, personality, and interest: evidence for overlapping traits. *Psychological Bulletin*, **121**, 219–245.

Anderson, N. & Ostroff, C. (1997). Selection as socialisation. In N. Anderson & P. Herriot (Eds), *International Handbook of Selection and Assessment*. Chichester: John Wiley.

Arnold, J., Cooper C.L. & Robertson, I.T. (1995). *Work Psychology: Understanding Human Behaviour in the Workplace*. London: Pitman.

Barrick, M.R. & Mount, M.K. (1991). The Big Five personality dimensions and job performance: a meta-analysis. *Personnel Psychology*, **44**, 1–25.

Bartram, D., Kurz, R. & Bailey R. (2000). *The SHL Competency Framework*. Internal SHL Memorandum, March 2000. Thames Ditton: SHL.

Bass, B.M. (1985). *Leadership and Performance Beyond Expectation*. New York: Free Press.

Beaumont, G. (1996). *Review of 100 NVQs and SVQs*. Moorfoot, Sheffield: Department for Education and Employment.

Belbin, M. (1981). *Management Teams: Why They Succeed or Fail*. London: Heineman.

Boam, R. & Sparrow, P. (1992). *Designing and Achieving Competency*. London: McGraw-Hill.

Borman, W.C. & Brush, D.H. (1993). More progress towards a taxonomy of managerial performance requirements. *Human Performance*, **6**, 1–21.

Borman, W.C. & Motowildo, S.J. (1993). Expanding the criterion domain to include elements of contextual performance. In N. Schmitt & W.C. Borman (Eds), *Personnel Selection in Organisations*, pp. 71–98. San Francisco, CA: Jossey-Bass.

Boyatzis, R.E. (1982). *The Competent Manager: A Model for Effective Performance*. New York: John Wiley.

Brannick, M.T., Salas, E. & Prince, C. (1997). *Team Performance Assessment and Measurement*. New Jersey: Lawrence Erlbaum.

Campbell, J.P. (1990). Modelling the performance prediction problem in industrial and organisational psychology. In M. Dunnette and L.M. Hough (Eds), *Handbook of Industrial and Organisational Psychology*, Vol. **1**, 2nd edn, pp. 697–731. Palo Alto, CA: Consulting Psychologists Press.

Campbell, J.P., McHenry, J.J. & Wise, L.L. (1990). Modelling job performance in a population of jobs. *Personnel Psychology*, **43**, 313–333.

Campbell, J.P., McCloy, R.A., Oppler, S.H. & Sager, C.E. (1993). A theory of performance. In N. Schmitt, W.C. Bormann et al. (Eds), *Personnel Selection in Organizations*, pp. 35–70. San Francisco: Jossey-Bass.

Carretta, T.R. & Ree, M.J. (2000). General and specific cognitive and psychomotor abilities in personnel selection: the prediction of training and job performance. *International Journal of Selection and Assessment*, **8**, 227–236.

Cassidy, T. & Lynn, R. (1989). A multifactorial approach to achievement motivation: the development of a comprehensive measure. *Journal of Occupational Psychology*, **66**, 171–175.

Conway, J.M. (1999). Distinguishing contextual performance from task performance for managerial jobs. *Journal of Applied Psychology*, **84**, 3–13.

Costa, P.T. & McCrae, R.R. (1992). *The NEO PI-R Professional Manual*. Odessa, FL: Psychological Assessment Resources Inc.

Digman, J.M. (1990). Personality structure: emergence of the five-factor model. *Annual Review of Psychology*, **41**, 417–440.

Dulewicz, D. (1989). Assessment centres as the route to competence. *Personnel Management*, **21** (9), 56–59.

Dulewicz, D. (1995). A validation of Belbin's team roles from the 16 PF and OPQ using bosses ratings of competence. *Journal of Occupational and Organizational Psychology*, **68**, 81–99.

Flanagan, J.C. (1951). Defining the requirements of the executive's job. *Personnel*, **28**, 28–35.

Fletcher, C., Baldry, C. & Cunningham-Snell, N. (1998). The psychometric properties of 360 degree feedback: an empirical study and a cautionary tale. *International Journal of Selection and Assessment*, **6**, 19–34.

Furnham, A. (1995). Personality at work. In P. Collett & A. Furnham (Eds), *Social Psychology at Work*. London: Routledge.

Gotoh, A. (1999). The evaluation of competencies predictors across nine studies in five countries. Unpublished MSc dissertation, Goldsmith College, London.

Gottfredson, L.S. (1986). Occupational aptitude patterns map: development and implications for a theory of job aptitude requirements. *Journal of Vocational Behaviour*, **29**, 254–291.

Guest, D. (1997). Leadership and management. In P. Warr (Ed.), *Psychology at Work*. London: Penguin.

Herriot, P. & Anderson, N. (1997). Selecting for change: how will personnel and selection psychology survive? In N. Anderson & P. Herriot (Eds), *International Handbook of Selection and Assessment*. Chichester: John Wiley.

Holland, J. (1959). A theory of vocational choice. *Journal of Counseling Psychology*, **6**, 35–44.

Holland, J. (1985). *The Self-Directed Search: Professional Manual—1985 Edition*. Odessa, FL: Psychological Assessment Resources Inc.

Hunt, S.T. (1996). Generic work behaviour: an investigation into the dimensions of entry-level hourly job performance. *Personnel Psychology*, **49**, 51–83.

Hunter, J.E. & Hunter, R.F. (1984). Validity and utility of alternative predictors of job performance. *Psychological Bulletin*, **96**, 72–98.

Kurz, R. (1999a). The structure of the "World of Work" (WoW) model. *Proceedings of the Occupational Psychology Conference*, pp. 246–251. Leicester: BPS.

Kurz, R. (1999b). Automated prediction of managerial competencies from personality and ability variables. *Proceedings of the Test User Conference*, pp. 96–101. Leicester: BPS.

Kurz, R. (2000). The facets of occupational testing: general reasoning ability, residual aptitudes and speed-accuracy balance. Unpublished PhD dissertation, University of Manchester Institute of Science & Technology.

Kurz, R. & Morley, R. (1996). Psychometrics in career guidance—validating AIMS with year 9. Paper presented at the BPS Annual Conference, Brighton, UK.

Kurz, R. & Morris, G. (1997). EXPERT career guidance via computer? Piloting the AIMS package. *Proceedings of the Occupation Psychology Conference*, pp. 161–166. Leicester: BPS.

Locke, E. (1968). Toward a theory of task motives and incentives. *Organizational Behaviour and Human Performance*, **3**, 157–189.

McCormick, E.J., Mecham, R.C. & Jeanneret, P.R. (1977). *Technical Manual for the Position Analysis Questionnaire*. Logan, UT: PAQ Services Inc.

Matthews, G. (1997). The Big Five as a framework for personality assessment. In N. Anderson & P. Herriot (Eds), *International Handbook of Selection and Assessment.* Chichester: John Wiley.

Miner, J.B. & Smith, N.R. (1982). Decline and stabilization of managerial motivation over a 20-year period. *Journal of Applied Psychology,* **67**, 297–305.

Mischel, W. & Shoda, Y. (1995). A cognitive–affective system theory of personality: reconceptualizing situations, dispositions, dynamics and invariance in personality structure. *Psychological Review,* **102**, 246–268.

Mitchell, L. & Bartram, D. (1994). The place of knowledge and understanding in the development of NVQs and SVQs. *Competence and Assessment, Briefing Series,* No. 10. Sheffield: Employment Department.

Norman, W.T. (1963). Towards an adequate taxonomy of personality attributes: replicated factor structure in peer nomination personality rating. *Journal of Abnormal and Social Psychology,* **66**, 574–583.

Pearlman, K. (1980). Job families: a review and discussion of their implications for personnel selection. *Psychological Bulletin,* **87**, 1–28.

Prediger, D.J. & Vansickle, T.R. (1992). Locating occupations on Holland's hexagon: beyond RIASEC. *Journal of Vocational Behaviour,* **40**, 111–128.

Ree, M.J. & Earles, J.A. (1991). Predicting training success: not much more than 'g'. *Personnel Psychology,* **44**, 321–332.

Ree, M.J., Earles, J.A. & Teachout, M.S. (1994). Predicting job performance: not much more than 'g'. *Journal of Applied Psychology,* **79**, 518–524.

Robertson, I.T. & Kinder, A. (1993). Personality and job competencies: the criterion-related validity of some personality variables. *Journal of Occupational and Organisational Psychology,* **66**, 225–244.

Rodger, A. (1952). *The Seven Point Plan.* National Institute of Industrial Psychology Paper No. 1. Windsor: NFER–Nelson.

Schein, E.H. (1990). *Career Anchors.* San Diego: Pfeiffer.

Schuler, R.S. & Jackson, S.E. (1999). *Strategic Human Resources Management.* Oxford: Blackwell.

Shippmann, J.S., Ash, R.A., Battista, M., Carr, L., Eyde, L.D., Hesketh, B., Kehoe, J., Pearlman, K., Prien, E.P. & Sanchez, J.I. (2000). The practice of competency modeling. *Personnel Psychology,* **53**, 703–740.

SHL (1992). *Motivation Questionnaire Manual & User's Guide.* Thames Ditton, UK: Saville & Holdsworth Ltd.

SHL (1995). *Work Profiling System.* Thames Ditton, UK: Saville & Holdsworth Ltd.

SHL (1999). *OPQ32 Manual and User's Guide.* Surrey, UK: SHL Group plc.

SHL (2000). *Career Pathfinder-Indepth Manual and User's Guide.* Surrey, UK: SHL Group plc.

Smith, C.A., Organ, D.W. & Near, J.P. (1983). Organisational citizenship behaviour: its nature and antecedents. *Journal of Applied Psychology,* **68**, 655–663.

Spearman, C. (1904). "General Intelligence" objectively determined and measured. *American Journal of Psychology,* **15**, 201–293.

Spokane, A.R. (1985). A review of research on person–environment congruence in Holland's theory of careers. *Journal of Vocational Behaviour,* **26**, 306–343.

Tesluk, P.E. & Jacobs, R.R. (1998). Towards an integrated model of work experience. *Personnel Psychology,* **31**, 321–356.

Tett, R.P., Guternamn, H.A., Bleier, A. & Murphy, P.J. (2000). Development and content validation of a "hyperdimensional" taxonomy of managerial competence. *Human Performance,* **13**, 205–251.

Tranberg, M., Slane, S. & Ekeberg, S.E. (1993). The relation between interest congruence and satisfaction: a meta-analysis. *Journal of Vocational Behaviour,* **42**, 253–264.

Van Dyne, L., Cummings, L.L. & Parks, J.M. (1995). Extra-role behaviour: its pursuit of construct and definitional clarity (a bridge over muddied waters). In L.L. Cummings & B.M. Straw (Eds), *Research in Organisational Behaviour,* Vol. **17**, pp. 215–285. Greenwich, CT: JAI Press.

Visser, C.F., Altink, W.M.M. & Algera, J.A. (1997). From job analysis to work profiling: do traditional procedures still apply? In N. Anderson & P. Herriot (Eds), *International Handbook of Selection and Assessment*. Chichester: John Wiley.

Viswesvaran, C. & Ones, D.S. (2000). Perspectives on models of job performance. *International Journal of Selection and Assessment*, **8**, 216–226.

Wagner, R.K. & Sternberg, R.J. (1985). Practical intelligence in real-world pursuits: the role of tacit knowledge. *Journal of Personality and Social Psychology*, **49**, 436–458.

Warr, P. (1999). Logical and judgemental moderators of the criterion-related validity of personality scales. *Journal of Occupational and Organizational Psychology*, **72**, 187–204.

Warr, P. & Bourne, A. (1999). Factors influencing two types of congruence in multirater judgements. *Human Performance*, **12**, 183–210.

Warr, P. & Connor, M. (1992). Job competence and cognition. *Research in Organizational Behaviour*, **14**, 91–127.

Woodruffe, C. (1992). What is meant by a competency? In R. Boam & P. Sparrow (Eds), *Designing and Achieving Competency*. London: McGraw-Hill.

PART III

CHAPTER 11

Organizational Effectiveness: The Contribution of Work and Organizational Psychology

Militza Callinan, Dave Bartram and Ivan T. Robertson

INTRODUCTION

This final chapter presents some common themes and questions that emerge from the writings of all the authors in this book. The previous chapters make clear that psychology has not a singular, but multiple contributions to make in understanding and attaining organizational effectiveness. Broadly, those contributions relate to three areas. The first area is knowledge about specific individual, group and organizational phenomena, the relations between them and their relations with overall effectiveness criteria. The second, related contribution of psychology is expertise in developing sound methodologies and procedures for collecting, analysing and evaluating information about complex phenomena. The third way in which psychology contributes assumes particular importance in the discussion taking place in this book. It is through an understanding of the social processes by which meaning is negotiated, questions are defined and knowledge is transferred between individuals and groups. Psychology provides the discipline for gaining this process knowledge.

Sparrow and West (Chapter 1) pose the question of whether psychology has influence, relevance, neither or both. The first two of the suggested contributions above can be used to support the *relevance* of psychological work to the pursuit of organizational effectiveness. The third area of expertise outlined is also about the phenomena of organizational life, but as suggested, has further significance. Hodgkinson and Herriot (Chapter 2) argue that the process knowledge held by psychologists is significant, actually critical, for the degree of *influence* that psychology gains within organizations in the future.

Organizational Effectiveness: The Role of Psychology
Edited by I.T. Robertson, M. Callinan and D. Bartram. © 2002 John Wiley & Sons, Ltd.

In fact, the first section of the book is as much about the effectiveness of the profession of work and organizational psychology, as it is about the effectiveness of organizations. It is a feature of psychology that the investigator may also be his or her own subject. The subject matter is just as relevant to how psychologists generate and validate knowledge, negotiate power and opportunity and work with others, as it is to those they help and advise. Hodgkinson and Herriot (Chapter 2) provide some direct self-analysis in their examination of the position and influence of psychology in the organizational arena and how those factors relate to the opportunities available to psychologists. The issues these authors introduce are fundamental, being about the often unspoken, underlying approaches that shape the activities of psychologists working in this domain. The debate adds a further dimension to the consideration of the other topics raised and it will be discussed first.

What emerges from that debate is the critical importance of process knowledge, not only for richer understanding of organizational functioning—a point echoed by many of the authors—but also for the health and progress of the profession itself. Two further themes that emerge from all the writings when viewed collectively will be discussed. The first of these themes is the need for holistic, integrative thinking about both organizations and individuals, which is being expressed both within psychology and in other domains. The second theme is, in fact, more of a characteristic way of seeing within the psychological approach. The basic assumption that people and the situations they occupy interact in a reciprocal way is inherent in most, if not all, of the work in this book.

THE INFLUENCE OF PSYCHOLOGISTS

So, are psychologists influential in organizations? According to Hodgkinson and Herriot, the answer is no. Psychologists have been "be-devilled" by a "vicious cycle" of non-involvement at the strategic level in organizations. Rather than being drivers or leaders of strategic activity, psychologists are more often reduced to "operational technicians". They have largely failed to ensure they are included in high-level organizational decision-making and so have limited the scope of opportunities to check and demonstrate the relevance of their expertise to solve real problems. This is surprising for a number of reasons.

Organizations were identified in the Introduction as being primarily social arrangements. Consequently, organizational effectiveness is necessarily a function of the nature and cohesiveness of the sets of social relations of which it is comprised. As Prusak and Cohen (2001) state it in their discussion of the importance of "social capital"; "strong relationships . . . are the grease of an organization. Business gets done without them, but not for long". In fact, current management thinking seems to be preoccupied with developing, coordinating and retaining human "assets" as a means of gaining competitive advantage.

Some may argue that such a commodity-based view of people is not a helpful starting point (e.g. Chalofsky, in Callahan & Ward, 2001). Sparrow and West do indicate that management may need convincing about the relevance of certain psychological concepts and their links with important outcomes. Nonetheless, understanding and managing people is firmly on the main agenda as one of the greatest challenges facing organizations. In spite of the fact that the content of psychology speaks directly to these issues, senior management (whom Hodgkinson and Herriot identify as the key stakeholders in organizations) do not call on psychologists to help them.

Another reason that this non-involvement is surprising is that the scope and flexibility of psychology surely makes a good psychologist exceptionally good value. In the Introduction, organizational effectiveness was noted to comprise at least four broad sets of factors—economic, technological, commercial and social. Potential was also identified for intervening at different levels of aggregation, from the organization to the individual. The work of the authors in this book has demonstrated that psychological research and practice are highly flexible, maybe uniquely so, in the range of issues and outcomes to which they can be applied and so are very fit for application to this purpose.

Sparrow and West describe substantial research concerned with three very different criteria of effectiveness—productivity, psychological well-being and innovation, at the level of the group and the individual—which relate to economic, social and commercial domains respectively. Dalgleish and Jacobs (Chapter 3) describe practical interventions addressing diverse problems including employee absence and accident rates, under-use of training places, changing manager behaviours, flow of job applicants and improving the success of job seekers. Their example of police officer selection in the US provides a notable illustration of how psychological expertise was utilized to meet the multiple goals of speed, cost, accuracy and diversity of outcome. This work also attends to the goals of multiple stakeholders—in this case, job applicants, the police department, ethnic minority groups and the general community. A wide range of relationships come under scrutiny, such as those between: peers in top management teams (Cartwright & Baron); managers and staff (Alimo-Metcalfe & Nyfield); recruiters and applicants (Murphy & Bartram) and service providers and clients (Dalgleish & Jacobs).

This flexibility stems from the fundamental nature of the phenomena with which psychology is concerned—the characteristics, behaviour, relationships and effects of people, individually and in groups. Consequently, there are few, if any areas of organizational life to which psychology cannot legitimately claim some interest. Even choosing and using technology is a people-driven process. If we consider as a contrast the disciplines of finance or economics, the end goal or focal point of activity must be pre-determined to some extent in that it must necessarily be the understanding or management of monetary issues. And as discussed, economic factors are only one set of criteria by which effectiveness can be judged. Marketing, also, is concerned with a particular and limited set of relations, those between customers and suppliers. Given the pervasive nature of psychology's subject matter, it would be expected to have a dominant presence in organizations.

So what is happening? Hodgkinson and Herriot argue that some of the causes of this situation may be found within the profession itself. Psychologists have been the architects of their own lack of influence because, unlike some competitors for organizational territory, they have been slow to adapt their approach to changes and challenges in the modern workplace. Specifically, they argue that adaptation is sorely needed in the underlying approach to knowledge generation and concomitant relationships both within psychology and with others.

The authors say that the traditional "scientific inquiry" approach of generating knowledge is still the bedrock of the field and it is helping to maintain a situation that is limiting psychology's impact and opportunities in the workplace. The approach has scientific evidence as a basis and assumes a traditional distinction between generalizable science and transitory specific application. A narrow set of stakeholders is involved in defining the questions to be addressed; and in the case of work psychology, the authors argue that the stakeholders are more often than not other researchers. Importantly, there is no concern for specifying how research findings might be translated into practice and no dialogue with practitioners and end users.

These sentiments are echoed by Johnson and Cassell (2001) who argue that work psychology, more than many other social science disciplines, has changed little in the way research is construed, undertaken and evaluated. The field, they argue, is "entrenched in positivism" at the expense of developing what they call "epistemological reflexivity"—the ability to question underlying assumptions—that would allow different, more organizationally-relevant questions to be considered valid in the research domain.

Certainly though, the importance given to sound evidence and theory is a particular strength of psychology. In fact, our people management colleagues in Human Resource Development (HRD) are becoming concerned that their discipline is actually too responsive to issues of the day and is being hampered by a lack of underlying theory (Swanson, 2000). But rigid adherence to a scientific inquiry approach is highly problematic for the relevance and influence of the profession. This is, simply stated, because it leads to research psychologists working only with each other, on problems defined by each other, with outputs validated according to criteria determined by each other. The consequence is that the research conducted is simply not dealing with the problems faced by organizations because their members are not included in the process of question definition and knowledge generation.

Hodgkinson and Herriot cite Argyris (1999) in calling the explicit theories and models, concepts and research, methods and instruments described in the chapters on specific topics psychology's "toolkit". They explain that it is possible to be highly expert in using this toolkit to improve specific aspects of an organization but incompetent at the same time because that improvement does not improve organizational effectiveness. Personnel selection research is held up as an indicative example of this uncoupling of research and practice.

The majority of personnel selection research has been concerned with establishing and replicating the reliability and validity of individual selection methods for predicting job performance criteria using sophisticated methodologies. However, as Murphy and Bartram (Chapter 4) explain, the research generally assumes the existence of conditions in the use of those methods that rarely apply in practice. So the levels of validity reported in the research literature can rarely be achieved in reality. Furthermore, managers are often more concerned with criteria other than job performance in a specific role. They are concerned with cultural fit and a person's general potential to perform a range of tasks because job roles change. Researchers in the field have simply failed to stay in touch with the realities of selection in organizations and have instead concentrated on pleasing each other with methodological prowess.

That is not to say that some of the fruits of this work are not valuable. The techniques of utility analysis, meta-analysis and validity generalization are notable achievements and add to the methodological expertise of psychologists. But in this case, Hodgkinson and Herriot argue, concern for scientific, technical advance has driven activity away from that which has real world relevance, becoming more of a liability than a strength.

Perhaps the apparent decline of the discipline of Operational Research should be a warning about the dangers Hodgkinson and Herriot suggest. The main thrust of work in operational research seems to be in achieving operational efficiency with the mathematical modelling of problems, the major areas of application being operations and logistics (Fildes & Raynard, 2000). An investigation by the profession's main society found that almost one quarter of the 99 operational research groups in organizations closed between 1990 and 1997. The conclusion of the investigation was that the discipline has over-emphasized the underlying science—mathematics—at the expense of relevance, and that operational research professionals need to get better at consulting skills, project management, marketing and responding to changes in clients' requirements. But the authors state that managerial culture, with its focus on "leadership and intuition at the expense of rationality", has left them ignored, suggesting that they are not entirely clear where they might fit into this new context.

THE IMPORTANCE OF PROCESS KNOWLEDGE

Looking forward at the future, Hodgkinson and Herriot see a clear place for psychology if changes are made to the profession. They describe an alternative knowledge generation process to scientific enquiry that is based on a "problem solution" approach. This approach is characterized by the inclusion of a wider range of stakeholders with the joint definition of questions and goals between the members of the group. Further, the group is more than likely to be multidisciplinary. The process of knowledge generation is one of a continuous feedback loop until the problem is addressed, rather than the linear scientific process moving from theory to application. In relation to the outputs of this approach, they are more likely to be in the form of procedural knowledge (how the problem was addressed) than explicit knowledge about the elements of the intervention. The authors do not suggest abandoning the scientific basis entirely but advocate a more balanced approach that allows more dialogue and connection to the issues of relevance whilst retaining important standards of accurate enquiry. They call such an approach "scholarly consultancy". Dalgleish and Jacobs (Chapter 3) refer to a similar concept when they discuss the need for psychologists to be "creative scientists" in organizations.

The approach to knowledge generation adopted and the nature of the relationships that psychologists have with others, including each other, are somewhat interdependent. In their discussion, although they do not specifically distinguish them, Hodgkinson and Herriot refer to both within-discipline and between-discipline relationships. Within psychology, they suggest there is a widening schism between research and practice. Presumably, this occurs as research becomes more distant from the real world problems that confront practitioners when they consult with clients.

Although practitioners may often be the intermediaries between academics and organizations, increasingly academics are themselves engaged directly with users of their research (Rynes et al., 2001). So the interface between psychologists and organizations, which may include relationships with managers and professionals from other disciplines, may include either research or practice psychologists, or both. It is worth noting here that unity within each community can be overplayed. Murphy and Bartram highlight tensions between personnel and organizational research psychologists, for example, with the former concentrating on individual differences and the latter on social systems. However, because currently the majority of the evidence base in psychology can be said to originate in the research community, it is the relationship between academia and practice that is critical to the transfer and utilization of new knowledge.

A recent article by Rynes et al. (2001) suggests that this discussion is really about more fundamental issues regarding the relationship and transfer of knowledge between academics and practitioners, regardless of the discipline. The authors argue that the gap between organizational research findings and management practices is part of a more pervasive gap between research and practice based on fundamental differences in the two communities. Even under good conditions knowledge transfer takes a long time. They provide the illustrative, but hardly motivational, example of the cure for scurvy being adopted by the Navy some 200 years after its discovery.

If we look for causes for this gap, it does seem that ambivalence on the part of some researchers may contribute to the separation. Rynes et al. find evidence that academics are deeply split about whether collaboration is actually good for scientific progress. Fears exist around the possibility for constraints on data collection, interpretation and dissemination. Also, it is feared that the nature of the problems addressed will be limited to those that are narrow, short-term and commercially relevant with a stance that favours managerial interest over that of employees. Further, there is concern that researchers can be subtly manipulated for the sake of corporate interests.

On the positive side, it is recognized that the unique insights of managers can stimulate new research questions and discoveries. Members of the organization can also expand the scope of the work by brokering wider participation and resources, as well as questioning the implicit assumptions of researchers. Rynes et al. conclude there is potential for both good and bad outcomes and the little information there is for evaluation of the claims provides mixed results.

However, the authors highlight some reasons to believe that the general climate currently favours collaboration. Namely resource dependencies have changed for university researchers making them more reliant on attracting private funding. In addition, research capability is no longer concentrated solely inside academic institutions but spread more widely, bringing greater competition for research opportunities. For organizations, intensified competition in combination with downsizing means they no longer have the resources to carry out research in-house and must seek partnerships to meet their requirements. For practitioners, any privileged knowledge that may help them help their clients gain competitive advantage is highly valuable. Given the intensity of global competition and the need to harness new knowledge quickly, national policies are also shaping the nature of collaborative opportunities by supporting industrial–academic partnerships.

If these opportunities are to be taken, the collaboration process will need to be managed in order to bring the desired gains in new knowledge creation and transfer. Using Nonaka and Takeuchi's (1995) model of knowledge creation, Rynes et al. argue that not only is the collaborative process between academics and practitioners inadequate, but knowledge generation *within* the academic community is itself sub-optimal. In the model, knowledge is created in a spiral of continual cycling from one type of knowledge creation to another. There are four interactive methods, which represent the possible combinations of conversion between tacit and explicit knowledge. It is the mobilization and conversion of tacit knowledge that is the key to the process—tacit-to-tacit conversion, called "socialization". Tacit-to-explicit conversion, or "externalization", is the next step, followed by "combination", which is explicit-to-explicit knowledge conversion. The last step in one cycle is "internalization", where explicit knowledge is converted back into tacit knowledge. The process begins at the individual level and moves upwards in a spiral to encompass interactions between groups.

Relating this model to scientific enquiry, we can see that the approach relies on only one stage of the cycle to transfer knowledge within the research community, explicit-to-explicit conversion, in the form of journal articles and presentations. The key stage of converting tacit knowledge is hidden, in that it is not reported or discussed, as evidenced by the declarative nature of research reports. It is for this reason that Rynes et al. suggest that research practices are flawed. Practitioners and managers, on the other hand, are far more likely to deal in tacit, procedural knowledge, creating a difference in the relative importance of the type of knowledge valued and employed and a barrier to communication between the two communities.

The chapter by Dalgleish and Jacobs provides a useful reference point for this discussion. The fact that this chapter is entirely different in nature from the rest of the chapters in the book—describing the "how" rather than the "what" of the interventions—is indicative of the points made about the relative use of procedural and declarative knowledge by practitioners and researchers. Their work also illustrates the critical importance of the process knowledge held by psychologists that is excluded from the dialogue in the research domain. In an example of externalization (tacit-to-explicit knowledge conversion) the authors have used their combined knowledge to formally outline a process model for organizational intervention which takes the form of a "continuous improvement loop" much like that advocated by Hodgkinson and Herriot.

The impact of ongoing feedback and dialogue between stakeholder groups is clearly demonstrated in a number of the examples provided. In the case of the selection of US bus drivers, revisiting the conditions under which the selection system works optimally was critical to the achievement of the expected impact. Dalgleish and Jacobs distinguish between "formative evaluation" of process and "summative evaluation" of overall impact, arguing that both are critical for making sure the intervention's impact is maximized and maintained.

Looking at the example from the public sector of developing and embedding a competency approach in line with desired organizational values illustrates the combination of knowledge and skills required by the "creative scientist". The science is seen in the definition of the competencies using procedures such as repertory grid and critical incident technique. But this development process is just the beginning of the intervention. The substantial practical task of embedding and activating that knowledge inside the organization must then be achieved. Dalgleish and Jacobs list five critical factors related to making competencies actually work inside the organization which have little relation to any of the research literature on the subject. In fact, Rynes et al. do draw attention to the incorrect assumption often made that knowledge transfer between academics and practitioners is always about transfer from the former to the latter. They suggest, in fact, that in some key areas it was practice that took the lead.

Some recommendations are made by Rynes et al. to the research community about how to move towards a more collaborative and productive working model. Some of the recommendations relate to the preferred location and style for publishing research reports and the policies of academic gatekeepers such as journal editors. But top of the list is to actively seek out those situations in which tension exists between ideas, because it is those situations that will lead to new knowledge creation. The face-to-face experience is emphasized, with simply more interaction needed between academics and practitioners. This is consistent with Hodgkinson and Herriot's emphasis on the socialization process in problem solving—a point that brings us back to the role of psychologists.

As psychologists, we should be well able to navigate changes to our own and others' characteristic ways of generating and evaluating knowledge. After all, our knowledge base includes understanding of human social, cognitive and emotional processes. Critically, we can also help organizations do the same thing. Hodgkinson and Herriot suggest that the process of collaboration between diverse groups of stakeholders in order to arrive at common definitions of the questions or problems that need to be addressed is one of the hardest tasks facing organizations. Psychologists can and should be facilitating that process whether or not the problem that emerges or solution required includes aspects of the psychological toolkit. The role suggested is akin to that of the conductor of an orchestra, who at specific times in particular pieces of music may leave the platform and join the orchestra to play a melody on an instrument in which he or she is particularly skilled.

It is fine to have visions, of course, but the profession will need to somehow manoeuvre from its current position to the new desired position, which means breaking the "cycle of non-involvement" described by Hodgkinson and Herriot. We have discussed some of the fundamental barriers to change. Dalgleish and Jacobs describe some practical realities associated with the way psychologists are employed today that will need to be challenged if the move to a problem-solving model is going to be achieved. In line with the image of psychologists as "operational technicians" an organization may seek a psychologist to design an intervention but not include that person in its implementation. In this situation, the psychologist does not have the opportunity to input into the definition of the issue to be addressed or to get feedback from the process of implementation. Time pressure means that there may simply not be time to gather information to evaluate impact and organizations have themselves moved on to new issues.

The harsh reality for individual psychologists is that they will need to persuade managers to pay them to be involved in parts of the change process that currently happen without them or do not happen at all. It is, therefore, particularly important that psychologists be able to demonstrate their impact in order to improve their persuasiveness in securing further more expansive opportunities.

It is paradoxical, of course, that an influential profession will be more able to create the working conditions and relationships in organizations that provide the opportunity to both have and demonstrate impact. The problem-solving model requires that psychologists work *with* rather than *for* organizations—being what Chalofsky calls "true partners" (Callahan and Ward, 2001). Chalofsky argues that HRD professionals cannot become true partners in organizational activity until they establish a set of core values about what they believe in to guide their interventions. Currently, without such guiding principles they behave like "stepchildren", doing whatever it takes to look good instead of what is really needed to help the organization. This situation, over-eagerness to deliver what management think they want rather than what will solve the problem, is perhaps what Hodgkinson and Herriot caution against when they suggest a scholarly consultant approach rather than a full-out problem-solving approach. But if we follow Chalofsky's thinking, work psychology, with its extensive and flexible toolkit, already has the basis for becoming the "true partner" of organization stakeholders.

Psychology has had the converse problem to HRD, that is a lack of responsiveness. But, of course, organizations have still been seeking solutions to their problems but from elsewhere. Other professions have been more willing to listen to and deal with the needs of organization members and, therefore, are perceived to be more appropriate partners in organizational planning and action, even when the subject is clearly people-related. Hodgkinson and Herriot suggest that one key reason psychological territory has been lost to others is that the way effectiveness is defined is not only consequential for organizational functioning as the Editors outlined in the Introduction, but its definition is highly consequential for the influence and viability of psychology in the workplace. Control of that definition process can lead to the dominance of particular agendas and effectiveness criteria.

By way of illustration, they argue that large accountancy practices have managed to subsume other disciplines, including psychology, because that profession has been highly successful in defining organizational success in purely financial terms, thus guaranteeing their own place at the helm of strategic action. Indeed there is some subtle support for such claims in a series of papers in the *Journal of Cost Management*. Sharman (2000) recognizes that cost efficiency is essentially a retroactive process but modern organizations need to be proactive in their management to survive. So, he argues that cost managers should become "value management specialists", "managing all aspects of value creation and value drivers" with "an emphasis on human behaviour". Another of Sharman's comments may suggest a further reason that psychology has been annexed by accountants in particular. He states that the core activity of auditing has become a "chore" and that "even the accountants want to do something else to make a living". Sharman's vision for the twenty-first century of cost management can be read as a convincing case for the importance of psychology—but practised by accountants.

It must certainly be helpful for psychology that the link between individuals, their behaviour and organizationally relevant outcomes is also being recognized and championed by others. And there are clear areas of convergence, if not interdependence between the two professions of finance and psychology in the context of organizations. The underlying view of the nature of people in the organization will determine to a large extent the nature of its financial structures (Cooper, 2001). Taking a psychological perspective on some recent research reports in finance journals also suggests how potentially fruitful and meaningful research questions can be stimulated by considering other professional domains.

For instance, the notion of hostility in takeovers was recently found to be a misnomer in economic terms, on the basis of accounting and stock performance data (Schwert, 2000). The investigator concluded that hostile and friendly takeovers could only be distinguished in terms of the bargaining strategies adopted by managers, such as use of the media. A psychological investigation might continue this enquiry and consider the impact of the perception of friendly or hostile situations on employee behaviour and subsequent outcomes. Such information may add an important dimension to top management's decision-making about how to weigh up the risks and benefits of particular financial bargaining strategies—especially given Alimo-Metcalfe and Nyfield's caution (Chapter 9) that the negative effects of mergers and acquisitions do not disappear over time but instead get more serious.

Another paper uncovers the critical impact of the judgement and decision-making of the lead underwriter in the price discovery process that occurs in the pre-opening period before trading of initial public offerings (IPOs) (Aggarwal & Conroy, 2000). This one team of people decides at what time to start trading and, crucially, set the first quote in the five-minute pre-opening window, both of which are strongly related to initial returns. With team outputs being so consequential, the composition and processes of these work groups are likely to be of certain interest to psychologists. It can also be imagined that finance researchers might usefully extend the investigations of psychologists by examining the economic implications of their work.

THE NEED FOR HOLISTIC THINKING

The examples above are about the combination of interests, expertise and measurements from each discipline, as opposed to the domination of one by the other. An integrative approach which is defined solely by finance people, or any other professional or stakeholder group including psychologists, runs the risk of assigning inferior status to other definitions and forms of effectiveness. And as Hodgkinson and Herriot note, "problems do not come discipline shaped", they are likely to be multi-faceted. A narrow focus on one set of criteria is a potential barrier to producing the kind of knowledge and activity that organizations need to leap beyond current thinking and find novel solutions to complex problems.

This introduces one of the central themes of this book, which is the need for inclusive definitions, understandings and interventions in relation to individual and organizational phenomena. Progressive solutions to organizational problems require a holistic perspective. We need to think more broadly about the reality of organizations and of individuals. Sparrow and West begin Chapter 1 by asserting that both managers and psychologists should think more broadly, the former about the definition of effectiveness, the latter about the range of potential contributions individuals make towards those overall criteria.

If we consider Sharman's vision for the future of cost management, underlying the desire to understand human behaviour is the motivation to harness those behaviours that are "value drivers" responsible for "driving significant cash flow". But people are more than simply "value drivers" for organizations. Organizations are more than just profit-making units. Each is a dynamic entity of interrelated parts with many simultaneous effects occurring at any one time. Change in one area will also impact on other areas, perhaps in undesirable ways, thus creating a solution to one problem only to create another problem elsewhere.

Psychologists have themselves been guilty of narrow thinking. For instance, in Chapter 4 Murphy and Bartram argue that selection research is typically characterized by the erroneous assumption that if you hire people who are better on some attribute, their job performance will change and everything else will stay the same. But although people with high levels of cognitive ability, for instance, may learn more quickly and make fewer errors, they may also become easily bored and be more likely to leave to pursue better opportunities.

Although Sparrow and West suggest that retail organizations can be described as "low human asset intensity" environments where potentially greater gains can be made by investment in technology than in sophisticated HRM practices, they also add a caution. It is not known what the cost of ignoring HRM would be over time should that strategy be taken. They introduce a concept that is helpful in understanding this point—the idea of "collateral damage" which may be related to organizational actions.

Of further relevance to this discussion, Sparrow and West suggest that whereas researchers tend to "measure to know", the usual approach of practitioners is to "measure to change". And there is a difference between domains that are predictive of performance and those that facilitate understanding. By way of illustration, in a study they describe looking at the relationship of organizational culture to overall performance, it was found that only eight of the 17 aspects of culture that were measured were directly related to productivity outcomes. But that result does not necessarily mean the non-productivity-related aspects of culture are not related to other criteria of importance to overall functioning and effectiveness. Such conclusions might usefully be delayed until enough is understood about the wider context.

Tharenou and Burke (Chapter 5) refer to the wider impact of taking action inside organizations in their discussion of training. They argue that the introduction of training is best considered more broadly, as a change programme, because the very process of offering training will itself affect employee attitudes and expectations. Anticipation of the broader impact of such actions potentially allows better risk management and less chance of "collateral damage". Alimo-Metcalfe and Nyfield (Chapter 9) also refer to the indirect and unintended effects of the "Pygmalion effect" in leadership. The expectations that leaders have about the capabilities and potential of their colleagues and staff can lead to self-fulfilling prophecies. The effect can occur in both a positive and a negative direction. A manager may unwittingly communicate low expectations to his or her staff, lowering their self confidence and subsequently, their performance levels.

Dalgleish and Jacobs explain the reason that understanding why things happen is important. They argue that measuring the overall impact of interventions is not enough. In the Hawthorne experiments, increases in productivity were found to be the result of the increased attention focused on employees rather than the actual intervention itself. That is why the processes underpinning the action must be evaluated too in order to determine which elements are critical to the result.

In the case of personnel selection and assessment, Murphy and Bartram argue that why assessments and tests work is often overlooked but crucially important for making inferences about the impact they may have on broader criteria. The implications for understanding and managing organizational activity may be very different depending on the cause of the overall result. In the case of interviews, for instance, do they work because they are measuring underlying job-related constructs? Or do interviews work because recruiters select applicants in the image of their own and managers' biases and prejudices, therefore getting new people that "fit in"?

In short, what is being argued here is that correlations between individual level phenomena and organizational level outcomes are a useful starting point and can direct attention and action to areas likely to have the greatest impact. But such correlations are just a starting point in achieving organizational effectiveness. Murphy and Bartram detail the attempts that have been made by psychologists to relate individual performance not only to organization level outcomes but further, to national productivity. The calculation can be computed using utility analyses, but the authors ask whether such cross-level inferences are even feasible. Because organizations are complex systems, improvements in one area do not necessarily translate into system-wide improvements.

We can look to the body of research attempting to link HRM practices and organizational performance, and that linking culture to overall effectiveness. In both cases, Sparrow and West detail work showing clear correlations between the sets of factors. But, similarly, they argue, the relationships cannot be simple and linear. They are better seen as sequences of causal factors at individual and team levels that lead to effectiveness. And in the case of culture at least, there is no consensus about the nature of those causal sequences.

Understanding of causation, how and why things are related, is necessary for effective intervention in organizations and specifying causal pathways and models is a particular strength of psychology. The work of Kurz and Bartram (Chapter 10) attempting to integrate diverse theories, concepts and measures into an overall model of individual performance provides strong evidence for that assertion. The starting point for this book was that psychologists have not routinely assessed the impact of their work at the level of the organization, although the exceptions are documented in these chapters. Perhaps one of the reasons for that is precisely because psychologists focus on unravelling those complex sequences of causal factors. End-to-end correlations may simply not seem like news to some psychologists because it is recognized that the usefulness of knowing that an individual level factor relates to an organization level factor depends on knowing why.

The pressing need for organizations to understand and coordinate how their various parts and functions work together is not new and is widely stated. Sharman's conclusions about the importance of human behaviour stem from his view that in the existing work environment "the pieces need to fit and work together". He refers to the elimination of "disconnects" in the inter- actions across business boundaries within the supply chain. Work on customer focus in the field of strategic marketing also asserts that coherence and flow be- tween the component parts, processes and people in the firm are necessary for a truly customer-facing organization. For instance, Whiteley and Hessan (1995) argue that "customer responsive flexibility and agility" can only be achieved by "superior collaboration both within and between business units in a company", turning the whole company into one "united effective team".

At the same time, it also seems that it is not coherence and coordination in relation to functional and geographical boundaries that is critical. New working patterns and technology are already eroding these structural aspects of orga- nizations. Prusak and Cohen (2001) describe the climate as one of "volatility and virtuality", which is seriously threatening for the development and mainte- nance of good social relationships between organization members. And it is these relationships, say Sparrow and West, the "soft-wired" psychosocial as- pects of organizations, that will be the key to the coordination of individual's activity going forward.

Cartwright and Baron (Chapter 8) add a further reason for focusing on the emotional rather than the structural aspects of organizations as a channel for creating and maintaining a cohesive and inclusive culture. They argue that glob- alization and increasing diversity in the workforce mean that organizations are becoming "multi-cultural"—they are characterized by increased cultural hetero- geneity. Individuals are members of many societal as well as work groups which means they will identify with others in diverse patterns, affecting the cultural context of the workplace. Consequently, valuing people and handling dissent will assume greater priority. The authors add that in addition to reconciling differences arising from diversity inside the organization, the need to adapt to external events can also challenge internal integration, as in the case of service companies who now require workers seven days a week and for hours outside the traditional working day.

The implications of "boundaryless careers" and a "careerist orientation" for organizations' cohesion is discussed by Arnold and Schoonman (Chapter 7).

Some researchers believe that individuals are increasingly taking more control of their own career development and progression. They are proactively seeking opportunities to fulfil personal goals and values and relying less on single organizations. In such cases, people's salient group identities are likely to concern workgroups or professions rather than the organization as a whole. If organizational ties are loosening it may be that quite individualized aspects of identity drive behaviour at work. Personal identities partly determine the rewards that employees are likely to value and the type of tasks to which they will be committed. Thus the fit between personal and organizational values assumes importance as a driver of commitment.

To help organizations achieve this psychosocial integration, work psychologists will need to understand and focus more on combination, on how individual factors work together inside organizations and over time. Arnold and Schoonman argue that the utility of motivation theories is limited by narrow thinking. They argue that the *direction* of effort has been overlooked in research, both in relation to individuals' choices and crucially in relation to "the coordination of different individuals' efforts to achieve multiple organizational goals". The value of motivated people in achieving overall effectiveness is greatly reduced if their activities are not co-ordinated.

Individuals need to be clear about which of the organization's goals they are contributing to and which to prioritize. It seems that conflicts between goals matter. Cartwright and Baron provide a concrete example of the effect on individuals' behaviour of competing organizational value and reward systems. An offshore oil company known to the authors was constantly stressing its commitment to safe working practices. It decided to base employee bonuses on the number of continuous days in the period for which no accidents were recorded. The effect of the bonus system was that employees ignored potentially unsafe practices and near-miss situations, in some cases actually concealing injuries sustained by colleagues—clearly not the intended outcome.

The coordination of organizational activities and reward systems to achieve what Tharenou and Burke call "single employee consistency"—a consistent message and effect from all the organizational practices and systems that impact on the individual—is the goal of performance management. They refer to both the "horizontal integration" of HR practices and the "vertical integration" of HR with organization strategy. In fact, Williams and Fletcher (Chapter 6) suggest that we know little about the effects of packages of interventions in combination. The growing research on links between HRM and organizational performance is discussed by both Williams and Fletcher and Sparrow and West, but that work does not seek to identify how the package of interventions is experienced by employees or how it affects their behaviour.

The influence of time adds a further dimension to the dynamic of combination. Tharenou and Burke argue that the impact of investment in training can only be determined some two to four years after the investment was made. Alimo-Metcalfe and Nyfield introduce the notion of the organizational life-cycle in relation to the style of leadership required. Research suggests that the style of leadership required varies as a function of the stage of growth of the organization. Monitoring and responding to the process of change in the external conditions influencing an intervention also features in Dalgleish and Jacobs' discussion. They illustrate how a selection process that is optimal when first implemented can lose efficacy over time. The distinction between an intervention "as designed" and "as delivered" opens up this area of evaluation. Although the design may be revisited at intervals, it is essentially static, whereas the delivery is an ongoing process that evolves over time, possibly into something different.

Another area of process that remains to be fully explicated is the overall process of employee recruitment and selection. According to Murphy and Bartram, few examinations of the validity of the end-to-end process have been conducted. As already noted, research has focused on the validity of individual assessment methods in isolation and assumed conditions of use that do not exist in reality. Hiring decisions are generally made by combining information from multiple sources and little is known about the effect of the nature of that combination process on the validity of final decisions. Further, selection and assessment is only one stage of the hiring process, the preceding stages of attraction and recruitment of applicants are also under-researched. That is despite the important fact that the effectiveness of selection is directly dependent on the size and quality of the applicant pool. Finally, in a failure to incorporate stakeholder perspectives, personnel psychologists have not fully explored the impact of applicants' decisions on the effectiveness of selection. Job applicants may decide to drop out of the process, or continue but refuse a job offer.

On a more positive note, there is at least one area where psychologists have used and championed the value of a wider perspective. The use of multi-rater feedback or 360-degree appraisal in leadership research and development interventions is analogous to the multi-faceted approach to organizational effectiveness being advocated in this book. Alimo-Metcalfe and Nyfield explain the increasing importance of managers' awareness of themselves and of the impact they are having on others. Obtaining and using multiple perspectives on an individual manager's performance in development interventions has been shown to be effective in bringing enduring changes in the behaviour of those managers.

At the level of the individual, there is converging thought both within and outside psychology about the value of a more holistic approach and an understanding of the whole person. It is not only in personnel psychology that there has been a tendency to focus on component parts rather than the whole. Arnold and Schoonman suggest the same is true of motivation research, which has focused on "individual task behaviour with little reference to the person as a whole". Some of their points about the relevance of understanding the self and identity have already been mentioned. These authors also comment that "there is something rather joyless" about motivation theories. They miss out the possibility that people may simply get enjoyment from carrying out their work.

Similarly, in relation to teams, Sparrow and West call on fundamental aspects of human nature to understand and explain some of the functioning and effects of team work. Underlying the tendency to work in groups, it is argued, is the fundamental human need to belong and hence to form strong relationships with others. Considering the presence or absence of aspects of belongingness in teams—such as frequent interaction, freedom from conflict and mutual affective concern—can help explain team members' behaviour and reactions. Sparrow and West highlight that the positive effects of group membership are related not just to work performance but also to the well-being of individuals.

From a more instrumental perspective, Prusak and Cohen (2001) lay down the business case for nurturing trust and community by providing meaningful work opportunities and acknowledging that employees are human beings. When people develop social bonds in the workplace and there is less separation between their home and work lives, it results in "ties that bind more deeply and positively" than economic incentives—that is, very low staff turnover. From an HRD perspective, Chalofsky (Callahan & Ward, 2001) also insists that when people are doing "meaningful work that they love, they will be more productive". In focusing narrowly on performance rather than learning and growth, he argues, we are forgetting the "essence of humanity that enables organizations to survive and thrive".

In general, there does seem to be a shift of thinking occurring away from the idea implicit in much psychology that people are made up of individual facets that relate to external criteria and not to other facets of themselves. It is being recognized that people are dynamic beings with interacting abilities, characteristics, values and needs.

The nature of individual performance is thoroughly explored by both Williams and Fletcher and Kurz and Bartram. From their work we can see that only some workplace behaviour can be considered to be goal- or job-related. But that is not to say that other categories of behaviour are not relevant for overall effectiveness. Contextual performance, or organizational citizenship behaviour (OCB), has proved to be one such important category. Sparrow and West suggest that OCBs provide an important link between individuals' well-being and organizational effectiveness. This is behaviour outside that needed to perform specific job tasks, such as helping others, that contributes to the wider social and psychological work environment. The emphasis on OCB in recent times, say Arnold and Schoonman, reflects the feeling that employees need to "go the extra mile" if the organization is to succeed in competitive times.

Although OCBs are often defined as non task-related, Kurz and Bartram caution that the label de-emphasizes the role these behaviours play in determining overall effectiveness. The willingness to engage in extra-role OCBs is related to individuals' levels of job satisfaction and organizational commitment. And it seems, say Sparrow and West, that underlying such behaviour are employees' notions of the fairness and trustworthiness of the organization. As such, OCBs are an indicator of the health of the social relations inside the organization, the "social capital" described by Prusak and Cohen (2001).

The key point here is that contextual performance is largely voluntary. It is precisely whether individuals *choose* to carry out these behaviours that is the important information about the organization's status as a cohesive social unit. Although it is suggested that some OCBs have begun to be included in formal job requirements in some instances, this type of employee behaviour is mainly outside the realm of performance management. Despite the fact that OCBs are probably "value drivers", managers cannot simply demand that they happen. Instead they must work to ensure that the social context in the organization provides the conditions under which people feel trust and justice. A narrow performance-focused view of individuals would miss this important category of human action.

THE PERSON–SITUATION PERSPECTIVE

Considering the influence of the context on individuals brings us to the final theme running through this book of chapters that we will discuss—the interaction of the person and the situation. This perspective, according to Hodgkinson and Herriot, is a part of psychologists' "intellectual heritage" although they say that the question of why the situation is as it is has not often been asked. Nonetheless, this brand of holistic thinking is evident in the vast majority of the work in these chapters.

The history of leadership research, described by Alimo-Metcalfe and Nyfield, can be used as an illustrative example of this approach. It reflects an evolution in thinking from the relative dominance of concerns about "who" makes a good leader—locating the cause of behaviour in the person—to the conditions under which people are viewed as leaders—locating the cause of behaviour in the situation—to the current recognition that both person and situation are important and interdependent. The authors conclude from the success of development interventions that although personal characteristics do account for some portion of the behaviour of effective leaders, there is plenty of room left for learning. We can see the same line of thought in relation to training. Tharenou and Burke state that the success of training transfer is linked to both inherent characteristics of the trainee and aspects of the work environment. That echoes the findings from research on the causes of innovative behaviour. Sparrow and West detail aspects of work design, such as autonomy, as well as individual differences, such as need for freedom and self-directedness, that are related to levels of innovation at work.

Most psychologists do now conclude that both people and situations are important causal factors. The notion of achieving a "fit" between particular people and particular situations or work contexts underlies personnel selection and assessment. As detailed by Dalgleish and Jacobs, the design of a selection system always begins with an analysis of the job context. The inherent assumption being made is that different people will be more suitable for different types of situations. The positive outcomes related to person–organization fit which include higher job satisfaction for the individual and lower staff turnover for the organization are described by Sparrow and West. Fit between the values held by organizations and individual employees is another area of emerging interest to psychologists as seen in the work of Arnold and Schoonman.

A final example of work psychologists' use of a person–situation approach is the work of Kurz and Bartram (Chapter 10). The basis for the development of their World of Work model is to create a conceptual framework that "ties together the influence of individual and organizational variables on performance and effectiveness". The model includes both person and situation categories of variables, as well as a category called "Working Life" comprised of factors that represent the interface between the two. The authors conceptualize competencies as "behavioural repertoires" that develop from interactions between person characteristics (determinants and antecedents of behaviour) and organizational characteristics which enhance or constrain the manifestation of competencies.

Williams and Fletcher (Chapter 6) also note the potential for the organization or work context to facilitate or hinder the achievement of desired individual actions. These authors argue that although performance management models include organizational context at a theoretical level, in reality they have focused exclusively on employee-centred interventions and failed to actually deal with the drivers and barriers within the work system. This comment raises an important point about the message being given in this book. It has been strongly emphasized that an organization is created and sustained through the collective behaviour of individuals. Effective individuals are a necessary but not sufficient input for organizational effectiveness, other aspects of organization are also critical. It is possible to go too far in locating the causes of all organizational phenomena within individual employees.

We have already drawn attention to Murphy and Bartram's questioning of the routinely made assumption that improving individual performance will improve the overall effectiveness of the organization. Although accepting this assumption to be a reasonable one, they argue that performance at higher organization levels is related to performance at lower levels, but not as a simple sum or average. Hence, a strategy of engaging in only employee-centred interventions to achieve overall effectiveness, whilst failing to consider the influence of the design of work and the psychosocial context in which it occurs, is inherently limited, just like many of the approaches described that are not based on a broader perspective.

SUMMARY

Taking an overview of the chapters in this book, consistent with the need for more holistic approaches to individuals, organizations and the relations between them, there is some coherence evident between the various domains of work psychology that have been covered. The authors of these chapters have shown many areas of agreement in the definition and importance afforded to particular concepts and future directions of research and practice aimed at improving organizational effectiveness. Psychology provides some useful concepts that allow the psychosocial aspects of work to be organized in a meaningful way that facilitates understanding and action—concepts that link into organizational research and thinking from other domains. Two dominant concepts are *culture* and *competencies*.

As well as being a central organizing concept in the psychological approach to organizations, the concept of culture has dominated management thinking about problems of adaptability and change according to Sparrow and West. Cartwright and Baron describe culture as being the "social glue that binds people together" performing the joint functions of internal integration and external adaptation. Many of the authors have outlined the cyclical links between their own domains of interest and organizational culture.

An organization's leadership is intrinsically linked to its culture, being described as "two sides of the same coin" by Alimo-Metcalfe and Nyfield (Chapter 9). Senior management shapes and maintains the cultural context of the firm. In fact, the task of leadership has been viewed as the management of shared meaning, in other words, attempting to bring about a cohesive culture. Of course, individuals bear on the creation and maintenance of cultural contexts. Murphy and Bartram discuss how recruitment and selection practices are reflections of the organization's culture and ways of dealing with people which impact on applicants' perceptions and decision-making. The authors suggest a "virtuous cycle" affecting recruitment whereby effective organizations are perceived as more attractive locations by job applicants which creates a larger applicant pool of higher quality candidates from which the organization can choose. This process suggests that the culture will be maintained because only those who fit the organization's requirements and who are also attracted to the prevailing values and attitudes will be employed. However, Cartwright and Baron suggest that recruitment can be used as a tool for cultural change. Although the strategy has been referred to as the "tactics of the machine gun", changing organizational membership is the quickest way to change its culture. Numerous other examples, including the impact on motivation of fit between individual and organizational values, can be found within these chapters detailing how specific areas of research and intervention influence and are influenced by the organization's culture.

Another important linking concept is that of individual competencies, the "sets of behaviours that are instrumental in the delivery of desired results or outcomes" as defined by Kurz and Bartram. Competencies provide a unit of analysis by which individuals' performance, desired and actual, can be explicitly linked with the goals and performance of teams and the organization. Kurz and Bartram provide a thorough description and explanation of competencies in Chapter 10. Importantly for psychologists and for the understanding of organizational effectiveness, discussing behaviour in relation to competencies provides common ground with strategic management thinking and practice—exactly the area on which Hodgkinson and Herriot suggest work psychologists should focus.

In the field of strategic management, competencies are used as an organizational level concept. An organization's competencies represent the sum total of individual members' knowledge and competencies and are defined as "the knowledge sets that distinguish the firm and provide competitive advantage" (Wilcox King & Zeithaml, 2001). Examples might be attracting and retaining top quality staff, or managing global customer relationships. According to the resource-based view of organizations, in order to be a source of competitive advantage, the competencies must be valuable, rare and difficult to imitate. Socially complex competencies, those that are embedded in organizational culture for example, are difficult and costly to imitate.

According to Sparrow (1997) there are two implications of organizational competencies for psychologists. Firstly, individual level competencies should be a reflection of the strategic capabilities of the organization. The second implication is that there are a set of conceptual abilities associated with the identification, modification and management of strategic capabilities. Sparrow argues that psychologists need to develop the skills to identify the competencies, or sources of competitive advantage, in an organization. Such skills would clearly make it easier to integrate work at the individual level with broader level goals. The need for the coordination of goals and values across individuals has been highlighted by Arnold and Schoonman as critical for the future.

However, it seems that developing the ability to identify organizational competencies is important not only for psychologists. Achieving consensus amongst senior and middle management about an organization's sources of competitive advantage and weakness is one of the most troublesome problems facing strategists (Wilcox King et al., 2001). One stream of thinking actually suggests that ambiguity is required about the links between organizational competencies and performance, even within the organization itself, for advantage to be gained. This has been termed the "causal ambiguity paradox". Research does suggest that causal ambiguity might be helpful in relation to a firm's weaknesses because it avoids them being exploited by competitors. But in relation to the firm's strengths, causal ambiguity is damaging because it prevents the development and nurturing of those competencies (Wilcox King & Zeithaml, 2001).

Logically, knowing clearly what needs to be achieved is critical to the integration of organizational activity. One of Williams and Fletcher's criticisms of the area of performance management is that it is based on the assumption that senior management has clarity about the mission and goals of the organization, from knowledge about its competitive advantage, which can be communicated in an unambiguous way to middle managers and their staff. The study by Wilcox King et al. (2001) shows, however, that the process of understanding where competitive advantage lies cannot be taken for granted. The cognitive approaches that psychologists have begun to apply to the strategic decision-making and shared mental models of top management has an important contribution to make in this area of convergence between the strategic and psychological approach to organizational effectiveness.

In conclusion, work psychologists have an extensive and flexible toolkit of concepts, models, theories and measures that are highly relevant to the pursuit of organizational effectiveness. The key area of knowledge in the field however, may be about the process of knowledge generation itself. It is this knowledge that provides the opportunity for psychologists to gain greater influence inside organizations. More opportunities are needed for psychologists to work with senior management and other professionals at a broader strategic level.

In order to create these more expansive opportunities, psychologists must regain organizational territory that has been lost to other professionals. Given the need for holistic and integrative approaches to individuals and organizations, however, this is perhaps not best achieved by supplanting psychological definitions over economic or other sets of definitions of effectiveness. The challenge is to be political and persuasive in ensuring the potential of psychology is recognized and included as a matter of course and to gain a high enough standing to be given access to influential roles, but to do those things without dominating at the expense of integrative action.

Work psychologists have the knowledge and capability to gain voice and influence by being primarily conductors of organizations' strategic activity. The social process of managing the careful orchestration of multiple perspectives, definitions and goals into a coherent organizational plan is the most difficult process organizations face. Psychologists are well placed to facilitate that process as well as themselves becoming performers when psychological expertise is required.

REFERENCES

Aggarwal, R. & Conroy, P. (2000). Price discovery in initial public offerings and the role of the lead underwriter. *Journal of Finance*, **55**, 2903–2922.

Argyris, C. (1999). *On Organisational Learning*, 2nd edn. Oxford: Blackwell.

Callahan, J.L. & Ward, D.B. (2001). A search for meaning: revitalizing the "human" in human resource development. *Human Resource Development International*, **4**, 235–242.

Cooper, R. (2001). Cost management: from Frederick Taylor to the present. *Journal of Cost Management*, Sept/Oct, 4–9.

Fildes, R. & Ranyard, J. (2000). Internal OR consulting: effective practice in a changing environment. *Interfaces*, **30**, 34–50.

Johnson, P. & Cassell, C. (2001). Epistemology and work psychology. *Journal of Occupational and Organizational Psychology*, **74**, 125–143.

Nonaka, I. & Takeuchi, H. (1995). *The Knowledge-creating Company*. New York: Oxford University Press.

Prusak, L. & Cohen, D. (2001). How to invest in social capital. *Harvard Business Review*, **79**, 86–93.

Rynes, S.L., Bartunek, J.M. & Daft, R.L. (2001). Across the great divide: knowledge creation and transfer between practitioners and academics. *Academy of Management Journal*, **44**, 340–355.

Schwert, G.W. (2000). Hostility in takeovers: in the eyes of the beholder? *Journal of Finance*, **55**, 2599–2640.

Sharman, P. (2000). Cost and performance management in the age of global change. *Journal of Cost Management*, Sept/Oct, 40–44.

Sparrow, P.R. (1997). Organizational competencies: creating a strategic behavioural framework for selection and assessment. In N. Andersen & P. Herriot (Eds), *International Handbook of Selection and Assessment*. Chichester: John Wiley.

Swanson, R.A. (2000). Theory and other irrelevant matters. *Human Resource Development International*, **3**, 273–277.

Whiteley, R. & Hessan, D. (1995). *Customer-centred Growth: Five Proven Strategies for Building Competitive Advantage*. New York: Forum Corporation.

Wilcox King, A., Fowler, S.W. & Zeithaml, C.P. (2001). Managing organizational competencies for competitive advantage: the middle management edge. *Academy of Management Executive*, **15**, 95–106.

Wilcox King, A. & Zeithaml, C.P. (2001). Competencies and firm performance: examining the causal ambiguity paradox. *Strategic Management Journal*, **22**, 75–99.

Index

Index compiled by Judith Reading